Adventuring

~~~ ALONG THE ~~~

Southeast Coast

The Sierra Club Adventure Travel Guides

Adventuring Along the Gulf of Mexico, by Donald G. Schueler

Adventuring Along the Southeast Coast, by John Bowen

Adventuring in Alaska, Completely revised and updated, by Peggy Wayburn

Adventuring in Arizona, by John Annerino

Adventuring in Australia, by Eric Hoffman

Adventuring in British Columbia, by Isabel Nanton and Mary Simpson

Adventuring in East Africa, by Allen Bechky

Adventuring in Florida, by Allen deHart

Adventuring in North Africa, by Scott Wayne

Adventuring in the Alps, by William E. Reifsnyder and Marylou Reifsnyder

Adventuring in the Andes, by Charles Frazier with Donald Secreast

Adventuring in the California Desert, by Lynne Foster

Adventuring in the Caribbean, by Carrol B. Fleming

Adventuring in the Chesapeake Bay Area, by John Bowen

Adventuring in the Pacific, by Susanna Margolis

Adventuring in the Rockies, by Jeremy Schmidt

Adventuring in the San Francisco Bay Area, by Peggy Wayburn

Trekking in Nepal, West Tibet, and Bhutan, by Hugh Swift

Trekking in Pakistan and India, by Hugh Swift

Walking Europe from Top to Bottom, by Susanna Margolis and Ginger Harmon

JOHN BOWEN

Adventuring

~~~ ALONG THE ~~~

Southeast Coast

THE SIERRA CLUB GUIDE TO
THE LOW COUNTRY, BEACHES,
AND BARRIER ISLANDS OF
NORTH CAROLINA, SOUTH CAROLINA,
AND GEORGIA

SIERRA CLUB BOOKS   SAN FRANCISCO

The Sierra Club, founded in 1892 by John Muir, has devoted itself to the study and protection of the Earth's scenic and ecological resources—mountains, wetlands, woodlands, wild shores and rivers, deserts and plains. The publishing program of the Sierra Club offers books to the public as a nonprofit educational service in the hope that they may enlarge the public's understanding of the Club's basic concerns. The point of view expressed in each book, however, does not necessarily represent that of the Club. The Sierra Club has some sixty chapters coast to coast, in Canada, Hawaii, and Alaska. For information about how you may participate in its programs to preserve wilderness and the quality of life, please address inquiries to Sierra Club, 85 Second Street, San Francisco, CA 94105.

Library of Congress Cataloging-in-Publication Data
Bowen, John, 1929–
    Adventuring along the Southeast coast : the Sierra Club guide
to the Low Country, Beaches, and Barrier Islands of North Carolina,
South Carolina, and Georgia / John Bowen.
       p.   cm.
    Includes bibliographical references and index.
    ISBN 0-87156-553-6
    1. Atlantic Coast (N.C.)—Guidebooks.   2. Atlantic Coast (S.C.)—
Guidebooks.   3. Atlantic Coast (Ga.)—Guidebooks.   I. Title.
F252.3.B68   1993
917.5—dc20   92-25831
                                                        CIP

Production by Robin Rockey • Cover design by Bonnie Smetts
Book design by Abigail Johnston • Maps by Hilda Chen

Printed in the United States of America on acid-free paper containing a minimum of 50% recovered waste paper, of which at least 10% of the fiber is post-consumer waste

10 9 8 7 6 5 4 3 2

Note to the Reader: Some area codes have changed. Area code 910 is now operative in the following counties that are in this book: Onslow, Pender, New Hanover, Brunswick, Sampson, Bladen, Columbus, and Duplin. If you experience difficulty in reaching a number listed in this book, please check with information.

CONTENTS

South of the Pamlico River 74

South of the Neuse River 77
New Bern 77, Tryon Palace and Gardens Complex 78,
Walking New Bern 80, Croatan National Forest 83,
Havelock and Newport 85

The Crystal Coast 85
Morehead City 86, Beaufort 87, Down East 89, Cape
Lookout National Seashore 91, Bogue Banks 95, Onslow
County 96, Hammocks Beach State Park 97

Cape Fear Area 99
Moore's Creek National Battlefield 99, Poplar Grove
Plantation 100, Wilmington 100, Cape Fear Coast 107,
Wrightsville Beach 108, Masonboro Island 108, Carolina
Beach State Park 109, Fort Fisher State Historic Site 109,
North Carolina Aquarium at Fort Fisher 110, Zeke's Island
111, Smith/Bald Head Island 111, The Western Bank 112,
Southport 112, Orton Plantation Gardens 114, Brunswick
Town State Historic Site 115

South Brunswick Coast 116
Oak Island 118, Holden Island 119, Ocean Isle Beach 119,
Rivers and a Swamp 120, The Green Swamp 120, River
Trails 121, Vereen Memorial Historical Gardens 122,
Shallotte 122, Calabash 123

The "Inland Coast" 123
Historic Halifax 124, Roanoke Canal Trail 125,
Murfreesboro 126, Tarboro 127, Goldsboro 129, The
Cliffs of Neuse State Park 130, Kinston 132, "Carolina
Bays" 132, Bladen Lakes State Forest 133, Jones Lake,
Singeltary Lake, and Lake Waccamaw State Parks 134

III **SOUTH CAROLINA 137**

Genteel and Close 139
History 142

The Grand Strand 143
Conway 146, The Myrtle Beaches 148, Waccamaw Neck
151, Brookgreen Gardens 151, Huntington Beach State

Contents

I A TURBULENT BUT BLESSED COAST 1

Nature Unleashed 3
History 6, The Area Today 9, Tourways 10, Recreational
Opportunities 12

II NORTH CAROLINA 15

The First Americans 17
Recreation 22

Outer Banks 24
Mackay Island National Wildlife Refuge 24, The Outer
Banks 25, Currituck National Wildlife Refuge 28,
Duck-Corolla 29, Kitty Hawk-Kill Devil Hills-Colington
Island 30, Jockey's Ridge State Park 32, Nags Head 33,
Cape Hatteras National Seashore 34, Bodie Island 34,
Hatteras Island 36, Ocracoke Island 40

Roanoke Island 42
Wanchese 46

The Albemarle Region 47
On and Off U.S. Route 17 47, Great Dismal Swamp
National Wildlife Refuge 49, Merchants Millpond State
Park 49, Elizabeth City 50, Hertford 53, Edenton 55,
Windsor 57, Hamilton 59, Albemarle Sound's Southern
Rim 60, Plymouth 61, Pettigrew State Park 61, Alligator
River Wildlife Refuge 64, Along the Pamlico Sound and
River 61, Lake Landing 66, Mattamuskett National
Wildlife Refuge 67, Swanquarter and Pocosin Lakes
Refuges 69, Belhaven 70, Historic Bath 70, Washington 72,
Goose Creek State Park 73, Greenville 74

Park 153, Pawley's Island 154, Georgetown 158, Belle Isle Garden and Battery White 160

Wilderness and Plantations 161
Tom Yawkey Wildlife Center 162, Santee Coastal Reserve 163, Francis Marion National Forest 166, Cape Romain National Wildlife Refuge 170, Capers Island 170, The Santee-Cooper Lakes 171, Cypress Gardens 172, Old Santee Canal State Park 173

The Charleston Area: North 174
Mount Pleasant 176, Boone Hall 176, Palmetto Islands County Park 177, Patriots Point 177, Fort Moultrie 179

Charleston 180
Fort Sumter 194, Charles Towne Landing 195, Ashley River Plantations 196, Drayton Hall 196, Magnolia Plantation 198, Middleton Place 200, Summerville-Harleyville Area 201, Francis Beidler Forest 201

Charleston Area: South 203
James Island 203, Island Beaches 203, Edisto Island 204, Jacksonboro 205, Bear Island Wildlife Refuge 205, Beaufort 206, Parris Island Marine Recruit Depot 208, Hunting Island 209, Bluffton and Other Sites 211, Pinckney Island National Wildlife Preserve 211

Hilton Head 212
Daufuskie Island 220, Savannah National Wildlife Refuge 221, Other Border Features 222

IV GEORGIA 225

Georgia's Colonial Coast 227
Hunting 236, Fishing 237, Biking 239, General 240

Savannah: Poetry of Nature 241
Saving Historical Places 243, Squares and Fountains 244, Historic District 245, Historical Living 251, Science Museum 253

Savannah's Surrounds 254
Bonaventure Cemetery 254, Thunderbolt 255, Isle of Hope 256, Savannah's Forts 257, Old Fort Jackson 257,

CONTENTS

Fort Pulaski 258, Oatland Island Education Center 259, Tybee Island 260, Skidaway Island 262, Wassaw Island National Wildlife Refuge 264, Williamson Island 265, Fort McAllister/Richmond Hill State Park 266, Fort Stewart 267, Midway 267, LeConte-Woodmanston Plantation 268, Sunbury 268, Ebenezer Church 269, Ogeechee River Tract 269, Tuckasee King Landing 270, Tuckahoe Wildlife Management Area 270

Golden Isles, Green Land 271
Ossabaw Island 272, Harris Neck Wildlife Refuge 274, St. Catherines Island 275, Altamaha River Sites 276, Sapelo Island 277, Blackbeard Island National Wildlife Refuge 280, Darien and Fort King George 281, Around Darien 284, Wolf Island National Wildlife Refuge 284, Hofwyl-Broadfield Plantation 285, Brunswick 285, The Triumvirate 287, St. Simons 287, Little St. Simons 290, Sea Island 291, Jekyll Island 292, Hazzard's Neck Wildlife Management Area 296, Woodbine 297, Kingsland 297, Crooked River State Park 298

St. Marys and Its Neighbors 298
Cumberland Island 302, Okefenokee Swamp 305, Jacksonville, Florida 310

APPENDICES 312

A. Recommended Reading 312

B. Climate 315

C. Flora and Fauna 316

D. Additional Information 336

North Carolina:
Accommodations 336, Biking 338, Boating 338, Civic Organizations 341, Conservation Organizations 341, Cultural Attractions 341, Ferries 343, Fishing 343, Golf 345, History 346, Hunting 347, Information Sources 347, Miscellaneous 349, Nature Sites 349, Tours 351

South Carolina:
Accommodations 351, Biking 353, Boating 354, Conservation Organizations 356, Cultural Attractions 356, Fishing 358, Golf 359, History 360, Hunting 360,

CONTENTS

Information Sources 361, Miscellaneous 362, Nature Sites 362, Tours 363

Georgia:
Accommodations 364, Biking 366, Boating 366, Conservation Organizations 368, Cultural Attractions 368, Fishing 370, Golf 371, History 372, Information Sources 373, Miscellaneous 374, Nature Areas 374

Index 377

PART ONE

A Turbulent but Blessed Coast

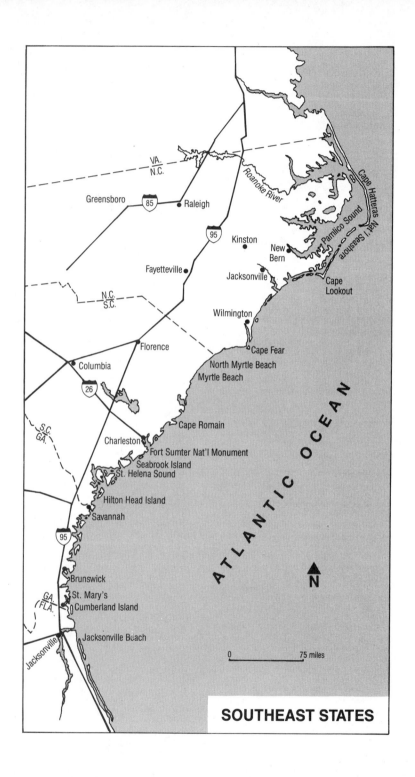

SOUTHEAST STATES

Nature Unleashed

STARTING WITH THE FIRST EUROPEAN EXPLORERS, SUCCEEDING GENER-
ations have frequently compared the Southeast Coast to Eden. "I
thinke in all the world the like abundance is not to be found," wrote
Captain Arthur Barlowe, one of the earliest English captains to explore the area. He saw an Indian dugout canoe burdened with fish,
"as deepe, as it could swimme."

Even considering the predilection of early explorers for exagger-
ation in order to promote settlement, that is high praise indeed. Nature invites such admiration by lavishing on this blessed coast some
of its greatest treasures—a chain of barrier islands, superb beaches,
copious marshes that stir poetic souls and sustain a rich wildlife, numerous bays and streams, and great forests. However, nature has
never shared these riches graciously; it reserves for this low country, on an intermittent basis, some of its harshest moods.

The coasts of the three states of the region—North Carolina, South
Carolina, and Georgia—extend about 600 miles, but the coastline
covers many times that number of miles because of numerous islands, sounds, and inlets and multitudinous contours. Contrasting
physiographical aspects are not unusual. For example, the barrier islands of North Carolina jut at an angle into the Atlantic; south of
these is a concave coastline known as the Georgia Bight. Behind the
ancient barrier islands are more recent marsh hammocks and even
an island that has developed in the last few decades.

The barrier island system extends almost the length of the region.
The northern and southern zones—the North Carolina coastline and
from roughly Garden City, South Carolina, through Georgia—are
screened by islands of various sizes. South Carolina's Grand Strand
is the only significant mainland section that fronts directly on the
Atlantic Ocean. Some geologists believe that barrier islands once

3

existed in this area, too, but have migrated against and become part of the mainland.

Although each barrier island differs somewhat in origin and history, they have a common linkage. The chain dates from events in the Pleistocene Epoch. At the beginning of the Ice Age about 15,000 years ago, river systems drained across the coastal plain. As water was absorbed in the ice cap and contracted by cooler temperatures, the sea level dropped to almost 300 feet below today's level, exposing much of the continental shelf. Then, as the planet warmed and the ice melted, the sea level rose steadily until about 4,500 years ago, when the rate of rise slowed dramatically. At the same time, land on the East Coast remained static or subsided slightly. This combination reworked the alluvial deposits on the continental shelf, deposited sand in reefs, and formed the estuaries and lagoons associated with them.

The estuaries and lagoons, especially the Albemarle and Pamlico sounds, are large in northern North Carolina, where the drift of the islands toward the coastline long has been stabilized. From southern North Carolina southward, the lagoons narrow and in some instances are little more than marshes. Although the barrier islands in Georgia, like those off the Grand Strand, have migrated faster than the lagoons behind them have widened, they haven't mated with the mainland because older barrier islands, probably from 100,000 years ago, impede their movement.

In many places behind the barrier islands are marsh islands or hammocks that develop when grasses growing on clay, silt, and peat trap material and hold it.

The coastline continues to be dynamic, constantly changing shape under alluvial, wave, and current actions. The islands are carved and curved by great river systems—the Chowan, Roanoke, Tar, and Neuse in North Carolina; the Waccamaw, Pee Dee, Santee, Edisto, Ashley, Cooper, Salkahatchie/Combahee, and Coosawatchie in South Carolina; and the Savannah, Ogeechee, Altamaha, and St. Marys in Georgia—and smaller streams that flow into shallow bays and sounds. In some instances, the rivers have a major impact on the barrier islands, creating shoreline dunes and ridges built by sand deposits carried downstream. Pounding winds and waves foster extreme dynamism. Storms design and redesign some of the islands, closing an inlet here to connect two former islands, opening a new one there. Otherwise, wave action is dominant in North Carolina and northern

South Carolina, while currents and waves are more important in the rest of the area.

The most important capes are Cape Hatteras, Cape Lookout, Cape Fear, and Cape Romain.

The crescent shape of the coastline from Cape Hatteras to southern Florida tends to force water toward the center of the curve. As waves ride over the continental shelf, they build up toward the center. Tides average about 8 feet along the Georgia coast, while they are less to the north and south. In addition, this phenomenon causes a large tidal flux. Consequently, the region has more than half of the rich and vital salt marshes on the East Coast (one-third are within a 100-mile strip of Georgia coast). These marshes, which flood twice daily, are a nursery for an abundance of fish and shellfish, especially shrimp, oysters, and crabs. Furthermore, the region accommodates what is known as a low-energy beach, with large grains of mineral sand and a high organic content in the water. Sand shifts normally are from north to south.

The offshore waters are among the most important in the world. The warm Gulf Stream, 30 to 60 or so miles offshore, gives vitality to ocean life. In the earliest days of exploration, Europeans learned that it also gave a 4-knot push to sailing vessels returning to Europe from Mexico and Central and South America. As the New World was settled, flourishing coastal and foreign trade turned this route into one of the major shipping lanes of the world.

A counterflow, the Virginia Coastal Drift—caused by lighter, low-salinity water exiting Chesapeake Bay, prevailing northeasterly winds, and the rotation of the Earth—moves south closer to shore. Ancient mariners also knew, and used, this advantage. However, this southerly flow is constricted by the Gulf Stream off Cape Hatteras, leaving only a narrow passage around the shifting underwater jetties of sand—the infamous Diamond shoals that have sent many a proud ship to Davy Jones's locker. (Generally, the Diamond Shoals name is used today to describe the complex of three pointed shoals that jut as much as 50 miles to sea, but oldtimers may use that name to describe only the large one that extends about 10 miles offshore and is the most treacherous.)

Nature wreaks some of its greatest havoc in the Southeast coastal region. The coastline off North Carolina's Outer Banks is internationally recognized as the "graveyard of the Atlantic." The ocean bottom there is strewn with the rotting hulks of more than 600 vessels that have gone down since the first recorded sinking in 1526—a Spanish brigantine off Cape Fear. Sturdy warships such as the Man of War *Huron,* lost in 1877, lie near ill-fated gold-bearing galleons; colonial transports; slave ships; pirate sailboats; blockade runners; merchant vessels loaded with coffee, logwood, and spices; and others.

While the turbulent waters off North Carolina grow calmer farther south until those off the Georgia islands are almost placid most of the time, no place is safe from the ravages of nature. Year after year, winds and waves batter the coast, sometimes in outrageous fashion. The area is part of the "hurricane alley," a moving course that begins east of the Caribbean and extends to the Gulf of Mexico and this part of the East Coast. Hurricanes come ashore with destructive force at indeterminable intervals. For example, in 1989 Hurricane Hugo devastated the Charleston, South Carolina, area, wreaking especial havoc in the less populated lowlands and forests. The effects still can be seen in many places.

History

For all of its violence, this region has an unusual affinity with humankind—taunting, tantalizing, and treating. Throughout recorded history, hardy people have lived, loved, and prospered on the barrier islands, fished the sounds, bays, and tiny rivers, hunted in the marshes and on the coastal plain, and traced the steady, but sometimes mysterious, footsteps of their ancestors.

Indians camped along the shoreline thousands of years ago. Pottery estimated to be 4,500 years old has been discovered. Ceremonial rings packed with oyster shells and other natural fillers date back at least 3,000 years. Giovanni da Verrazano, a Florentine in the employ of France, explored the coastline in 1524 and provided the earliest first-person description. He was impressed by the wealth of natural resources, including trees, wildlife, and fresh water. The natives were generally friendly, returning to the ship a sailor who had fallen overboard. Perhaps influenced by the prevailing view that Asia lay just beyond the American coastline, Verrazano thought he could see the fabled Orient across Albemarle and Pamlico sounds.

Spain, apprehensive about Verrazano's trip, accelerated its efforts to claim all of the New World, sending explorers in 1525 as far north as Cape Fear in search of gold. Spain also tried unsuccessfully to found a settlement there. In addition, Hernando De Soto, marching north from Florida, rambled into North Carolina in 1540 but spent most of his time in the mountains before turning westward. Establishment of St. Augustine in Florida in 1565 facilitated Spanish settlement of the coastline. Within a year, soldiers and missionaries began leap-frogging from island to island. They built small forts and founded missions as far north as Parris Island, South Carolina, which they called Santa Elena.

The fort at Parris Island, 200 miles from the explorers' base in Florida, was abandoned in 1586 after repeated Indian attacks. Missions on the islands closer to St. Augustine were longer lived, although they too were frequently attacked and many were wiped out in a massive Indian attack in 1597. One of the most important, Santa Catalina de Guale, which probably was located on St. Catherines Island, Georgia, remained open until 1683 when Britain was established in South Carolina and was aggressively coveting the Georgia coast.

The colonial histories of the three states in this region are organically linked. The first English attempts at colonization were made in North Carolina (then known as "Virginia") but were unsuccessful. This charter was revoked and, ultimately, roughly what is now North and South Carolina was given by King Charles II as a payoff to eight men who helped him gain the British throne.

South Carolina was settled first. North Carolina's first land seekers drifted down from the growing colony in today's Virginia. Then, Welsh and Scottish settlers moved from Charleston and elsewhere to the Cape Fear region and organized the first forest "plantations" that supplied the naval stores Great Britain needed to remain a world power in the 18th century. North Carolina soon had a population larger than South Carolina's. Georgia was a separate colony from the start, but it was founded in part to defend Charleston from Spanish attacks. Georgia's first fort at Darien was garrisoned largely by South Carolina volunteers.

In time, the bountiful land created great plantations that sent forth ships laden with precious sea island cotton, rice, hemp, indigo, and tobacco. Charleston and Savannah were the first social arbiters and commercial centers. Out through their ports flowed bulk products, in came manufactured goods from the North or foreign countries. The merchants built elegant homes furnished with imports from Great Britain or France and read books popular in other countries.

Their affluence made them attractive to pirates in the late 1600s and early 1700s. After a British–Spanish accord drove Calico Jack, Half-Bottom, Gentleman Harry, and other freebooters with equally colorful nicknames from their bases in Tortuga, Jamaica, and the Bahamas, they moved to the protected harbors of North and South Carolina. Though most of the pirates were of English origin, that did not preclude attacks on vessels sailing the two active English sea lanes. When action was slow at sea, they plundered coastal communities too weak to resist effectively.

In some cases, the pirates may have benefitted from official acquiescence. Appointed governors in North Carolina and New Jersey were suspected of looking the other way in exchange for receiving a share of the loot or of buying their own peace and protection at the expense of others. It was said of South Carolina, for example, that rich pirates were tolerated and poor ones were hanged. The most notorious buccaneers were Captain Edward Teach, a.k.a. Blackbeard, and Captain Stede Bonnet. Blackbeard made his headquarters in Pamlico Sound for a time, forgoing depredations in the immediate area in exchange for sanctuary. Bonnet, a retired British army major who maintained a gentlemanly bearing through all his bloody deeds, holed up in the Cape Fear River area.

This pirate presence has left many legends of treasure, especially on the barrier islands. The stories make interesting reading and enliven visits to the sites, even attract the attention of historians at times. However, whatever the justification for the tales, the treasure troves remain largely undiscovered.

Cotton and rice plantations dominated the islands and immediate coastal mainland prior to the Civil War. The last African slaves were unloaded—illegally—on the beaches of Jekyll Island in 1858 by the ship *Wanderer*. However, the incident was discovered and the owner of the ship was prosecuted.

The blockade of the Confederate coastline was one of the significant Union victories of the Civil War. Many of the Southeast islands and much of the adjacent mainland were either occupied or raided periodically by Union forces. The plantations declined after the planters fled. Union General William Tecumseh Sherman wanted to turn the coastal islands from Charleston, South Carolina, to the St. John's River in Florida into an independent state for freed slaves, with St. Catherines Island as the "capital." Congress, however, did not endorse the scheme.

The ports of this region helped revive the prostrate South after the war. The seafood industry and farming were important as well. In the latter decades of the 19th century, wealthy Northern and Midwestern industrialists began to purchase some of the islands as private hunting, fishing, and recreational retreats. New resorts were created, some of them lavish. After World War II, the resort trend changed to a more egalitarian mode and has become one of the phenomena of the modern era, with cottages, condos, and hotels lining major strips of beachfront from one end of the region to the other.

The Area Today

This history has naturally left an abundance of historic sights: colonial farmhouses and towns, plantation mansions, old forts, shipwrecks, the "cottages" of the rich and famous at Jekyll Island and elsewhere, and even the sandy site at Kill Devil Hills in North Carolina where the Wright Brothers inaugurated the era of modern flight.

Each state has one major coastal city: Wilmington in North Carolina, Charleston in South Carolina, and Savannah in Georgia. Most other communities are relatively small seafood or farm centers or resorts. Fishing boats leave from picturesque ports to harvest the bounty of the Gulf Stream or net the shrimp and fish closer to shore. Farming remains the largest industry in the region. Traditional crops include tobacco, corn, and peanuts. The white cotton tufts so familiar in the pre–Civil War era once again wave in fields as far north as northeastern North Carolina. Logging continues on major coastal tracts in all three states.

The development of major resorts is the most significant social phenomenon of the modern era. Motels, condos, cottages, and summer homes, sometimes mixed with the older water activities, dominate the coastlines of all three states. Today, more than anything else, it is a vacation coast, visited annually by millions of people. Some small communities have literally exploded in the last 20 years. In the Myrtle Beach area, a chain of resorts extends virtually uninterrupted for about 50 miles.

Such changes are transforming the character of the region and, in a way, exacerbating a long-standing social dichotomy. Coastal society, until the influence of modern communications began homogenizing lifestyles, was a reflection of the sea and the soil. The coastal region developed culturally and commercially earlier than the "up country" or interior. As a result, a socio-psychological division developed; coasters felt superior and inlanders were suspicious of those along the coast. This, in turn, created an important political division as the center of population shifted to the interior. Many coasters resent the modern commercial intrusion much as they once resented regional differences. And some of the most determined foot-draggers and exclusionists are transplants from other states. The resort trend, sometimes in harmony with nature and sometimes not, seems inexorable, however.

Like other areas, terminology in this coastal region may not always be precise. For example, "low country" often is used in a generic sense to describe the coastal plain immediately adjacent to water. People in each state may refer to their own particular coastal area that way. In some places in South Carolina, the words are often used in a capitalized form to denote the coastal area south of Charleston.

As might be expected, this is seafood country. The abundance of marshes in the region nurses a teeming sealife, both inshore and offshore. Blue crab is a delicacy, often served deviled in the shell or in cakes. Soft-shelled crabs are prized when they are available. Fish caught in the bays, sounds, and ocean move quickly to shops and restaurants.

But even in a region devoted to seafood, certain areas stand out. Calabash, North Carolina, has given its name to a kind of deep-fried seafood that has spread to the surrounding areas as well. While restaurants in Wrightsville Beach, North Carolina, may no longer feature newspaper-covered tables piled with delicious family-style eating, the community is still frequented by seafood lovers. She-crab soup is not limited to Charleston, of course, but often seems to taste better there. An oyster roast anywhere in the area is an event to remember; Charlestonians sometimes compare themselves at an oyster roast to sharks in a feeding frenzy.

Venison and other game meats appear frequently on private tables, seldom in restaurants.

Tourways

Familiarity, we are told, breeds contempt. This is not true of this three-state area along the southeast coast of the United States. The mixture of bountiful nature, history, and mysticism make the region forever fresh. The long history of hosting recreational-minded visitors has helped shape the region—for good and bad. Some people visit the area year after year. When the warm months roll around, the regulars flock like lemmings from inland North Carolina, South Carolina, and Georgia and the Hampton Roads area of Virginia to North Carolina's Outer Banks and barrier islands farther south. Those who once rented or owned rustic cottages may now rent or own high-rise condos and homes. Their soft Southern accents mingle with the more precise speech of visitors from other regions — many of whom eventually join the permanent residential or business community. A vacation on the Outer Banks does not rank as high on the social scale as it once did, but those at Sea Island and Hilton Head have climbed several notches in the last few decades. The Southeast region has two distinct climatic zones. Most of the North Carolina coast (a case can be made for including the South Brunswick area in the subtropical zone) belongs to the moderate climatic area that also includes the states immediately north of it. South Carolina and Georgia coasts are subtropical. The farther south one goes, of course, the more tropical the climate becomes.

This means that some place in the area is visitable at any time of year, although January and February usually are regarded as off months. It can be very pleasant in Savannah or Cumberland Island, Georgia, in late February; at times, this is true as far north as Charleston, South Carolina. Spring and autumn, which avoid weather extremes and the worst insect periods, are good times to visit. Summers usually are hot and humid, but that does not deter the beach lovers, and this is high season throughout much of the region.

Exploring is easy because three routes — Interstate 95, U.S. 17, and a combination of U.S. 258 and 117 and North Carolina 701 — open up the entire area. The choice is a matter of preference and interests.

Interstate 95 in general forms a practical — not a natural — boundary for the coastal region. The coastal band east of the thruway is wide in the north and tapers as it runs southward, at some points coming within a few miles of the coast. A north–south run starts in the Piedmont region of North Carolina. It angles toward the coast, skirting cities and towns, crossing rivers, and cutting through forests until it reaches the coast at Charleston, South Carolina. From there, it more or less follows the coastline through Georgia into Florida.

In areas where I-95 is close to the coastline, especially in southern Georgia, the coastal area covered in this book overflows the interstate barrier to coast-related sites such as the Okefenokee Swamp.

Paralleling I-95, and crisscrossing it at times, is U.S. Route 17. This artery — sometimes called the Ocean Hiway — is a more leisurely route that passes through towns and cities. It also is the most direct approach to the historic cities and plantations, major resorts, barrier islands, ocean and river fishing, and much, much more. Route 17 is one of the oldest roads in America; parts of it roughly follow what was known in colonial times as the "King's Highway" because it connected colonies farther north with the Carolinas and Georgia. Route 17 is dualized through most of North Carolina and South Carolina. Despite substantial roadside development in recent decades, it retains some of its former picturesque qualities, such as places where the road is bordered by trees hung with Spanish moss.

A combination of U.S. 258 and 117 and state Route 701 connects North Carolina's inland river ports, provides access to interior forests, and extends into South Carolina before reaching the coast at Georgetown.

Amtrak passenger service almost parallels I-95 and accesses the coast at Myrtle Beach and Charleston, South Carolina, Savannah, Georgia, and Jacksonville, Florida.

Key airports are located at Raleigh/Durham, North Carolina, Myrtle Beach and Charleston, South Carolina, Savannah, Georgia, and Jacksonville, Florida. A number of smaller airports, a few with scheduled service, are spotted throughout the region, including Beaufort, Englehard, Frisco, Hatteras, Hertford County, Jacksonville, Kitty Hawk, Kenansville, Mount Olive, South Brunswick, and Washington in North Carolina; Florence in South Carolina; and Brunswick in Georgia.

Boaters also have another well-developed highway—the Intracoastal Waterway. This route, which extends the length of the East Coast from New England to Florida, is especially interesting in the Southeast area. It passes through canals, winds along scenic rivers, and goes from sound to sound along the back side of nearly all of the barrier islands. In some instances, the Waterway is the best way to view unusual natural phenomena along the shoreline. At least one swinging bridge crosses the waterway, at least for the time being, along with newer high-level bridges and ferry routes.

Recreational Opportunities

The pervasive presence of nature on a coastal plain protected by barrier islands makes this prime outdoors country. Pristine areas such as the Mattamuskeet National Wildlife Refuge, Cape Lookout National Seashore, Francis Marion National Forest, St. Catherines Island, Cumberland Island National Seashore, and Hunting Island State Park rank with any of their kind in the nation. Even the new resort developments include areas of green.

Many offshore islands are accessible via ferries and bridges; those that are not can be reached by private or charter boat. Public access to beaches is generally good, especially in the resort areas and national, state, and municipal parks. Short diversions from the Intracoastal Waterway access even the most isolated of the islands and the resorts and principal cities. Longer diversions up navigable streams open up virtually the entire coastal region. Public docks and private marinas are well situated and plentiful.

Beaches come in all sizes and configurations. Almost all serve multiple purposes: sunbathing, beachcombing, surfcasting, research, and so on. Resort beaches naturally are packed during the summer months. Those on less-accessible islands are less crowded. Beaches on some islands are lightly visited, even in peak season.

So many people sportfish from boats, beaches, piers, and bridges that recreational angling is challenging commercial fishing in economic importance. Inshore waters offer sea trout, bass, whiting, flounder, and other finfish species, as well as crab and shrimp. Offshore catches include king mackerel, snapper, dolphin, and billfish. Charter and "head" boats (the latter combine unrelated individuals into a group) leave from marinas in sheltered coves on a daily basis from spring through autumn and on a spot basis in December, January, and February. They head for such fertile areas as the Gulf Stream, Gray's Reef, Snapper Banks, and manmade reefs or the numerous sounds, bays, and rivers. The biggest catches usually come during seasonal migrations, but some success is likely at all times. Fishing tournaments are plentiful.

The numerous rivers and tributaries provide ample opportunities for canoers; while streams may be less demanding than in some other areas, the trails frequently pass through magnificent wild scenery.

Extensive forests and an abundance of game make marksmen of ordinary hunters. The region is flecked with woods and marshes designated as gamelands. Hunts also are conducted on refuges for conservation purposes. Even a few supposedly general-purpose parks seem to exist primarily for the benefit of hunters. Private game clubs have their own lands. White-tailed deer and game birds are the primary targets, but black bear, bobcat, feral hogs, and small game also are sought.

The region is on the Atlantic flyway for wildfowl of many types, and the pastoral nature of the area provides ample food. Field crops such as corn, peanuts, sorghum, soybeans, and rice are attractive to ducks and geese. Wild pondweed and smartweed, the acorns of pin oak, and reeds and rushes form part of their diet as well. Hunting seasons vary widely from place to place, but are lengthy in some instances. The abundance that makes the region popular with hunters also attracts bird-watchers, who may indulge themselves year-round. In addition to the gamebirds, shore birds and wading birds harvest the beaches, ignoring the human activity around them, and songbirds fill the forests. Spring and autumn migratory periods are especially rewarding and exceptional on some of the more isolated barrier islands that are reachable only by boat, such as Blackbeard.

The forests and parks also provide a variety of wilderness trails for hikers—and some for bikers and motorbikers. Marked bike trails using lightly traveled sideroads crisscross the coastal region—in some instances traversing mile after mile of countryside, skirting harbors and inlets, and crossing forests and marshes. States provide maps and lists of campsites.

The region, like other vacation destinations in the United States, has demographic difficulties. Some sites are overused; others remain delightfully undervisited. In addition, natural sites such as the Great Dismal Swamp are threatened and pollution problems arise from time to time, such as the 1991 release of radioactive tritium into the Savannah River and the discharge of dioxin over a number of years into Winyah Bay in South Carolina. Yet the region has to some extent avoided the excesses that have debased land, sky, and water in other regions of the nation. The murkiness of these coastal waters is more likely to result from rich sediments and natural decay than pollution.

During the warm months, mosquitos, gnats, and ticks are a problem in wilderness areas, especially on some of the barrier islands and marshy areas. Visitors should be prepared for reasons of both comfort and health. Malaria is no longer the serious problem it once was, but health officials are increasingly taking note of the potential for lyme disease, despite a low incidence thus far. Although the agent or agents for transmitting lyme disease are not known, suspects are the adult black-legged tick (*Ixodes scapularis*) and the lone star tick (*Amblyomma americanum*). Information is available from the Southeastern Cooperative Wildlife Disease Study, College of Veterinary Medicine, University of Georgia, Athens, GA 30602 (404/542-1741).

As always, visitors should be wary of alligators, present in most of the wilderness areas of the region, and other wild animals.

A Lost Colony. Pirates. Revolutionaries. Governors sneaking away from luxurious mansions at night to avoid capture. Fabled wilderness islands and glitzy resorts. These are the things that legends are made of—and legends aplenty exist along this blessed coast.

PART TWO

~~~~~~~~~

North Carolina

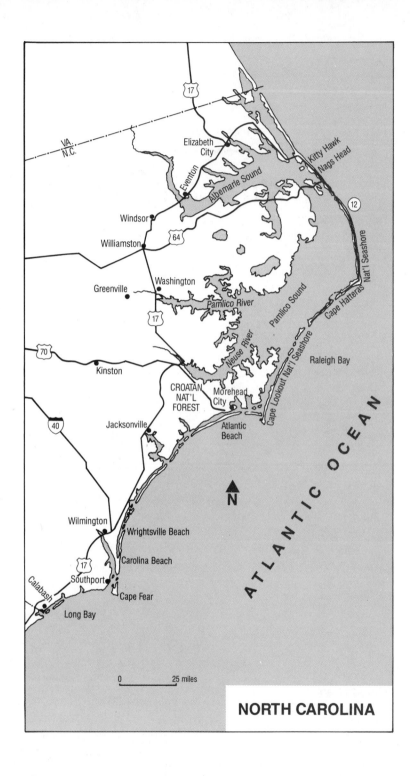

NORTH CAROLINA

0 ——— 25 miles

VA.: N.C.

Elizabeth City

Kitty Hawk
Nags Head

Edenton

Albemarle Sound

Windsor

Williamston

64

17

12

Cape Hatteras Nat'l Seashore

Greenville

Washington

Pamlico River

Pamlico Sound

Neuse River

Cape Lookout Nat'l Seashore

Raleigh Bay

70

Kinston

CROATAN NAT'L FOREST

Morehead City

Atlantic Beach

40

Jacksonville

N

ATLANTIC OCEAN

Wilmington

Wrightsville Beach

17

Carolina Beach

Calabash

Southport

Cape Fear

Long Bay

The First Americans

SIXTEENTH-CENTURY COLONIES WERE FRAGILE THINGS, TEETERING ON the edge of extinction. The Native Americans alternately traded and warred with the settlers, whose well-being depended on the thin lifeline to the mother country and the rapidity with which they could adjust to the new land. Both failed at times.

That was the fate of the first English attempt to colonize North America. In 1585, Sir Walter Raleigh established a colony on Roanoke Island. There was born Virginia Dare, the first English child delivered in America. There, too, Indian chief Manteo was baptized an Anglican and made the lord of Roanoke Island, the first grant of English noble title to an Indian. Both events were obscured by the fate of the colony. When resupply vessels returned in 1590 after a long delay occasioned by the Spanish Armada and other causes, the colonists were gone. The only clue to their fate was a single word—"Croatoan"—carved into a log. The mystery of this "Lost Colony" has excited historians to this day, producing various theories—all unproved.

As a result of this failure, the first permanent English settlement in the United States was at Jamestown, Virginia, in 1607. For the same reason, what is today North Carolina became part of other grants. The charter of the company that established the Roanoke Island colony covered land between 34 and 45 degrees latitude, or from Cape Fear to Maine, but it was revoked in 1624. The Carolinas were crown land again only briefly; King Charles I granted to Sir Robert Heath the land between 31 and 36 degrees north latitude, or roughly from Albemarle Sound to the Florida border. This grant in turn was revoked by King Charles II, who gave the Carolinas to eight political supporters. These Lords Proprietors, as they were called, included some of the most powerful noblemen in England, including Anthony Ashley Cooper, the Earl of Shaftsbury—for whom the two rivers at Charleston, South Carolina, are named—and a former Virginia governor, Sir William Berkeley.

The charter gave the proprietors power to levy taxes and raise an army, but also provided that laws were to be passed with the "advice, assent and approbation of the Freemen of said Province, or the greater part of them, or their Delegates or Deputies" in an assembly held from time to time. Anglicanism was to be established, but religious toleration was permitted—and indeed was practiced in the early period.

In the meantime, Virginia settlements had expanded southward into the Albemarle region. The first permanent settler in what is today North Carolina, Nathaniel Batts, was an Indian trader who built a home on the western shore of Albemarle Sound. By 1663, at least 500 people had emigrated from Virginia and, two years later, Albemarle County had its own governor and a functioning legislative assembly, patterned after that in Virginia.

The first settlement created by the Lords Proprietors was Charles Towne (today's Charleston, South Carolina). It was an established port city by the time the Proprietors became actively interested in populating the North Carolina area and divided their domain into three counties: Albemarle and Clarendon (today's North Carolina) and Craven (now South Carolina). Early attempts at colonizing North Carolina were tentative. In 1662, Puritans dissatisfied with life in New England settled in the Cape Fear area, but apparently did not remain long. A pioneering group from Barbados was equally transient. In the early 1700s, settlers began to move from South Carolina, Pennsylvania, and Delaware into the Cape Fear River Valley. By 1730, so many individuals of Welsh descent were cultivating individual farms that the area was often described as the "Welsh Tract." Published descriptions of this growth encouraged further immigration.

Lord Shaftsbury, with the assistance of philosopher John Locke, drafted a Fundamental Constitution that, though it never became a governmental document, gave philosophical support to such ideas as trial by jury, religious toleration, and freedom from double jeopardy.

In the early 18th century, pirates roamed and raided the coastline of the new British colonies in America almost at will. Royal governors came and went, without being able to muster enough manpower in the right place at the right time. There were many reasons for this. In the first place, it was difficult to hit a moving pirate target. The shallow and sometimes befuddling coves of Pamlico Sound, where vessels frequently ran aground at low tide, provided a haven for pirates. Additionally, North Carolina did little, if anything, to dislodge them. And many merchants in cities such as Charleston, whose shipping lanes were being raided, accepted goods without questioning their origin. Pirate vessels regularly unloaded cargo and/or took on stores from the eastern end of Long Island.

The most notorious pirate was Blackbeard, who made his visage more frightening in action by twisting slow-burning fuses into his coal black beard. The pirate cleverly had a number of bases and moved frequently. There were many rumors that he had formed a secret alliance with Governor Charles Eden; it was even rumored that Blackbeard had married Eden's daughter, although the governor had no daughter. In the shallow waters of coastal North Carolina, Blackbeard enjoyed the protection of nature, if not of the royal governor.

Whatever peace Eden may have bought through association with pirates, it did not extend to the adjacent colonies. Blackbeard's frequent depredations were a constant political embarrassment and costly to life and property. Furthermore, the costs of Virginia Governor Alexander Spotswood's defensive measures mounted year after year without achieving appreciable results. When efforts to enlist Eden in a joint crusade against Blackbeard failed, Spotswood launched his own. He posted a reward for the pirate and commissioned two sloops commanded by Lieutenant Robert Maynard and a crew of volunteers to hunt him down in North Carolina.

Maynard's attack on a windy November day did not begin auspiciously; his vessels ran aground on shoals behind Ocracoke Island. Blackbeard sought to take advantage of Maynard's distress but his own vessel grounded on another shoal. Maynard deceived Blackbeard by hiding his crew below deck; seeing only a few men on his foe's deck, Blackbeard boarded. The hand-to-hand combat between the boarders and sailors pouring from the hold is the kind of thing of which legends are made. Blackbeard's pistol misfired; Maynard's shot only grazed the pirate. They fought with cutlasses; Maynard's was broken. A nearby sailor shot Blackbeard in the neck, virtually ending the battle.

Maynard sailed to Edenton with Blackbeard's head hung from the bowsprit, then back to Virginia, the captured pirates prisoners in the hold. There, they were tried and all but one was executed.

Stede Bonnet, a retired British army major who had made a fortune in Barbados before turning to piracy, met a similar fate from a South Carolina expeditionary force in 1718. Colonel William Rhett led two sloops into the Cape Fear River, where they and the pirate vessel *Royal James* clashed briefly before all of them ran aground. They continued to fire at each other, but the turning tide cleared the smaller South Carolina vessels first and Bonnet's crew, fearful of being blown out of the water, forced him to surrender. They were carried to Charleston, where Bonnet and one of his officers escaped with the apparent connivance of friends or business associates. Unfortunately, their small boat could not beat its way north against prevailing winds and they were forced to return to land for suppliers. They were captured on Sullivans Island, again by Colonel Rhett, and eventually hanged.

North Carolina continued for a while longer to be known as a haven for pirates, but the passing of Blackbeard and Bonnet marked the end of the "golden age" of piracy in American coastal waters.

The North Carolina coast is the wildest, most unpredictable along the East Coast. The northernmost barrier islands jut at an angle out into the ocean. At the point of the angle, Cape Hatteras, three shallow and dangerous pointed shoals — the infamous Diamond Shoals — extend as much as 50 miles to sea. Northeasterly winds and the strange water action created by the northward flow of the Gulf Stream meeting the southward flow of the Virginia Coastal Drift combine to intensify storms, which can come up suddenly and develop unbelievable intensity.

The barrier islands are separated by shallow, treacherous inlets. Behind these islands and inlets are two large sounds that are not as benign as one would expect. The mainland coast features a variety of low areas, including marshes and freshwater lakes. The coastal plain is serrated by numerous coves and streams, including rivers that drain most of the state and part of Virginia. These rivers can be just as treacherous, in their own ways, as the waters closer to the ocean. The coastal plain stretches inland to a phenomenon known as the Sand Hills.

Little wonder that seamen have always respected these waters. The Outer Banks — and Cape Hatteras in particular — are known as the "graveyard of the Atlantic." Even a casual visit will show why; the remains of one of the more than 600 recorded losses has been hauled ashore as an exhibit. Undoubtedly, numerous smaller or clandestine vessels have gone unrecorded to oblivion along a coastline legendary for smuggling right into the modern era. Records prior to 1800 are sketchy; wrecks during the early decades of the 19th century are better documented because newspapers carried complete accounts. By the mid-1800s, so many wrecks were occurring that they lost their edge as news, but bureaucratic recordkeeping was well developed by then.

Such harsh weather conditions breed stories of miraculous escapes and heroic rescue efforts. Starting about 1794, lightships and lighthouses were built to warn vessels approaching a dangerous coastline. In 1874–75, the federal government recognized the need for an organized rescue operation and began building lifesaving installations where needed, including North Carolina.

The focus of private rescue efforts was not always on saving human lives. Some men with seaworthy boats made a livelihood saving precious cargoes — or what part of them could be salvaged — for personal use or sale for profit. Sometimes, valuable cargo from wrecked ships floated ashore on the barrier islands. Many houses built along the coastline in the 19th century incorporated salvaged or washed-up materials. Naturally, many attempts were made to locate the gold and silver carried by sunken Spanish treasure ships.

The storm threat is greatest during the hurricane and winter months — for example, in August of 1750, vessels were lost at Cape Hatteras and Drum, Topsail, and Currituck inlets — but the mayhem goes on year-round. Ships ranging from the largest, most seaworthy naval vessels to small schooners and barks have gone down in every month of the year. Full-time residents invariably recall years according to the major storms, ranking them according to severity.

Despite such difficulties, one of the most profitable trade routes followed the coast. Spanish galleons laden with gold, silver, and precious stones from Mexico returned home that way because the Gulf Stream pushed their vessels along rapidly as far as Cape Hatteras, where they turned eastward across the Atlantic. Merchant vessels sailed almost in line to reach Wilmington, a major port linking the hinterland of North Carolina and the world at large.

The port was particularly active during the Civil War when blockade runners, guided by pilots familiar with the shifting channels and shoals, used their knowledge to elude federal warships. They maintained a lively commerce between the Confederate States of America and the outside world almost until the end of the war. The cost was heavy for both sides. The famous ironclad *Monitor* went down off Cape Hatteras in a storm. At least 13 other federal blockading vessels and transports were lost during the war. The toll of blockade runners was even greater since they moved mostly at night; it was particularly heavy between April 1863 and January 1864, when 13 were lost.

Coastal communities like Edenton and New Bern tended to be small and picturesque. They retained their primacy as social and political centers even after inland riverports developed at Murfreesboro, Tarboro, Halifax, and elsewhere. In time, the coastal influence extended considerable distances inland — for example, Historic Halifax on the Roanoke River is almost 140 miles from the entrance to Albemarle Sound. In the relative isolation of the backcountry, the promises of democratic action put on paper in the Tidewater area became reality. The settlers became a fiercely independent people who drafted the Halifax Resolves demanding independence before the representatives of the colonies adopted the Declaration of Independence.

Recreation

North Carolina hunting laws are a bit complicated and vary widely from county to county. Special rules apply to game lands, which also may shorten the seasons individually. Check with local officials. However, generally, antlered deer season for bows and arrows is mid-September to early October, for muzzle-loading firearms is early October, and for other firearms is mid-October to January 1. Does may be taken from late November through December in a few counties, for a few days in late November and early December in others. Permits for hunting on wildlife refuges and military bases usually are available early October to January 1. Season bag limit is four; possession limit is two. In general, using a light to blind deer is prohibited.

Bear hunting (season limit one) is allowed in certain places, generally in November. Bobcat may be taken mid-December to late January or early February, while wild boar are sought from mid-October to late November and mid-December to January 1. Raccoon and opossum are hunted late October to the end of February or, depending on the county, in certain areas during November and December. Small game seasons include fox squirrel, mid-October to the end of year, and rabbit, mid-November to the end of February. Fox hunts with dogs are permitted year-round.

North Carolina has short seasons for waterfowl hunting: mid-December to the first week of January for ducks; first of October to the middle of January for sea ducks. Wild turkey, not plentiful in the coastal area, generally may be hunted in late April and early May; rails, moorhens, and gallinules, early September to early November; doves, early September to early October, late November and mid-December to early January; woodcock, early December to mid-January; grouse, mid-October to end of February; pheasant, mid-November to February 1; and quail, mid-November to end of February.

Significant opportunities for both freshwater and saltwater fishing exist in close proximity. A world record lunker red—94 pounds, 2 ounces—was taken in the area. Catches of 50 pounds or so are common. The Outer Banks hold 10 of the 16 world-class line records. Huge Pamlico Sound offers many opportunities, and brackish Currituck Sound is bass rich. Charter and "head" boats carry fishers into deep water in search of sailfish, marlin, dolphin, and other species. Lines are cast from numerous piers for more than 20 species of game fish. Fishing normally is permitted in game-land waterways. Surf-casting is also a popular sport.

North Carolina enforces minimum sizes on most species. For example, striped bass must be 16 inches in length, and only three per day may be kept. There are no limits on the number of spotted sea trout (12-inch minimum), red drum (14-inch minimum), flounder (13-inch minimum), or on nongame fish.

Combination hunting and fishing licenses are available. So are one-day and three-day fishing permits.

Pleasure boats of all kinds dot the sounds and streams. The large, protected sounds and broad rivers with limited commercial traffic are ideal for sailing. Channel 16 monitors the U.S. Coast Guard.

Along North Carolina's 300-mile coastline a few lightly traveled roads beckon bikers. Even the heavily traveled areas have off-peak periods when bikers need not feel threatened by traffic. The terrain is flat and especially interesting in remote areas. Prevailing winds, averaging about 12 mph, come from the south.

Marked bike trails crisscross the state, but roads usually do not have separate bike lanes. The 300-mile Ports of Call path parallels the coastline from Virginia to South Carolina and passes through colonial ports such as Edenton, New Bern, Wilmington, and South-port. Segments of longer east–west trails run through lightly populated coastal areas, such as U.S. Route 264 through Hyde County to the Outer Banks and Cartaret County. Though the highway through the Cape Hatteras National Seashore is not part of the statewide system, bikers use its paved shoulders. Maps and campground directories are available from the state's Department of Transportation. Bikers should prepare for rain showers and insects.

Outer Banks

NEAR ELIZABETH CITY, U.S. ROUTE 158 MARKS A PARTING OF THE WAYS. Eastward lies the famous Outer Banks, a string of vacation communities and coastal wilderness refuges. In the other direction lies the Albemarle region, a large, sparsely settled but historic zone around North Carolina's largest sound. Most visitors turn toward "The Banks," as they are known to regular visitors.

"The Banks" usually refers to the "capitalized" Outer Banks, which in the minds of vacationers normally includes the resort islands from Corolla to the southeren tip of Ocracoke Island. Actually, the outer banks (uncapitalized) includes all the barrier islands that cover the state's entire coastline.

Mackay Island National Wildlife Refuge

The northernmost of the outer banks cannot be reached by the traditional route to the resorts. Mackay Island has two entry points—North Carolina Route 615 from Virginia Beach, Virginia, and the free ferry between Currituck and Knotts Island—but it has not received much attention from tourists. While an occasional RVer from Canada and elsewhere may venture there, for the most part the people seen fishing and crabbing in this 7,800-acre site live in the vicinity.

That does not mean it is without attraction. The causeway (Route 615) that crosses the refuge to adjacent Knotts Island, open year-round, is a good place to watch the annual wildfowl migrations, especially the greater snow goose, and to experience the phenomenon of water rising and falling like tides because of wind action. The .3-mile Marsh Trail off this road winds through a maritime forest alive with wildflowers and passes a pond and marsh covered by a sea of grass.

A gravel road into the south end of the refuge, also open year-round, parallels a borrow canal that provided the materials to build the road. A 6.5-mile Live Oak Point hiking and biking trail that can be shortened to 4 miles leaves from the end of this road and follows the banks of the east and middle impoundment ponds. This trail is open mid-March through mid-October.

Mackay Island was set aside in 1960 as a wintering ground for ducks, geese, and swans, in particular the greater snow goose. More than 180 species of birds have been spotted, including bald eagle, osprey, peregrine falcon, herons, ibises, hawks, sandpipers, owls, ruby-throated hummingbirds, and doves. More than 40 types nest on the refuge. The most common songbirds are the prothronotary and prairie warblers, cardinal, Carolina wren, brown thrasher, and mockingbird.

Sportfishing is permitted on canals and bays between mid-March and mid-October, and year-round on Corey's Ditch, the north canal, and Marsh Trail. The east and middle ponds are closed. A boat ramp is located at the island causeway. Catches include freshwater varieties such as largemouth bass and catfish and brackish water swimmers such as puppy drum and flounder. The causeway bridge over Corey's Ditch, which connects Virginia's Back Bay and the North Landing River in North Carolina, is a favorite fishing and crabbing spot for locals.

Hunting normally is not permitted. Certain areas are closed during controlled deer hunts.

A visitors center at the entrance to the causeway is open weekdays from 10 a.m. to 5 p.m. from mid-March to mid-October.

The visitor may not be aware of entering Knotts Island except for an historical marker noting that about 3 miles north of that point, on March 16, 1728, commissioners began work on settling the boundary dispute between North Carolina and Virginia. Knotts Island is privately owned, with a general store where licenses can be obtained.

The Outer Banks

The Outer Banks Chamber of Commerce
P.O. Box 1757
Kill Devil Hills, NC 21948
919/995-4213

Dare County Tourist Bureau
P.O. Box 399
Manteo, NC 27954
919/473-2139

For an area whose tricky waters bear a "graveyard" reputation, the Outer Banks have done all right.

Isolation and unpredictable weather made the islands seem inhospitable to early settlers. The first arrivals chose protected Roanoke

Island, whose lush forests were more inviting than the scrub vegetation on the windswept outer rim and were easier to defend against possible Spanish attack. The first European towns on the outer islands were composed largely of commercial fishers and pilots who assisted merchant ships through Oregon Inlet and other tricky straits so they could reach mainland ports. Not everyone was helpful; according to rumors, some islanders were not above luring unsuspecting captains onto the shoals so they could salvage their cargos.

A few venturesome vacationers began visiting the settlements at Portsmouth and Ocracoke as early as the mid-1700s; but, year after year, little seemed to change until visitors discovered the vacation potential of the islands in the early decades of the 19th century. In the 1830s, Nags Head became the first actual resort, with increasing numbers of vacationers boating to the island to soak up the sun and view the natural wonders. This trend was slowed by the Civil War and its aftermath. When the Wright Brothers initiated the Air Age at Kitty Hawk and Army Air Corps General Billy Mitchell made practice bombing runs that would help prove the mastery of air power, few people were there to interfere—or even watch.

It was the building of a bridge in 1931—since enhanced by other links—that turned the Outer Banks into a premier vacation spot. In the middle decades of the 20th century, it was fashionable for mainlanders from North Carolina and the Hampton Roads area of Virginia to rent a summer cottage for a week or two. Some families made an annual pilgrimage to an area that was now readily accessible but still seemed somewhat exotic. In recent decades, the pace of development quickened, invading large areas that until then had remained wild.

Today, the Outer Banks is one of the most popular vacation spots on the East Coast. Cottages, condos, and sunbathers crowd the beaches (it is a matter of prestige whether the place faces the ocean or the sound on the back side of the island). A number of public ocean beach access points are located between Kitty Hawk and Oregon Inlet. Underwater sports are significant. Hang gliding is a regular activity, and some of the most important contests in this sport are held there.

Fishing, the number-one participant sport, can be practiced more or less year-round. Outer Banks anglers regularly account for nearly 75 percent of the fishing citations in the state. Billfish and surf fishing tournaments are held on a regular basis between May and November. While all kinds of ocean and sound fishing are common, the Outer

Banks are especially known for deep-sea fishing. Charter and "head" boats begin invading deeper water in April for tuna, dolphin, and blues; May for marlin, sailfish, swordfish, and other big game fish. Night swordfishing requires special arrangements with charter-boat captains and marinas. Ocean casting closer to shore is rewarding for channel bass, bluefish, spot, croaker, mullet, and trout.

Surfcasters drag many of these species onto the beaches, as do fishers at one of the eight piers situated almost at regular intervals along the oceanside. Inland waters, including Albemarle and Pamlico sounds, yield striped bass, largemouth bass, flounder, spot, croaker, and other species. In the brackish waters of Kitty Hawk Bay, Colington Bay, and Currituck Sound are found freshwater yellow and white perch, bass, and catfish.

The year opens by mid-March with runs of channel bass as big as 60 pounds, whiting, flounder, spot, trout, croaker, and small bluefish. Cobia peak in late May and June. Species available in summer include bluefish, Spanish mackerel, flounder, spot, and even a few tarpon. September is good for pompano and tarpon. Autumn is usually regarded as the best time; blues weighing 15 pounds or more, Spanish mackerel, spot, channel bass, and gray trout are plentiful. Striped bass swim in late in the season.

Bait includes shrimp and crab pieces, fish pieces, bloodworms, and, for mackerel and blues, metal lures.

Public boat ramps include those at Kill Devil Hills (Durham Street), Manteo waterfront, Oregon Inlet, and Hatteras Island. A number of private marinas also have ramps.

In spite of development that will astonish a visitor who has been away for a few decades, the Outer Banks remain unlike any other area on the East Coast in size, diversity, and romance. Large chunks of the dogleg-shaped series of sandy islands still are in a natural state as wildlife refuges and preserves, including long stretches of beach and dunes — 70 miles in one instance.

Bridge entry to the Outer Banks may be made in the north at Kitty Hawk on U.S. Route 158 or near the center of the island chain via Roanoke Island on U.S. Route 64. A first-class highway extends from Corolla to the southern tip of Ocracoke, joined at Hatteras Village by a free ferry. Fee ferries connect Ocracoke Island with two mainland points, Swan Quarter and Cedar Island.

Traffic normally flows smoothly, even in peak periods. Reservations for the Ocracoke-mainland ferries are advisable. Storm periods are another matter, knocking out power and sometimes stranding people if bridges are damaged. For example, in October 1990, a dredge broke loose and slammed into the sturdy Herbert C. Bonner Bridge across Oregon Inlet — the only highway egress from Hatteras Island. In such instances, state police advise motorists, and ferries may operate continuously 24 hours a day until the backlog is evacuated.

Driving on the beach is prohibited in most areas during the warm months. Licensed vehicles are allowed in certain designated areas on Hatteras and Ocracoke islands at other times.

Occasionally, traveling the Outer Banks may require some adjustment in vocabulary. References to "milepost" or "M.P." numbers mark the progress down the main highway from north to south and are helpful where no place names exist along stretches of natural areas. As a general rule, avoid pulling off pavement onto sandy shoulders. In particular, obey signs to that effect posted in some areas!

Currituck National Wildlife Refuge

When most people think of the Outer Banks, they think of developed places like Duck, Kitty Hawk, Nags Head, or Hatteras. But the northern tier of barrier islands are little known, even to those who have vacationed at the Outer Banks for years.

That is slowly changing. In 1983, the purchase of the property of the Monkey Island Hunt Club provided a core for the Currituck National Wildlife Refuge. The Nature Conservancy donated the site of the Swan Island Hunt Club in 1984, and a site at the village of Corolla was added in 1988 through a trade with Currituck County. The 1,787 acres are managed from Mackay Island Wildlife Refuge.

The refuge encompasses marshland, beaches backed by dunes, and some highland dominated by scrub live oak. A 50-acre section is flooded annually as a feeding and resting place for ducks and geese, including Canada and snow geese, tundra swans, mallards, black ducks, and gadwalls. Many birds that forage elsewhere fly to the marshes of the refuge and just north of it to roost at night. The dunes are protected. Piping plover nest there.

Currituck Refuge can be reached only by boat. In general, the refuge is off limits to visitors. However, part of the beach on and off the eastern boundary of the refuge may be used for daytime hiking, birdwatching, and photography. Visitors are banned from climbing or crossing the dunes. Hunting and camping are not allowed.

Duck-Corolla

Just north of the Kitty Hawk entrance to the Outer Banks is the most intensive development in recent years—the resorts, condominiums, and time-share facilities at Duck and Corolla. Multistory buildings, handsome in design, are surrounded by manicured lawns and serviced by shopping centers in what was virtually a wilderness a few decades back.

Not all has been lost, however. A 24-mile section has been designated a wild horse sanctuary, protecting the vestiges of a feral population that used to roam the islands. Only a few descendants of the Spanish and English horses, first introduced in 1523, survive. An estimated 14 roam the sanctuary, and they generally remain in the Corolla area. The greatest danger is their vulnerability to automobile traffic; in recent years, 11 have been killed at night by cars. The gradual decimation of the herds prompted citizens to organize the Corolla Wild Horse Fund, which has been instrumental in protecting the few remaining horses. Signs alert motorists to the possible appearance of the animals on the highway. In 1990, developers cooperated in building a mile-long fence to separate the horses from beach users to the extent possible. A county ordinance makes it illegal to approach closer than 50 yards or feed, touch, harm, or kill them. That is good advice. It is dangerous to approach these unpredictable animals.

Another positive development is the Audubon Society's designation of a strategic area of tufted dunes and beach a dozen or so miles south of Corolla as the Pine Island Sanctuary. Pullouts allow viewing, but the sanctuary is posted against trespassing.

The 158-foot-high Currituck Beach Lighthouse at Corolla and the lightkeeper's dwelling, constructed in 1873, are part of the chain of land installations devised to protect seafarers. Originally, the lighthouse held a five-wick mineral-oil lantern and Fresnel lens, but it was modernized and automated in 1939.

Visitors may climb the 214 steps to the top for a spectacular view of the sound and commingled rugged terrain and housing development along the shoreline. The "stick style" lightkeeper's house was shipped in precut pieces to the island on barges and assembled on the site. The Outer Banks Conservationists leased it from the state in 1960, with the objective of restoring it and eventually opening it to the public as a museum showing how lightkeepers and their families lived.

The lighthouse and residence were placed on the National Register of Historic Places in the 1950s. The site is open 10 a.m. to 6 p.m. June-September, 1 to 6 p.m. the remainder of the year, closed Sunday. The sports fishing in Currituck Sound rises and falls with the amount of rainfall. In good seasons, the sound is one of the best shallow-water spots for largemouth bass. Fly fishers catch as many as 40 per day; some weigh as much as six pounds, but most are in the two-pound area.

Kitty Hawk-Kill Devil Hills-Colington Island

South of the Kitty Hawk causeway to the Outer Banks lies the area that gave the barrier islands their reputation as a premier resort community. A four-lane road runs straight through the most heavily developed area on the Outer Banks, past telltale signs of a modern vacation spot: motels, automobile service stations, numerous restaurants, souvenir shops, and a variety of other stores and service companies. Standing tall to the east, by the oceanfront, are the unpainted residential buildings typical of the Outer Banks and additional hotels.

This section of the Outer Banks also harbors the greatest concentration of historical memories and mementoes and holds its own with legends. A handsome monument on the highest hill in the area makes that readily apparent; it is part of the Wright Brothers National Memorial commemorating the advent of manned-powered flight.

On gentler land below, a large granite boulder marks the spot from which the frail, cloth-covered craft took off on four flights. The first on December 17, 1903, piloted by Orville Wright, lasted 12 seconds and extended 120 feet. "Damned if they ain't flew!" exclaimed an eyewitness. Subsequent flights the same day reached ever-increasing distances, the last soaring 852 feet and covering 59 seconds. The Wrights knew they had made history. In a telegram to his father in Dayton, Ohio, Orville reported four successful flights "from level with engine power alone" and suggested he "inform press." However, it was almost strictly local news at the time; a Norfolk, Virginia, newspaper was the only one actually covering the event. The telegram even misspelled Orville's first name. It would be several years before the world in general recognized that the flights signalled a revolution in transportation.

The problems confronting the Wright Brothers and the manner in which they achieved a breakthrough are themes in the visitors center. Big Kill Devil Hill was a favorite test site for glider pioneers, including the Wright Brothers, for a number of years prior to Orville's epic powered flight. The Wrights made almost a thousand glider flights in preparation for their step up to power. Another display explains in Wilbur Wright's own words how the test site was selected: "I chose Kitty Hawk because it seemed the place which most closely met the required conditions . . . ." A replica of the Wright Brothers biplane, which had a 40-foot wingspan and two propellers, is on display. (The original, damaged beyond repair by a gust of wind after the last flight and never flown again, is in the Smithsonian Institution in Washington, D.C.)

The simple uninsulated frame buildings where the Wrights lived and worked to prepare their plane for its historic event have been reconstructed to show the Spartan conditions they endured for the sake of success. As visitors view the interior of the building where they lived or walk the nearby Wright plane flight path, chances are a small plane or two will take off from a runway a short distance away that almost parallels the historic flight path. The airport is screened from the historic site by a line of trees and offers excursion flights and accommodates small planes.

Visitors may hike across the field or along a road or drive to the base of Big Kill Devil Hill, on which the monument stands, then climb the slope to the 60-foot-tall pylon made of marble from Mount Airy, North Carolina. Panels on the monument's stainless steel and nickel door, busts of the Wrights, and a map depict key players and achievements in the conquest of the air. The observation deck overlooks the flight-test area used by the Wrights and also affords a splendid view of the surrounding countryside.

Erection of the monument was approved in 1929. However, stabilization of the 26-acre hill, which had moved steadily southwestward since the Wright Brothers experimented nearby, took three years. The planting of Bermuda wire grass, shrubs, and bitter tannic for that purpose also beautified the area. At times, the monument has been functional, as well as decorative. It was used for a time as a nautical beacon and during World War II housed a system used to detect German submarines off the coast.

Three anniversaries associated with the Wrights create special opportunities for visitors. On December 17, the anniversary of the first powered flight is commemorated. In April, when Wilbur Wright's birthday is observed, the pylon is open so visitors may climb to the top. August 19, Orville's birthday, is also observed as National Aviation Day. Among other major events is a hang-gliding program in May. Otherwise, the monument is open daily 9 a.m. to 7 p.m., last week of June to Labor Day, 9 a.m. to 5 p.m. at other times, except Christmas Day.

Colington Island, off the main road on the sound side, is primarily a residential community with a few seafood packing houses and other businesses. It does, however, provide a faint resemblance to a working community on the Outer Banks before tourism took over.

Jockey's Ridge State Park

A spectacular natural phenomenon, the highest active dune system in the United States, survives because a feisty woman named Carolista Baum sat down in front of a bulldozer in 1973 and refused to move. Faced with such determined resistance, developers withdrew crews sent to level the dunes. Carolista's heroic act inspired an organized effort to save the unique site, long a popular spot with visitors and local residents alike. Indeed, according to tradition, Jockey's Ridge received its name because local residents caught and raced wild ponies in the flats at the base of the dunes. Spectators sat on the sloping banks.

The dunes are true sand hills or medanos, shifting mounds without vegetation. Their height varies from about 110 to around 140 feet, depending on the time of year. Prevailing winds blow sand away, only to return it when they shift direction.

The park also encloses other habitats more common to the Outer Banks: clusters of maritime forest trees such as live oak, loblolly pine, and bayberry and thickets of low-slung wax myrtle; marshes; persimmon; wildflowers such as beach heather, dandelion, salt marsh pink, and swamp rose mallow; and grasses and bushes growing from a sandy soil. These are viewable along a 1.5-mile self-guided nature trail that heads directly from the parking lot toward Roanoke Sound and includes a loop at the water end. Like the medanos, the sights along this path change according to conditions. However, the wind-blown route emphasizes the interrelation between the various habitats and the life they support: white-tailed deer, gray fox, raccoon, opossum, moles, frogs, snakes, and migrant birds such as ducks, geese, and herons. A boardwalk trail makes many of these features accessible to handicapped persons.

The park is a popular place for hang gliding. Using year-round winds in the 10- to 15-mph range, enthusiasts take off from Ridge

Top and other hills and soar above the high dunes. Kite and model-airplane flying also are popular.

The state purchased 152 acres in 1975 and since has increased the size to 414 acres. The more than 500,000 annual visitors make it the third most visited park in the state.

The park is open 8 a.m. to 9 p.m. June–August; 8 a.m. to 8 p.m. April, May, and September; 8 a.m. to 7 p.m., March and October; and 8 a.m. to 6 p.m. November–February.

Nags Head

Place identification has never been a precise art among visitors to the Outer Banks. Once upon a time, when vacationing was much simpler, this community was held in such esteem that most travelers to the Outer Banks said they were going to Nags Head.

It may have lost that edge, but those who want to see why it had that reputation may leave the main road and drive along Old Nags Head Road, which is closer to the beach. Furthermore, Nags Head yields to no one in the colorfulness of its legends. The name, so 'tis said, derives from the local method of luring ships onto the shoals. Shipwrecked sailors-turned-pirates would hang lanterns on the necks of nags and walk them across the sand dunes. The bobbing of the lights resembled a ship at safe harbor. If vessels headed in that direction, they ran ashore and were easy prey for the pirates. The seal of the Town of Nags Head recognizes the legend by including a horse's head with a lantern around its neck.

The Outer Banks tourism industry began at Nags Head in the 1830s, but most of the buildings in that era were located on the sound side to avoid the full fury of the storms. The resort flourished until the Civil War. As the resort revived after the Civil War, vacationers began to build homes on the ocean side.

Nags Head remains one of the premier spots on the Outer Banks for deep-sea fishing. Furthermore, the Roanoke Sound side of the island has a reputation for excellent fishing for those not seeking deep-sea varieties. That commercial fishermen drop gill and pound nets in these waters is a sure indication of the abundance of fish, as well as oysters and clams. In addition, air and pontoon boats explore the shallow waters shared by wading birds, otters, and other species.

Nags Head Woods Ecological Reserve, operated by The Nature Conservancy, is open to limited public use. A visitors center at the end of West Ocean Acres Drive off Route 158 Bypass operates Tuesday, Thursday, and Saturday from 10 a.m. to 3 p.m. Two short loop trails explore forests, dunes, swamps, and ponds. The Friends of Nags Head Woods provide support.

Cape Hatteras National Seashore

This string-bean national park extends more than 70 miles across three islands — Bodie, Hatteras, and Ocracoke. Along the way, North Carolina Route 12 passes through or skirts eight villages, provides access to five campgrounds, and leads to three lighthouses and other historical sites. A free ferry connects Hatteras and Ocracoke islands.

Normal beach acivities may be supplemented by dark night walks when the crests of waves project a greenish glow called "living lights." This bioluminescence occurs when heavy concentrations of small organisms called *noctiluca* are agitated by wave action.

More than 400 species of birds have been identified, especially at numerous tidal flats, the Pea Island and Bodie Island ponds, the salt ponds at Cape Hatteras Point, the woods at Buxton, and the thickets on Hatteras and Ocracoke islands. Brown pelicans, once threatened by use of the pesticide DDT, have recovered and may be seen year-round diving for mullet, menhaden, and silversides. In March, they nest on small islands in Pamlico Sound.

Interpretive programs in the warm months cover a wide range of topics: crabbing, casting a fishing net, catching a safe wave, kite flying, flight experimentation, Elizabethan pleasures, erosion and other ecological subjects, history, birds, and hurricanes, to name a few. In addition, the National Park Service and the North Carolina Beach Buggy Association sponsor a photo contest for visitors to this national seashore.

Bodie Island. Bodie (pronounced "body") Island is a prime example of the dynamism of the Outer Banks. It is no longer a separate island, as it once was. Indeed, it included part of what is now Hatteras Island. Oregon Inlet, which now separates Bodie and Hatteras islands, was cut by a hurricane in 1847. One historian contends there have been eight inlets within a distance of 15 miles at various times. Since Bodie Island is listed on maps and sometimes mentioned by "Bankers," visitors should keep the name in mind.

South of the information center at Whaleboat Junction near the causeway to Roanoke Island, the Cape Hatteras National Seashore

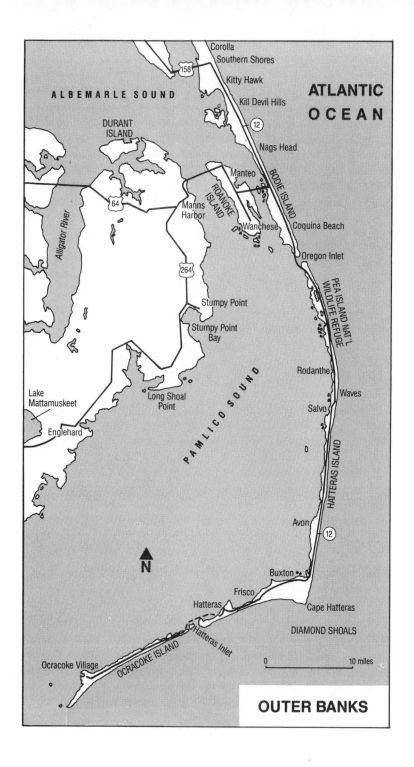

begins. For most of the route to the bridge to Hatteras, the highway is bordered by low-slung vegetation; periodic pullouts provide beach access, and platforms facilitate viewing the natural surroundings.

Coquina Beach is the largest and best known. There, across tufted dunes, lies a wide sandy beach with pounding waves—one of the best on the Outer Banks. The ruins of the 629-ton, four-masted sailing ship *Laura A. Barnes,* one of the last commercial vessels of its kind, which ran aground June 1, 1921, are presented like a museum exhibit beside the parking lot. Just a few decades ago, the stark bones of such hapless vessels could be seen at places offshore. These have deteriorated, but submerged hulks in deep water contribute to superior scuba diving and a teeming underwater population.

One underwater hulk that is readily identifiable is the *U-85,* 15 miles offshore in more than 100 feet of water. In 1942, it became the first Nazi submarine sunk by Americans during World War II.

The Bodie Island Lighthouse was part of the effort initiated in 1837 to upgrade the ship warning system along the dangerous coastline. Heavily used Oregon Inlet is one of the most unpredictable straits in the region and is responsible for causing grief to many a ship. Indeed, a report justifying additional lighthouses observed that "more vessels are lost there than at any other part of our coast."

The first 54-foot lighthouse, completed in 1848, had immediate problems. It leaned and its light mechanism did not function properly. However, it remained in service until it was dynamited by Confederate troops as federal units took over the islands during the Civil War.

The current 150-foot structure was built in 1873 at a new location because erosion threatened the former one. The site, about a mile off the main highway, is virtually unaltered and thus has considerable value. The lighthouse can be inspected from a distance; it is not open to the public. The exterior of the double lightkeeper's house has been restored to its original appearance; renovation of the interior as a visitors center and museum is underway.

A nature trail at the Bodie Island Visitors Center explores the sound side of the island. A marina and ramp are located at Oregon Inlet.

Hatteras Island. A sign at the first pullout on Hatteras Island reads, "Strong currents, deep water and sudden drop-offs make this shore dangerous." This introduction is symbolic of its history and nature. Attractive as it is, Hatteras Island is principally responsible for the region having an international reputation for disaster.

Natural areas dominate the length of the island, broken occasionally by residential and commercial enclaves like Rodanthe, Waves, Salvo, and Avon. The largely pristine terrain changes, as one drives southward, from thickets of wax myrtle and related plants of varying heights to low dunes with less vegetation and then to maritime forests before resumption of the familiar low tufted dunes. Salt flats, impoundment areas, beaches, and other features are located off the highway.

The northern 12 miles of the island are part of Pea Island National Wildlife Refuge. The refuge covers about 5,900 acres of the island and almost 26,000 acres of adjacent Pamlico Sound. Flocks of snow and Canada geese, whistling swan, and more than 25 kinds of ducks winter on the refuge; the greatest numbers may be seen in January, but the largest variety normally occurs in October and November. Least tern, willets, black skimmer, and oystercatcher nest in the dunes habitat, while herons, egrets, and ibises favor the impoundments and Pamlico Sound marshes. Peregrine falcon, bald eagle, eastern brown pelican, cormorants, kestrels, merlins, hawks, and black-bellied plover also are seen. In all, more than 250 birds appear regularly and another 50 show up occasionally.

On dark summer nights, loggerhead turtles crawl slowly ashore to lay their eggs. Muskrat and nutria build mounds in the marshes, and otter may be seen swimming in ponds. Hognose, black racer, and banded water snakes (but not venomous ones) are common, as are diamondback terrapins and snapping turtles. Blue crab, oysters, clams, croaker, spot, speckled trout, bluefish, drum, flounder, Spanish mackerel, sea mullet, pompano, and menhaden thrive in the waters. Fishing is especially good near the bridge over Oregon Inlet.

About 5 miles south of Oregon Inlet, the half-mile North Pond Nature Trail follows a dike between two ponds through a managed ecosystem that is attractive, according to season, to thousands of migrating wildfowl, shorebirds, wading birds, and songbirds. Canada and snow geese, egrets, yellowthroats, cardinals, sparrows, and warblers are common, and ring-tailed pheasant have been spotted on occasion. Low platforms facilitate viewing. A 4-mile walk around the North Pond also is possible. The dikes were constructed in the 1930s and early 1940s by the Civilian Conservation Corps (CCC).

The less interesting New Inlet Trail leads from the parking lot at the refuge headquarters through a marsh and perhaps is best at sunset. More than 12 miles of beach are open to swimmers, beachcombers, surf fishers, and surfers. Crabbing near Oregon Inlet is best in July and August.

The site is managed with periodic flooding of impoundment areas and controlled burning. Some sectors are left untouched to vary habitats. Endangered species are monitored, and waterfowl are banded. Chicamacomico Lifesaving Station is a living reminder of the vital service provided by such installations along a turbulent coast. On numerous occasions, surfmen rowed across tricky shoals in crashing waves and high winds to rescue sailors in distress on vessels such as *Strathairly, Fessenden,* and *Mini Bergen.* On August 16, 1918, they rescued 42 crewmen from the British tanker *Mirlo,* which had been torpedoed offshore by a German submarine.

The station, established in 1874, is one of the most complete U.S. Lifesaving Service/Coast Guard stations on the East Coast. The oldest structures on the site are the board and batten boat house, the original station, and the 1874 cookhouse. The larger main house was finished in 1911 and modified in 1928. The station was decommissioned in 1954.

The shipwreck artifacts collection of the Fearing family is exhibited in a building on the site. In the yard is a bell, cast in 1904 by A. Williams and Son in Jersey City, New Jersey.

Commemorative lifesaving drills are part of the historical interpretation at 2 p.m. every Thursday from mid-June through August.

South of Chicamacomico Station are the populated areas with the names Rodanthe, Waves, and Salvo where fishing, windsurfing, and water skiing are popular pastimes. At Frisco, there is a Native American Museum and Natural History Center. At first thought, this seems to be an odd place for such a facility, but reflection changes that: What better location could there be than the region where English settlers and Indians first met? Visitors may view a dugout canoe, baskets, examples of weaving, primitive weapons and tools, and other artifacts from 10 a.m. to 6 p.m. daily July–August and the same hours Friday to Sunday at other times.

The terrain alongside the road for the remainder of Hatteras Island, except for the populated areas, is the way coastal nature was intended to be seen—a mixture of high and low dunes, grasses, and wax myrtle thickets, the amount of vegetation declining as one moves south toward the cape.

Cape Hatteras, whose name once sent shudders down the spines of mariners, doesn't seem all that threatening today. The highway separates the neat houses, condos, and stores, with the 208-foot-tall lighthouse standing tall in the distance.

At the lighthouse complex itself, people seem more interested in the beach and crashing waves than the potential danger of this dog leg in the island and dangerous shoals. Sun worshippers stretch out on blankets on the broad beach, while surf fishers drop their lines into the crashing waves. Those waves bring out tanned young men who, surfboards under their arms, walk into the water and paddle out, then ride the crest of a returning wave.

The lighthouse is a constant reminder, though, of the dangers to navigation that exist at what one captain called "the most dangerous point on our whole coast." The United States Congress authorized a 90-foot lighthouse with a sperm oil lamp in 1794, but it was not completed until 1803 and then was roundly criticized. As late as 1850, captains complained they could not see the light or that it was out because storms had broken the windows. These problems were solved by raising the height to 150 feet and installing a Fresnel lens in the mid-1850s, but the lights went out again during the early stages of the Civil War. The Union captured a damaged tower after a series of battles in 1861 and had it back in operation by 1862. Seven years later, it was decided to erect a new tower—the present one, the tallest in the United States. It went into service in 1870. It stands on a "floating" foundation—yellow pine timbers placed crossways below the water table—that have deteriorated little since they were placed.

Erosion is an ongoing concern. One reason the original tower was abandoned was the threat of erosion. The old tower, considered dangerous, was destroyed when the new one went into service. The present tower stands 600 feet from the original site, but erosion over the years has reduced its land buffer. Indeed, waves lapped around its base in the 1930s, causing transfer of the light to a steel tower at another site. A natural decline in erosion, plus beach restoration work, permitted reopening of the tower in the late 1930s.

The National Park Service and the Coast Guard share the facility— the Coast Guard maintaining navigational equipment and the Park Service guarding the tower as an historic landmark. As a result, the tower is not open to the public. It is an impressive sight, however, and one of the most photographed objects on the Outer Banks.

The lighthouse operates in conjunction with a signal placed at the outer edge of infamous Diamond Shoals. The first of a series of lightships dropped anchor in 1824; a Texas tower took over the duty in 1967.

The Assistant Keeper's Quarters, where two families lived, serves as a visitors center and museum (open 9 a.m. to 6 p.m. daily in summer, closed at 5 p.m. the rest of the year and all day December 25).

Displays consist largely of photographs but include some artifacts; they explore such topics as the improvement resulting from invention of the Fresnel lens; fishing as a livelihood; hunting with decoys; the effect of the Civil War on the Outer Banks; and "torpedo alley," the destruction caused by German subs in offshore shipping lanes during World War II.

A healthy maritime forest that includes oak, cedar, yaupon holly, and wildflowers dominates the land for a few miles south of Cape Hatteras before the terrain returns to the familiar tufted dunes appearance.

Hatteras Village is one of the largest commercial and social centers on the Outer Banks. A large fleet of charter boats operates from its docks and marinas. At Hatteras Village, a free ferry crosses protected waters to Ocracoke Island.

Ocracoke Island. Ocracoke is historically one of the most isolated of the Outer Banks islands. Indeed, the famous Banker ponies that now have almost disappeared may have been present when the first British settlers arrived in the 1500s, perhaps descendants of Spanish horses that swam ashore from shipwrecked galleons. At one time, more than 1,000 probably grazed on the island's abundant marsh grass and obtained fresh water by digging shallow wells with their hooves.

Sir Walter Raleigh's advance party visited the island before deciding on Roanoke Island as the place for a settlement. In 1585, the *Tiger,* the flagship of Raleigh's second expedition under Sir Richard Grenville, ran aground. That gave it the dubious distinction of being the first recorded English shipwreck along the Outer Banks. One theory is that the "Lost Colony" survivors sailed for Ocracoke before vanishing into history.

The isolation appealed also to pirates such as Blackbeard, who hid in the shallow inshore waters of the barrier island between forays against Spanish and British ships. In November 1718, Blackbeard was cornered and defeated near Ocracoke Inlet by two Virginia ships under command of Lieutenant Robert Maynard. Tradition places the site of his death at Teach's Hole Channel in Pamlico Sound about 1 mile south of Ocracoke Village.

Even today, with regular ferry connections at both ends sending a steady stream of visitors along North Carolina Route 12, Ocracoke still has a feeling of isolation. Sixteen miles of wilderness beach on the ocean side accommodate sunbathers, swimmers, beachcombers, and surfcasters. A small herd of semi-wild ponies is kept in a fenced enclosure near the northern end of the island; until 1959, they roamed wild and contributed to colorful island customs, such as an annual mostly-for-fun roundup and mounted Boy Scout troop, whose members each had to catch and tame one horse.

Not far from the pony pen are a campground and ¾-mile loop, Hammock Hills Nature Trail. The trail crosses a sand hill and explores woods and marshes where, during annual bird migrations, large numbers of herons, sandpipers, willets, indigo bunting, cardinal, grosbeaks, and warblers are visible. In addition, brown pelicans nest on Pelican Island, while gulls and terns at times cover Sand Castle Rocks.

Population is concentrated, as it has always been, in Ocracoke Village at the southern tip. By 1715, the town was a base for pilots guiding sailing ships through treacherous Ocracoke Inlet. Commercial fishing reigned until World War II, when a 500-man naval base (since closed and dismantled) was constructed at the harbor. Despite the invasion of modern tourism, the commercial seafood industry still exerts a strong influence. Thus, the village has a relaxed atmosphere, where the Methodist Church and public school are leading social centers, front porches encourage neighborliness, and picket fences are handy racks for drying shoes and seashells.

Maps of the village are available at the ferry landing at the end of Route 12, but most visitors will be able to explore the town by following their instincts and signs, which point to principal features such as the lighthouse on the National Register of Historic Places.

The appearance of the Ocracoke Lighthouse is not as impressive as some others on the Outer Banks, but it is the oldest active lighthouse in North Carolina and is second in continuous service in the United States only to the Sandy Hook, New Jersey, beacon. The 75-foot brick tower, painted white, was constructed in 1823 by Noah Porter of Massachusetts. The old kerosene burner in the Fresnel lens was not electrified until 1938. Today's lighthouse shines a steady white beam visible up to 14 miles. An earlier lighthouse on Shell Castle Island was destroyed by an 1818 storm.

Ocracoke Village only recently began to take advantage of its other historical attributes. Exhibits in the visitors center explore themes associated with the island: shipwrecks and resulting formation by 1715 of a base for pilots to guide sailing ships through the risky Ocracoke Inlet; the experiences of early settlers as expressed in drawings by John White, chronicler of the Raleigh expedition; tourism and its effects; and feral horses.

Howard Street, still a sand lane with a number of traditional island houses and a section of maritime forest, provides a glimpse of how the community looked before most of the streets were paved, starting in 1942. In the British Cemetery, the Union Jack flies over four sailors who washed ashore in May 1942 after the *HMS Bedfordshire* was torpedoed by a German U-boat. The altar cross in the Methodist Church was carved from a piece of another vessel torpedoed during World War II.

During the summer months, the large Coast Guard station at the harbor provides information on that service's activities.

A walking tour guide is available at the visitors center near the ferry landing.

Portsmouth Island, part of the Cape Lookout National Seashore headquartered in Morehead City, is most accessible by boat from Ocracoke. The ghost town on the island, which thrived as a transshipment point before the Civil War, is protected. A self-guided walking tour visits abandoned churches, houses, commercial buildings, and cemeteries.

Ferries. Ferries from Ocracoke make it possible to reach the mainland without backtracking. Runs to Cedar Island take about 2¼ hours and leave about that often every day from 7 a.m. to 8:30 p.m. in summer, four times a day from 7 a.m. to 3 p.m. in winter. Trips to Swan Quarter (about 2½ hours) run twice daily throughout the year, departing Ocracoke at 6:30 a.m. and 12:30 p.m. and Swan Quarter at 9:30 a.m. and 4 p.m. Schedules are available from the Department of Transportation (see Appendices).

Roanoke Island

SIR WALTER RALEIGH'S "NEWE FORTE IN VIRGINIA," LOCATED ON THE northern tip of Roanoke Island, was not the first British attempt to colonize the New World. A 1584 expedition had scouted and explored, made contact with friendly Indians, and taken two of them to England as part of the process of deciding to found a colony. The first settlement was abandoned because of hardship, but another expedition was sent out to establish itself in the Chesapeake Bay. Because the ship's pilot would take them no farther than Roanoke Island, they wound up at the site of the colony abandoned earlier and there entered history.

Fort Raleigh National Historic Site recalls the first great mystery in what became a series of wealthy colonies and then a new country. While ships were away obtaining additional supplies, 115 men, women, and children vanished. "The Lost Colony" has ever since tantalized and baffled historians and buffs alike. The only clue the missing colony left was the word "Croatoan," the name of a nearby island, carved on a log; the prearranged maltese cross symbol indicating trouble was not present. Historians and archaeologists study any new artifacts from the period in the hope of proving one of many theories, including those that the colonists joined the Indians, were massacred by Indians, attempted to sail to an island near Cape Hatteras known to them as Croatoan, and were lost or tried to march overland to resettle in the Chesapeake Bay area where the colony was intended to be. A definitive answer thus far has eluded them.

Actually, the colonists were the second group to vanish. Fifteen soldiers left to protect the site after the first colonists abandoned it also disappeared without trace.

The national park interprets the "dawn of English colonization of the New World" through a reconstructed earthen fort; demonstrations and commentary by costumed interpreters on the daily activities of the colonists and other aspects of their lives; horticulture and a trail through a forest much like that the pioneers would have seen; a museum examining the life of the colonists and Indians, including contemporary drawings; an introductory film in a visitors center theater whose foyer is a recreated paneled Elizabethan room; and a full-length outdoor drama during the warm months.

The Lost Colony is America's oldest outdoor drama. It opened in 1937 and has been repeated annually since, excluding the World War II years. With this play, author Paul Green established a pattern that he and others would successfully implement at dozens of other sites in the United States. Performances are held nightly from early June through late August in Waterside Theater, which stands on the ground where the real-life drama of the colony took place.

Nearby, the short Thomas Hariot Nature Trail circles through woods hung with Spanish moss and includes an overlook on Roanoke Sound. Narrative panels along the route point out the importance of the resources of the new land to the colony, which was expected by its sponsors to send back "marketable commodities" that would turn a profit. Loblolly pine forests were expected to provide masts for sailing ships, cedar and oak were to be used for furniture and buildings, and even the spoonleaf yucca plant was viewed as a potential source of material for clothing. Here, as they did later at other colonies, sponsors dreamed of establishing a silk industry, apparently on the assumption that the indigenous red mulberry tree would feed the worms.

One narrative panel compares a drawing by colonist John White, whose depiction of the Indians and region is an important research tool, with a photograph taken recently. They show that much of the southwest corner of the island that John White knew had since eroded.

Life at the settlement was not easy. The colonists borrowed from Indian agriculture, based on corn, beans, and tobacco, and learned from them to boil acorns as a substitute for bread when eating fish and game. Holly was used to make an adhesive that caught and held small birds. However, the supply line to Britain was tenuous, the settlers were not accomplished woodsmen or farmers, and Indians did not always have goods to share. Furthermore, exploring could be hazardous to health; while searching for copper mines up the Roanoke River, one group lost its supplies and almost starved to death. Reported Governor Ralph Lane, "We found nothing to eat but a pottage of sassafras . . . ."

The Elizabethan Gardens adjacent to the historic site depict a gentler side of the era when the first settlers sailed across an ocean to transplant English civilization. While not the kind of thing settlers struggling to survive in a wilderness would have been concerned with, it is considered a "living memorial" to them and was common in the homeland they left behind. Walking along tree-shaded pathways to the 22 features of the garden—including roses, herbs, wildflowers, and a terrace overlooking Roanoke Sound—is also an escape from the cares of the everyday world. The most spectacular feature is the sunken garden, a formal arrangement with geometrical parterres and an ancient fountain with balustrade.

The gardens, created by the Garden Club of North Carolina, Inc., are open daily year-round (except Saturday and Sunday in December and January) from 9 a.m. to 5 p.m. and later on nights *The Lost Colony* is presented.

The Elizabeth II State Historic Site adjacent to the downtown area of Manteo is another link with the period. The reconstructed 69-foot-long, three-masted, 16th-century wooden sailing vessel is similar to those that brought the first colonists to these shores in 1584.

Elizabethan Gardens, Roanoke Island. PHOTO BY H. APPLEWHITE.

The reconstructed vessel, fully operable and expected to serve as a roving ambassador when not on display, at first was almost as unfortunate as the lost colonists. Its 8-foot draught was too deep, and it was not able to move from its mooring until a new channel was dug in the harbor. Incidentally, a situation of that type was not unknown to sailors in these waters 400 years ago.

Visitors are taken on a guided tour of the vessel and may inspect the top deck and the dark, airless 'tween decks where 25 or 30 passengers, regarded as cargo, generally were confined for most of a voyage that might last as long as 41 days. Both decks are fitted out as they would have been in Raleigh's time, except for changes required to make the vessel operable under current laws. In addition, a compromise was made in construction of the vessel so tourists could stand erect on the 'tween decks; in Raleigh's day, the distance between deck and overhead was 4½ feet.

Two museums are located in the Elizabeth II visitors center. One describes the colonization voyages of 1584, 1585–86, and 1587; life in Elizabethan England; Indian dress, religion and lifestyle; and the transplantation of the antagonism between England and Spain to the New World. The other, the Outer Banks History Center, holds temporary exhibits of items such as ancient maps, drawings of sea life, and Civil War sketches.

The Elizabeth II is open from 10 a.m. to 6 p.m. daily April–October, 10 a.m. to 4 p.m. Tuesday–Sunday the rest of the year.

Roanoke Island was occupied by Union troops during the Civil War and became a haven for freed or runaway slaves. Many were employed to help restore forts and, for a time, a colony of free blacks existed on the north end of the island. The community dwindled when many blacks enlisted in the Union army and others sought work after the war.

Roanoke Island is a full-service tourist destination. In addition to its unique historic relics, it houses one of the three branches of the North Carolina Aquarium. Though small, the facility emphasizes animals found in the predominantly fresh waters of Currituck and Albemarle sounds and their tributaries and nearby saltwater marshes and ocean. A score of tanks house marine fishes such as striped bass and sharks, invertebrates, and reptiles; at one large tank, children may touch horseshoe crab, sea star, and other marine life. Temporary displays cover subjects such as the hurricanes that periodically threaten the coast; the Carolina alligator, a threatened species; and the red wolf, which recently was reintroduced into the Alligator National Wildlife Refuge on the mainland a few miles away.

Programs cover a variety of topics, from sharks and their relatives and blue crab to beachcombing. Special events include Coastweeks in late September to early October and the Marsh and Sea Fest in early October. The aquarium also sponsors field trips to places such as nearby Pea Island National Wildlife Refuge and Fishermans Island National Wildlife Refuge in Virginia.

On the grounds of the aquarium overlooking Croatan Sound, a nature trail explores the symbiotic relationship between land and sea that is ever present in this area. Osprey nest on a tower near the aquarium.

Pleasure boats tie up at Pirate's Cove Yacht Club at the end of the causeway from Nags Head. Charter and "head" boats are available there also.

Wanchese. Quiet but winding state Route 345S, which traverses pine forests and low marshes and passes only a few houses, leads to Wanchese on the southern tip of the island. This community projects a different image from the rest of the island. It is a working seafood community, where visitors may watch the watermen come and go and work on their boats.

The Albemarle Region

Historic Albemarle Tour, Inc.
P.O. Box 759
Edenton, NC 27932
919/483-7325

On and Off U.S. Route 17

THE ENTRY INTO NORTH CAROLINA ALONG THIS ROUTE IS AN INTRO-
duction to the symbiotic relationship between land and water in the
northeastern flatlands of the state. At the first rest stop, about 3 miles
south of the Virginia–North Carolina border, boats traveling along
the Intracoastal Waterway may tie up at a dock beside a parking area
for automobiles and commercial vehicles moving along U.S. Route
17. Picnic tables face both ways and demonstration gardens are
planted with some of the principal crops of the region — cotton,
peanuts, and tobacco.

This North Carolina visitors center is a small recognition that the
Great Dismal Swamp extends across the border into North Carolina.
While the best access to this marvelous natural phenomenon is located
in Virginia, the waterway passing the park is the Dismal Swamp Canal,
which connects Virginia's Elizabeth River and North Carolina's Pasquotank River. Opened in 1805, the canal was an important commercial route until modern transportation methods made it obsolete.
The canal is now a National Historic Civil Engineering Landmark.

The Virginia–North Carolina border symbiosis has time-honored
precedent. The northeastern section of North Carolina was explored
and mapped prior to 1585, but it was to a large extent an extension
of the successful colony at Jamestown, Virginia, after 1607. By the
mid-17th century, expansionists from Jamestown were settling along
the streams in what is now northern North Carolina and carving
tobacco plantations from wilderness purchased from the Indians, so
many of them, in fact, that the area was often described as "South
Virginia."

The settlers tried to cultivate good relations with the Indians and
were successful for a time. However, their steady encroachment on
land and hunting grounds led to the Tuscarora War of 1711. After

it was put down, most of the Indian tribes migrated to New York. The first Dismal Swamp Canal roadhouse, which opened in 1802 just south of the Virginia border, became famous as a refuge for runaway lovers wanting to take advantage of North Carolina's accommodative marriage laws, duelers, and n'er-do-wells seeking a temporary hideout. The flight of youthful lovers to North Carolina actually continued into the 20th century.

This northeast corner of North Carolina is an area where nature exists in a somewhat jumbled state. The principal geographical features are Albemarle Sound and the rivers that flow into it and numerous offshore islands. Albemarle Sound makes the deepest penetration of any in North Carolina, extending more than 55 miles into the mainland. No less than seven rivers flow into the shallow sound, the largest being the Chowan and Roanoke. The rivers create a series of small peninsulas along the north shore of the sound. While much of the coastline is marsh and maritime forest, there are places where rich farmland cozies up to the coast while a large wetlands area lies farther inland. The area is rich in natural resources and large chunks of it have been set aside as national and state parks preserving wildlife and spectacular natural features. Some of these, especially along the Outer Banks, are extensively used; others such as Alligator River National Wildlife Refuge are used mostly by local people and savvy travelers.

There is no precise definition of the Albemarle region. To some people, "The Albemarle" means only the land area immediately around Albemarle Sound. To others, it may mean a ten-county area or the entire northeastern corner of the state. This last definition has been given local endorsement by the creation of a self-guided Historic Albemarle driving tour that extends from the Outer Banks to Historic Halifax to the fossil museum in Aurora.

The streams serrating the mainland coast have greatly influenced the history of the region. They were rivers of commerce for the first farms, later to become plantations with fine manor houses — somewhat more modest than those in Virginia and South Carolina, but handsome and functional. A few of them remain, including the oldest brick structure in the state. North Carolina's great colonial cities were in this area: Bath, Edenton, Halifax, and others. And much of the pirate lore of the East Coast has its roots in this area.

Today, the forests and countryside are more impressive than pretty, which is symbolic of the rustic lifestyle of the region where cotton, peanut, tobacco, and vegetable farming and fishing mix comfortably. In places at picking time, white puffs of cotton from short plants line the highway like ghostly reminders of the Deep South. And along the rivers of the region are the types of homes and cottages, some of them trailer homes, that traditionally have provided summer relief for middle-class urbanites from Virginia and North Carolina cities.

Great Dismal Swamp National Wildlife Refuge

The swamp may be seen along U.S. Route 158, either going to Merchants Millpond State Park or to the Outer Banks. Good views of the nature of the swamp can be obtained from the highway, but they give no indication of the size and complexity of the phenomenon. The Great Dismal Swamp covers 106,000 acres in North Carolina and Virginia, with about 60 percent of it in North Carolina. It abounds in wildlife, including bear, bobcat, deer, smaller animals, and birds. Despite its name, it has been user-friendly throughout its recorded history. Sailors prized the dark-colored water for its purity. Its trees were cut for spars and other equipment on sailing vessels. George Washington surveyed the swamp in 1763.

The roads and canals that reach into the depths of the swamp were cut to avoid logging operations, which continue in a reduced form even today. For example, a sawmill along Route 158 west of Route 17 cuts the cypress and other timber hauled by a logging train from as deep as 7 miles within the refuge.

The main entrance to the park is located in Suffolk, Virginia. In addition, a feeder ditch at Wallacetown, just north of the North Carolina line, connects the Dismal Swamp Canal and Lake Drummond, a 3,100-acre freshwater lake.

Merchants Millpond State Park

This unusual park requires a 20-mile diversion along U.S. Route 158 and through the swampy woodlands of the southern end of the Great Dismal Swamp.

The park entrance on Route 158 accesses the family campground in a wooded area and gives little indication of the substantial attributes of the park. At the canoe landing a few miles down state Route 1403, the natural beauty of the area, a rare mingling of coastal pond and Southern swamp forest, begins to reveal itself. The surface of the pond at this point is green from floating duckweed. A veritable forest of bald cypress and tupelo gum extends as far as the eye can see. The pond, which covers about 760 acres of the 2,700-acre park, has two canoe trails laid out—a half-mile orange trail and a mile-long yellow trail. Campsites are located at the end of each. Confirmed canoers will want to go beyond that and paddle along a channel through Lassiter Swamp, where the large cypress trees identify an ancient forest and the trunks and limbs of tupelo have been molded into unusual shapes by mistletoe. Fishers haul in largemouth bass, chain pickerel, bluegill, and black crappie.

Hiking trails reach all areas of the hilly uplands section of the park. The forests are a mixture of hardwood and pine with stands of American beech, whether along the mile-long trail from the family campground to the canoe landing or at the backpacking camp about 3 miles from the family campgrounds. Some of the trails reach the swamp where the big cypress and gum, decorated with Spanish moss and resurrection fern, grow.

The rare combination of habitats sustains a diverse wildlife, including large numbers of warblers and waterfowl among more than 170 species of birds, river otter, beaver, mink, and a number of reptiles and amphibians.

The park is open year-round: 8 a.m. to 9 p.m. June–August; 8 a.m. to 8 p.m. April–May and September; 8 am. to 7 p.m. March and October; and 8 a.m. to 6 p.m. the remainder of the year. The most popular seasons are spring and autumn.

According to local legend, the privately owned "Old Brick House" (circa 1700), about 3 miles north of Elizabeth City on Old Brick Road off Route 17, was home to the pirate Edward Teach, a.k.a. Blackbeard, when he hid out in the area. A boat ramp at the end of the road stands on the site where he supposedly landed.

Elizabeth City

Although scattered settlements already existed in the vicinity, Elizabeth City owes its creation to the digging of the Dismal Swamp Canal in the 1790s. The Pasquotank River became the southern terminus of the canal and Elizabeth City, at the "narrows," was the first transshipment point. By the early 1800s, it was an important agriculture and logging port with vessels from the West Indies and more distant places sailing in and out. First named Reding, and later Elizabethtown, it was renamed Elizabeth City in 1801.

Elizabeth City was not seriously affected by the War of 1812, but

Boardwalk, Merchants Millpond State Park. PHOTO BY JOHN BOWEN.

was occupied by Union forces during most of the Civil War. However, like other Southern communities, it revived slowly after the war. Recovery was led by a climate that averages 252 frost-free days a year and new advances in agriculture, including the first planting of soybeans in the United States at nearby Bayside Plantation.

Small as it is, with perhaps 15,000 population, Elizabeth City is today a leading business center of the Albemarle region. Though no longer a major commercial port, it is an important stopping point on the Intracoastal Waterway, a jumping-off point for recreational activities in the sound and Atlantic Ocean, and a major Coast Guard center. It is a market town for its agricultural hinterland. Light industries include seafood processing, a cotton mill, and wood products.

A visit to Elizabeth City should begin at the city's roots—its waterfront. There, Mariners Park has slips where itinerants may tie up free for up to 48 hours. Many of the arriving boaters are greeted by "Rose Buddies" who continue a tradition begun in 1983 by Joe Kramer and Fred Fearing, who gave free refreshments and a rose from Kramer's garden to new arrivals. At the end of East Main Street is Moth Boat Park, little more than a boardwalk overlook, which memorializes the 11-foot-long sailing craft that was invented there in 1919 by Captain Jack Van Sant. Charles Creek Park hosts picnic facilities.

The historic district naturally lies near the waterfront. Although a number of early 20th-century structures are in the district, its best feature is the division between antebellum and late Victorian structures, business and government buildings, and residences. Details include marble window sills and Tiffany-style windows. The greatest number of historic buildings stand on Main Street; these include the Southern Hotel (circa 1874), a classic example of the period; the Courthouse (circa 1882), with a Corinthian porch and clock tower; the stuccoed Greek Revival-style Farmers Bank (circa 1855); the Shannon-Hollowell House (circa 1850), a Greek-Revival original with a late Victorian addition; and the 1853 Charles Harney House, another example of mid-century Greek Revival style.

Some of the most striking structures are located on other streets. The Gothic Revival-style Christ Episcopal Church and Parish house, built about 1856, and the Federal Greek Revival-style First Masonic Lodge (circa 1827), for example. The L-shaped Cobb building (circa 1850) on South Road Street originally was a combination store and residence. The Grice-Fearing House on the same street dates from about 1800 but was enlarged in 1840 and 1885. Some of the city's late 19th-century brick paving is preserved on Seldon Street. A self-guided walking tour covers 32 sites. A map can be obtained at the Chamber of Commerce office on Ehringhaus Street. Traditionally, Elizabeth City is the alter ego for the area around it. Thus, appropriately, the Museum of the Albemarle is located about 2 miles south on U.S. Route 17 (a downtown site has been chosen for later relocation). Exhibits cover the history of the region in chronological order, starting with the Algonkian Indians and their encounters with the first English settlers and extending to logging, farming, Coast Guard, and tourism—activities that shape the economy today. Antique duck decoys and other displays identify hunting as one of the area's favorite seasonal pastimes; other displays include 18th-century English porcelain, homemade farm equipment, handmade quilts, and a pumper fire engine (circa 1888).

The free museum is open from 9 a.m. to 5 p.m. Tuesday–Saturday and 2:00 to 5:00 p.m. Sunday.

Principal annual events are the River Spree Festival in late May, at which musicians and craftspeople combine their talents, and the Albemarle Craftsman Fair in September, at which the latter dominate. The Moth Boat Regatta is held in autumn.

Hertford

This historic and picturesque community is the seat of Perquimans (pronounced per-*kwim*-ans) County. In this largely agricultural and timber county, hunting is such a passion that signs warn gunners not to shoot along highway rights-of-way. The county also is strongly influenced by the broad Perquimans River, whose calm surface provides many sailing, canoeing, and fishing opportunities.

Perquimans is a Yeopim Indian word meaning "land of beautiful women." The land north of Albemarle Sound was home to the Weapemeoc nation, an Algonkian branch, at the time the English explorers arrived in the 1580s. Indian villages stood on high land beside waterways and near hunting and fishing grounds. The natives also cultivated corn, beans, peas, squash, and pumpkins.

Hertford, incorporated in 1758, retains many historic buildings. A self-guided walking tour of the town (brochures available at the Municipal Building on Grubb Street) passes 23 structures, most of them private residences, dating from the 19th century or earlier.

Among them are the Wood-Winslow House (circa 1772), with a Federal-style entrance and checkerboard-pattern stenciled hallway floor; the Skinner-Whedbee House (circa 1775), a Federal-style building with double-tiered porch; the 1818 Edward Wood House, with a 2½-story coastal design; the Federal-style brick courthouse (circa 1825); the Edy Wood House (circa 1832), a one-story coastal cottage; the 1849 Gothic Revival-style Church of the Holy Trinity; and the two-story 1851 Old Temperance Hall, typical of meeting centers of the period.

The most important is the Newbold-White House (circa 1685), located on a 7-acre site on state Route 1336 about 1½ miles east of U.S. Route 17. The name is modern rather than historical, but the structure is the oldest house in North Carolina and a direct link to the state's earliest years. In addition, because its owner let courts and the state General Assembly sit there at times, it is the state's oldest seat of government.

Even without that primacy, the two-story, four-room structure has special qualities. It combines medieval and colonial styles. Variations in the regular Flemish bond design, such as exterior glazed headers and angle patterns on the sides, make it unusually handsome for a period when similar houses elsewhere sacrificed beauty for simplicity and functionality. The work was so fine and the design so solid

Newbold-White House. PHOTO BY JOHN BOWEN.

that some of the original glaze still can be seen. Crushed oyster shells were burned to obtain lime for mortar for 18-inch-thick walls.

Inside the 25-by-40-foot house, the heavy beams over the large fireplaces hold the weight as well as they did more than three centuries ago. The first-floor fireplaces are large for the size of the building—so large that a visitor may stand in them and look up at the fine workmanship of the chimneys. Large storage closets flank each fireplace. Some of the original heart-of-pine floors and paneling on the second floor provided the design for restoration of the remainder. Two sections of original plaster, also made with burned oyster shells, are displayed under glass. The glass and lead for windows probably were imported.

The original house remained intact, but additions were made from time to time. In 1973, the Perquimans County Restoration Association returned the house to the appearance chosen by Joseph Scott, a farmer who also served as a Justice of the Peace and was elected to the provincial legislature, when he built it on a 640-acre land grant. Scott was already established in the area by the time he raised this house, having earlier farmed land on the north bank of the Perquimans River. In November 1672, Scott entertained the Quaker missionary, George Fox, and joined with his neighbors in organizing the first church in North Carolina.

The house is open from 10 a.m. to 4:30 p.m. Monday–Saturday between March 1 and December 22.

This wilderness settlement is a good introduction to the next stage of social development in the English colonies, the formation of hub communities such as Edenton.

Edenton

Edenton is the kind of place that sticks pleasantly in the memory: tree-lined streets, handsome colonial structures, a beautiful waterfront setting once viewed by royal governors and pirates, and a laid-back ambience. This special quality is evident from the moment one enters the historic district, which is listed on the National Register of Historic Places.

Appropriately named and lined with historic structures, Broad Street points directly at Edenton Bay. The waterfront is the soul of the town, just as it was in 1722 when the first government of the royal colony was established there and when a later governor irritated Virginians by ignoring the presence of marauding pirates in nearby coves. Even without the trade of pirates, it was a prosperous port, clearing hundreds of ships for the West Indies and other foreign destinations in the 18th and early 19th centuries.

Edenton had a non-violent form of "tea party" prior to the Revolutionary War; one of the first collective political actions undertaken by women in colonial America was a meeting on the Courthouse Green on October 25, 1774, at which the housewives agreed to forgo the "pernicious custom of drinking tea." During the Revolutionary War, ships defying a British blockade unloaded cargo for George Washington's struggling Continental Army at Edenton docks.

The Barker House (circa 1762), the visitors center for Historic Edenton, is a good place to start a tour. In rooms where Thomas Barker, a colonial agent, and his wife once lived, a 20-minute audiovisual program introduces Edenton. Double porches look out over Edenton Bay and toward the neat row of homes and Revolutionary cannon on East Water Street. Guided tours of the Cupola House, Iredell House, Courthouse, and St. Paul's Episcopal Church start from there. The visitors center is open 10 a.m. to 4:30 p.m. Monday–Saturday and 2 p.m. to 5 p.m. on Sunday, except major holidays.

The white frame Cupola House (circa 1725) may be the finest wooden Jacobean-style house in the South. Its reproduced Georgian interior, paintings, and antiques recreate the lifestyle of the early 18th century. An 18th-century-style formal English garden reflects the love of order and detail of the period.

The Iredell House complex, a few blocks away on East Church Street, represents an upper middle-class town residence of the late 18th century. Built about 1773 and enlarged about 1816, it is noted for its finely restored interior. Four ancillary buildings are located on the property. The house was built by James Iredell, who emigrated to North Carolina in 1768 and became a lawyer. His essays were an important factor in North Carolina's ratification of the U.S. Constitution. He later was appointed by President George Washington as an Associate Justice of the U.S. Supreme Court. His son, James Iredell, Jr., was governor in 1827–28.

The Chowan County Courthouse, a 1767 red brick building with a white cupola, is the oldest courthouse in continuous use in North Carolina and one of the oldest in the nation. It is also a fine example of Georgian architecture.

St. Paul's Church, organized in 1701, has the oldest charter and is the second oldest church building in North Carolina. The red brick structure, begun in 1736, partially burned in 1949 but was restored to its original appearance. Three colonial governors, including Charles Eden for whom the city is named, are buried in its graveyard.

A map of the 1½-mile self-guided walking tour prepared by Historic Edenton pinpoints 27 key buildings, including those on the guided tour. Other important structures include the 18th-century Homestead, whose architecture is reminiscent of designs used in colonial homes in the West Indies; Blair House (circa 1776), for many years the home of Confederate General Thomas Courtland Manning; Charlton House (circa 1760), one of several with a gambrel roof and brick chimneys; the 1805 Skinner-Bond House, fronting on the Courthouse Green; the 1810 Beverly Hall, a handsome Federal-style building that once housed a bank; the 1840s Greek Revival-style Pembroke Hall, with spacious grounds; Paine House, a coastal cottage from the 1850s; and the Leary Building, distinguished by an elaborate Victorian pressed-metal front.

Some of the private historic homes are open during the Edenton Pilgrimage, held in the spring of odd-numbered years.

Windsor

Windsor has understated charm. Neat, well-kept houses, many of them historic, surround a small municipal and commercial zone that serves as county seat and as an agricultural and timber center. The town was formed in 1768 at a site known as Gray's Landing and became the seat of Bertie County in 1794.

Evidence of a long, prosperous history is everywhere. The visitors center at the end of York Street (follow U.S. Route 13 to the business center and continue straight when it turns right) occupies the 1840 Freeman Hotel, a splendid example of the kind of hostelry that served steamboat and railroad clientele in the region right into this century. The restored Greek Revival structure was moved to its present site after restoration preserved the original external appearance and its floors and stairs.

The historic district centered on King Street is composed mainly of private homes with an unusual variety of styles and architectural features for a small community. Among the key structures are the 1790 Gillam Bell House, Elmwood (Watson-Mardre House) (circa 1836), Briar Patch Hall (Burden-Rascoe House) (circa 1840), early 1850s Liberty Hall, and Britten-Bell House (circa 1890). The Bertie County Court House, built in 1887, is among several buildings on the National Register of Historic Places.

Hope Plantation. PHOTO BY JOHN BOWEN.

Visitors may view the exteriors of these homes at any time on a self-guided tour; in the spring, usually in May, the Windsor Area Chamber of Commerce sponsors a guided tour that visits many of the homes and includes lunch at St. Thomas' Episcopal Church, an 1848 brown-frame structure serving a congregation that dates back to the early 18th century.

A stroll through Cashie Park reveals a different side of Windsor. The park overlooks the tree-shaded Cashie River; its strategically located boat ramp provides river access to Albemarle Sound. A mini-zoo is the principal feature of Livermon Recreational Park.

Four miles northwest of Windsor on state Route 308 is Hope Plantation, sometimes described as the "crown jewel of Bertie County's historic legacy." The elegant mansion built in 1803 by Governor David Stone, like Thomas Jefferson a "Renaissance man," is the centerpiece of a 38-acre multifaceted historical offering that opened in 1972 under the auspices of the Historic Hope Foundation, Inc.

John Tyler, chairman of the board, says the Lords Proprietor granted the plantation to the Hobson family in the 1720s. Later, Jedekiah Stone of Massachusetts married the widow of a Hobson descendant and in 1770 became the father of the builder of the mansion, an attorney who also served as a judge and as United States congressman and senator before becoming governor.

The house is architecturally significant because it reflects the transition from the 18th-century Georgian style to the neoclassical style popular in the 19th century. It also has a full above-ground basement in the English style, with warming pantries and storage room. The first floor has a large central hallway separating a parlor and dining room and two bed chambers. On the next floor are a 30-by-40-foot drawing room, a library, and two bedrooms. A service stairway extends from the basement to the attic, where a ladder leads to a small roof platform from which the governor could observe his plantation fields.

The house, furnished according to the inventory at the time of Governor Stone's death in 1818, includes one of the best collections of regional furniture in the southeast, including cabinet work done in the region during the Federal period.

The 1763 King-Bazemore House, which depicts a more modest lifestyle, is part of the guided tour. It was moved 4 miles to its current site, restored, and authentically refurnished. The Samuel Cox House, considered a typical North Carolina farmhouse from about 1800, presently is used as a caretaker's house.

The modern Roanoke-Chowan Heritage Center, which opened in 1992 in Hope Woods, is both the visitors center and an educational institution. Among other things, it houses a research facility that includes the reconstituted library of Governor Stone and galleries exploring the history of the region chronologically. Nature trails will be laid out in the nearby woods during the next five years. An interpretive program that presently includes flower and vegetable gardens, crafts, and Halloween and Christmas programs is being expanded to include 19th-century cooking demonstrations, weaving, and blacksmithing.

The complex is open from 10 a.m. to 4 p.m. Monday–Saturday, 2 p.m. to 5 p.m. Sunday from March 1 through December 23, except Thanksgiving Day.

Hamilton

Southwest of Windsor, via U.S. 17 to Williamston and state Routes 125 and 903, sits the historic Roanoke River port of Hamilton. Incorporated in 1804, it was prior to the Civil War a significant stopping point for shallow-hull steamboats loading cotton for European textile factories. After the war, some of the previous prosperity returned as farmers shipped peanuts and tobacco through the port.

Hamilton contains about fifty historic sites from these two periods. Among them are the 1840 Greek Revival-style Hamilton House; Hickory Hill (circa 1848), later modified twice, the 1850 Wethersbee-Anthony House with Doric columns on the porch; the Queen Anne-style Baker-Ballard House (circa 1888), notable for its exterior wood-work and iron fence; and Gothic-style St. Martin's Church (circa 1879), with a three-staged tower. The Sherrod House (circa 1815), south of the town on Routes 125/903, reflects several styles.

Fort Branch, an earthen fort about a mile east of Hamilton along state Route 1416, was constructed by the Confederacy to prevent Union naval forays up the Roanoke River. When Confederates abandoned the fort in 1864 after General Robert E. Lee's surrender at Appomattox, they threw the fort's eleven cannon into the river. Eight of those and partially restored earthworks are part of the presentation at the site, which is open on weekends April through November. An annual November battle reenactment includes the first North Carolina Volunteers, which maintains a headquarters at the site.

From Williamston, U.S. Route 17 continues due south to Washington, another historic community. However, many will want to approach Washington by a broad loop that takes them through one of the most interesting areas of the North Carolina coastal region. The uniqueness of the area will become readily apparent to those who take state Route 308 east toward Plymouth. About 10 miles from Windsor, the unpaved Sans Souci Road (state Route 1500) leads to a ferry landing in a sylvan setting on the Cashie River. A sign advises, "Blow horn for ferry." The Sans Souci Ferry, one of the last of the breed of two-car, flat-barge ferries, is used primarily by farmers and those living in the vicinity. The free ferry takes about four minutes to reach the landing at an unpaved road on the opposite shore.

Albemarle Sound's Southern Rim

The peninsula south of Albemarle Sound is the largest in North Carolina — and one of the most diverse. This sparsely settled farming region has extensive wide open spaces, attractive but widely separated settlements, and a history that ranges from plantations to a major engineering effort to drain a lake to provide more cropland. The Intracoastal Waterway utilizes the broad Alligator River and a canal that cuts through a largely wilderness area along the Atlantic waterfowl flyway.

U.S. Route 64 makes an almost straight run to the tip of the peninsula at Manns Harbor and then goes on to Roanoke Island and the Outer Banks. From Manns Harbor, U.S. Route 264 follows the varied coastline, sometimes marshy and sometimes solid farmland, along the eastern and southern shores of the peninsula all the way back to Washington. A detour onto state Route 90 is required to reach Bath, one of the state's most historic communities.

Plymouth

A trip through this region is full of surprises. For example, now largely bypassed Plymouth was one of North Carolina's busiest ports prior to the Civil War and had the only federal customs house in the northeastern section of the state. It was also the site of significant fighting for control of the region and the strategic Roanoke River, then an important inland waterway. In April 1864, occupying federal forces, mainly from Connecticut, Massachusetts, New York, and Pennsylvania, were attacked by Confederates supported by the ironclad ram *CSS Albemarle*. They surrendered the town on April 20. Six months later, the ironclad was sunk and Union forces recaptured the town.

Plymouth retains much of its antebellum aura at Ausbon House (circa 1840), where bullet holes left by fighting are still visible around an upstairs window and other buildings. The Port O' Plymouth Roanoke River Museum, which rotates theme displays such as the battle of Plymouth near the anniversary date of the battle, sponsors a living history weekend featuring demonstrations by Civil War reenactors. Museum hours are 10 a.m. to 5 p.m. Wednesday–Saturday, except holidays.

Pettigrew State Park

Lake Phelps covers 16,600 of the 17,743 acres enclosed in this park. The 5-by-7-mile lake is both a wildlife sanctuary and active recreational area. This expanse of water, coupled with the flat terrain of nearby farms, creates a continuing breeze that makes for ideal sailing in shallow-draft catamarans and sunfish. The water can be rough at times, however.

The park's boat ramp is the only public access to Lake Phelps. Fishers cast for largemouth bass, yellow perch, pumpkinseed, bluegill, and bream. An attempt to reintroduce white perch in the 1980s after a natural kill in 1979 was only marginally successful. The lake is especially beautiful at sunset when the right conditions turn the descending sun into a ball of fire that paints its rays over the dark waters.

Although only a small portion of the park is forested, some of the state's most spectacular flora grow there. Devil's walkingstick, sugarberry, sweetleaf, pawpaw, and swamp tupelo on the grounds have been declared state champions in a single year by the American Forestry Association. Towering specimens of bald cypress (examples of canoes made from this tree more than 1,000 years ago have been found), sweetgum, yellow tulip poplar, cherrybark oak, laurel oak, swamp chestnut oak, shagbark hickory, and sycamore also overlook a dense understory that includes Virginia willow, spicebush, beauty berry, pepperbush, poison ivy, wild grape, dayflower, jack-in-the-pulpit, and jewelweed.

Nature trails are a long-standing tradition. A scenic carriage route was laid out in the 1800s around part of the lake by the owner. Today, approximately 5 miles of hiking trails follow the contours of the lake on high ground and explore a cypress swamp and forests. A 3-mile trail starts behind the park office and ends at the Moccasin Canal Overlook, a 350-foot boardwalk that extends through a cypress swamp to the edge of the lake. This is a popular spot in November and December for viewing migrating waterfowl, especially tundra swan, Canada geese, pintail, bufflehead, hooded mergansers, and mallards. At other times, bald and golden eagles, osprey, great blue, white, and Louisiana herons, great white egret, killdeer, pileated woodpecker, hummingbirds, and numerous other birds are spotted. Another trail starts at the campground and passes Somerset Place, an 1840s plantation mansion, to reach an overlook near the Bee Tree Canal, so named because of nearby nests of honeybees. A spur trail reaches the cemetery of the Pettigrew family whose estate, Bonarva, also bordered the lake; Confederate General James Johnston Pettigrew, for whom the park is named, died at an early age because of wounds received in the Confederate retreat from Gettysburg.

Nature programs occur throughout the year. Events normally are held weekly from Memorial Day to Labor Day and monthly the rest of the year. These include waterfowl watches, listening to night sounds, and slide shows and lectures on snakes, birds, animals, and astronomy. During Indian Heritage Week late in September, Algonkian artifacts found in the state are displayed and presentations are made on such subjects as building dugout canoes, making arrowheads, hunting, and making pottery.

The origins of the lake, sitting on one of the highest elevations in the area, remain a mystery. It may have been created by underground springs, glacial activity, meteorite shower, peat burn—or a combination of events. Human presence is more easily verified. Thousands of pottery shards, spear points, and even canoes sunk in the lake as much as 4,400 years ago have been recovered. Indians are believed to have entered the region as early as 8,000 B.C.

Pettigrew Park, the state's largest, preserves part of what once was the largest plantation in North Carolina. Its development also shows a common pattern in the low-lying coastal area, where draining was often attempted to create new farmland and families slowly increased their acreage. The plantation was founded by Josiah Collins, who emigrated from Great Britain to Edenton and became a successful merchant. In 1795, in association with other Edenton entrepreneurs, he formed the Lake Company, which purchased 100,000 acres adjacent to Lake Phelps and dug a 6-mile-long canal to the Scuppernong River to transport lumber cut and sawed on the site, rice, and corn.

Collins bought out his partners in 1816 and named it Somerset Place, after his birthplace in England. It was enlarged on several occasions until it was one of the largest plantations in the state, with more than 300 slaves. Somerset was a focal point of social life in the region; the Christmas celebration, for example, included banquets, music recitals, and poetry readings. Slaves held their own celebration, called "John Kooner," which mixed African and Caribbean influences. Federal occupation of the region during the Civil War forced the Collinses to flee, and the family fortunes never recovered after the war.

Lake Phelps and a few hundred acres holding the mansion and other well-preserved buildings were acquired by the state in 1939. After a thorough archaeological evaluation, extensive restoration was begun in 1951.

Today a tree-lined lane leads to the handsome 14-room Greek-Revival mansion with large porches nestled among trees near the shore of the lake. The house, administered by the state's Department of Cultural Resources, is furnished according to the style of the 1830s, when it was built. However, tours focus on the lifestyles of the owners, house servants, and a free black during the 1840s. Outbuildings, including a salting house with meat and fish, smokehouse, summer kitchen, and laundry, emphasize the work of the plantation.

Interpreters make candles and lard at open hearths, show how laundry was done, and perform other everyday tasks. A reunion of the descendants of slaves is held every other year on Labor Day weekend. The plantation owners kept records that show some slaves earned money by raising vegetables and hiring out to other farmers, which gave them the means to buy clothing, jewelry, and other items at a plantation store. The mansion is open 9 a.m. to 5 p.m. Monday–Saturday, 1 to 5 p.m. Sunday April through October, and 10 a.m. to 4 p.m. Tuesday–Saturday, 1 to 4 p.m. Sunday the rest of the year.

Alligator River Wildlife Refuge

Those who like roughing it will love this refuge, which not only is lightly used but is largely inaccessible to all but the most determined visitors. While most of its 200 miles of old logging roads are open year-round during daylight hours, regular cars and similar vehicles cannot negotiate them. In addition, heavy rain or a long wet spell can make the roads almost impassable even for four-wheel-drive vehicles.

Still, those who make the effort will be thrilled by pocosin habitats, the tangled pine and hardwood forests that include stands of Atlantic white cedar, and the chance to view animals in as wild a state as exists along the East Coast. The 150,000-acre size of the refuge, which covers most of the thumbnail-shaped peninsula between the Alligator River and Croatan Sound, makes sighting of animals chancy, however.

One of the first programs initiated after the refuge was acquired in 1984 was to block manmade drainage ditches and canals as a means of restoring natural water conditions. This action should support increasing numbers of migratory wildfowl, barred owl, red shoulder hawk, black bear, bobcat, otter, mink, red and gray foxes, and other creatures. Some 3,800 acres are cooperatively managed with local farmers, who leave portions of their crops to sustain wildlife. The creeks, canals, and small lakes are open to fishing.

Because of its relative isolation, Alligator Refuge was chosen as the site of reintroduction of the red wolf (*Canus refus*) into the wild. Red wolf, one of three wild canids native to the United States, once roamed at will over the southeast; by the 1960s, the species was confined to a small area on the Texas-Louisiana border and was in danger of extinction. In the late 1970s, 17 pure animals were captured and bred selectively in captivity. Four pairs were sent to the Alligator River Refuge in 1986. They were released the following year after being gradually adapted to a diet of wild prey. Radio monitoring shows the experiment, the first of its kind in the world, is thus far successful and that the wolves have adapted to the wild. They are seldom seen by visitors, however. Most sightings have been at night along highways through the refuge.

Hunting for mourning dove, geese, swans, ducks, snipe, quail, and woodcock is good. Other possible bags include deer, squirrels, rabbits, opossums, and raccoon. Permissible hunting methods differ from section to section: Dogs are not allowed in the Gum Swamp Unit along the Alligator River but can be used in some other sectors; they may be used only to retrieve birds in still other areas. Some sections are off limits to hunters. In addition, several large sections are not part of the refuge. The use of lights in hunting or construction of platforms and blinds is prohibited.

The easiest way to penetrate the wilderness may be by boat. Milltail Creek is open to both canoes and motorboats. American alligator and cottonmouth snakes live in the creek. Whitetail deer, black bear from one of the largest concentrations in the Mid-Atlantic region, and smaller mammals sometimes are seen near the stream. Numerous birds, including the prothronotary warbler, sing from the forest canopy. Bald eagle and peregrine falcon sometimes soar in the skies.

Buffalo Creek Road, which runs to Milltail Creek near East Lake, opens up other possibilities. It leads to the ruins of an old logging village. Several old logging roads in this area, while not prepared trails, may be walked for short distances.

More casual travelers may get an idea of the scope and nature of the refuge by driving along U.S. Route 64 and 264, which divide the refuge roughly into thirds. Alligator River, of course, is frequently used by fishers and pleasure boaters. It is part of the Intracoastal Waterway.

The refuge plans ultimately to build a visitors center on Roanoke Island. There, in comfortable surroundings, visitors will be given vicarious views of the inaccessible refuge, including live red wolves and an interpreted nature trail.

Along Pamlico Sound and River

Lake Landing

U.S. Route 264 continues through countryside settled 400 years ago. One of John White's early drawings, of a Pomeloc Indian Village, was made in this area. Farmlands and forests border the highway most of the way, but occasionally it breaks out within sight of Pamlico Sound or one of its inlets. Side roads also lead to waterfront villages with names like Middletown, founded in 1787, Stumpy Point, and Gull Rock. Englehard, whose docks stand at the head of an inlet, is the largest community and the site of an annual May seafood festival, but the most interesting is Lake Landing, whose development was spurred by several attempts to drain nearby Lake Mattamuskeet.

Lake Landing Historic District stretches out along U.S. Route 264 and state roads east and south of Englehard. Three buildings on the main highway are regularly open to the public: the 1857 Octagon House, restored by a non-profit organization, and two churches. The architecture of the six-room stucco Octagon House, built by Dr. William T. Sparrow, is unusual; its walls are made of 1-by-3 boards laid on top of each other without uprights except at doors and windows. A large central chimney vents four fireplaces. The original Greek-Revival interior of Amity Methodist Church, built between 1850 and 1852, is basically intact. St. George's Episcopal Church, a Gothic-Revival frame structure raised in 1874, is likewise little changed.

A number of private residences along the highway were constructed from the early to late 1800s by Henry W. Gibbs, Hugh Jones, James Robinson Fisher, and others. Signs trace their lineages. The highway crosses the Great Ditch and Bennett Rose Canal, designed to help drain Lake Mattamuskeet into Pamlico Sound.

Off the main highway, along state Routes 1108 and 1110, are nine historic structures, including the Federal-style Carter-Swindell House (circa 1810), the 1850 Spencer-Gibbs Store, the 1872 Middletown Christian Church, the Gibbs Family House (circa 1810), one of the least altered in the area, and the 1890s Queen Anne-style George Israel Watson House at Nebraska.

A map available at the Chamber of Commerce office in the Octagon House (open 1 to 4 p.m. Wednesday–Sunday) identifies 25 sites.

One of the real-life legends of the region—the church "moved by the hand of God" — occurred in the small town of Swan Quarter. In 1876, members of Providence Methodist Church could not acquire the site they wanted so they built a new church elsewhere. Along came a hurricane and floated the new church down the street and around a corner to the preferred site, where it has been ever since. U.S. Route 264 through this region is part of the extensive network of roads that North Carolina has designated a bike route.

Mattamuskeet National Wildlife Refuge

Shallow Lake Mattamuskeet, the largest natural lake in North Carolina, is the dominant geographical feature of the region. In a way, it also has been a dominant historical feature, inspiring prodigious efforts to drain it in order to access the rich bottom for farming. The drainage idea was broached as early as 1789, and two canals dug around 1808 lowered the water level enough to encourage further consideration. The North Carolina General Assembly authorized the project in 1835, but nothing was done at the time. Beginning in 1914, more than 2,000 miles of ditches and canals were dug as intakes and outflows for the largest pumping station in the world. Rice, corn, soybeans, flax, sweet potatoes, wheat, barley, and other crops were planted on as much as 12,000 acres of reclaimed land before the project was abandoned in 1932. One reason was recurring financial problems. Margaret Silverthorne of Lake Landing recalls that a man who drove tractors there told her one company paid out $25 for every dollar it made.

The 49,925-acre site was sold to the U.S. government in December 1934 and made into a wildlife refuge by presidential order. As the lake gradually refilled to its average depth of 3 feet, Civilian Conservation Corps (CCC) workers converted the pumping station into a hunting lodge and observation tower. The lodge closed in 1974 after the number of migrating fowl on the lake declined drastically.

Evidence of this history may be seen in the remnants of canals on and off the refuge and at the refuge headquarters at the end of a dirt road on the southern shore. The pumping station/lodge remains closed, but its restoration as a motel to serve the 50,000-plus visitors to the site each year is occasionally discussed.

The 40,000-acre, 18-mile-long lake within the refuge is encircled by a thin barrier of land totaling about 3,500 acres. Another 6,400 acres is freshwater marshes. Water-control structures, burning, planting, and other methods are used to manage the site to enhance habitats for the wildlife.

Most visitors hunt (swans, ducks, and coots on special dates), fish, and crab. Fishing for bass, catfish, bream, and other species is permitted on Lake Mattamuskeet from March to November and year-round from canal banks and water-control structures. Canal and lakeshore fishing is especially productive in the spring and autumn. Ramps for small boats and canoes are located at state Route 94 and the refuge entrance road, at park headquarters, and on Rose Bay Canal at the western end of the lake.

An increasing number of visitors engage in passive pursuits such as wildlife viewing and photography. Wildfowl may be observed either from vehicles or on foot. A dirt wildlife drive starts at the refuge headquarters and parallels a canal through a pine and mixed-hardwood forest before it breaks out on the shore of the lake. Blinds used for controlled duck hunting are located at the end of this road, which has limited turnaround opportunities. The main canal road and Waupoppin Canal Road also are open to vehicular traffic from March through October.

Hiking is permitted year-round on all dikes and roads.

The easiest way to view ducks and geese that winter on the lake is along the 7-mile causeway (state Route 94) that crosses the lake. While no prepared parking areas are available, the wide shoulders of the road have plenty of room. Fairfield, just north of the lake, is on the National Register of Historic Places.

Mattamuskeet is noted especially for the number of tundra swan — perhaps 20,000 — that winter there each year. Another 7,000 Canada and snow geese and 22 species of ducks, including black ducks, mallards, teals, and canvasbacks, arrive each fall. They are replaced by songbirds and marsh birds during the warm months.

Interpretive programs vary from year to year and include such events as canoe handling, nature studies about the white-tailed deer and small mammals on the refuge, building songbird nests, and environmental studies.

The ancient history of the lake is just as unsettled as the modern one. Its name is Indian for "dry dust"; a tradition describes a peat-bog fire that burned for 13 moons. Geologists believe the lake was once a large juniper swamp that burned down through the layer of peat.

Swanquarter and Pocosin Lakes Refuges

Two other national wildlife refuges (NWR) are located within a short distance of Mattamuskeet.

Swanquarter NWR covers about 15,000 acres of loblolly pine forest, coastal marshlands dominated by black needle rush and sawgrass and islands, and 27,000 acres of open water in Pamlico Sound. About 8,000 acres are included in the National Wilderness Preservation System. Wildlife includes the American alligator, water snakes, and turtles in the wetlands and white-tailed deer in the forests. Among wintering wildfowl are whistling swans, Canada geese, scaups, buffleheads, ruddy ducks, mallards, and wigeons. Bob-white quail and pileated woodpeckers are among plentiful songbirds, shorebirds, wading and marsh birds.

The refuge is only partially developed and thus is lightly visited. A 2-mile road leads from U.S. Route 264 through the forest in a section known as Bell Island to a fishing pier. Waterfowl hunting is permitted on about 6,100 acres of marshland. Boat ramps are located along Oyster Creek Road near the refuge.

Pocosin Lakes NWR, northwest of Lake Mattamuskeet, encompasses about 111,000 acres of varied terrain put together by combining a number of parcels. The 12,000-acre Pungo NWR on state Route 45 was the first. In 1989, the Conservation Fund donated an additional 93,000 acres of adjacent wetlands. Another 6,000 acres north of Frying Pan Lake were ceded later by Alligator NWR. The enlarged refuge includes 2,800-acre Pungo Lake, 4,100-acre New Lake, and 2,000-acre Frying Pan Lake and borders on the Scuppernong and Alligator rivers.

A good example of a pocosin is visible from state Route 94 about ½ mile south of the northwest fork of the Alligator River. There, thickets of broadleaf evergreen shrubs grow with pine wood, dwarf pine pond, and pitcher plant. Near the Scuppernong and Alligator rivers are bottomland hardwood forests featuring black gum, Carolina ash, loblolly pine, Atlantic white cedar, red maple, water tupelo, and bald cypress. About 400 acres of marsh lie along the Alligator River.

The Pungo refuge is a spectacular bird area. In winter, Lake Pungo attracts large numbers of snow geese, as well as other wildfowl. Overall, 207 species, including the loggerhead shrike, fulvous whistling duck, and western sandpiper, have been spotted. A wildlife drive parallels old canals and passes Pungo Lake. An observation tower stands at the southeastern tip of the lake. Bob-white quail prefer another area of the Pocosin Lakes refuge south of Lake Phelps.

Black bear are present on the north side of Lake Phelps; white-tailed deer and other animals roam many areas. Archers may hunt deer during the state season on about 12,000 acres; shotguns and primitive weapons may be used on certain days in October on about 7,000 acres. Only 200 permits per day are issued by lottery.

Belhaven

Many visitors along U.S. Route 264 merely pass through Belhaven en route to more historic towns such as Bath and Washington. But it is worth a stop, if only to recognize its unusual search for identity. First named Aquascogoc by Algonkian Indians, it was later called Jack's Neck by English settlers. Its first business was founded by Solomon J. Topping, son of an entrepreneur who built a summer cottage there, but it grew rapidly after arrival of the railroad in 1891. At that time, the city decided it needed a more prestigious name; Belhaven, "beautiful harbor" in French, was the first choice, but another community with a post office already had that name. Belle Harbor, the second choice, was used until the post office in the other Belhaven closed in 1893. The town on Pantego Creek prospered as a seafood, lumbering, and agricultural center, with even the Rockefeller interests participating, and in 1928 became a stop on the Intracoastal Waterway.

A few relics survived even such a pragmatic existence. One is the large Victorian mansion on East Main Street where entrepreneur John A. Wilkinson lived among leaded-glass windows, crystal chandeliers, and eleven fireplaces with carved oak mantels. It is now a hotel-retaurant named River Forest Manor. Another is the old Town Hall, whose second floor holds a museum office described as "attic" in format: a complete country kitchen, thousands of buttons, a dress worn by a 700-pound woman, late 19th-century farm equipment, and dolls. The museum is open daily from 1 to 5 p.m.

Historic Bath

The current side-road status and size of North Carolina's first town—Historic Bath is situated on state Route 92—is deceiving. From this one-time port on the Pamlico River flowed the mainstream of colonial North Carolina life. Settled as early as 1690 and chartered in 1705, it was the pioneer political and economic hub of the state, as well as the center of the prosperous farming region around it. The early years were, as an historical marker points out, a "period of turbulence." Out of the first official port of entry flowed naval stores, furs, and tobacco. The first meetings of the colonial assembly held there brought together politicians, merchants, plantation owners, and humble pioneers. Thomas Harding built the first shipyard in the colony in Bath and built ships that expanded the commerce of the region; the notorious pirate Edward Teach, better known as Blackbeard, probably did not harass Bath because he was allowed to live there unmolested during the eight-year governorship of Charles Eden. Naturalist and historian John Lawson lived there later.

Historic Bath may disappoint some visitors when they first arrive because it has no dominant focal point, no governor's palace. But its understated charm grows on visitors as they walk cobbled streets, attend the play *Blackbeard — Knight of the Black Flag* (Thursday–Saturday, June through mid-August), and tour historic structures.

A number of exceptional colonial buildings, including the two-story Palmer-Marsh House (circa 1744) on Main Street, are part of tours that start at the modern visitors center on Route 2 (Carteret Street). The hospitality of North Carolina's surveyor general and customs collector, Colonel Robert Palmer, was praised by no less than Governor William Tryon, whose mansion in New Bern became the epitome of luxurious living. The frame Van Der Meer House (circa 1790) is more modest, but was quite comfortable and large by frontier standards. The Bonner House (circa 1830), an excellent example of North Carolina coastal architecture with large porches front and rear, also has a fine memorial garden. Red brick St. Thomas Episcopal Church, built in 1734–62, is the oldest church building in North Carolina; its cemetery has headstones dating back to the earliest years of the colony.

Another interesting house is the white frame Glebe House (circa 1835), the mid-19th century home of the publisher of *Farmer's Journal,* John F. Tompkins.

Historic Bath is best viewed on foot, following its tree-lined streets past the historic homes to places that reveal the beautiful waterfront setting of the town, such as Bonner (Town) Point overlooking Bath Creek and Jarding's Landing, where a public dock is located. Guided tours that include house visits are conducted 9 a.m. to 5 p.m. Tuesday–Saturday, and on Sunday afternoons. A self-guided walking tour map can be obtained at the visitors center (9 a.m. to 5 p.m. Monday–Saturday, 1 to 5 p.m. Sunday).

Washington

In the region, this community is often referred to as "little" Washington to distinguish it from the national capital. There is nothing small about it historically or visually, however.

Sir Walter Raleigh's first expedition visited the area in 1585, and the first settlers arrived about a century later. A town named Forks of the Tar was founded in the 1770s on the farm of James Bonner; a change in 1776 made it the first community named after George Washington, the Revolutionary War hero and later first president. Washington was a strategic port, especially after the British occupied Charleston and Savannah. It remained an important port until the Civil War, when it was occupied by Federal units. Many buildings burned when a fire set to destroy stockpiles by retreating Federals got out of control. Another disaster occured in 1900 when a faulty flue started a fire that burned much of the business district.

As a result, this vital, vibrant community has an eclectic assortment of historic structures—and historic memories. A self-guided walking tour passes more than 25 points of interest in a 19-block area. These range from colonial houses to a turn-of-the-century train station. All the houses are private residences or business offices, but most have authentically restored exteriors.

The Chamber of Commerce office on Stewart Parkway, a riverfront drive just off U.S. Route 17 that replaced unused commercial docks and warehouses, is a good place to start. A small park on the shore has a ½-mile-long promenade that overlooks the active Tar River, its boat ramp on the opposite shore, and Castle Island, whose name derives from the smokestacks of industrial kilns that once stood there.

Side-by-side on Water Street, a few blocks east, are three buildings built in the late 18th century. A Civil War cannonball is lodged in the wall of the Marsh House (circa 1795). This building and the adjacent Myers House (circa 1789), the oldest in Washington, were used by Federal forces as offices and quarters. The appearance of the Hyatt House, built about 1785, has been altered; what the ghost supposedly haunting the third floor thinks about that has not been determined.

Other historic concentrations are located on Main and Market streets. Among those with colorful backgrounds are the Havens House (circa 1820), a West Indies-style cottage built by a shipping merchant from Long Island, New York; the Riverside-Winfield

House (circa 1886), once the hotel and depot for the "Jolt and Wiggle," the nickname of Washington's first railroad, the Jamesville and Washington; the Mayo law office (circa 1830), an interesting example of Federal commercial architecture that later was used as a school and funeral parlor; and the Cravens Warehouse (circa 1820), a naval stores facility that somehow survived the fires.

A few historic buildings can be visited. The Old Town Hall (circa 1884) and the long brick train station built in 1904 house museums — the latter the displays of the Beaufort County Arts Council. The original courtroom in the Old Beaufort County Courthouse (circa 1786), the second oldest in North Carolina, is open.

Two late 19th-century church buildings replaced structures burned during the Civil War: the 1867 First Presbyterian Church on West Second Street and St. Peter's Episcopal Church (circa 1867) on North Bonner Street. According to legend, the bells of St. Peter's tolled as the church burned in 1864. The First Methodist Church building on North Second Street, dedicated in 1899, is the fourth to be used by the congregation.

Goose Creek State Park

This 1,200-acre park on the Pamlico Park 8 miles east of Washington off U.S. Route 264 is described by Ranger David Curtis as "almost pure nature."

More than 6 miles of hiking trails explore varied habitats: planted pine forests, bottomlands along Goose and Mallard creeks, cypress swamps and live oak along the riverbank. Boardwalks through a marsh area show the transition from freshwater to brackish species.

The Ragged Point Trail is an excellent place to experience wetlands and see shorebirds. Black bear, which live around a landfill outside the park, sometimes wander onto the preserve. Bobcat, white-tailed deer, beaver, muskrat, mink, otter, nutria, and raccoon are among other mammals seen there. The park is not noted for wildfowl, but quite a few greater scaups, canvasbacks, wood ducks, and other species fly in. The endangered red cockaded woodpecker is often seen.

A boat ramp provides access to both freshwater casting for bass, bream, and catfish, and brackish-water fishing for flounder, speckled trout, croaker, spot, mullet, and bluefish, among others. Nature programs, held monthly, cover such subjects as wetlands, reptiles, astronomy, and birds of prey. Bird and night hikes are conducted.

Every summer, a sandy beach on the river is cleared and roped off for swimming. The mixture of sand and mud at that point creates a solid bottom. Twelve primitive campsites are available.

Greenville

This agricultural market center is the big city of the region, with nearly 50,000 residents and several times that number of transients each year. It is one of the largest tobacco markets in the world and the home of East Carolina University, which conducts a year-round program of educational and cultural activities. A Voice of America broadcasting station admits visitors, Monday–Friday from 9 a.m. to 3:30 p.m.

South of the Pamlico River

Pamlico County Chamber of Commerce
P.O. Box 23
Bayboro, NC 28575
919/249-1851

FOR MANY PEOPLE, THE PENINSULA BETWEEN THE PAMLICO AND NEUSE rivers is "just there." In one of the most isolated places along the North Carolina coastal plain, people divide their attentions between farming, forestry, and seafood—as they have for centuries. A limited number of tourists find their way to this area, most of them just passing through on the Intracoastal Waterway.

Still, the area has attraction for savvy travelers. State Route 33 parallels the northern shore of the peninsula through a sparsely settled flatland area broken by short inlets and maritime forests. En route to the three principal points—Aurora, Hobucken, and Oriental—the driver will see occasional settlements, pass a boat ramp/wildlife point about a mile west of the Pamlico County line, enjoy a profusion of wildflowers along the highway, and encounter numbers of trucks carrying logs and slow-moving farm equipment.

Aurora is a crossroads community that also is located at the head of an inlet. It is best known for the Aurora Fossil Museum, whose audiovisual show and exhibits emphasize the geologic influences that over millions of years created the coastal plain, fossil discoveries including shark's teeth, and the possibility of prehistoric humans in eastern North Carolina. The museum is open Tuesday–Saturday during the warm months and Monday–Friday at other times of the year.

At Goose Creek Island, whose 1929 bridge (soon to be replaced by a high-rise span) swings open to allow vessels on the Intracoastal Waterway to pass, one can find the down-home simplicity and suspicion of outsiders that once characterized the entire coastal region. It takes a while—sometimes years—for newcomers to gain social acceptance.

There has been no major development on the island. The main settlement, Hobucken, remains a simple water-oriented community, with a seafood processing plant and docking facilities. It is literally where the pavement ends. From that point, a dirt road leads into an area known locally as "the Marshes,"which is covered with grass and scrub as far as Middle Bay and Sow Point. Several places to put boats in the water are located along this road.

Hobucken stands farther from the tip of the peninsula than it did in the early decades of this century when a ferry operated across the Pamlico River to Washington. After a storm washed away much of the community in 1913, it was rebuilt at what was considered a safer site. The site is still low, however, and the mosquito problem, according to June Lang, has been known to persist from February to December.

Some of the homes that survived the storm were moved in sections to the new site and reassembled. Eight houses in the community, all private residences, are more than a century old but most have been modified over the years. The oldest is believed to be the Robinson-Lupton house.

According to legend, the pirate Blackbeard buried treasure in the area while he was living unhindered at Bath, a little farther upstream on the opposite shore of the Pamlico River. As the pirates dug, legend has it that they refrained from talking for fear the treasure would disappear if they did. Mysterious night lights also have been sighted in the marshes along the coast.

The community of Lowland, at the end of a side road that deer sometimes cross, is similar in character. Most of the docks for fishing boats on Goose Creek Island are located there, and sailboats may be seen at the inlet where the road ends. Lowland also is the approach to the state refuge on Pamlico Point, where an impoundment was constructed to control the habitat and aid hunting.

Six separated parcels of state forest around Hobucken, covering about 7,600 acres, are known collectively as the Goose Creek Game Lands. They are managed by burning, and in some areas clover planting, but overall are as primitive as almost any place in coastal North Carolina simply because so few people know about them. Since they are lightly used, the forests abound in wildlife—white-tailed deer, squirrels, rabbits, quail, snipe, woodcock, and other species. Hunting is permitted in some areas in October and December, the later hunters being chosen by lot.

The largest segment, the Goose Creek Wildlife Management Area, lies along paved state Routes 33 and 304; the others require travel across dirt roads or use of a boat. Hikers may enter the forests, using old, untended roads and a primitive trail at the segment on the Pamlico River near Spring Creek. Pamlico Point, where impoundments in a former military bombing impact area attract waterfowl, is accessible by boat.

The forest headquarters is located on state Route 306 south of Grantsboro, but prospective users should contact the North Carolina Wildlife Commission (919/638-3000).

Oriental, via state Routes 304 and 55, is just the opposite of Hobucken. For one thing, the natural attributes of the community are much more pleasant to the eye. Located on high ground overlooking the Neuse River, it has a beautiful harbor and a number of inlets that increase the water frontage and add to the aesthetics. For another, huge real-estate promotion signs and sales offices strategically located on the main road—one of which dispenses general information about Oriental, as well as the properties it sells—announce that it is open. Real-estate developments are tucked away in the pine forests of the area.

Retirees and boat lovers supplement the community's economic base, which seafood once sustained. The self-styled "sailing capital of the world" has a municipal harbor for both private and shrimp boats, several marinas, a sailing school and yacht club, among other facilities. A 10-foot channel extends to the Intracoastal Waterway. Fishers seek both saltwater and freshwater varieties; charter boats are available. In addition, there is hunting nearby for wildfowl, bear, deer, small animals, and doves.

A township was founded at what is now Oriental in the 1870s after Louis B. and Robert P. Midyette and their families settled there, but it had no name when the time came to open a post office. Rebecca Midyette owned the nameplate of the ship *Oriental,* which had gone down in 1862, and suggested using that name. The town was incorporated in 1899, and now has approximately 1,100 residents.

At Minnesott Shores on state Route 306, a free ferry connects the tip of the peninsula to the south shore of the Neuse River, especially Havelock and the Croatan Forest, historic New Bern, and the Crystal Shore area around Morehead City.

South of the Neuse River

Craven County Convention & Visitors Bureau
P.O. Box 1413
New Bern, NC 28563
919/637-9400

New Bern

MENTION OF NEW BERN IMMEDIATELY BRINGS TO MIND TRYON PALACE. The association is fully justified; the reconstructed governor's mansion is one of the finest colonial buildings on the East Coast. But New Bern is hardly one-dimensional. It contains other fine colonial buildings. Its Swiss origins are reflected in its City Hall, as well as the city's bear flag and name. It includes a beautiful waterfront setting, where the sun rising over the Neuse River can be spectacular. Riverfront marinas suggest that the use of the river today for sports is just as heavy as it was for commercial purposes in the colonial era.

Chautauqua Indians occupied the region when a hardy band of Swiss and German Palatinate settlers landed in 1710. The Europeans not only had difficulty adjusting to the hot climate and new diseases, but faced hostile Indians who massacred many of them in 1711. They managed to defeat the Indians, who fled northward and founded what is today Chautauqua, New York. However, the problems of the colony's leader, Baron Christopher deGraffenreid, were far from over. Financial difficulties induced him to mortgage the colony's lands to Thomas Pollock, a wealthy planter from the Chowan area, after which deGraffenreid returned to Europe.

In time, the Swiss and German influence waned and New Bern became an anglicized community. It prospered as a port trading with the Mother Country. North Carolina's first newspaper, the *North Carolina Gazette,* was printed there in 1751 by James Davis, who also brought in the state's first printing press in 1749. In 1766, Royal Governor William Tryon located his capitol in New Bern; the last royal governor, Josiah Martin, fled in May 1775 when the American Revolution broke out. New Bern's pivotal role in North Carolina history was over; it languished for several decades after the Revolutionary War until it began to turn nearby pine forests into profitable naval stores. The large number of Federal-style buildings in the community attests to its wealth in the early 1800s.

Pollock Street follows the route known in the colonial period as Kings Highway because it connected Virginia to the Carolinas and Georgia, where the possessions of the British king ended at the border of then-Spanish Florida.

Tryon Palace and Gardens Complex. Tryon Palace actually is the centerpiece of a complex that includes four other historic structures and their gardens.

Flanking the entrance road are two early 19th-century houses relocated to the site: the John P. Daves House (circa 1813), built by a wealthy planter and now the Tryon Palace shop, and the neoclassical Dixon–Stevenson House (circa 1828–33), built by merchant-tailor and mayor George W. Dixon and later enlarged. Federal and Empire furniture in the latter house reflects tastes during the first half of the 19th century. At the rear of this house is a garden planted entirely in white seasonal flowers.

The elegant John Wright Stanly House on George Street was constructed by a man who arrived in New Bern in the 1770s. Built in 1783, it has fine interior woodwork and is furnished primarily with American Georgian-style pieces. President George Washington, who stayed there during his visit to New Bern in 1791, described it as "exceeding good lodgings." During the Civil War, Union General

Ambrose Burnside used the house for a time as his headquarters. It then became a Union army hospital. After 1935, it was used as the city's public library for 30 years. It has been restored and furnished according to an inventory made by Stanly.

Tryon Palace itself, when completed in 1770, was regarded as the finest government building in America. This first permanent meeting place for the government of the colony personified the symmetry and massiveness (its walls were 3 feet thick) typical of Georgian architecture. Its beauty and elegance did not impress cash-poor frontier families, who were among those being taxed to pay for it. They revolted but were defeated by Governor Tryon's forces at the Battle of Alamance. Tryon, despite a record of religious tolerance and support of education, stayed in the palace only a year and, in a decade, royal rule was no more.

After the Revolutionary War, the palace remained the state capitol until 1794. The first president of the United States dined and danced there during his 1791 visit. In 1798, all but one wing was destroyed by fire, and in 1945 much of the site was paved over to extend George Street. In 1959 the surviving wing was restored and the remainder of the Georgian-style palace reconstructed on the original foundations.

A guided tour today is as much an account of the people and events associated with the mansion as of the furnishings. Tours are conducted Tuesday–Saturday, Easter Monday, Memorial Day, and Labor Day from 9:30 a.m. to 4 p.m., Sunday from 1:30 to 4 p.m.; closed Thanksgiving, December 24–26, and January 1.

The mansion is authentically decorated. Curtains and chair covers are changed according to the season, as they were during the colonial era. Gardens reflect 18th-century British traditions.

The interpretive program includes drama tours during which costumed actors portray Governor Tryon, members of his household, and visitors. Cooking and blacksmithing are among the crafts regularly demonstrated. Special events, held in every season, include Colonial Living Day in mid-May, when costumed craftspeople make things the old-fashioned way and children demonstrate colonial games. For the annual two-week Christmas program, the houses in the complex are decorated according to their antecedents, Tryon Palace is festooned in green cuttings and fruit wreaths, candlelight tours are conducted, a groaning board displays colonial-era foods, and a colonial-style ball is held.

The New Bern Academy, the oldest school in the state, is now a museum administered by Tryon Palace. It was founded in 1766 when the state legislature levied a tax to support it. The present four-room brick building (circa 1809) remained in service until 1971, except for a period during the Civil War when it was used as a hospital. Restored in 1985 by the New Bern Academy Historical Commission, it now houses artifacts such as an Indian log canoe, dueling pistols, 1792 porcelain, furniture made in New Bern, and a Civil War battle flag and artillery piece. Narrative exhibits cover contacts with Indians; New Bern's status as the "Athens of North Carolina" in the late 18th and early 19th centuries, when it was a center of culture and education; methods of teaching in the academy in its early years; the city's role as a port; and architectural influences evident in New Bern.

Walking New Bern. After a tour of Tryon Palace and its related buildings, a walk around the old section of New Bern (maps available from visitors center at 219 Pollock Street) traces the city's history through various periods and unearths numerous anecdotes. Scattered throughout the district are historic structures housing modern uses—the 1797 Harvey House, now a restaurant, and the Victorian home (circa 1880) that is now the Aerie bed and breakfast establishment, for example. Others range from colonial homes and churches to an art nouveau-style former automobile service station. Many of the historic buildings open to the public are concentrated on Pollock Street.

From the palace, Pollock Street in either direction displays historic buildings. In the westerly direction lie a number of private houses: the Federal-style Jones House (circa 1808), where Confederate spy Emeline Pigott was imprisoned during the Union occupation; John Horner Hill House, a Georgian structure built between 1770 and 1780; the well-preserved Henry H. Harris House (circa 1800), an example of vernacular Federal style; the Alston–Charlotte House, with a gambrel roof, built before 1770; the story-and-a-half Osgood Cottage (circa 1830); and others.

A stroll east along Pollock reveals more variety. A modern building at the corner of Metcalf Street intrudes into this historic setting. However, its contents—the New Bern Civil War Museum—are appropriate since New Bern was captured in March 1862 by Union General Burnside and occupied for the duration of the war. The museum, open daily 10 a.m. to 6 p.m. except holidays, holds a superior collection of arms from the period, photographs of North Carolina soldiers, and uniforms and personal equipment used by combatants. Curator Will Gorges is recognized as an authority on Civil War memorabilia.

The Renaissance Revival-style Edward R. Stanly House on the corner of Hancock Street was built by a descendant of John Wright Stanly about 1849. On the other side of the street is the art nouveau gasoline station known as the "Old Blue Gable." When a proposal was made to tear it down, elementary schoolchildren organized a petition drive to save it. On the corner of Middle Street is an unobtrusive marker identifying the site where pharmacist Caleb D. Bradham created in 1898 a soft drink first called Brad's Drink. Later, the name was changed to Pepsi-Cola.

Christ Episcopal Church, established by Governor Tryon in 1715, is one of the oldest Anglican dioceses in North Carolina. The original 1750 church, sometimes known as "King's Chapel," burned in 1877. The current red brick building incorporates the old walls and retains the communion service and Bible and prayer book sent in 1752 by King George II. According to local tradition, the cannon in the churchyard was taken from a British warship during the Revolutionary War.

City Hall at the intersection of Pollock and Craven streets is more interesting for its style of architecture than its history. Its spire with a clock, added in 1910, mimics architecture frequently seen in old Swiss cities, including Bern for which the North Carolina city is named. The handsome buff-colored structure was built in 1897 and used as a post office, courthouse, and customs house before the city acquired it in 1936.

The visitors center on Pollock Street occupies a house built in 1847.

A diversion from historic tracing is justified to view the beautiful New Bern waterfront at the point where the Neuse and Trent rivers meet. A right turn off Pollock onto Craven Street leads to a promenade overlooking the Trent River; across busy U.S. 20 is Union Point Park, which overlooks the Neuse River. The latter is a special place at sunrise when the red orb slowly appears above the forested shore and transforms the river into a canvas of colors.

North along East Front Street stand a number of historic homes that are private residences. Some of them are usually among the dozen or so private houses and gardens and numerous churches opened for tours during the annual Spring House and Gardens Tour in early April.

A 1,000-year-old cypress tree in the backyard of a residence at 520 East Front Street is among only 23 listed in the Hall of Fame of American Trees. Early colonists and Indians met under its branches to conclude treaties; later, Revolutionary War generals took oaths there. President George Washington knew of the tree's history and asked to see it during a visit in April 1791. The tree is partly visible from the street; visitors should ask permission of the property owners before entering the yard to touch it.

Two blocks west on New Street is the tall white eminence of the First Presbyterian Church, built between 1819 and 1822 with an African-American woman as one of its founding members. It was used as a Union hospital and lookout post during the Civil War; the belfry still bears the initials and names that lookouts carved while on duty. In the nearby Federal Building paintings depict scenes from the city's history.

The Firemen's Museum on Broad Street depicts the courage and devotion of fire units, including two of the oldest continuous companies in the country, through displays of early 19th-century firefighting equipment, maps, and photographs. Open Tuesday–Saturday, 9:30 a.m. to noon, 1 to 5 p.m., and Sunday 1 to 5 p.m.; closed Thanksgiving, Christmas Day, and New Year's Day.

Catty-cornered across Broad Street is the Attmore-Oliver House (circa 1790), the headquarters of the New Bern Historical Society. The house is decorated with 18th- and 19th-century furniture and regional historical relics. It is open Tuesday–Saturday afternoons.

Town tour tapes are available at the Chamber of Commerce. A guided New Bern at Night Ghost Walk sponsored by the New Bern Historical Society visits six candlelit late 18th- and early 19th-century homes where the antics of allegedly ethereal squatters occur among antiques, Federal-style woodwork, cast-iron hitching posts, an in-house ballroom, and handsome mantels. The annual Chrysanthemum Festival in mid–October features a variety of events, including regattas, concerts, demonstrations by volunteer firemen, and Revolutionary War and Civil War encampments. Tryon Palace gardens are open at no charge.

New Bern's extensive waterfront continues to pull attention in that direction, though primarily recreational now. The Neuse River is half a mile wide at New Bern and bulges downstream. The channel to the Intracoastal Waterway usually has depths of 8 to 12 feet, but the clearance can be 2 feet greater or less depending on the wind. A strong easterly or northerly wind raises the level, while a westerly wind lowers it. There is little tidal influence. In the warm months, sapling stakes, white flags, or floating plastic bottles identify nets placed by area residents to trap fish and mark crabpots. The Trent River is narrower but still wide enough for a full range of boating activity—sailing, power boating, water skiing, fishing, crabbing, and so on. Docking facilities of all types dot the shores of both rivers.

Canoeists may follow either of the rivers or a number of interesting creeks and inlets. From the Trent River, Brice Creek makes numerous turns as it cuts deep into forested countryside alive with wildlife. East of New Bern, much of the Neuse River's southern shoreline lies within the boundaries of Croatan National Forest and the Cherry Point Marine Air Station. The northern shoreline is indented by a series of creeks that wind deep into sparsely settled territory.

The array of masts that inhabit the marinas on both the Neuse and Trent rivers show how devoted area residents are to sailing. Several motels have docking areas for power boats as well.

Croatan National Forest

The Croatan National Forest extends almost from New Bern to the coast, covering an area of more than 157,000 acres. It encompasses a variety of ecosystems—upland hardwood forests, stands of loblolly and longleaf pine, pocosins, and bottomland—that sustain quite a few rare species of wildlife, including the red-cockaded woodpecker, bald eagle, and alligator. It hosts five genera of insectivorous plants—Venus fly-trap (*Dionaea muscipula*), pitcher-plants (*Sarracenia sp.*), round-leaves sundew (*Drosera rotundfolia*), butterworts (*Pinguicula sp.*), and bladderworts (*Utricularia sp.*), as well as the rare shrub Zenobia. It contains 40 miles of streams and 4,300 acres of lakes yielding largemouth bass, bluegill, chain pickerel, warmouth, yellow perch, and other varieties, although lake fishing generally is poor because of acidity in the water. The forest is actively managed by burning in early summer and winter, harvesting of pine, replanting, and other activities. Hunting and trapping are allowed at certain times.

U.S. Route 70 cuts through the forest. Side roads lead to various sections of the park where maintained features are accessible to the public. A public recreation area for swimming, fishing, camping, and picnicking at Flanner's Beach, 10 miles south of New Bern off U.S. Route 70, is usually open April through November. Boats may be launched at Brice Creek, Cahooque Landing, Haywood Landing, Catfish Lake, Great Lake, and Cedar Point, which also are favored spots for fishing, primitive camping, and picnicking. Hikers may reach Cedar Point any time of year; normally, others are allowed

April through October. The limited facilities at Fishers Landing, about 8 miles south of New Bern, are open year-round. Primitive camping generally is permitted anywhere hikers can reach along old roads and trails.

Three prepared trails of different lengths explore different sections and habitats of the forest.

The half-mile loop of Island Creek Forest Walk, which starts on state Route 1004 about 7 miles past the airport at New Bern, winds through a rare sight in eastern North Carolina—a beech climax forest. Along the canopied trail are loblolly pine, yellow poplar, dogwood, black walnut, sweetgum, bald cypress, American holly, umbrella magnolia, mockernut hickory, American beech, white oak, red oak, and at least 30 varieties of wildflowers, including ferns, wild aster, bloodroot, columbine, cinquefoil, wild ginger, honeysuckle, Indian pipe, jack-in-the-pulpit, partridge berry, pipsissewa, rattlesnake plaintain, and birdfoot violet. The trail passes Island Creek, under-laid with marl, a stratum of fossilized seashells deposited millions of year ago when the region was under water.

The Neusiok Trail, which starts at the Pinecliff Recreation Area on the Neuse River, covers about 20 miles of sandy beaches, hardwood ridges, cypress–palmetto swamps, pine flatlands, dense brush, pocosins, and swamps and crosses paved and dirt roads en route to the Newport River near the coast. Wildlife seen in these habitats includes the rare red-cockaded woodpecker, southern bald eagle, American alligator, white-tailed deer, black bear, wild turkey, quail, and other small animals. Snakes—including copperheads, cottonmouth, and the eastern diamond rattlesnake—and insects are a problem at times. Fall, winter, and early spring are the best times to try this path.

The coastal Cedar Point Tideland Trail at the mouth of the White Oak River, also a short loop, offers blinds for viewing wildlife, including migratory shorebirds and waterfowl. Part of the trail winds through a hardwood and pine forest; boardwalks cross marsh and open water. Egrets, hawks, woodcocks, flycatchers, peregrine falcon, and owls frequent the area.

The rangers office is located on U.S. Route 70.

The nearby 27,600-acre Hoffman State Forest is similar in nature to Croatan, but is not geared for casual visitors. However, U.S. Route 17 cuts through it, giving drivers a look at its attributes. The forest, a state game land with foxes, doves, raccoon, and deer, is open to hunting during regular seasons.

Havelock and Newport

Havelock on U.S. Route 70 evokes a single image: the Cherry Point Marine Corps Air Base. It is the Marine Corps' largest aviation facility and by far the largest employer in the area. A 100,000-square-foot Marine museum, opened in 1992, contains a tower that overlooks the base and runways. Exhibits include 45 planes spanning the history of Marine Corps aviation from the fragile, fabric-covered DH-4 of World War I and World War II Japanese Zero to the contemporary F-4 Phantom Jet and Iroquois helicopter; examples of modern technology; simulators; and old photographs. The museum is named for Major Alfred A. Cunningham, the first Marine Corps pilot and commander of the first Marine Aviation force during World War I.

Despite its military image, Havelock has more to offer. It is centrally located for those using the Croatan Forest, and it hosts the annual North Carolina Chili Cookoff in October.

Nearby Newport, a largely residential community, was settled in the early 1700s as a port and producer of naval stores. The name probably derives from "New Port" to differentiate it from the old port of Beaufort. However, when a post office was opened in 1859, the name was Shepardsville. It officially became Newport in 1866. Newport has an annual pig cooking contest in early April.

The Crystal Coast

Carteret County Tourist Development Bureau
P.O. Box 1406
Morehead City, NC 28503
919/637-9400

WHILE THIS NOMENCLATURE IS A MODERN PROMOTIONAL INVENTION, it has a certain authenticity. The region is a shining example of merging human and natural development.

The Crystal Coast extends from the ferry landing at Cedar Island (from Ocracoke) to the White Oak River. It includes Morehead City and the barrier islands east and south of it. Outside the Morehead City-Beaufort area, the mainland is divided between fishing villages and other residential enclaves and long stretches of forested and marshy countryside. A few of the islands hugging the mainland, like Harker's Island, have become famous in their own right. The Core Banks—the islands oceanward of Core Sound—remain virtually in a wild state. The Bogue Banks, where the mainland turns more westward behind Bogue Sound, are fully developed.

This is an area where isolation is historical—and even a bit traditional. Until modern times, mailboats made regular runs to maintain links between the mainland and island communities. They carried not only mail, but passengers and cargo.

In general, the visitor will benefit from viewing the region as one unit, as the locals do. The undeveloped barrier islands, which have splendid beaches for sunbathing, shell collecting, surfcasting, and other activities, are reachable only by boat. Docks are available even on the isolated Shackleford Banks, where ponies run wild. Commercial car-carrying ferries operate to several points on Cape Lookout National Seashore, which accounts for the large number of four-wheel-drive vehicles that one sees on the island with rows of fishing poles sticking up from front bumpers. More formal fishing events include the Big Rock Blue Marlin Tournament in early June, Cap'n Fannie's Billfish Tournament in July, Band the Billfish Tournament in early August, and the Atlantic Beach King Mackerel Tournament in mid-September.

Indians inhabited the region when it was first explored by English colonists. The communities established by the British were small and usually devoted to the fishing industry. In the early 18th century, the tricky sound and numerous inlets provided a convenient haven for ships flying the Jolly Roger, including Blackbeard before he was killed in 1718. Indeed, Blackbeard is supposed to have put down a mutiny by marooning the troublesome crew members on the shore of Beaufort Bay. It was not until Morehead City was chosen as a railroad terminus in the 1850s that the region began to expand.

Morehead City

In 1853, former Governor John Motley Morehead acquired a mainland site at today's Morehead City for the terminal of a new railroad. The city was incorporated in 1861 and named for the gover-nor/railroader. The city's aspirations to rival Nags Head as a resort were never quite achieved, but it grew rapidly and ultimately be-came the largest city on the Crystal Coast. It remains, even in this era of mass tourism, workaday in nature.

The waterfront is its fortune. The visitor entering on U.S. Route 70 will pass several marinas on inlets before reaching the main part of city. Elsewhere, numerous other marinas mix and match com-mercial and sports fishing craft. Morehead City is a well-known center for charter boat fishing, although some of this has shifted to nearby communities. One marlin caught off the coast weighed over 1,000 pounds. A stroll or drive down Evans Avenue, just one block off U.S. Route 70E, confirms this city's water orientation. Side by side are marinas, seafood houses, restaurants, tour boats, and the headquarters of the Blue Marlin Fishing Tournament.

Morehead — locals sometimes contract the name — is North Caro-lina's second largest port, handling about 2.5 million tons of dry bulk and general cargo a year from 5,500 feet of wharf frontage on the Newport River and Bogue Sound. It is an outlet for the wood chips and phosphates produced in the surrounding countryside and an im-porter of finished products.

The wide through streets — for the most part four lanes — are sym-bolic of Morehead City's role as a jumping-off place for an interest-ing region, rather than a tourist destination in itself. That does not mean the city is without redeeming cultural values. The Carteret County Museum of History with Indian artifacts, a prehistoric oys-ter, and diverse memorabilia and art is located in the heart of the city, near the Crystal Coast Civil Center and Carteret County Com-munity College, the scene of frequent cultural activities. It is open from 1 to 4 p.m. Tuesday–Saturday. In addition, it is the headquarters of the North Carolina Seafood Festival the first weekend in October, where mouth-watering down-home seafood cooking rivals in pub-lic affection events such as street dances, musical programs, races, demonstrations, and fireworks.

Beaufort

Beaufort often comes with the prefix Historic, which is justified. It is the third oldest town in North Carolina and was founded in 1709 by British sailors and French Huguenots and incorporated in 1722. Quakers later came in substantial numbers, followed by other religious and ethnic groups. It became a prime vacation site late in the 19th century and has never relented.

Nearly 100 restored structures in a 21-block historic district recreate a tight little 18th- and 19th-century community frequented by both sailors and plantation owners. Many of these are private homes viewable only from the outside. Five buildings are open year-round (Monday–Saturday 10 a.m. to 4 p.m., Sunday 2 to 4 p.m.) as part of a guided walking tour sponsored by the Beaufort Historical Association. The tours start at the visitors center in the Josiah Bell House (circa 1825) on Turner Street, which has several rooms furnished in the style of the period. Also on the tour are the 1767 Joseph Bell House, painted coach red with white shutters and furnished with 18th-century antiques; the 1796 Carteret County Courthouse, whose authentic furnishings include an original 13-star American Flag; the Carteret County jail (circa 1829) with two cells and keeper's quarters; and the Apothecary Shop and Doctor's Office (circa 1859), where many of the instruments, bottles, and prescription files are original.

Another way to tour the historic district is by English double-decker bus, which on Wednesdays and Saturdays offers narration of the stories of buildings such as the modest Samuel Leffer Cottage (circa 1778), home of a schoolmaster and typical small residence of the period, and the Rustell House (circa 1732), an example of an historic building preserved as a shop. The First Methodist Parsonage dates from 1820 and the present St. Paul's Episcopal Church was constructed about 1857. The Old Burying Grounds, shaded by gnarled live oak, is listed on the National Register of Historic Places.

The annual Old Homes Tour and Antiques Show the last weekend of June opens up eight to ten private homes. The ticket also includes admission to the regular tour buildings.

The North Carolina Maritime Museum brings this ancient history into the 20th century and emphasizes the natural attributes of the region. The entrance hallway is decorated with a large collection of seashells and molds (some using actual skin) of the great white shark, dolphin, and various fish caught in nearby waters. Live fish and snakes from the region are kept in large tanks in another room.

Among other displays are about 30 hand-carved duck decoys; a 1910 dead-rise skiff built in Beaufort using natural knees of red cedar; an early 20th-century pole-driven duck hunting boat used in Currituck Sound; navigational instruments; models of ships such as the U.S. Navy Schooner *Boxer* and a 1690 Dutch frigate; visuals on the North Carolina estuarine community; photos and equipment of oystering; a sealable "life car" developed in the 1890s to aid in coastal rescue operations; and a bamboo coracle from the Mekong Delta in Vietnam.

Museum hours are 9 a.m. to 5 p.m. Monday–Friday, 10 a.m. to 5 p.m. Saturday, and 1 to 5 p.m. Sunday. Interpretive programs include boat trips to Shackleford Banks and Bird Shoal, canoeing on the White Oak River and to Phillips Island, observation of boatbuilding, birdwatching, study of ecology, identification of wildflowers, workshop on coastal reptiles and amphibians, and demonstration of ship model building. The museum uses a boat from the Duke University Marine Laboratory at Beaufort for "trawl and dredge" trips.

Beaufort is a handsome, pleasant city that invites strolling. It has an attractive harbor, crowded with sailboats and shrimp boats. The Beaufort Boardwalk is a good stopping place for boaters. The Jolly Roger flag sometimes appears in the harbor on the mast of a 54-foot reconstructed pirate vessel under command of "Captain Sinbad."

The Strange Seafood Festival in mid-August, a little twist on a common theme, serves up chef-prepared exotic foods from the water such as stingray, shark, and calamari.

The Beaufort waterfront looks out on the Rachel Carson Estuarine Sanctuary, a complex of artificial islands, tidal marshes, tidal flats, sand flats, and eel-grass beds sustaining a herd of wild ponies, red fox, more than 160 species of birds, and other animals. Boaters may land there for swimming, hiking, shell searching, fishing, clamming, birdwatching, and primitive camping. It is named for an author whose works in the 1940s, in part based on research at this site, heightened ecological awareness.

Down East

This generic term encompasses a large, diverse peninsula beside U.S. Route 70/state Route 12 that lies generally east of the North River. Settlements generally cling to the coast or highway intersections. It is not a pretty area, with extensive flatlands broken by marshes and scrub forests. It is not without charm, however. In the small communities live families whose ancestors arrived before the Revolutionary War. They are artisans and farmers, hunters and fishers, as their ancestors were.

Harkers Island once was so famous for the wooden boats built there that mere mention of its origins was enough to authenticate a boat's sturdiness. Boatbuilders, who learned their skills as youths and continued all their lives, carefully selected the wood used in the vessel. The boats were truly handmade, using only a minimum of tools and often crafted from a "rack-o'-the-eye" design that existed only in the head of the builder. A boat took many months to build. Few men carry on the tradition in this era when fiberglass boats can be manufactured quickly and cheaply. Those who do, like 75-year-old Julian Guthrie who works behind his home, are folk heroes. Guthrie, for example, has been declared a North Carolina Living Treasure.

U.S. Route 70/state Route 12 is fairly heavily traveled because of the ferry connections to Ocracoke Island and to Cape Lookout National Seashore. The route traverses many miles of flatlands and stunted woodlands, passing solitary service stations, towns like Davis, and an occasional fish house on an inlet before heading straight across the marshes to the ferry landing near the eastern tip of the area.

Cedar Island National Wildlife Refuge occupies about 12,500 acres at the tip of the peninsula, including 10,000 acres of salt marsh dominated by black needlerush, saltgrass, and saltmeadow cordgrass and 2,500 acres of maritime forest, mostly longleaf and pond pine, wax myrtle, gallberry, red bay, yaupon, and fetterbrush. Water levels are controlled through impounding and the excavation of potholes, and wigeongrass is planted as food for ducks. Established in 1964 primarily as a refuge for wild ducks and geese, it attracts more than 270 species of birds, including osprey, brown pelican, red-tailed and marsh hawks, great horned owl, and the secretive black rail. White-tailed deer, otter, mink, raccoon, marsh rabbit, and muskrat also are present. Black bear are rarely seen.

Each arrival of the Ocracoke-Cedar Point ferry disgorges and takes on scores of vehicles, including many trucks, but these usually pass through without stopping. Thus, the refuge is minimally used except by locals who know its many attributes. About 400 acres of marsh on the shore of West and West Thoroughfare bays are opened to waterfowl hunting. Facilities include an observation area, boat landings, and a campground. A motel stands near the ferry landing.

The road to the ranger station passes a few houses. The station site, formerly a radar tracking post, is an excellent overlook on Core Sound. The refuge is open year-round during daylight hours.

Other Down East ferries provide regular car-carrying service to Cape Lookout National Seashore.

Cape Lookout National Seashore

This dogleg-shaped barrier island park stretches from Ocracoke Inlet in the north to Beaufort Inlet in the south, a distance of 55 miles. It has two distinct segments, the Core Banks that generally extend northeast–southwest and Shackleford Banks at the elbow that run almost east–west.

While the Core Banks are not the "promontorium tremendum" or "horrible headland" mentioned on a 1590 map, the terrain is untamed and a bit monotonous. There is almost no shade or shelter. On the Atlantic Ocean side, wide sandy beaches are backed by low dunes stabilized to some degree by thin growths of sea oats and other grasses. At places in the interior there are flat grasslands bordered by dense scrub vegetation. Facing the sound are large salt marshes. Forlorn relics of human presence — weathered tarpaper shacks and abandoned vehicles among them — intrude now and then on the landscape.

Weather conditions may change quickly (Coast Guard information is available at 919/726-7550). Afternoon thunderstorms occur in summer, and squalls can come at any time. Lightning sometimes strikes dunes, beach, and water. Tidal flats may flood rapidly at high tide if wind conditions are right.

Carol Lohr, director of the Carteret County Tourism Development Bureau, often refers to this park as the "South Outer Banks." The Cape Lookout National Seashore, geographically a continuation of its more celebrated neighbors, is today not unlike Hatteras and Ocracoke were before the tourist deluge began. The surf fishing, especially in autumn and spring, and shell collecting are regarded as among the best on the Atlantic Coast. An excellent beach for sunbathing and hiking is backed up by a variety of natural features.

The wildness of the area at places stirs the blood. There is ample wildlife, especially birds — more than 275 species. A few pairs of piping plover and large numbers of least tern, gullbilled tern, common tern, and black skimmer nest on the islands. The threatened eastern brown pelican is sometimes seen. Loggerhead turtles lay their eggs on the beaches. Rabbits, raccoon, shrews, river otter, snakes (none venomous), frogs, diamondback terrapin, and box turtle inhabit more protected areas. Nearly 100 species of fish — such as black sea bass, scamp, porgy, hogfish, purple reef fish, and yellowtail reef fish — swim above the offshore ledge.

Still, it is not suitable at present for the casual visitor. There is no land access at any point. Visitors must arrive by boat and make their own way around the islands. Since there are no maintained roads and those that exist are mostly sand, four-wheel drive is essential. Visits require a certain amount of dedication: the ferries are not cheap and the outings tend to be all-day affairs. In addition, mosquitos, greenhead and deer flies, ants, chiggers, and ticks are a serious problem in woods, shrublands, grassy areas, and wet meadows from May through October.

Swimmers should avoid places where currents are likely, including inlets, channels, and breaks in sandbars. Sharks are offshore year-round, but are especially noticeable in the fall when they follow schools of fish along the shore. Stinging jellyfish are a summer problem.

Car-carrying ferries operate from Davis to near Shingle Point and from Atlantic to North Drum Inlet. Passenger ferries run from Harker's Island, Atlantic Beach, and Beaufort to the landing near Cape Point and from Ocracoke directly to the ghost town of Portsmouth Village at the northern tip of the park.

The most visited places are Cape Point near the Cape Lookout Lighthouse and Portsmouth Village at the northern tip of the national seashore.

From the ferry dock near Shingle Point, drivers maneuver four-wheel-drive vehicles with fishing poles stuck in front bumper racks along primitive sandy roads marked by the Park Service and along the hard-packed beach to the sharp, windswept point where the ocean and Onslow Bay meet. At times, Cape Point resembles a parking lot more than the tip of an idyllic island. Car owners stand on the water's edge casting lines into the surf. Cape Point also is an excellent place to collect shells, including sand dollars, especially in winter and spring.

This fishhook-shaped southern end of the South Core Banks is historically the most frequented part of the island. An old Coast Guard station, whose tower provides an excellent view of the nearby vegetation and distant beaches and lighthouse, is now used by the Park Service. The remains of World War II concrete gun mounts, now offshore, illustrate the dynamic nature of the island. They were on solid ground when constructed; a few still are, hidden among the dunes.

The point of the fishhook is Power Squadron Point, a sand spit that overlooks both Onslow Bay and Cape Lookout Bight, 40 feet deep in places and one of the most protected anchorages in the world. The bight is a natural fish trap and is used both for commerce and study. Fishing boats drop their nets close to shore in this area in search of drum, spot, croaker, whiting, bluefish, Spanish mackerel, and other species.

The 150-foot lighthouse, completed in 1859, is a long walk from a National Park Service dock and nearby ferry landing along a sandy road that meanders through tufted dunes. The present tower, which replaced a 96-foot structure built in 1812, is still functioning and thus is not open, but is impressive from the outside. It was the model for a number of other Outer Banks lighthouses constructed later. The unusual diamond pattern painted on it results from an 1873 determination that lighthouses should be painted differently. Cape Lookout was to be "checkered, the checkers being painted alternately black and white."

The tower and 1873 lighthousekeeper's house stand on a site with a beautiful view. A visitors center in the keeper's house is manned mostly by volunteers and has only a few exhibits.

Primitive overnight camping is permitted throughout the island except in designated areas. A few cabins are located in the Great Island area, near the ferry landing from Davis and a Park Service dock. Hunting is permitted at times. Nesting areas are closed during certain periods.

The North Core Banks, about 22 miles long, have ferry landings at the northern tip near the ghost village of Portsmouth and north of Old Drum Inlet. Designated sand roads and beach may be used by four-wheel-drive vehicles. A cabin area is located at Long Point and primitive overnight camping is permitted in areas not posted. The dunes east of Portsmouth Village are regarded as a good site. The southern tip of the islands and a long strip of the northern end are salt flats subject to flooding.

Portsmouth Village was established in 1753 as a transshipment and lightering place for cargos. Goods unloaded there could be sent to the mainland on barges or boats and the lightened oceangoing vessels could cross the shallows at Ocracoke Inlet and proceed to river ports such as Bath and Beaufort. In 1842, more than two-thirds of the state's exports passed in this manner through Ocracoke Inlet. For a time, Portsmouth Village was the largest community on the North Carolina barrier islands. Shoaling in Ocracoke Inlet and the creation of the Hatteras Inlet by a storm in 1846 reduced Portsmouth's importance and it never recovered from the Civil War blockade and occupation by Union forces. It turned to fishing and, in 1894, a life-saving station was established there. However, the population gradually declined. The last two residents left in 1971.

The 250-acre ghost village, listed on the National Register of Historic Places, stands virtually as it did when abandoned. The buildings and yard are maintained in neat condition by the National Park Service. In several enclaves, divided by marshes and Doctors Creek, are the homes of Roy Robinson, Jesse Rabb, Ed Styron, T. T. Potter, George Dixon, and others, the 1840 post office/general store, the Methodist Church (rebuilt after being destroyed in a 1913 storm), a school, the life-saving service complex, and the cemetery. A visitors center is maintained in the Salter-Dixon House, a short walk into the township from the Haulover Point Dock.

A self-guided walking tour passes 21 buildings depicting the lifestyle of a working coastal community. The church and Salter-Dixon House are open to provide a sense of the lively years when "Governor" John Wallace started the lightering business, when the streets were crowded with the lusty sailors handling valuable cargos, and the time in 1903 when the whole community helped save 421 immigrants aboard the 605-ton brig *Vera Cruz VII,* which ran aground on Dry Shoal Point. Other buildings are occupied by Park Service personnel or persons holding Park Service leases.

Now, as throughout its existence, the town is subject to the vagaries of nature, such as storms, swarms of insects, and shallow waters with shifting shoals, which should not be entered without local advice and navigational charts. The oceanfront beach and Wallace Channel Dock are about a mile east of the village across a sand flat that is subject to flooding when north or northeast winds are blowing.

The 8-mile-long, 2,500-acre Shackleford Banks, situated perpendicular to the main banks and separated from them by Barden Inlet, are a fascinating combination of recovering nature and public use. This is a typical barrier island, with wide beaches, extensive grassy dunes separated by grasslands, and a sizable maritime forest near its western end. The highest elevation is about 50 feet.

Originally, the island was covered by substantial forests, but these were virtually demolished by severe hurricanes in the late 1800s. Since then, low-growing bushes have replaced the taller trees in most upland places.

Coree Indians were the first known inhabitants. John Shackleford purchased the island in 1714, but apparently did not develop it. English colonists began building permanent homes by the 1760s and, by the mid-1800s, 600 people lived in several communities. The largest was Diamond City at the eastern end, which reportedly was named about 1885 for the diamond pattern visible on the Cape Lookout Lighthouse across the inlet. Its 500 residents prospered as fishers and whalers; indeed, the care with which the processors cleaned, salted, and packed the fish made mullet from Diamond City famous. In 1899, a severe hurricane tore houses from their foundations, wrecked boats and gardens, and littered the area with debris. Most of the discouraged residents left, some moving their houses to sites in Morehead City, Harkers Island, and Beaufort.

Little evidence of the towns remains, principally the ruins of a few fishers' shacks and family graveyards. As a result, the island is largely in a wild state and is best known for its feral horses, which roam the island at will. The island, accessible only by boat, is largely undeveloped for tourists. It has a local reputation as an excellent place for a beach outing. Primitive camping is permitted.

Bogue Banks

This 25-mile-long east–west island hard by the mainland is just the opposite of Shackelford Banks. It is fully developed residentially and is accessible by bridge at both ends. The main road down the island, state Route 58, moves through a succession of communities: Atlantic Beach, Pine Knoll Shores, Salter Path, Indian Beach, and Emerald Isle, the latter ones developed since the 1950s.

Still, the island has a good number of tourist attractions, especially in the Atlantic Beach and Pine Knoll Shores areas. It also has marinas, handsome condos and beach homes, motels, campgrounds, and amusement parks. Four fishing piers are located at strategic spots along the shoreline.

North of Atlantic Beach, along state Route 58, is Fort Macon, an excellent example of an early 19th-century coastal fort. Now part of a 385-acre state park, the five-sided fort was completed in 1834. Robert E. Lee, later to lead Confederate forces during the Civil War, was among the engineers supervising early construction. Fort Macon was lightly defended at the outbreak of the Civil War and was captured by Confederate forces in 1861. A year later, Union forces occupied Beaufort and other coastal areas and established a siege base on the Bogue Banks. The isolated fort repulsed a naval attack, but surrendered after a day-long bombardment from the land side that disabled many of its batteries. After the war, it was used until 1876 as a federal prison and was garrisoned again during the Spanish-American War. It was closed in 1903 and acquired by the state in 1934. Visitors may circle the now-dry moat around the restored main fort, visit its counterfire outposts, walk the parade ground, and inspect some of its 26 casements now devoted to historical exhibits. The fort is open weekends throughout the year and daily June through Labor Day.

The road into the park runs through a maritime thicket of wax myrtle, yaupon, red cedar, and live oak. The .4-mile loop Elliott Coues Nature Trail traverses a scrub thicket and tufted dunes en route to the beach on Beaufort Inlet. Herons, egrets, sanderlins, dunlin, purple bunting, warblers, and other species may be seen. Beaches may be hiked or combed for sea stars and coral. At low tide, the base of a jetty reveals the symbiosis of water and land. In winter, the jetty attracts birds such as purple sandpiper and common elder usually associated with rocky places.

Swimming in the ocean, surf fishing, and picnicking are permitted at a beach near the park entrance. Rangers conduct nature programs on a regular basis.

At Pine Knoll Shores is the 265-acre Theodore Roosevelt Nature Area, which preserves a large maritime forest and freshwater pond on the sound side of the island. Trails with observation decks open up wide woodland and coastline vistas.

Located within the park is the Pine Knoll Shores version of the North Carolina Aquarium. A 12,000-gallon tank holds a "Living Shipwreck" exhibit that shows the effects of ships that went down in the "Graveyard of the Atlantic." Other exhibits include live regional sea life in tanks and a touch tank. Interpretive programs are held on a regular schedule. The aquarium is open 9 a.m. to 5 p.m. Monday–Saturday and 1 to 5 p.m. Sunday.

Route 58 on Bogue Banks is paralleled by state Route 24 on the mainland. The two meet at Cape Carteret, a small community of about 1,400 people, including many retirees. Just north of the town, on Route 58, the Crystal Coast passion play, *Worthy Is the Lamb,* features horsedrawn chariots, camels, and sheep as props for local actors. It is staged June through Labor Day.

Onslow County

A large section of this county's coastline is taken up by the U.S. Marine Corps' Camp LeJeune. Indeed, coastal state Route 172 crosses the base. A guard at the boundary of the base waves civilian drivers on without much scrutiny but the "tank crossing" signs and sideroads to training areas emphasize the martial nature of the base.

The civilian communities include Jacksonville, whose attention is focused on the Marine Corps base, and villages and recreational sites oriented toward the water and hunting for deer, waterfowl, quail, and wild turkey.

Swansboro, a quaint village on the White Oak River, dates back to 1730 when Jonathan and Grace Green established a settlement. A town of Swannsborough, named after a former speaker of the North Carolina House of Commons, was laid out ten years later and incorporated in 1783. It was an active port until after the Civil War, then became a fishing and farming center.

Swansboro, today a charter fishing center and convenient stop on the Intracoastal Waterway, remains water-oriented. The placid waters of the river and Bogue Sound are ideal for boating. Rivers, sounds, inlets, and the ocean yield king mackerel, wahoo, croaker, spot, flounder, amberjack, dolphin, and sharks. An annual Mullet Festival is held in early October. At Christmas, Santa arrives in a flotilla of pleasure craft. The ferry to Hammocks Island State Park leaves from Swansboro.

Residents have preserved the town's historic flavor by restoring many pre-Revolutionary and later homes.

Swansboro is connected to Jacksonville by a 19-mile bike route. One of Onslow's most favored loop bike trails extends about 50 miles from Haws Run, south of Jacksonville, to Richlands, traversing upland forests and country farms.

On state Route 24 near Jacksonville, in a stand of dogwood and oak trees, the handsome Beirut Memorial commemorates the 268 Marines and sailors from Camp Lejeune who were killed by terrorists in their barracks in Beirut in 1983 and the Marines who died in the invasion of Grenada later. Hubert Park, 6 miles east on route 24, has a half-mile nature trail marked with interpretive signs. Jacksonville's New River Park has a lighted waterfront boardwalk. The Pelletier House (circa 1850) is shown by appointment. There are two other recreational parks in and around Jacksonville.

Hammocks Beach State Park

Tiny Bear Island south of Bogue Inlet has one of the widest and most beautiful beaches in North Carolina. Many of the people who live along the Crystal Coast, not exactly deprived of coastal settings, have a special affection for this 4-mile stretch of sand along the Atlantic Ocean. In summer, sunbathers, surfcasters, swimmers, walkers, shell hunters, and picnickers vote with their feet.

Behind the beaches of this 892-acre park are sparsely vegetated dunes that rise as high as 60 feet, shrub thickets, and tidal mud flats supporting a wide variety of wildlife, including deer, raccoon, herons, egrets, and terns. Loggerhead turtles lay their eggs on the beaches.

The park is accessible only by boat, and the number of visitors each day is limited. Ferries carry only passengers from the end of state Route 1511 near Swansboro to a dock about 1½ miles from the beach. They operate daily June 1 through Labor Day but are halted when the maximum number of visitors is reached. Primitive camping is permitted, except on full-moon nights during the summer turtle-nesting period.

Snead's Ferry on the New River also retains much of its colonial flavor, but is primarily a fishing, snorkeling, and boating center. A Shrimp Festival in mid-August brings out lovers of down-home cooking. Just south of the village, state Route 210 loops to highly developed Topsail Island, through resort communities such as West Onslow Beach, Del Mar Beach, Surf City, and Topsail Beach and back to Route 172 at Holly Ridge. Topsail Island has seven fishing piers and three places of public beach access; the public-access area near Topsail Beach has an elevated pavilion for observation. A kite festival is held annually in late April.

At Folkstone, state Route 172 merges with U.S. Route 17 for a run through forested countryside that requires quite a few fire towers. At Hampstead, a change occurs, with signs advertising condos and resorts dotting the roadside.

Cape Fear Area

Cape Fear Coast Convention & Visitors Bureau
24 North 3rd Street
Wilmington, NC 28401
919/341-4030 or 800/222-4757

Moore's Creek National Battlefield

THE REVOLUTIONARY WAR WAS NOT A SIMPLE US VERSUS THEM AFFAIR. Indeed, this early battle pitted North Carolina patriots against North Carolina loyalists, led by kilted, broadsword-swinging Scots Highland immigrants.

On February 27, 1776, patriots gathered to hold a key point in the road between Fayetteville and Brunswick, an assembly point for loyalists being recruited by exiled royal Governor Josiah Martin in an effort to reassert British authority. At first, the patriots camped on both sides of Moore's Creek, but at midnight they abandoned their forward position, removed the planks from the bridge across the creek, and took positions inside an earthen fortification on the eastern bank. At dawn, kilted Scots led an attack across the slippery framework of the bridge, many of them falling into the dark water below. It was a short battle—three minutes perhaps—but the patriot fire exacted "great execution" on the attacking loyalists. The survivors retreated.

This 86-acre battlefield, 27 miles west of route 17 on state Route 210, preserves many of the elements of the battle along a .7-mile historical trail, including parts of the colonial wagon road, remnants of the earthworks held by the patriots, and a 2-pounder cannon of the type apparently fired by patriots. A boardwalk shaded by tall pines and bald cypress crosses the creek and adjoining marshland to the point from which the loyalists launched their attack. Plans call for reconstructing the bridge in the skeleton form it had during the battle. Memorials honor both sides; Pvt. John Grady of Dublin County is remembered as the "first martyr in the cause of freedom in North Carolina" and Molly Slocum, who may have helped nurse the wounded, represents "the heroic women of the lower Cape Fear" and all women "who endured hardship and danger in the struggle for independence."

A .3-mile Tarheel Trail loops through the kind of pine forest that made the region prosperous during the 1700s. Sign boards and exhibits show how the forest provided the naval stores that were important to British policy.

In the visitors center, a short audiovisual presentation, a diorama recreating the battle, and weapons such as a Brown Bess musket and broadsword provide an introduction to the battlefield. The battlefield is open 9 a.m. to 5 p.m. daily year-round, 8 a.m. to 6 p.m. on Saturday and Sunday from Memorial Day through Labor Day.

Poplar Grove Plantation

Historic Poplar Grove Plantation, just off U.S. Route 17 a few miles from Hempstead, contains a number of antebellum structures, including an 1850 mansion furnished in antiques. Guided tours (9 a.m. to 5 p.m. Monday–Saturday, 12 to 5 p.m. Sunday, except during January) emphasize the plantation's association with the Foy family, which owned it for 175 years. It came under the supervision of a foundation in 1971 and was opened to visitors in 1980. Ancillary buildings include a detached kitchen, tenant house, herb cellar, and smokehouse.

The grounds and gardens of the 16-acre plantation, which are open at no charge are a pretty and active setting for a number of annual festivals and shows, including a March Peanut Festival, Easter Egg Hunt, and Halloween Haunted Barn and Trail. Thus, the plantation serves as an appropriate introduction to perhaps the most active region on the North Carolina coast — Wilmington and the Cape Fear Valley.

Wilmington

Locally, Wilmington is sometimes called the "capital" of the North Carolina coastal region. The claim has a certain historical validity; no place has had a greater impact than this protected river port of 60,000 inhabitants. At the least, it is first among a handful of focal points.

Wilmington's history is tied directly to the Cape Fear River. Settlement of the Cape Fear Valley, including Wilmington, received priority in the early 1700s because England was badly in need of pine products — spars, boards, tar, and pitch for ships and turpentine for pharmaceutical products — to keep its navy afloat and to preserve the health of its citizens. To encourage settlement, the king granted "plantations" of up to 640 acres to those who would supply the wood products needed.

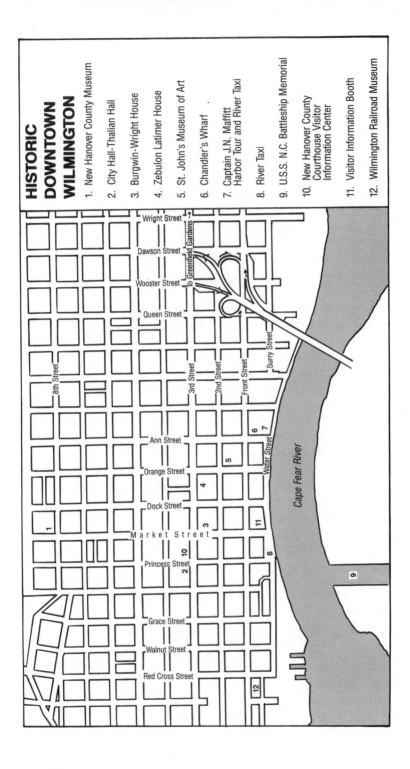

HISTORIC DOWNTOWN WILMINGTON

1. New Hanover County Museum
2. City Hall-Thalian Hall
3. Burgwin-Wright House
4. Zebulon Latimer House
5. St. John's Museum of Art
6. Chandler's Wharf
7. Captain J.N. Maffitt Harbor Tour and River Taxi
8. River Taxi
9. U.S.S. N.C. Battleship Memorial
10. New Hanover County Courthouse Visitor Information Center
11. Visitor Information Booth
12. Wilmington Railroad Museum

Newton, as the city was first called, was established in 1734 by John Watson on a land grant. In 1739, when it was incorporated, the royal governor named it after a British friend, the Earl of Wilmington. Millions of board feet of almost indestructible heart of pine flowed to England through the port. The Cape Fear region remained the largest producer and shipper of naval stores right into the 20th century.

This tradition influenced the language of the region. The "tarheel" nickname for North Carolinians began with joking references by merchants in Liverpool and London. The word "plantation" in this area originally meant a stand of pine trees, not a farm raising tobacco, cotton, or rice, as it did in many other places. Even today, when old-timers speak of "corking" a boat, they are talking about caulking it.

Not all settlers—English, Scottish, Welsh, and Irish, and blacks from the Caribbean, both slave and free, dominated colonial immigration—were mesmerized by the forests. At various places along the river, some plantation owners took advantage of the abundance of water and moderate climate to create rice plantations as large as 10,000 acres.

As the break with the mother country approached in the latter half of the 18th century, Wilmington citizens actively resisted the Stamp Act and similar repressive laws. In 1765, they poured into the streets to burn an effigy and prevent the landing of stamp paper from a British naval vessel. The first Revolutionary War battle in North Carolina was fought at Moore's Creek about 20 miles northwest of the city. British forces occupied Wilmington in 1780, and Lord Cornwallis made it his headquarters during the 1780–81 winter.

With the advent of steam power, Wilmington became a railroad center, with five lines radiating outward. For a time, the Wilmington-to-Weldon line was the longest in the world. Utilizing the railroads and a new machine that could compress cotton, and thus double the number of bales a ship could carry, Alexander Sprunt became the world's largest transshipper of cotton. Wilmington's second wave of immigration, mostly continental Europeans, coincided with this period.

Wilmington, protected by strong Fort Fisher at the entrance to the river, was the last Confederate port to fall during the Civil War. For most of the war, sleek blockade runners discharged munitions and scarce manufactured goods and took on cotton and tobacco. The port continued to sustain Wilmington through good times and bad in the post-Civil War period. Steamers and sailing ships filled the river at times, taking on cotton, lumber, and other bulk commodities. It remained North Carolina's largest city until the early years of the 20th century.

Wilmington still is North Carolina's largest seaport. The port area, 6,000 feet of concrete quays equipped with giant cranes to handle containerized cargos, stands inconspicuously downstream from its historic location at the city center—but is still 26 miles from the mouth of the river. Cigarettes and manufactured tobacco, textiles, and wood products are the primary exports now. Tours can be arranged in advance (919/763-1621).

Wilmington's historic area today bears little resemblance to the colonial city. Wilmington burned three times when fires at a waterfront piled high with barrels of turpentine, cotton, and other flammable materials spread out of control. Conflagrations in 1778 and 1819 were caused by drunken sailors. The 1840 destruction followed the explosion of an old train.

A walking tour of the city with Guide Bob Jenkins (919/763-1785), which starts at the foot of Market Street, probes the influences that made Wilmington a port and transportation center. He also discusses the architectural styles used on a number of historic structures, including the handsome 1859 Bellamy Mansion, used as Union headquarters after Wilmington was captured during the Civil War, and Kenan Fountain at the corner of Market and Fifth streets. From the corner of Third and Market streets, the visitor can see at one time more examples of the work of famous American architects than at any other single spot in the United States. Most of the pre-Civil War construction work was done by black artisans.

A horse-drawn carriage tour also winds through the historic district. Historical markers and memorials are numerous; the Confederate monument at Third and Dock streets was designed by the same Henry Bacon who planned the Lincoln Memorial in Washington, D.C. Wilmington has been home to many famous people: President Woodrow Wilson lived there as a youth; Mary Baker Eddy, founder of the Christian Science movement; and the subject of one of the most famous American portraits, Whistler's mother, were born there.

The self-guided seven-block Historic Wilmington Tour starts with an introduction at Thalian Hall, the theater section of the 1858 governmental center that houses the nation's oldest community theater organization, started in 1788. The tour traverses an area of 18th- and 19th-century houses and includes a visit to the 1771 Burgwin-Wright House and gardens, a good example of a colonial planter's townhouse. The first building on the site was the city jail, which is now the basement of the house. It is often referred to as the Cornwallis house because the British general stayed there in 1781 while the British occupied the city. The complex has a separate three-story kitchen. A tunnel under the house was built sometime between 1740 and 1770, but its purpose is undocumented. Also visited are the four-story Italianate Zebulon Latimer House, built in 1852 and still containing the original furnishings, and the Federal-style Governor Dudley Mansion (circa 1825), owned by the first North Carolina governor elected by popular vote.

Wilmington's skyline is jagged with steeples belonging to historic places of worship, including Gothic Revival-style St. Thomas Church (1845–47); Carpenter Italianate Chestnut Avenue Presbyterian Church (1858); St. Paul's Evangelical Lutheran Church (1859–69); early English Gothic-Revival First Baptist Church (1859–70); St. Mark's Episcopal Church (1871); Moorish-style Temple of Israel (1875–76), the oldest Jewish Synagogue in North Carolina; and Spanish Baroque Revival-style St. Mary's Roman Catholic Church (1908–11), a structure employing no steel, wood, or nails.

The oldest building in the city is the Smith–Anderson House at 102 Orange Street, built about 1740 but later modified. Another old structure, later modified, is the Cameron-Hollman House (circa 1800) at 512 Surry Street. Noteworthy public buildings include the 1892 New Hanover County Court House, whose cavernous entrance hall and high-ceilinged rooms hold, among other things, a visitors center; the Tileston School, built in 1871–72 and modified later; the Chamber of Commerce office (circa 1855), an Italianate structure with stick-style porch; and the Museum of the Lower Cape Fear, which holds a model of the city's waterfront in 1863 and a good collection of Confederate relics.

Georgian/Federal-style St. John's Masonic Lodge, which dates from 1803–5 and is the oldest building of the order in the state, now is part of a three-building complex that houses St. John's Museum of Art. Others are the Cowan House Studio (circa 1830) and the former St. Nicholas Greek Orthodox Church (1943). The museum's permanent collection emphasizes North Carolina artists but includes a large number of color prints by Mary Cassatt, turn-of-the-century expatriate American Impressionist artist who worked for a considerable time in France.

Wilmington's preservation movement began in 1966. A survey of 65 blocks showed that 200 architecturally or historically significant buildings had been lost. That shocking disclosure led to the creation of an historic district and the Historic Wilmington Foundation. Two hundred blocks were placed on the National Register of Historic Places and plans were implemented to highlight major aspects of the city's history, including the creation of the Wilmington Railroad Museum in 1979 to recognize the city's chief provider for more than 100 years. The museum was moved to the old Atlantic Coast Line Railroad freight office in 1981 and now includes a 1910 steam locomotive and other rolling stock, as well as photographs and small articles such as table settings and railroad watches from the 1840 Wilmington and Weldon Railroad to the present.

The Cape Fear River can be viewed a number of ways. A 13-block riverwalk, created in 1980, leads to small Riverfront Park and preserves an unobstructed view of the river, darkened by tannic acid from decaying flora upstream. Its 39-foot depth at low tide—tidal action is roughly 5 to 7 feet—makes it a deep-water port although the ocean is 27 miles away. The river divides at Wilmington, its left fork extending 170 miles into the Piedmont region and its right fork meandering 150 miles but remaining a coastal river. On the land side, the riverwalk exposes a line of historic structures, including the Cotton Exchange, and handsome new buildings that harmonize aesthetically with the old district and its cobblestone streets. Shops and restaurants occupy structures such as the 1879 Ellers Building. In a parking lot, the oldest tugboat in the United States, the *John Taxis,* has its final mooring.

Another viewpoint is available aboard *Henrietta II,* namesake of an 1818 merchant vessel that made port often during her 40 years of sailing. The new version bucks currents as high as 8 knots or more on daily cruises and dinner cruises during the warm months. Still a third river experience is the river taxi *Captain J. N. Maffitt,* a former Navy launch named for the captain of the Confederate raider *CSS Florida,* which shuttles between downtown and the battleship *USS North Carolina* between Memorial Day and Labor Day. It also takes 5-mile cruises from May through September.

The World War II battleship, also easily reached by highway, is moored on the opposite shore in plain view of downtown. Beached may be a better word to describe its situation; the warship is embedded fast in river-bottom mud. In 1960, the schoolchildren of North Carolina contributed pennies, nickels, and dimes to help retrieve the highly decorated vessel from mothballs and make it one of the state's top tourist attractions. A self-guided tour covers nine decks and levels and includes a visit to the bridge, walks on the main deck under 16-inch cannon and around 5-inch and antiaircraft gun mounts, inspection of the interior fire controls of one of them, closeups of the OS2U Kingfisher float reconnaissance planes the battleship carried, and visits to officers and crew quarters.

During the summer months, a sound-and-light program, *The Immortal Showboat*, recounts the story from its construction and commissioning at the Brooklyn Navy Yard in 1941 through its wartime career in the Pacific, which included every major offensive from Guadalcanal to Okinawa.

Despite a certain commercial hardness throughout its history, Wilmington exhibits an environmental side, with tree-lined streets and a surprising number of outdoor oases scattered around the city and environs.

Within the city, 180-acre Greenfield Park, located in a residential area off U.S. Route 421, is the most versatile. A paved bike trail follows the contours of the lake, passing wooden boardwalks that overlook a detritus-strewn pond lined with cypress, dogwood, and pine trees and plantings of azaleas, Cherokee rose, camellias, and other flowering plants. Nature trails winding through the woods include a bridge over the lake. A 5-mile driving tour also circles the lake, which was created in colonial times as the race for a grist mill.

The 10-acre Herbert Bluethenthal Memorial Wildflower Preserve on the campus of the University of North Carolina at Wilmington (state Route 132) holds a variety of flowering plants native to the region. Interlocking trails lead through stands of pond pine, sweet gum, red maple, and cypress, with an understory of ferns and blossoms of wildflowers that change with the seasons. The trails also pass an insectivorous garden, a manmade pond, and a pocosin.

Despite modern development, unusual habitats remain along the banks of the Cape Fear River. The extensive freshwater tidal marshes south of the city support a large population of alligators. And inland along the southern shore of the river, wet and dry habitats at Bryant Mill (Greenbank) Bluff sustain a number of unusual plants, including the large-leaved grass of Parnusses.

Wilmington joins with nearby beaches and other neighbors to sponsor several weeks of Christmas season programs, including 5 miles of lighting on Carolina and Kure beaches and illumination of Riverfront Park; the world's largest lighted tree; Yule illumination of the *USS North Carolina*; Old Wilmington by candlelight; and a Christmas festival at Poplar Grove Plantation.

Other annual sporting events include the East Coast King Mackerel Tournament at Carolina Beach in late July and several at Wrightsville Beach. In a fall triathlon, contestants swim across sound-side Banks Channel at Wrightsville Beach, cycle to Carolina Beach, and end at Wilmington. Ten golf courses in the Wilmington area are open to the public.

Eagle Island in the Cape Fear River is rated good for duck hunting.

Cape Fear Coast

The peninsula and barrier islands east and south of Wilmington unabashedly form a summer vacation complex competitive with the Outer Banks. Motels, condos, and cottages line up along mile after mile of white sandy strands at Wrightsville Beach, Carolina Beach, and Kure Beach. Charter and "head" boats depart small coves in search of deep-sea varieties such as marlin, swordfish, and king mackerel or for the smaller coastal blues, flounder, and spot in the more placid sound waters. Each of these communities has devoted followers, but they are similar in character and outlook. Nearly 100 public beach-access points are spotted along the coastline, varying from facilities with restrooms and showers to simple dunes crossovers.

Development of these beaches began in earnest in the late 19th century. The first resort community to be incorporated was Wrightsville Beach, in 1899, after construction of the Ocean View Railroad to haul vacationers from Wilmington to the oceanfront. The erection of several dance halls in the early 1900s made Atlantic Beach on Bogue Banks a popular rendezvous. Carolina Beach was incorporated in 1920 and Kure Beach followed in 1947. However, a resort boom occurred after World War II.

The approach roads from Wilmington are as fully developed as the oceanfront. U.S. Route 74 to Wrightsville Beach, where many open fields and forests remained only a generation ago, is now almost fully developed. And the colorful old-time, family-style seafood restaurants with newspapers on tables then spotted infrequently at the water's edge have been succeeded by numerous stylistic versions, motels, real-estate offices, and shopping malls. Harbour Island, which the causeway to Wrightsville Beach crosses, also hosts numerous restaurants and shops, as well as a few marinas. U.S. Route 421 south from Wilmington likewise is developed for many miles, then breaks out into countryside en route to Carolina and Kure beaches.

However, these routes are not without redeeming natural values.

Airlie Gardens, off U.S. Route 74–76 on the approach to Wrights-ville Beach, has a 5-mile drive through extensive azalea and camel-lia plantings. The gardens are open in the spring when the azaleas bloom. The New Hanover County Extension Service's 6.5-acre ar-boretum, on U.S. Route 17 south of Bradley Creek, is a developing teaching center that ultimately will include native shrubs, trees, or-namentals, roses, oriental plants, herbs, vegetables, and fruits. It also will contain a pond with an island in the middle.

Wrightsville Beach. This small island community 10 miles east of Wilmington traditionally rates high in the affection of the people of the region. Now intensively developed, it consists of side-by-side hotels, restaurants, shops, offices, churches, and private residences along two major thoroughfares. However, it also has miles of fine, sandy beach shared by sunbathers, swimmers, surfers, surf fishers, and beachcombers; marinas hosting deep-sea fishing boats and sail-boats; and fishing piers at each end of the island. The sailboat season of the Wrightsville Beach Ocean Racing Association extends from April to October.

Annual events include the king mackerel tournament and wind-surfing regatta in September, Azalea Festival in April, Wachovia Cup Offshore Yacht Race, and Cape Fear Open Marlin Tournament in May.

Masonboro Island. Accessible only by boat, this unspoiled island just south of Wrightsville Beach is part of the North Carolina Na-tional Estuarine Research Reserve, established in 1982. In all, four North Carolina islands with related marshes and mud flats have been set aside as part of a national system of living laboratories along the east, Gulf, and west coasts.

Masonboro, the largest undisturbed barrier island along the south-ern North Carolina coast, is unusual because its fresh water comes from upland runoff, not a tidal river. At low tide, several thousand acres of salt marsh and mud flats are exposed. Its 8 miles of white, sandy beach are an important nesting place for terns. Other shore-birds frequently seen include brown pelican, black skimmer, Ameri-can oystercatcher and willet. Loggerhead turtles struggle ashore in spring and summer to lay eggs.

Despite its isolation, the island is not difficult to reach. It has a dock where boaters may tie up (or they may anchor offshore, being careful not to be caught by tides). In addition, Wrightsville Beach

Water Taxi runs a shuttle service and tours guided by a marine biologist Tuesday–Sunday.

Carolina Beach State Park. This 1,773-acre preserve is ecologically one of the most diverse parks in North Carolina, with sand ridges, savannah, and lime sink ponds. It borders both the broad Cape Fear River and narrow manmade Snow's Cut that connects the Intracoastal Waterway and the Cape Fear River. Its most famous plant is the insect-eating Venus fly-trap, but it abounds in coastal wild-flowers, live oak, and other flora. Large numbers of songbirds perform from the branches of its trees.

More than 5 miles of interconnecting trails traverse all aspects of the park. Sugarloaf Trail passes swamp, three ponds, clusters of wild-flowers, and the live oak atop Sugarloaf dune, the most prominent natural feature of the park, before it breaks out onto the banks of the river. The 60-foot-high dune is a good place to observe the river and nearby terrain. The Swamp Trail leads back to the camping area, but a diversion past bladderworts, pitcher plants, and sundews ends at the loop around a pocosin with a large growth of Venus fly-trap.

Nature walks and slide shows are among the interpretive programs presented on a regular basis during the summer and by arrangement at other times.

Carolina Beach State Park, open year-round, is located on Dow Road a short distance off U.S. Route 421. A 42-slip marina can handle boats up to 6-foot draught. The family campground has 83 tent and RV sites.

Route 421, which ultimately ends at a ferry connection to Southport on the mainland, passes through largely residential Kure Beach en route to the ruins of one of the Civil War's strongest forts.

Fort Fisher State Historic Site. Pictures taken during the Civil War show huge cannons behind massive mounds of sand. They imply the strength of the fortification that guarded the entrance to the Cape Fear River, but not the scope or complexity. The sand and earth fort had 22 batteries lined up along a mile of shoreline, with a lightly equipped flank guarding the land approach. Nor do the old photos signify the importance of this single installation to the Confederacy; long after other major ports were lost, Wilmington remained open, thanks to the strength of this fortification and the unpredictability of the waters offshore.

Sleek, darkened blockade runners waited in the lee of the fort until dark, then made a run for the sea—the route depending on the captain's experience and cunning and daring. Inbound vessels knew they were safe from Union patrols when they came within range of the fort's heavy cannon. Union forces perfected amphibious operations at numerous other coastal locations before attempting to take Fort Fisher on Christmas Eve in 1864, and still failed on the first attempt. The second effort in Juanuary 1865 was successful; Union troops landed farther up the peninsula and attacked the fort from the land side. They were the two largest land-sea battles in history up to that time.

Only a small portion of the fort remains, principally ruins near the northern angle where the seaside and land flanks met, but they adequately convey the powerful nature of the entire fortification. A trail around the base of the largest remaining mound has narrative boards that explain the construction of the fort, named for Colonel Charles F. Fisher, who was killed at the Battle of First Manassas in Virginia; the river road sally port (near a marsh crossed by a boardwalk) where Union troops broke through in 1865; a bombproof shelter at Sheppard's Battery with a 63-foot entrance tunnel leading to a 13-by-18-by-5-foot underground room; and details of the fighting for the fort.

Other preserved earthworks are located on the beach side of U.S. Route 421, near a monument on the site of the headquarters of the Confederate fort.

Displays in the visitors center include relics recovered from sunken blockade runners like the *Stormy Petrel,* which ran aground in December 1864, and engravings of such famous Cape Fear blockade runners as *Ellie and Annie, Anglia, Lizzie, Lady Davis, Robert E. Lee, Marion,* and *Colonel Lamb.* Other displays include a bell from the *Luzon,* which apparently sailed nearby waters before the Civil War, and cannonballs, rifles, and other relics of fighting at the site. An audiovisual program provides an introduction to the fort. The center is open 9 a.m. to 5 p.m. Tuesday–Saturday, 1 to 5 p.m. Sunday.

Displays on underwater archaeology are kept in an auxiliary building.

North Carolina Aquarium at Fort Fisher. The tanks teeming with aquatic wildlife emphasize creatures indigenous to the Cape Fear area, including sea horses, pipefish, skates, and rays. Visitors may touch, hold, or view at close range starfish, horseshoe and hermit crabs, and other marine life. A 20,000-gallon tank, the largest in the state, is devoted to sharks and large game fish, while a nearby exhibit lines up 18 sets of shark jaws found in North Carolina. A 6,000-gallon tank houses *koi* or Japanese colored carp. A waterfall in a rocky den provides a habitat for two North American river otter. Other exhibits include a 49-foot replica of a female humpback whale and an explanation of fish-farming methods.

The aquarium sponsors an extensive year-round interpretive program on topics such as shell makers, armored animals, endangered wildlife, and ditch denizens. Field trips include canoeing, crabbing, clamming, beach exploration, food from the sea, sun printing, Japanese fish printing, and nature crafts.

The aquarium is open from 9 a.m. to 5 p.m. Monday–Friday year-round and 1 to 5 p.m. Saturday–Sunday April–October. It is closed Christmas Day.

Beyond the aquarium is a state recreation area—a section of beach open to the public.

Zeke's Island. This small island is part of the North Carolina National Estuarine Sanctuary. A 3-mile-long jetty known as "the Rocks," built after the Civil War, creates a lagoon known as "the Basin" and blocks the flow of the Cape Fear River through the estuary. This places two different systems—the river and ocean/estuary—side by side. Ocean waters flowing through the inlet give the lagoon a salinity level similar to the ocean.

People walk across "the Rocks" to beaches or to look for Atlantic bottlenose dolphin. "The Basin" is a popular fishing site. Large ibis, heron, and egret rookeries on nearby Battery Island and colonies of red-tailed hawk and osprey make the isolated island a birdwatching destination.

Smith/Bald Head Island. This 12,000-acre island at the tip of Cape Fear peninsula is best known locally as Bald Head Island. The island is being developed for residential and resort purposes but is free of high rises and cars. Golf carts and bicycles are the only vehicular forms of transportation to the fine white sand beach, 18-hole championship golf course, croquet lawn, and other facilities.

About 10,000 acres form a lush nature preserve with a large salt marsh and a maritime forest dominated by cabbage palm and live oak. Birds and land animals are abundant and loggerhead turtles nest there in large numbers. The nonprofit Bald Head Island Conservancy conducts walks on trails in the maritime forest and along beaches backed by sand dunes and anchored by sea oats. The organization also administers a nationally recognized loggerhead turtle hatching program.

Bald Head Lighthouse, located at the southwestern end, was turned on in 1817 to replace a 1796 lighthouse threatened by erosion. Octagonal-shaped "Old Baldy," now North Carolina's oldest lighthouse, stands 110 feet tall. It was reopened to visits in late 1992 after being closed for many years. Cape Fear lies at the southeastern tip.

Off the island is the infamous Frying Pan Shoals. The first recorded ship to come to grief there was a Spanish vessel, which went down in the 1520s. Survivors constructed a new vessel in the vicinity of Southport, which is reputed to be the first European vessel to be built in what is now the United States.

Evidence has been found of an ancient Indian settlement, dating from about 300 A.D. The Spanish explored the island in the 1400s but the British later settled the region. As mainland settlements grew, pirates began using use Bald Head Island as a base of operations. Earthworks were raised there during the Revolutionary War, when the British occupied the island, and the Civil War, when Fort Holmes was part of the Confederate complex guarding the entrance to the Cape Fear River.

A 20-minute ferry ride from Indigo Plantation at Southport passes between Battery and Oak Islands and lands at a marina near "Old Baldy." From there, South Bald Head Wynd follows part of the island's 14 miles of sandy beaches and North Bald Head Wynd and Federal Road parallel Bald Head Creek and adjacent salt marshes.

The Western Bank

There is so much concentration on the sun and sand of the Cape Fear Peninsula that the western bank of the Cape Fear River is almost the "left" bank. To ignore the area, however, is to miss much that is pivotal in this section of North Carolina.

Southport. While the ferry sends many visitors through Southport, not all of them adequately appreciate this historic community. Spanish sailors explored the area as early as 1521, and at least five Indian villages existed when the first British settlers arrived. The town was laid out in 1792 and incorporated in 1805. Quiet, leafy Franklin Square Park dates from that original plat. In that period, it was a popular vacation spot for residents of Wilmington. Subsequently, it was a county seat, fishing village, and center for harbor pilots.

Originally named Smithville after Benjamin Smith, an early governor of the state, the name was changed in 1887 during one of its greatest growth periods. Bonnet's Creek is named for Stede Bonnet, the "gentleman pirate" who once tried to repair a vessel at the mouth of the stream.

Southport retains much of its historic quaintness. A walking tour of the historic district that begins at the 1854 City Hall, since modified, passes more than a dozen 19th-century structures and a number of later ones. The oldest, the Walker–Pyke House, dates back to about 1800. The 1868 T.M. Thompson House on Bay Street, facing the Intracoastal Waterway, was the home of a successful Civil War blockade runner who lived to enjoy the rewards of his wartime exploits; the house has a cupola and widow's walk. The Frink–Cotton House (circa 1890) was built by the grandfather of actor Joseph Cotton and the Brunswick Inn (circa 1859) continues to host, some say, the spirit of an Italian harpist who drowned while sailing.

Historic churches include 1860 St. Philip's Episcopal Church, used as a hospital during the Civil War, and 1871 Southport Baptist Church. The Old Smithville Burying Ground, opened before 1804, has a memorial to lost harbor pilots that reads, "The winds and the sea sing their requiem and shall forever more."

A walk along the Southport waterfront is a must. Bay Street, in addition to the historic structures, has many majestic live oak trees. From Riverside Park, visitors may see the Bald Head Island Lighthouse, the oldest in North Carolina; Oak Island Lighthouse, once said to be the brightest in the United States; and Battery Island. Near the park is the site of star-shaped Fort Johnson, established in 1745. Joseph Martin, the last royal governor of North Carolina, spent his final night ashore there after the Revolutionary War broke out. Confederates took it during the Civil War; afterward it was used by the U.S. Army Corps of Engineers and the Army Transportation Corps. Relics include the Officers Quarters, an 1805 structure built around an earlier wood barracks, and the hospital (circa 1852), relocated a few blocks away in 1889 when it became a private residence.

The Boat Harbor at the end of Bay Street has a busy kind of picturesqueness. The modern facility, dedicated in 1965, almost always has some boats tied up that have interrupted their journey along the Intracoastal Waterway. In the summer and autumn, shrimp boats leave the harbor in the predawn and return in the afternoon. Unloading continues into the night. The harbor is one of the most photographed places in the town.

In Keziah Memorial Park is a live oak tree reputed to be over 800 years old. It was bent as a sapling by Indians to mark a trail to the Shoals fishing ground.

Southport hosts the annual North Carolina Fourth of July Festival with a large fireworks display, a freedom run, arts and crafts under the live oak in Franklin Park and along the waterfront, street dancing, and other entertainment. The U.S. Open King Mackerel Tournament, held each year the first weekend in October, normally attracts more than 400 boats. The annual Christmas by the Sea Festival in early December includes a Holiday Boat Flotilla, judging of home decorations, and a tour of homes.

Located on the grounds of the Sunny Point Military Ocean Terminal are a large number of limestone sinkholes, some perhaps as old as 1,000 years and others still being formed as a layer of limestone well below the surface collapses. The more than 80 water-filled sinkholes, most of them less than an acre in size, support 20 or more rare plants, including pondspice and dwarf bladderwort. Base permission is required to visit the area.

Another natural phenomenon, the privately owned Boiling Springs Lake wetlands complex northwest of the intersection of state routes 21 and 133, combines Carolina bays, pocosins, and savannahs. Rare plants include the rough-leaf loosestrife.

The Carolina Power & Light visitors center 2 miles north of Southport on state Route 87 shows movies on the nearby nuclear power plant and the history of energy and has hands-on exhibits that use a bike to generate electricity, rate household appliances according to energy consumption, measure radiation levels of natural and manmade objects, and show the parts of a nuclear fuel bundle. It's open 9 a.m. to 4 p.m. Monday–Friday year-round except holidays and 1 to 4 p.m. Sunday June–August, including July 4.

Orton Plantation Gardens. Beginning in the late winter and spring, a succession of flowering plants and trees—azalea, camellia, pansy, rose, dogwood, peach, cherry and apple trees, day and water lilies, rhododendron, oleander, magnolia, gardenia, summer annuals, and crepe myrtle among them—keep the expansive lawns and ponds of this old plantation alive with bright colors. Avenues of live oak, cypress, and pine shade many of the garden walks on the 20-acre site. The Scroll Garden, where sculpted hedges complement beds of annuals, overlooks a lagoon and fields where rice was grown until the end of the 19th century.

The gardens were laid out in 1910 by James and Luola Sprunt around the house and the tombs of the first owner, Roger Moore, and his family. Moore migrated from South Carolina in 1725 and established the plantation at the northern edge of the rice growing region. Nicknamed "King" because of his imperious manner, he also was one of the founders of the town of Brunswick.

The 1½-story brick house he built about 1735 was elevated to two stories in 1840. Four fluted Doric columns also were added at that time. Union forces used the building as a hospital after the fall of Fort Sumter and it fell into disrepair after that. It was acquired in 1884 by the great-grandfather of the present owners. Two wings were added in 1910, giving it the appearance seen today. The mansion, considered an excellent example of Greek Revival architecture, is part of the gardens but is a private residence and not open. Harmonious Luola's Chapel was built in 1915.

The gardens, located on state Route 133 about 10 miles north of Southport and 18 miles south of Wilmington, are open March 1–November 30.

Orton Pond, a millpond, and the adjacent uplands support large populations of anhinga, osprey, red-cockaded woodpecker, alligator, and fox squirrel. The rare snail *planorbella magnifica* also is present.

Brunswick Town State Historic Site. Founded about 1725 as a business venture by Maurice Moore and his brother, Roger, Brunswick quickly became one of the most prosperous ports in the southeast, rivaling Wilmington in the export of lumber and naval stores. In 1748, it was captured by Spanish privateers from the ship *Fortuna,* who held it for three days. When the Brunswick settlers counterattacked, the surprised sailors accidentally set fire to munitions on their ship and blew it up. On the eve of the Revolutionary War, citizens protesting the Stamp Act placed Royal Governor William Tryon under house arrest. In 1776, British soldiers burned the town, and it never recovered. However, during the Civil War, the Confederate States of America constructed a strong earthworks fortification, Fort Anderson, on the town site.

The foundations of the colonial buildings, including the impressive walls of 1768 St. Philip's Anglican Church, have been excavated and are maintained as archaeological exhibits. Narrative displays are spotted around the village area. Artifacts excavated at the site are displayed in the visitors center.

The remains of Fort Anderson are a good example of Civil War earthen fortifications. Fort Anderson held out for 30 days after the fall of Fort Fisher.

A nature trail passes under cypress and other trees hung with Spanish moss and by insect-eating Venus fly-trap, visits a spring used by colonists, and follows the banks of a pond.

The park is open year-round 9 a.m. to 5 p.m. Monday–Saturday and 1 to 5 p.m. Sunday April–October, 10 a.m. to 4 p.m. Tuesday–Saturday and 1 to 4 p.m. Sunday the rest of the year.

Town Creek, which flows into the Cape Fear River between Brunswick State Historic Site and Wilmington and was once deep enough for steamboats, is an interesting canoeing stream whose wild inhabitants include alligators.

South Brunswick Coast

South Brunswick Islands Chamber of Commerce
P.O. Box 1380
Shallotte, NC 28459
919/754-6644

THE COASTAL AREA BETWEEN CAPE FEAR AND THE SOUTH CAROLINA LINE, where the coastline runs almost east–west, is known as South Brunswick since it is the southern part of Brunswick County. Four barrier islands with long, sandy beaches—more than 47 miles of them, according to the Chamber of Commerce—have been virtually taken over by resort developments. Nevertheless, each of the islands—Oak, Holden, Ocean, and Sunset—has to some extent its own character. Only two of the islands—Ocean and Sunset—are connected; consequently, visiting all of them requires backtracking to the mainland across causeways.

The wide, white beaches are made up of fine sand that compacts when it gets wet—a plus for runners and joggers. The beaches are backed by dunes, tufted with sea oats, that survived Hurricane Hugo. Cottages and other structures generally are set behind the dunes. Public access points to the beaches are marked on all of the islands. Each isle has at least one fishing pier. The Intracoastal Waterway passes behind the islands.

The relationship between the resort islands and the mainland is symbiotic. Traditional centers such as Shallotte and Calabash, greatly influenced by the tourist traffic, stand near a number of handsome upscale resort communities with excellent recreational facilities, including golf courses that are their bread and butter. There are more than a dozen 18-hole courses in the area. Charter and "head" boats leave from many marinas.

Residential developers have changed the natural order in the area but have shown some concern for natural and historical values. Resorts often preserve outstanding natural features and submit to historical interests. For example, at Sea Trail Plantation, a golf path was designed to follow the original route of the "King's Highway." At the Winds Carriage House Inn at Ocean Isle Beach, owner/manager Miller Pope demonstrates how vegetation from both the subtropical and northern zones thrives in the area. He has planted numerous kinds of palm trees and other subtropical plants, including Florida needle palms and a Mediterranean variety, in a garden between the motel and the beach. Pampas grass imported from Argentina flourishes in his garden—as it does at other places in the area. On the other hand, the saltiness of the air is deadly to regular North Carolina pines; the variety most seen on Ocean Isle Beach is Japanese pine.

Although the resort atmosphere dominates, the area retains some of its traditional character, especially at fishing villages such as Calabash and Varnamtown, where docks are lined with big trawlers, men brave the ocean depths in much smaller boats, and sometimes call any dry land "the hill." Commercial catches of finfish, shrimp, oysters, clams, and crabs are still one of the major industries of the area. The Calabash style of cooking seafood has become so popular that restaurants serving it are no longer confined to the community of Calabash.

Sports fishers who boat out to the Gulf Stream return with sailfish, king mackerel, red snapper, grouper, and other species. In the Inland Waterway and nearby marshes are trout, channel bass, croaker, and other varieties.

A number of cooperative events are held annually. The largest, with about 30,000 participants, is the North Carolina Oyster Festival in mid-October. It satiates seafood and hush-puppies lovers against a backdrop of entertainment and arts and crafts. Labor Day weekend sees anglers competing in the South Brunswick Islands King Mackerel Tournament.

Historic interests remain. This is an area where visitors may profit by turning off state Route 179 to follow streets to the waterfront. For example, at the end of Gause Landing is the old landing once used by a plantation.

Between Southport and Holden Beach, travelers along the Intracoastal Waterway see an unusual sight—the Yellow Banks. For a distance of a mile or so, bluffs 40 to 50 feet high stand on both banks of the waterway.

Oak Island

Oak Island is an elongated sliver of sandy soil at the eastern end of the line. Local people sometimes refer to the whole island as "Long Island." It has three beaches—Long, Yaupon, and Caswell—and a long inlet at its western end known as the Big Davis Canal. Fishing piers stand at Yaupon and Long beaches. In some places, the island retains the natural look, including sizable stands of trees and scrub vegetation that existed before humans began to manicure them for resort purposes. It has a high rate of permanent population for the area.

Oak Island has a long history of use. Fort Caswell, which has served the country in four wars, is now on the grounds of the North Carolina Baptist Assemblies. The church, which acquired the property in 1949, cooperates with local organizations in conducting tours and presenting cultural programs in its auditorium.

Brick and concrete gun emplacements, shorn of their cannon, and casements look seaward from this strategic point at the eastern end of the island. The extensive fortifications that remain, including domed cisterns and artillery mounts, incorporate elements of various periods, although most of the construction dates from World War I. The first fortification was raised in 1825 and was manned by the Confederates between 1861 and 1865, when it was part of the defenses of the Cape Fear River. The fortress was upgraded during the Spanish-American War and World War I and was used as a U.S. Navy supply station during World War II.

Visitors who want to visit the fortifications should telephone the Baptist Assembly in advance to determine if programs are being held. This end of the island is a good place to watch from a distance the annual Fourth of July fireworks display at Southport.

The road to Fort Caswell passes the tall Oak Island Lighthouse and a Coast Guard station. Still in operation, the lighthouse is not open to the public.

The Brunswick County Parks and Recreation Department conducts guided programs such as a bicycle ride from the Yaupon Beach fishing pier to Caswell Beach Lighthouse.

Holden Island

The wide sandy beach on Holden Island has been favored for a long time by sunworshippers and shell collectors, but the 11-mile-long island developed slowly as a resort. It projects a "family beach" image and has about 20 public beach access points, one of which has a 90-space parking lot with restroom facilities. Most of the commercial development is on the approach to the causeway to the island.

This island historically was noted for its boatbuilding, based on expertise stored in the memories of craftsmen who passed it from father to son. A few such builders still are active. An oceanfront pier is available to fishers. Shrimp boats operate from a dock on the Intracoastal Waterway.

The North Carolina Festival by the Sea, featuring coastal food specialties, entertainment, and arts and crafts, is held annually the last weekend in October.

Ocean Isle Beach

Ocean Isle Beach is unabashedly a resort, with all the visible signs: rustic cottages, luxurious summer homes, inns and hotels and restaurants serving mostly generic cuisines. Its 7 miles of sandy oceanfront are crowded in summer and the shoulder seasons with sunbathers, swimmers, fishers, and beachcombers. A long pier caters to fishers and provides a vantage point for viewing the sweep of the shoreline and relaxing in salty ocean breezes.

Near the center of the island, the Museum of Coastal Carolina creates a capsule view of the fertile waters. In one large room with floor and wall murals, visitors view lifesize replicas of sharks, turtles, and other sea life as though the visitors are walking on the bottom of the sea. Other key features are a large collection of seashells and shark's teeth, animal and bird life displays, and Civil War relics.

Ocean Isle Beach was purchased in 1950 by developer Odell Williamson for the express purpose of development. The town was incorporated in 1959.

A picturesque one-lane swinging pontoon bridge, often opened to allow vessels to pass through Tubbs Inlet, connects the western end of Ocean Isle and Sunset Beach, which is predominantly residential. Naturally, proposals to replace this low bridge with a high span are controversial locally. Sunset is the smallest of the islands, barely 3 miles long, but is accreting. In some places, people now have to walk considerable distance from their homes across sand dunes to reach the beach. An oceanfront lot at the end of Sunset Boulevard is open to the public. A fishing pier is located on Main Street.

Bird Island, west of Sunset Beach, is uninhabited and privately owned. However, a few locals go there by walking across the mud flats between the islands at low tide — an act that requires deference to the tide charts. Bird Island has a sizable maritime forest.

Rivers and a Swamp

Brunswick County's reputation for exceptional natural phenomena is deserved. For example, the North Carolina Natural Heritage Program has catalogued more than 500 rare plants, animals, and significant natural communities — far more than in any other county in the state. Among them are more than 20 natural areas regarded as having national and statewide significance, including the extensive estuarine marshes that border blackwater rivers as they flow through the area. South Brunswick also contributes in other major ways to the county's reputation. The ponds on the mainland across from Sunset Beach are the only place in the state where wood storks gather, in late summer. The Green Swamp, an inland pocosin, is perhaps the most striking phenomenon.

The Green Swamp. Many people speak of North Carolina's Green Swamp, which at one time covered about a third of Brunswick County, with awe. Despite the name, the area today is predominantly high ground with significant wet areas, largely the result of draining for cutting and to plant tree farms. Historically, the area was mysterious and wild and considered dangerous because it was believed to be a haven for outcasts and escapees from organized society. And it was populated with alligators and other predators that feasted on the unwary and ill-equipped.

The Green Swamp, a vaguely defined area generally west of U.S. Route 17 on both sides of state Route 211, appears on few maps. Some aspects of the area seem timeless. Certain forested areas, where people have seen as many as 30 to 40 deer gathering at dusk, retain an almost primeval quality. "Hog" bear (the local name for black bear) sometimes wander across the roads, insectivorous Venus fly-trap and pitcher plants (at least 15 have been identified, including the uncommon horned bladderwort) and various types of orchids grow amid stands of longleaf pine trees that look like prehistoric forests. In small communities like Crusoe and Exum, families that go back many generations have not lost the ability to use the resources of the swamp—to make furniture or a dugout canoe for fishing or to capture snakes for sale to zoos and others, for example.

Yet the swamp is no longer isolated. A hunt club is located on Route 211. A 13,000-acre section is game land. Nearly 16,000 acres abutting Route 211 5 miles north of Supply are set aside as a nature preserve and bear sanctuary (one of 12 in the North Carolina coastal region). The preserve encloses a large pocosin system, a longleaf pine savannah with an abundance of wildflowers and orchids and 14 insectivorous plants. White-tailed deer, American alligator, and diamondback rattlesnake are common and the red-cockaded woodpecker is among avian inhabitants.

The Nature Conservancy (919/967-7007) conducts field trips and allows deer hunting on part of the preserve in season. Driving on the preserve is not allowed.

Although most of the Green Swamp land is privately owned, wilderness buffs may proceed with permission on their own along dirt roads, provided they are careful not to make too many turns and get lost. The roads provide access to fire breaks that can be hiked and to Juniper Creek near its confluence with the Waccamaw River, an interesting canoeing experience. Sandy areas along the stream can be used for overnight camping. Other streams are too overgrown for easy paddling.

Some local people advise against entering the swamp without a guide. Grissetown artist Ken Buckner, who left Connecticut about 15 years ago and is familiar with the swamp, says people trying to go alone often become lost.

Properties adjacent to Green Swamp sometimes are visited by wild animals. A few years ago, men clearing a site flushed a wild boar, for example. Bears sometimes stray off the preserve onto nearby properties in search of food.

River Trails. The abundant natural features of South Brunswick include worthwhile canoe and kayak trails. The Lockwood Folly and

Waccamaw rivers are suited to paddling, but both require portaging at times to avoid natural obstructions. Paddlers will be rewarded at places by densely forested banks visited by birds such as pileated woodpecker and various kinds of hawks.

Boats can be put into the short Lockwood Folly River at Routes 211 and 17 for a downstream trip through the kind of terrain the original settlers saw or to watch nesting osprey. The alligator population has increased in recent years, according to local people, because those caught in the process of building new golf courses have been transplanted to the river. Some paddlers start in the forests farther upstream, too.

One legend attributes the river's unusual name to a man who built a boat with a draught too deep for the river.

While the Folly is a short trip, canoers can spend days following the Waccamaw into South Carolina and passing some areas seldom visited by humans. However, the results of clearcutting for timber are evident at other places along the route.

The Brunswick County Parks and Recreation Department conducts an overnight canoe trip to Shelter Creek near Burgaw.

Vereen Memorial Historical Gardens. An orderly kind of outdoors area lies on state Route 179 near its intersection with U.S. Route 17 just north of the South Carolina line. Vereen Memorial Historical Gardens is a peaceful escape from the stream of vehicles along both roads and the related commercial bustle, including real estate offices and signs for developing resort communities.

A nature trail traverses a forest with more than 60 varieties of plants, including American holly, longleaf pine, water and live oak, dogwood, hickory, myrtle, and wild ginger. The trail crosses the first road cut through the wilderness, the King's Highway. The gardens are open during daylight hours.

Shallotte

Settled in the 1880s and incorporated in 1899, Shallotte was first a port on the Shallotte River. It has since dropped much of that role, but sometimes provides a haven for coastal ships during hurricanes. Now primarily a Route 17 commercial center for the South Brunswick area, its name is an Indian word for "healing waters." Drinking the water and swimming in the river were considered cures for many illnesses.

The 20-acre Shallotte Township District Park has a nature trail, canoe trail, and fishing-viewing platforms among its extensive facilities.

Calabash

This community was originally named Pea Landing, apparently in recognition of the peanuts shipped from its docks to Wilmington. In the late 19th century, when the villagers decided to shuck that name, they remembered a common sight—gourds hanging on walls: Calabash is an Indian word for gourd. Until 1989, Calabash had about 200 permanent residents. A decision to merge with the nearby Carolina Shores Resort increased that five-fold.

Calabash today is known for its cuisine. The self-styled "Seafood Capital of the World" each year feeds succulent Calabash-style seafood to about a million people at 20-plus restaurants. Some people drive long distances to sample the batter-dipped, deep-fried cuisine, whose quality belies the tradition that the best seafood is served in plain-looking places.

The town's nautical origins remain apparent at the small harbor on the Calabash River. Shrimp boats and charter boats share space with pleasure boats sailing the Intracoastal Waterway.

Calabash is a fitting transition place for entry into South Carolina because the mixture of active fishing village and tourist culinary destination continues at Little River and other places at the upper end of South Carolina's Grand Strand.

The "Inland Coast"

TRADITIONALLY, NORTH CAROLINA'S COASTAL REGION HAS EXTENDED inland as far as ships could sail. Early ports were located a few miles upstream because the sites provided some protection from Spanish marauders and pirates. As the population moved inland, carving farm enclaves into the forests along river banks, river ports linked the Piedmont farms with the rest of the world. As a result, the coastal region of North Carolina is deeper than that of most Eastern states.

Interstate 95 is in the western fringe of the zone and provides quick access to many of the sites. U.S. Route 258 cuts through the heart of this area to Kinston. U.S. routes 13, 117, and 701 and state routes 53 and 211 take over to complete a drive through this "inland coast." Relatively short diversions from coastal U.S. Route 17 to many of these sites also are feasible.

Historic Halifax

Halifax County Tourism Development Authority
P.O. Box 144
Roanoke Rapids, NC 27870
919/535-1687

The site of this town was its fortune. Located on the south shore below the rapids of the Roanoke River, it also stood astride major north–south and east–west roads. Thus, when new Halifax County was created in 1758, the small village was chosen as its seat. Its "golden age" had begun.

It quickly developed into a river port for the rising number of tradesmen, shippers, politicians, and inland farms raising tobacco, corn, produce, and pork. Rich planters took an interest in politics and this, combined with Halifax's wealth and role as communications center between the west and east, made it a center of political power. In 1776, the Halifax Resolves approved by the North Carolina provincial congress authorized North Carolina members of the Continental Congress to "concur with the other delegates of the other colonies in declaring independency" — the first official action by any colony in support of independence. Halifax was a military depot and recruiting center during the war, but was affected directly only when Cornwallis marched through en route to defeat in Virginia.

Halifax reached a peak about the time of the American Revolution and, for the next 60 years, was one of the most prosperous and influential towns in the state. It began to decline in the 1830s when a change in the state Constitution reduced its political power and the railroad bypassed it. The Civil War seriously affected the plantations of the Roanoke River Valley. Halifax's only continuing role was as county seat.

The aura of the lusty river town remains, despite the intrusion of modern structures and activities. Yards are largely unadorned, the buildings are widely dispersed, and a path leads from the Old Market Square past a natural gardens to Sally-Billy House, set off in the woods—just the way frontier communities looked in the early 19th century.

The past is still visible in the restored buildings that constitute Historic Halifax. Visitors may walk the streets and look at the bright exterior of 1790 Eagle Tavern, where Lafayette was entertained during his early 19th-century visit to America; the 1832 brick clerk's office and the 1838 brick jail; and the 1760 Owens and the 1808 Sally-Billy houses.

The houses, which can be visited on guided tours, disclose the orientation of even hard-headed businessmen. On the first floor of the small Owens house is a merchant's office, while the second floor holds living quarters. An unusual glass painting is among the decorations. The larger Sally-Billy House is comfortably furnished in antiques; an engraving of a horse identifies one of the passions of Halifax's leading citizens—horse racing. Another was cock fighting.

A modern visitors center, open from 9 a.m. to 5 p.m. Tuesday-Saturday and 1 to 5 p.m. Sunday, except holidays, reconstructs history through displays and an audiovisual introduction to the historic area. Guided tours start from this point. A formal garden of shrubs, trees, and flowers is adjacent to the center.

Roanoke Canal Trail. Between 1819 and 1825, a canal was built to bypass the rapids on the Roanoke River west of Halifax, whose churning 44-foot drop in 300 feet led the Indians to call the Roanoke the "River of Death." This canal was to be part of an extensive system that would connect the coast with the Blue Ridge Mountains. The system provided a short-term economic boost, but declined as railroads expanded. In the 1890s, it was converted to generate power, a use that continued until the 1920s.

The impressive and well-preserved remnants of the cut between Weldon and Roanoke Rapids are now an exceptional nature/history trail through a forest of loblolly pine, hardwoods, and native wildflowers inhabited by deer, quail, and songbirds. The trail follows the towpath on the north wall of the cut; rustic footbridges span gaps that have developed since the canal was abandoned. The approximately 3-mile trail also crosses an aqueduct across Chocoyotte Creek.

The trail was opened in 1990 by the nonprofit Roanoke Canal Commission, Inc., which owns a strip 3.2 miles long and 165 feet wide. Parking lots are located at both ends — near the aqueduct and on River Road at Roanoke Rapids.

The four locks built at Roanoke Rapids may still be seen, but are undeveloped.

Murfreesboro

Thirty-five miles east of Halifax on Route 158 is Murfreesboro, another colonial frontier river port. English explorers reached the area in the late 16th century and the first settlers arrived by 1710. Historic structures date from later, more settled periods.

The Chamber of Commerce is located in the Roberts-Vaughan House (circa 1790) on Main Street (Route 158) and the other buildings are within walking distance. Among them is the Murfree-Smith Law Office (circa 1800), named in part for William Murfree, an Irish immigrant whose landing for imports and exports became the nucleus of a town on land he donated; the 1811 Hertford Academy of Arts, first a school run by an individual and then the ancestor of Chowan College; the impressive 1814 brick John Wheeler House on East Broad Street, which served as a store as well as a home; the 1872 frame Winborne Law Office and Country Store; and the William Rea House, built in the opening years of the 19th century by a Boston merchant who conducted extensive trade between Murfreesboro and New England and now a museum.

Maps showing the locations of these buildings are found behind the Rea Museum (on 4th Street just off Route 158) and at the end of the wooden footbridge across the gully to the Hertford Academy. Near the museum map is a 150-year-old dugout canoe used for transportation across the Chowan River at Barfields Ferry and for fishing.

Chowan College, a junior college with approximately 1,000 students, stands on another site. "The Columns," as its administrative building is known, was constructed in 1851.

Dr. Walter Reed, conqueror of yellow fever, grew up in Murfreesboro; the white frame house where he lived as a youth fronts on Main Street.

In Gatesville, on state Route 37, the Federal-style courthouse dates back to 1836.

Tarboro

Tarboro Chamber of Commerce
12 West Church Street
Tarboro NC 27886
919/823-7421

The name of this delightful community is doubly appropriate. Not only is it situated at the navigable extreme of the Tar River, but it also was a colonial river port shipping naval stores as well as cotton from nearby farms to the outside world.

The Tarboro area was settled mainly by people from southern Virginia, beginning about 1720. Tarboro was incorporated in 1760 basically as a real-estate venture. Among the five commissioners appointed to develop the 150 acres of land was Elisha Battle, ancestor of a family still prominent in eastern North Carolina. His 1742 mansion at Old Town Plantation, east of Rocky Mount, is one of the ten oldest houses in the state.

Tarboro quickly became a center of activity, primarily because of its position at the westernmost point on the river. It enjoyed prominence throughout the 18th century and in the 19th century until the Civil War interrupted commerce and drained its resources. Tarboro revived but not greatly until after World War II, when an influx of small industries reduced the town's agricultural orientation. Despite these changes, the population has remained almost static.

Tarboro is proud of its heritage — in a businesslike way. Its 45-block historic district is on the National Register of Historic Places. At a time when many communities are devouring unused land, it retains a 24-acre Town Common created in 1760 as an outdoor haven. Ancient oaks shade a few memorials; a symbol of the town's agricultural side, a huge 1860 cotton press; a small herb garden; and the McBryde Trail, a brief walk along a planted hillside beside a gully with slow-moving water.

Most of the town's colonial, antebellum, and Victorian structures are carefully preserved so they can be used for modern purposes. Among the numerous homes still in private hands is the Porter House (circa 1790), the town's oldest building. Other significant private homes are the deBerry House (circa 1795), the 1803 Irwin House, 1810 Theophilus Parker House, 1830 Pender-Lanier House, Hyman-Philips House (circa 1840), Norfleet House (circa 1858), and Howard

Holderness House (circa 1890). The two-story Porter-Bass House (circa 1869) is now a real-estate office.

The mainly late 19th-century Main Street, which has excellent examples of facade decorations from the period, is being revitalized by a joint private/government program involving the National Trust for Historic Preservation, local businesses, and the state government.

Two historic houses are open to the public year-round: the Federal-style Blount-Bridgers Mansion (circa 1808), which devotes its second floor to the more than 200 works in the Hobson Pittman Memorial Art Gallery, and the 1810 frame structure housing the Pender Museum. A guided tour of the Blount-Bridgers House, originally the nerve center of a 300-acre plantation known as The Grove, introduces visitors to its inhabitants, starting with its builder, General and Congressman Thomas Blount, and his wife. Blount and his brothers, who owned a large mercantile business, used the house as their Tarboro office and residence. Furnishings from the Federal, late Federal, and Victorian periods and the original cedar floors reveal the lifestyle of Blount and subsequent owners, such as Louis Dicken Wilson, a proponent of public schools and libraries for whom the city of Wilson was named, and Captain John Bridgers, owner during the Civil War period, who added its Italianate wraparound porch about 1850. Open 10 a.m. to 4 p.m. Monday–Friday and 2 to 4 p.m. Saturday–Sunday.

The Blount-Bridgers House was acquired by the community in 1930 and used for various purposes, including library and school offices, until it was restored in 1980 as an exhibition building.

Handsome red-brick Calvary Episcopal Church, with columns on the face of its steeple, dates from 1857.

A map available from the Chamber of Commerce shows a walking or driving tour that passes more than 90 historically or architecturally significant buildings.

Spotted unobtrusively in Riverfront Park's cypress lowlands and landscaped gardens are walking trails and a boat ramp that gives fishers and boaters access to the Tar River. Indian Lake Park has a stocked freshwater pond in a wilderness setting. Livesay Lake Park is urban greenspace with walkways through woods and landscaping. A boat ramp is located on state Route 44 just northwest of Tarboro.

Goldsboro

Wayne County Chamber of Commerce
308 North William Street
Goldsboro NC 27533
919/734-2241

From its broad main street to the narrow side streets, this city bustles. That is appropriate because the Wilmington and Weldon Railroad, the longest in the world when it was completed in 1838, turned a small, unnamed village into a bustling community. It was selected as the new site of the county seat in 1845 and incorporated in 1887. It was even named for the railroad's assistant chief engineer, Major Matthew T. Goldsborough.

The Civil War drained the city of manpower—the Goldsborough Rifles and Goldsborough Volunteers were immediately dispatched to garrison Fort Macon on the coast—but was little touched until late in the war when Union General William T. Sherman defeated Confederate forces at Bentonville Battlefield about 25 miles away. After the Confederate defeat, General Sherman's 100,000-man army camped in and around Goldsboro.

The city has remained true to its heritage as a transportation and farm market center, but it has developed new interests over the years. During World War II, the conversion of the local airport into a training center for Air Force ground-crew mechanics began an ongoing love affair. The small installation grew in time into Seymour Johnson Air Force Base, home of the Tactical Air Command's 4th Tactical Fighter Wing and the 68th Air Refueling Wing. The base played an important role in Operation Desert Storm.

Goldsboro today reflects its business origins. Its major historical structures are located on and near Center Avenue, the traditional business core. These are being preserved and restored under a Main Street revitalization program managed by a public-private nonprofit organization. The exteriors of a number of structures already have been restored for modern uses. The handsome City Hall, with a dome and flanking roof statues, sets the tone for rows of ornate late 19th-century buildings on both sides of the street. Among them are the 1882 Paramount Theater, the 1867 Keaton Fonvielle Jewelry Store, and 1868 L.D. Gliddens & Son Jewelry Store. The clean, impressive lines of the 1856 First Presbyterian Church dominate an adjacent block of Ash Street.

The Wayne County Museum on North William Street continues the local history lesson. Opened in 1988 in a building donated by the Woman's Club, it explores subjects such as Southern furniture, Indian culture, World War II, the War Between the States, and black history through permanent and changing exhibits. It is open 2 to 5 p.m. Tuesday, Thursday, and Sunday.

A view of rural life in the same era is depicted at the Charles B. Aycock Birthplace about 11 miles north of Goldsboro on U.S. Route 117. There, preserved as a state historical site, is the simple farmhouse in which the state's first 20th-century governor was born and a one-room schoolhouse typical of those used in later decades of the 19th century. From this humble beginning, Aycock became one of the most influential men in state politics and a major proponent of public-school education.

The Aycock Birthplace is open 9 a.m. to 5 p.m. Monday–Saturday and 1 to 5 p.m. Sunday April–October, 10 a.m. to 4 p.m. Tuesday–Saturday and 1 to 4 p.m. Sunday the remainder of the year.

Bentonville Battlefield State Historic Site, slightly more than 2 miles off U.S. Route 701 near Newton Grove, preserves some of the earthworks and the Harper farmhouse around which the last major battle of the Civil War swirled. There, on March 19 to 21, 1865, Confederate General Joseph E. Johnston tried to halt Sherman's inexorable march. The farmhouse, used as a hospital during the battle, is equipped as it was then, with the family furniture and possessions pushed aside for pallets and operating table. Each year, near the anniversary of the battle, "reactivated" Civil War units hold an encampment, demonstrate use of weapons, and explain medical care during the period.

The site is open from 9 a.m. to 5 p.m. Tuesday–Saturday and 1 to 5 p.m. Sunday year-round. A visitors center contains displays on the battle and its significance.

The Cliffs of Neuse State Park

This park, about 15 miles from Goldsboro on state Route 111, is a good place to overdose on the beauties of natural phenomena. For a distance of more than 600 yards, multicolored layers of sand, clay, seashells, shale, and gravel rise steeply as high as 98 feet above the dark, slow-moving Neuse River.

More than 420 species of plants grow in six distinct community zones: mixed pine–hardwoods, deciduous hardwoods, river margin, xeric coarse sand, disturbed, and aquatic. The first, which includes wild azalea, dwarf sumac, goldenrod, Maryland golden aster, and muscadine grape under oaks, loblolly pine, hickory, sweet and red bays, black gum, and Virginia willow, is widespread throughout the park. Though the fall line is 40 miles farther west, plants normally associated with all three regions of North Carolina are found in the park. In close proximity are cypress and live oak found in coastal regions, oak-hickory forests typical of the Piedmont area, and galax, red oak, and Virginia pine common in mountain habitats farther west. Half a dozen orchids, prickly pear, and trillium are among scores of wildflowers. Furthermore, this is the western limit of Spanish moss in the state.

Four trails less than a mile in length and an observation path and deck give visitors views of the cliffs and river from several perspectives. The descending Bird Trail follows the riverbank to a lower vantage point, then circles back through gums, maple, ash, oaks, beech, walnut, loblolly pine, bushes, and ferns along Still Creek, where federally operated stills once made whiskey. Nearby Mill Creek powered a gristmill that supplied the stills and made cornmeal. Today, the creeks and river are open to fishers who hook catfish, crappie, bluegill, and largemouth bass. In the summer, white and hickory shad migrate through the park. The Spanish Moss Trail loops along the cliff and through a forest where the sharp, rhythmic tapping of woodpeckers can be heard.

Small animals such as squirrels, raccoon, foxes, river otter, beaver, and reptiles are common, while white-tailed deer are scarce. Northern parula nest in Spanish moss and prothonotary warblers live along the river. Migrating waterfowl stop in the park.

An 11-acre manmade lake has a sandy beach for sunbathing and swimming and a boat rental facility. A 35-site camping area is open from June 15 to November. Rangers hold interpretive programs year-round.

An audiovisual program in a museum near the observation point explains the formation of the cliffs by a shift in the fault millions of years ago. Exhibits deal with the culture of the Tuscarora and Saponi Indians and European settlers who established a trading center at Seven Springs (then named Whitehall) just east of the park. The shallow-bottom Confederate ironclad ram *CSS Neuse,* which saw action only briefly before it was destroyed to prevent capture, was built there. Later the town was a well-known spa until the 1920s.

The 521-acre park was first proposed in 1944 by Lionel Weil and created largely by private donations. Park hours are seasonal: 8 a.m. to 9 p.m. June–August; 8 to 8 April, May, and September; 8 to 7 March and October; and 8 to 6 November–February.

Kinston

The ruins of the ironclad *CSS Neuse,* raised in 1964, are displayed in Kinston, about 15 miles east of Goldsboro. Also located on the Caswell-Neuse State Historic Site is a memorial to Governor Richard Caswell, a Revolutionary War hero and first governor of the state. Relics are on display and a sound-and-light program depicts his military and political career, from 9 a.m. to 5 p.m. Tuesday–Saturday and 1 to 5 p.m. Sunday.

"Carolina Bays"

In southeastern North Carolina and northeastern South Carolina, thousands of lakes and depressions interrupt the forests and fields. These range in size from 500 to 8,000 feet long, the largest covering about 6,000 acres. Many are covered by wet organic soil and swamp-type vegetation, but their round and oval shapes remain clearly visible from the air. The name "bays" derives from the vegetation that surrounds them—sweet, loblolly, and red bay trees. Many scientists have speculated about their origin; meteor showers, underground springs, glaciation, wave action, and dissolution of subsurface minerals all have been suggested at one time or another. Yet, no one knows for certain how this spectacular but little known Lakes District was formed. Most of the bays have no inlet or outlet, and, thus, are dependent on rainwater.

It has been an attractive phenomenon since it was discovered, however. The region was settled in the colonial era by farmers who planted cotton and other crops along lowlands bordering the extensive water system. In addition, the forests were for more than a century a prolific source of naval stores such as timber, turpentine, and pitch. Statewide interest in preserving the phenomenon emerged as early as 1827–28 in North Carolina and, in 1911, lakes of 500 acres or more in Bladen, Cumberland, and Columbus counties became state property. In 1919, this was expanded to include any lake of 50 acres or more. Between 1936 and 1939, the federal government purchased submarginal farmlands and conservation areas, some of which was used for recreational purposes. The property was turned over to the state in 1939.

Bladen Lakes State Forest. This is North Carolina's largest forest, covering more than 32,000 acres. Inside the boundaries are four of the most spectacular of the "Carolina Bays," some of which are accessible in state parks. In addition, the North Carolina Division of Forest Resources carries on an active program that includes educational tours, trails, camping, protection of endangered species, 72 acres of seed orchards, planned cutting and burning and artificial regeneration, fence-post and pine-straw sales, and experimental studies in zoology, botany, geology, and other subjects. Hunting is permitted on gamelands within the forest.

Part of the tract off state Route 242 north of Elizabethtown has been set aside as Bladen Lakes Educational State Forest, which synthesizes the natural surroundings and human use of it. Ranger Cynthia Jackson conducts guided tours for groups, covering such subjects as the meaning of tree rings, predators and their prey, products obtained from trees, and wildflowers in a managed forest.

However, the course is laid out so individuals can follow it in their own automobiles, stopping to enjoy the Turnbull Creek, Post and Pine Straw and Fire Control trails, and related exhibits. At the Naval Stores area is a turpentine still built in the 1880s and once used in Swansboro, the earthworks of old tar kilns, and a mockup of a kiln. At the Forest Resources site are equipment for baling pine straw and making fence posts. Fire-control explanations at this site are supplemented later by a T-34 Scout plane of the type used to drop water on forest fires and a scaled-down fire tower. The Turnbull Creek Trail descends from an upland forest featuring loblolly pine, dogwood, American holly, yellow poplar, red bay, and other species to the creek carrying large floes of what look like soapsuds but are actually the result of natural oxidation. Growing in the bottom are bald cypress hung with Spanish moss, sparkleberry, and other flora. Signboards along the trail identify important trees — including the pignut hickory more common to mountain habitats — and note human application — such as using the ends of sweetgum branches as toothbrushes. White-tailed deer and smaller animals may be seen near the trail if no traffic has been there recently.

In another area of the forest, the South Swamp covers about 9 acres and contains an unmarked trail. It was drained in the 1970s.

Endangered species such as white wicki, Venus fly-trap, red-cockaded woodpecker, and barrens tree frog are protected at the 4,773-acre Carolina Bays Natural Area. Isolated White Lake, part of the state park system, is one of the best fishing holes in the region.

Jones Lake, Singletary Lake, and Lake Waccamaw State Parks. Similar in character, these parks differ in size and function. Jones Lake Park covers 2,208 acres and caters to families and individuals; Singletary is a thin 649-acre land area around a 572-acre lake and caters primarily to groups. Both are open year-round.

Aquatic activities predominate at Jones Lake Park, which actually encompasses two lakes that are sustained by rainfall and thus subject to depth changes. Since special permission is required to use Salters Lake, located in wilderness at the end of the park, most of the activity is centered at Jones Lake, whose depth averages 8.7 feet. The lake is not especially good for fishing because of its acidity, but catches include yellow perch, sunfish, chain pickerel, catfish, largemouth bass, and warmouth. Pleasure boating is aided by a boat ramp and pier. A sandy beach west of the pier encourages sunbathing and swimming.

Self-guided trails include a 3-mile circuit of Jones Lake that traverses a typical bay habitat of boggy soil covered by dense vegetation, including bay trees, bald cypress hung with Spanish moss, white cedar, longleaf pine, blueberry, fetterbush, and delicate blossoms such as the white titi. Since the park is adjacent to gamelands, white-tailed deer, wild turkey, black bear, bobcat, cottontail rabbits, and gray fox tend to shelter in the park, which also houses river otter, Virginia opossum, numerous reptiles, and frogs (often heard on summer nights). A 1-mile nature trail follows the shoreline and then loops through a bay forest area.

More than 100 species of birds, including the endangered red-cockaded woodpecker, have been spotted. The most common species include Carolina wren, Carolina chickadee, and black vulture, but other frequent sightings include ducks, owls, warblers, pileated woodpecker, white-eyed vireo, red-tailed hawk, great blue heron, American woodcock, mourning dove, ruby-throated hummingbird, red-winged blackbird, chipping sparrow, and rufous-sided towhee.

An interpretive center near the beach is staffed on weekends during the summer. Twenty wooded campsites are available.

Singletary Lake Park is named for Richard Singletary, who received a land grant in 1729. This handsome park opened in 1939 for use by Boy Scouts, 4-H clubs, and other organizations. Today, two organized group camps near a swimming and sunbathing area are available to nonprofit adult and youth organizations. Camp Loblolly Pine, open year-round and accessible to the handicapped, has space for 48 people. Camp Ipecac, named for an herb common in the park, houses 88 persons but is closed during winter.

When group camps are not occupied, others may use a prepared trail and fish in the lake, though acidity keeps fish counts low. The trail, extended early in 1992, begins near the pier and winds through a forest of longleaf pine, turkey oak, bay shrubs, cedar, cypress, gums, and poplars. Some of the cypress trees lining the lake are 400 years old.

The 133-acre Turkey Oak Natural Area near the northeastern shore of the egg-shaped lake encompasses a sand ridge and bay bog. Turkey oak is the predominant tree in the preserve, but all the types of plants associated with a Carolina bay are present, as is the rare white wicki and insectivorous species.

The animal population is similar to that at Jones Lake Park but may be larger because of the gamelands near Jones Lake.

Singletary Lake facilities have been used as an evacuation center in recent emergencies. During World War II, the park was part of an anti-aircraft school at Fort Davis.

At Elwell, east of Singletary park along state Route 53, is another of those charming two-car ferries. This one crosses the Cape Fear River.

Lake Waccamaw State Park, located on state Route 1757 (Jefferson Road) 4 miles off U.S. Route 74-76, is under development and has minimal facilities. The nearby town of Lake Waccamaw enjoys a beautiful lakeside location and has a small Depot Museum on Flemington Drive. A public boat ramp lies off the road to the park entrance.

Lake Waccamaw, fed by a number of streams, is the source of the Waccamaw River, which parallels the coastline into South Carolina. The acid entering the lake is neutralized by limestone outcroppings. As a result, the 9,000-acre lake has an abundance of fish and other aquatic life. The Waccamaw silverside and Waccamaw darter are indigenous species; the Waccamaw killifish also is found in Lake Phelps in the Albemarle region. Mollusks, crayfish, alligators, and turtles also are found in large numbers in and around the lake. Since it is only 25 miles from the ocean, sea birds sometimes enlarge an already populous bird life.

PART THREE

~~~~~~~~~

South Carolina

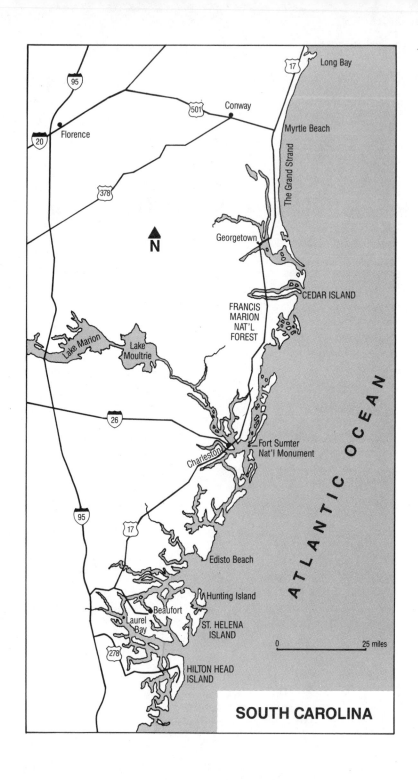

Genteel and Close

THANKS TO THE REPUTATION OF CHARLESTON, THE IMAGE OF THE PAL-
metto State oozes with gentility. In a way, this is justified. Yet the
nickname alone suggests that it also has a wild side. In that instance,
too, the reality lives up to the image.

South Carolina extends only 198 miles along the Atlantic Ocean
yet contains more than 3,000 miles of land adjacent to bays, sounds,
rivers, and other waterways — most of them on the coastal plain. This,
naturally, has been a boon to the tourist industry — and some areas
have taken advantage of it. Altogether, about 15 million out-of-state
tourists visit the state each year, most of them headed for the coastal
region. The Grand Strand, a 60-mile stretch of virtually side-by-
side motels, condos, and cottages, is one of the greatest vacation
meccas on the East Coast, and so is Hilton Head Island.

South Carolina has more than 500,000 acres of coastal marshes,
including about 335,000 acres of salt marshes that feed the microscopic forms that anchor the coastal food chain. It has two kinds of
estuaries, bar-built inlets such as Murrells and North, and drowned
river valleys such as the Santee River Delta.

About 400 species thrive in these waters, ranging from the feisty
striped bass to furtive flounder. Offshore fish include tuna, dolphin,
sea trout, cobia, channel bass, grouper, and other species. Shellfish,
especially shrimps and crabs, also are plentiful. Altogether, commercial and sportfishing add about $350 million a year to the state's econ-
omy, directly and indirectly.

Commercial fishing directly contributes about $25 million each
year, indirectly much more. Between 700 and 1,200 boats are licensed
year after year in places such as Edisto Beach, Rockville, and Awendaw to net white, brown, and pink shrimp. More than 5 million
pounds of blue crab also are sent each year to pickers in McClel-
lansville, Yemassee, Burton, and Frogmore. Clams valued at more

than $2 million are dug, raked, and dredged. Oysters are harvested by permit.

Sportfishing is a year-round activity. For example, February is a good month for catching striped bass in the lowcountry bays and sounds, as well as rivers such as the Edisto and Pee Dee and the Intracoastal Waterway. In April, cobia migrate through Port Royal Sound on the northern end of Hilton Head Island. Weights average about 30 pounds but may reach twice that figure.

Twenty-two artificial reefs have been created offshore, most of them 6 to 12 miles out. A few are closer inshore, including two that can be fished from piers and two in estuarine waters. The most distant is Edisto Offshore Reef, about 20 miles off Stono Inlet. A triangle of sites lies between Little River and Myrtle Beach. Three are off Murrells Inlet and five are off Winyah Bay. Other key reefs are located off Fripp Island, Hunting Island, Port Royal Sound, and Hilton Head.

South Carolina created the first artificial fishing reef in the U.S. in the 1830s. A few accidental wrecks, such as the sinking of the *General Sherman* in 1874 off Myrtle Beach, also contributed, but no organized follow-up occurred until the 1960s when other states such as Florida and California had mature programs. Since then, both private and state agencies have sunk thousands of tires, boats, barges, and other objects from Little River to Hilton Head Island. The *Betsy Ross,* a.k.a. *Cor Caroli* when it served in the South Pacific during World War II, is the largest single object deliberately sunk. It lies about 18 miles off Hilton Head in 85 feet of water.

No license is required for saltwater fishing. Size and catch limits apply to many freshwater and saltwater species. For example, in the Savannah River, largemouth bass must be at least 12 inches. Many types migrate at certain seasons. Personal-use crabbing and shrimping do not require a permit. Oysters for personal use may be harvested from public oyster grounds and state shellfish grounds, both marked by signs, between the first of May and middle of September. Taking terrapin is prohibited between April 1 and July 15. Sea turtles are protected.

In South Carolina, all streams adequate to handle general pleasure boating (power boats) are considered open to public use. Land above the average high-water mark is private and should be used only with the permission of the owner. For motorboaters, trips of considerable length are possible, like a 170-mile journey from Columbia in the Piedmont region to coastal Charleston using the Congaree River, a diversion canal, Moultrie and Marion lakes, and the coastal Cooper River.

Coastal rivers also have areas suitable for canoeing. The Little Pee Dee, Black, Santee, Cooper, Edisto, and Ashpoo rivers and short Wambaw Creek are accessible, scenic, and navigable at adequate water levels, provided care is taken to avoid obstacles. Naturally, trips are faster at high stages. Some streams have marshy areas where canoeists may view rare plants.

South Carolina has 16 barrier islands. The sandy soil on these offshore islands supports mainly scrub vegetation, despite the semitropical climate. In this sparse habitat, a small subspecies of deer has developed on three islands—Hunting, Hilton Head, and Bull. The same kind of stunted deer is found on a few islands in states farther south. A few miles can make a big difference in the size of deer, however; full-size deer are obtainable on the mainland only a short distance inland.

The lowcountry deer hunting season—mostly for the full-size white tail—runs almost five months and begins early in most coastal counties. This means that hunters in or near the mid-August opening date have a chance to bag a buck in velvet, rare in Southern states. Early deer hunting requires a tradeoff. The heat and humidity are oppressive at times, but many hunters minimize the risk by going to stands just before dusk or dawn. Insects, especially mosquitos, flies, and ticks, and poisonous snakes also are problems. The cooler months of November and December are considered the best time. As they prepare for winter, the deer follow pretty much the same trails to food in the forests and nearby crop fields.

Both public lands and private hunting clubs—at least 600 of them by one count—are available. Guns and bows may be used at the same time. The near absence of natural predators make the deer plentiful throughout the season, which ends January 1. From a statewide deer herd estimated at 800,000, about 100,000 are killed each year by about 175,000 hunters. Despite the damage caused by Hurricane Hugo, the 250,000-acre Francis Marion National Forest and other prime hunting areas are experiencing overpopulation.

Non-resident annual, 10-day, and 3-day licenses are available, in addition to resident licenses. Big game requires a separate fee.

South Carolina's coastal rice and sorghum fields are attractive places for duck hunting. Statewide seasons are announced September 1, but usually run from mid–December through early January. Seasons for woodcock, common snipe, and marsh hen are set at the same time. Quail season runs from October through March.

Statewide dates are set for mourning doves (early September to early October, mid- to late November, and mid–December to mid–January); crow (September 1 to January 1); rabbit (late November to early March); and bobcat (late November to early March). For bear, check with appropriate officials.

The flat coastal plain and mixture of terrains make bicycling a pleasure. South Carolina has marked a number of lengthy routes that cross the state in both directions and can be cut into shorter trips if desired. The Coastal Route, the state's leg of the National Bikecentennial Virginia to Florida Route, generally parallels the coastline, but lies somewhat inland to avoid the major cities and heavily traveled tourist ways. The trail passes through scenic farm countryside, small woodlands, and the huge Francis Marion National Forest, visits high river bluffs, and crosses streams of various sizes. Relatively short side trips will reach swamps, planned gardens, and some of the historic Charleston mansions. Lowland segments of the east–west Savannah River Run and the Walter Ezell Route also are available to coasters.

The abundance of forests, coastal wetlands, and barrier islands ensures a bevy of beautiful birds, many of them migratory. Hiking trails opening up varied terrains are spotted throughout the region. These include a 20-mile path in the Francis Marion Forest.

History

South Carolina was explored within 30 years after the discovery of America. Attempts at settlement were made by the Spanish at Winyah Bay in 1526 and by French Huguenots near Parris Island in 1562. The failure of these villages put South Carolina behind Florida, Virginia, and Massachusetts in settlement. What is today South Carolina was part of larger grants made and rescinded by successive English kings, finally ending in the hands of eight Lord Proprietors named by King Charles II. South Carolina's first permanent settlement at Albemarle Point (Charleston) in 1670 developed rapidly, however. It was England's first outpost to block Spain's coastal crawl, and its wealth of resources and rich soil helped it become prosperous. Britain considered it so important it later established a new first line of defense in what is today the state of Georgia.

By the mid–1700s, plantations stood along the waterways indenting the South Carolina coastline and on the barrier islands offshore. The backcountry was being settled, too; there, lack of representation and a tradition of freedom made the settlers resentful of the richer coastal area where the political power—including the power to tax—lay.

South Carolinians were among the first to resist the Stamp Act and governance from abroad, and the state's strategic location made it a Revolutionary War battlefield. More armed clashes were fought there than in any other state. The "Swamp Fox," General Francis Marion, became a national hero by adroit use of terrain to frustrate the invading British. The successful defense of Fort Moultrie was the first major victory of the war for the struggling Continentals.

The plantation economy, based on rice, indigo, and cotton, boomed in the early decades of the 19th century, but planters constantly chafed at Northern attacks on slavery and tariff restrictions. South Carolina was the first state to secede from the Union in 1860 and the site of the first armed conflict of the Civil War—the capture of Fort Sumter in Charleston harbor. The plantation economy was ruined by the war and the boll weevil. In modern times, the great cash crops of the 19th century have been replaced by logging and truck farming. Commercial fishing has remained active throughout the state's history.

The South Carolina coastline has only one major city—but what a city! Charleston was where it began and Charleston remains the soul of the state, despite the steady transfer of political power inland as the centuries passed.

The most notable modern development has been the creation of a chain of resorts along the coast, especially in the Myrtle Beach area, and a few of the islands. These are the primary reason that perhaps 30 million people visit the South Carolina coastal region each year. Other communities tend to the small side.

The Grand Strand

THE TRANSITION TO SOUTH CAROLINA IS SMOOTH. INDEED, THE APPEARance changes little at first either along U.S. Route 17 or Interstate 95. Inland Dillon, known primarily as a marriage center, is one of the late bloomers in the region. The house of James W. Dillon, the city founder, now a museum open on major holidays and by appointment, dates from 1890. Eleven miles southeast of Dillon on state Route 57, Little Pee Dee State Park introduces the sandhills area of central South Carolina with a forest of bottomland hardwoods, pine and scrub oak, and a small swamp. The 835-acre park has facilities for boating, fishing, and camping and a nature trail.

Along the coast, the village of Little River has the same intensive commercial development on U.S. Route 17 as do Calabash and other nearby North Carolina towns. The Little River waterfront at the end of Mineola Avenue is commercialized, too, with restaurants famous for their seafood and ticket offices fronting charter firms that take "party boats" out 10 miles or so in search of black sea bass, porgy, and snappers and deep-sea fishers to the Gulf Stream about 50 miles out to cast for swordfish and other gamefish.

Little River is still a commercial seafood port, too. Early in the morning, vessels chug about 80 miles offshore to cast their nets.

Few tourists realize, as they pass through Little River, that they are treading on historic ground. Indians were the first settlers, and the protected harbor was explored by the Spanish in the 1500s. Pirates found the cove to their liking before regular settlement produced naval stores and a seafood-oriented economy. Near the intersection of today's U.S. Route 17 and Mineola Avenue stood the home of James Cochran, George Washington's first stop in South Carolina during his 1791 Southern tour.

Little River is not entirely water oriented. In season, the young man selling charter-boat tickets may be eagerly awaiting the time when he can leave and drive inland to hunt for deer, turkey, quail, and bear in the Lewis Ocean Bay Wildlife Management Area, better known locally by its former name, the Biust.

This forest lies along state Route 90, which angles inland at Little River. Route 90 cuts through mile after mile of flat, forested countryside broken only occasionally by human habitation. Two-thirds of the area is still covered by game-rich forests. Of this, the Lewis Ocean Bay Wildlife Management Area, created in 1989 to preserve the "bays" and significant vegetation such as Venus fly-trap, covers about 11,600 acres. About 6,400 acres are owned by the state and the remainder are leased from a paper company. The main gate is located off Route 90 on Old Kingston Road.

At the end of the road is the Peter Horry Wildlife Refuge, now being developed. Its boardwalks explore marshy area in the vast forest.

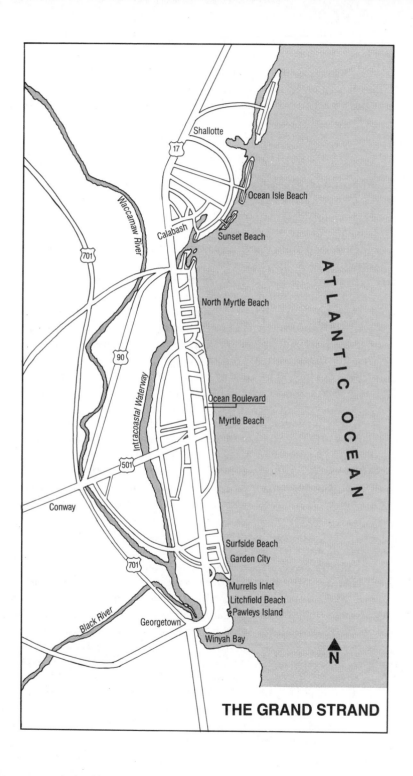

Shallotte

17

Ocean Isle Beach

Calabash

Sunset Beach

Waccamaw River

701

North Myrtle Beach

90

Intracoastal Waterway

Ocean Boulevard

Myrtle Beach

501

Conway

701

Surfside Beach

Garden City

Murrells Inlet

Litchfield Beach

Pawleys Island

Black River

Georgetown

Winyah Bay

ATLANTIC OCEAN

N

THE GRAND STRAND

The Waccamaw River has been the traditional lifeline of the region. This unusual river, which begins in North Carolina, flows through northeastern South Carolina almost parallel to the coast and enters the sea at Georgetown.

Conway

Conway Area Chamber of Commerce
P.O. Box 831, Conway SC 29526
803/248-2273

The largest community in the Grand Strand hinterland reached that status only slowly. Laid out in 1734 as one of twelve communities in a grand design to open up the South Carolina interior and first named Kingston, the community had only about 200 inhabitants a century later. Although a few properties were classed as plantations, the inhabitants were predominantly small farmers who also tapped the vast pine forests for turpentine as a source of cash.

Periodic subdivision of political jurisdictions eventually led to the formation of Horry (pronounced oh-ree) County, named for Revolutionary War General Peter Horry. Conwayborough, named for General Robert Conway, became the county seat. The Civil War halted growth temporarily—Conway was occupied by Union troops for a time after the war—but it resumed in the 1870s because of the demand for lumber and naval stores. The name was shortened in 1883. This new prosperity continued into the early 1900s when much of the downtown business area was constructed.

Conway's heritage as an agricultural center and river port is visible today in its historic district, predominantly from the early 19th century. Ten of the buildings are listed on the National Register of Historic Places.

A walking/driving tour of 40 sites in the historic area starts at the old Horry County Courthouse, built in 1824–25 during the administration of architect Robert Mills, designer of the Washington Monument and other important structures in Washington, D.C. Now the City Hall, the building's records room contains massive masonry arches. Nearby are the 1857 Kingston Presbyterian Church, housing a congregation established in 1756 by early Scotch-Irish settlers; the C. F. Quattlebaum (circa 1807) and 1850 Paul Quattlebaum houses and the 1860 Quattlebaum office, representing a family prominent in the city's 19th-century business life; and the Beaty-

Spivey House (circa 1870). On Applewhite Lane is the Barnhill-Weston-Timbes House, whose front section was built around 1847. The house was enlarged in 1863 by Plowden C. J. Weston, lieutenant governor of the state, who bought it as a refuge for his family after fleeing his plantation during the Civil War.

The red-brick Horry County Museum on Main Street, formerly a post office, houses a small but stimulating collection of artifacts, drawings, and photographs dealing with natural and local history, the displays are especially good at explaining the development of the state's inland river ports. The museum is open 10 a.m. to 5 p.m. Monday–Saturday.

In front of the museum is the stately Wade Hampton Oak, for many decades the focal point of public gatherings, including that to hear General Wade Hampton when he ran for governor in 1876. The tree stands today because Mrs. Mary Beaty brandished a loaded shotgun at railroad construction workers sent to cut it down. Her act of courage motivated the town to save this and many others; today, one of the most lasting impressions of Conway is of the live oaks hung with Spanish moss that line residential streets.

The striking Gothic-style First Methodist Church building across the street dates from 1898, but the congregation was formed in 1842. Related buildings were built in 1910 and later.

At the end of Elm Street is a city marina, boat ramp, and campground.

Like Conway, the string of resorts along the coast had a slow beginning. Indeed, Conway residents were the first to use the beaches as a resort. U.S. Route 501 between Conway and the Myrtle Beach area shows how great a change has taken place. The four-lane divided highway no longer cuts through vast forests but is virtually saturated with commercial outlets and government buildings. A Grand Strand visitors center is located on the highway just east of Conway.

Although some in North Carolina claim the South Brunswick area is part of the Grand Strand, South Carolinians came up with both the concept and the name and, therefore, are entitled to exclusive use of it.

Waccamaw and Winyah Indians lived there more than 500 years ago, calling the area Chicora. Early settlers paid scant attention to the beaches that are today's economic lifeblood. Consequently, history is concentrated largely in Georgetown; the beaches are modern inventions and, thus, one of the few places along the Southeast Coast that are virtually devoid of tradition and history.

The Myrtle Beaches

Myrtle Beach Area Chamber of Commerce
P.O. Box 2115
Myrtle Beach SC 29578
803/626-7444

Soon after it enters South Carolina, U.S. Route 17 veers toward the coast and for a way actually runs east of the Intracoastal Waterway. As a consequence, it is the main access route to the Grand Strand, a string of resorts stretching 60 miles from Little River to Georgetown and including eight major communities.

Myrtle Beach, the largest, was a small, isolated summer cottage community known simply as "New Town" in the 19th century. The first hotel was built in 1901 by Conway interests, and a Chicago developer began selling waterfront lots in 1912. Arcady, a resort for the affluent, followed in the 1920s. The first golf course was laid out about 1928. Myrtle Beach, whose name was changed in a contest, was incorporated in 1938 and severely damaged in 1954 by Hurricane Hazel.

The explosive development that began in the 1960s has literally fused Myrtle Beach and its neighbors—North Myrtle Beach, Surfside Beach, and Garden City—into a contiguous resort strip. There, the visitor can drive for miles along canyons of business and residential structures screening the reason for all of them—the fine oceanfront beach. And only small natural areas and the peculiarities of the coastline separate this strip from Murrells Inlet, Litchfield Beach, and Pawley's Island, traditional resorts in their own way. All are today unabashedly resort communities. Myrtle Beach is the commercial and social hub.

Even people who knew the area a few generations ago may be surprised at how thoroughly developed the region is now. For example, the Grand Strand has more than 50,000 hotel rooms, 7,000 camping sites, 60 golf courses (resort hotels offer golf packages), 150 tennis courts, 1,100 restaurants, and numerous entertainment options, from amusement parks to night clubs—not to mention its *raison d'être,* the beaches. The climate normally is amenable to outdoor activities during three seasons, but summer is the top season. In June, the season-starting Sun Fun Festival features more than 100 events, including live musical entertainment, beach games, beauty pageants, and a parade with a national figure as grand marshal.

Myrtle Beach. PHOTO BY JOHN BOWEN.

Water-oriented activities naturally dominate. Numerous marked public-access points admit surfcasters, as well as sunworshippers, to the beaches. The value of these access points varies; some are little more than paths, while others offer adjacent parking spaces. It is not always clear, however, whether these parking spaces belong to hotels or the public. Generally, access points north of 3rd Street in Myrtle Beach have parking areas. So do those in North Myrtle Beach.

Charter boats carry anglers into the deep waters of the Gulf Stream in search of dolphin, marlin, king mackerel, snapper, and grouper. Four king-mackerel tournaments are held annually, and a billfish tournament is held at the end of May each year. Litchfield Beach sponsors a Crawfish Festival. Myrtle Beach permits cars to back onto the beach to launch sailboats at 77th Avenue North and 29th Avenue South.

The long stretches of Ocean Boulevard beckon to bikers, but the U.S. Route 17 connections are so heavily traveled that safety may require bikers to favor one section or another. The long stretch of Ocean Boulevard in Myrtle Beach is designated a bike route.

Cultural events are subordinated, but not ignored. For example, the Myrtle Beach Convention Center at 21st Avenue North sponsors Christmas events and various programs at other times of the year. The convention center is also the repository of the South Carolina Hall of Fame, which houses portraits and memorabilia of South Carolinians ranging from eight signers of the Declaration of Independence and U.S. Constitution to an astronaut who walked on the moon and a Nobel Prize-winning physicist.

Myrtle Beach contains the upscale shops usual for a major resort area, in addition to crafts specialties such as hammocks patterned after designs brought back from Africa many generations ago by sailors. Christmas Elegance Park has appropriate items and decorations year-round.

The other communities are less commercially oriented, but all have limited year-round residency. Family-oriented North Myrtle Beach, at the eastern end of the strip, has the broadest beaches and at least 20 public-access points. Residents retain a provincial attitude. Most still regard themselves more as residents of their neighborhoods — Cherry Grove, Ocean Drive, Crescent Beach, and Windy Hill (named by George Washington in an offhand remark) — than of the city at large despite merger in 1968. Atlantic Beach remained out of the conglomerate.

Myrtle Beach State Park, just southwest of the city, mirrors seasonal changes in much the same manner as the resort strip. Since most people go to the park to use the beach and its facilities, it bustles during the peak seasons and is nearly deserted at other times.

Seven boardwalks cross sand dunes stabilized by sea oats from parking areas to the white sand beach. Narrative boards near the parking areas discuss topics such as loggerhead turtles, which nest on the beach, and warn against damaging the environment. A new pier, completed in 1992, generally divides those swimming in the ocean and those using the beach for surfcasting. The park also offers a swimming pool, which is open between Memorial Day and Labor Day. Other facilities include 350 camping sites, five cabins and two apartments, bathhouses, laundry facilities, outdoor showers, and picnic areas.

In contrast to the resort beaches, however, this 312-acre oceanfront park, developed in the 1930s by the Civilian Conservation Corps (CCC), has more than 100 acres of maritime forest. The Sculptured Oak Nature Trail, which starts at the entrance road, winds through a typical South Carolina coastal forest that includes live oak, pine, maple, dogwood, and magnolia on generally level ground and ends at the beach.

Naturalists lead nature and beach walks, shellfish workshops, and other programs on a year-round basis. During the summer, fireside stories for youth are shared in an amphitheater.

Surfside Beach and Garden City, predominantly cottages, condominiums, and single-family residences, lie between Myrtle Beach and Murrells Inlet. Garden City has numerous public beach-access points, usually at the ends of streets.

Waccamaw Neck

Definitions of this area may differ. Generally, maps identify the tip of the land between the Atlantic Ocean and the Waccamaw River as Waccamaw Neck, but locals sometimes stretch the term as far as Murrells Inlet. As a result, visitors may hear it applied to the southernmost beaches of the Grand Strand, as well as the attractions closer to Winyah Bay.

Murrells Inlet, which according to tradition is named for a pirate who established a base in the marshy cove, witnessed its share of plundering and smuggling in former centuries. Thus, it is home to almost as many legends as people, from the hair-raising story of a bloody rampage by a drunken buccaneer to the touching story of a young girl's lost love.

Its modern reputation rests on more savory or solid ground—as an Atlantic Ocean boating and fishing center. Charter and "head" boats exit the large natural harbor on deep-sea fishing expeditions as far out as the Gulf Stream. Docks also provide good facilities for visiting boats venturing into the ocean. The Murrells Inlet Public Boat Landing has a boat ramp and short pier. An antebellum home, the Hermitage, is open to visitors in season. Murrells Inlet restaurants have a reputation for seafood.

Between Murrells Inlet and Litchfield Beach on U.S. Route 17 are two of the Grand Strand's premier nature attractions: Brookgreen Gardens and Huntington Beach State Park. Both were part of an estate purchased in 1930 by Archer M. Huntington and his sculptress wife, Anna Hyatt Huntington. The property includes what were Brookgreen, Springfield, The Oaks, and Laurel Hill rice and indigo plantations in the colonial period. Carolina golden big-grain rice, ancestor of today's long-grain rice, was developed in the 1830s at Brookgreen Plantation.

Brookgreen Gardens. Officially described as a "garden museum of American sculpture," Brookgreen is that and more. Two readily apparent features—the "Fighting Stallions" statue at the entrance and signs warning against feeding or harassing the alligators—symbolize the symbiosis of art and nature sought by Anna Hyatt Huntington when she and her husband founded the park in 1931 "for the appreciation of American sculpture and the preservation of southeastern flora and fauna."

The success in melding the two may be immediately perceived as the visitor enters the park, passing the massive statue at the entrance and driving along a road bordered by loblolly pine, live oak, gums, and dogwood, a few of the 1,600 wild and planted species in the park. Sometimes, a deer crossing the road may reinforce the impression. Other animals living in a wild state in the park include alligators, turkey, raccoon, foxes, squirrels, grasshoppers, and snakes.

A more intimate brush with wildlife is possible at the Native Wildlife Park. There, located along a ¾-mile trail covered in 40 minutes with a guide, are otters, alligators, foxes, raccoon, deer, and a variety of birds, including waterfowl, herons, egrets, ibises, bald eagle, owls, and red-tailed hawk. Many of these animals were brought there in an injured condition and probably could not survive in the wild. One of the aviaries is built over a natural cypress swamp. The deer savannah, where a herd of about 40 roams, covers 20 acres. Also along the trail is a native plant garden with more than 70 species native to the southeast, including insectivorous Venus fly-trap and pitcher plants, cattails, roundleaf birch, blue star, wild grapes, cherries, strawberries, blueberries, and the beautyberry bush, whose purple berries were used as rouge in the colonial period. A few small sculptures are spotted along the walkway.

The main feature at Brookgreen is its 10 acres of formal gardens, where planting-art combinations create an aesthetic effect that is both satisfying and soothing—as they were intended. Gardens featuring plants such as day lilies, rose of Sharon, dwarf box, barberry, laurel, American holly, trifoliate orange, glossy abelia, pineapple guava, loblolly bay, camellia, Irish ivy, and coral bean are laid out so the visitor may wander from one to the other with little pre-planning.

More than 525 sculptures by about 230 American artists, including Anna Hyatt Huntington, are skillfully situated amid various types of plantings and pools. For example, *Diana of the Chase* by Hyatt stands at the center of a reflecting pool; beyond is the focal point of the gardens, the 250-year-old Live Oak Allee from Brookgreen Plantation. Huntington's *Jaguar* is poised in flora beside a wall in this section. A striking gold *Dionysius* by Edward McCartan, sculpted in 1936, harmonizes with the greenery in the Center Garden. The figures of Swedish-American sculptor Carl Miller soar over the Fountain of the Muses. The oldest sculpture, *The Fisher Boy* by Hiram Powers, dates from 1846. *Alligator* by David H. Turner was added as recently as 1990. More than 150 small sculptures are artfully arranged on a patio around an outdoor pool in a building inspired by a Moorish structure in Spain.

Historical precedent for a sculpture garden on the site was set when Washington Allston, considered the greatest American painter of the Romantic period, was born at Brookgreen Plantation in 1779. A marker on the grounds notes that George Washington stayed there during his 1791 Southern tour. Of the original buildings, only a detached kitchen survives. Brookgreen mansion burned in 1901.

The gardens, open from 9:30 a.m. to 4:45 p.m. year-round except Christmas Day, are striking at any season. A good time to witness the brightest colors is mid-April when the dogwoods and azaleas bloom. Small demonstration gardens grow crops historically important to the economic life of the region — rice, cotton, indigo, and sugar cane — and herbs used in folk medicine. Guided tours and slide shows and movies are held daily; lectures and workshops are held regularly.

Huntington Beach State Park. Like Brookgreens Gardens, this 2,500-acre park helps fulfill the Huntington's dream of preserving elements of the coastal environment in their natural state. Since it was turned into a state park, development has been limited to further this objective.

The park is distinguished by having several habitats in close proximity. Its large saltwater marshland, the most productive environment in the world, is separated by a causeway from a freshwater lagoon. Oaks Creek runs through the marsh. A long stretch of Atlantic Ocean beach fronts a parcel of high land that includes dunes and a maritime forest.

These features support a variety of outdoor activities. Huntington Beach Park, home to osprey, marsh hen, herons, egrets, purple gallinule, laughing gull, Eastern brown pelican, oystercatcher, clapper rail, marsh hawk, and other species, is an excellent birdwatching place. A drive on the entrance road past old-growth trees, stunted trees, and tangled underbrush is a learning experience in the properties of a maritime forest. A paved rock fishing and crabbing jetty is located a short walk from North Beach. The short Sea Oats Nature Trail winds through an oak-pine forest and follows the edge of the lagoon to an observation deck; observation decks on the causeway overlook this area and the marsh. The marsh boardwalk angles out into the swamp to a covered observation deck. A paved pathway extends under arches made by the leafy limbs of trees from Atalaya, the Huntington home, to the park entrance. The park has picnic facilities and two camping areas with a total of 127 sites and bath facilities and water and electric hookups. Two sites are designed for handicapped persons.

Huntington Beach is open year-round and observes longer day-use hours during the summer months than at other times of the year. The park has not fully recovered from Hurricane Hugo's destruction, despite the planting of many new trees.

Atalaya remains open in an unfurnished state. The walled rectangular one-story house, designed to resemble the Moorish architecture of the Spanish Mediterranean coast, has a large open courtyard with a cloister-like walkway and living quarters on three sides. Common rooms such as the sunroom, dining room, library, and some living quarters face the ocean, while wings hold bedrooms, Mr. Huntington's study, and the artist's studio with a 25-foot skylight. Fireplaces and mantels are made of brick, and the windows are covered with Spanish-style iron bars. Auxiliary structures are located adjacent to the rear entrance to the courtyard. Sabal palmetto and Phoenix palm (*butia capita*) are planted in the courtyard, whose walls are decorated with vines.

The mansion, built in stages during the 1931–33 Depression years by local labor, takes its name from the Spanish word for watchtower. During World War II, an Air Force gunnery range was located at the north end of the beach. The Huntingtons last visited the house during 1946 and 1947. The state leased the site from Brookgreen Trustees in 1960. The residence is open in summer months during park hours.

An historical marker near North Beach recalls that a fish club established before 1816 built its first clubhouse on nearby Drunken Jack Island and later moved to several nearby sites before being disbanded during the Civil War.

Pawley's Island

Pawley's Island was one of the first resorts established on the East Coast. George Washington visited the Pawley family during his 1791 Southern tour. Rich plantation owners took their families to the island during the malaria season prior to the Civil War.

Today, the community retains much of that early mystique and casual appearance. In some places, hammock and other specialty shops

Seagull, Pawley's Island. PHOTO BY JOHN BOWEN.

stand beside placid lagoons. A few of these buildings date back a half century. At Christmas, an angelic glow emanates from more than 100,000 pin lights stretched out on trees, terraces, and eaves. The low-key atmosphere of the resort makes it a good place for biking.

The southwestern end of the island is set aside for public use. A large parking lot and walkway across the tufted dunes provide access to the broad, sandy beach for sunbathing, surfcasting, beach-combing, watching the antics of gulls, terns, and shorebirds, and other activities. From this vantage point, one can view a solid line of weathered cottages facing the Atlantic Ocean.

Just before U.S. Route 17 reaches the two river bridges that approach Georgetown, a sign on the highway reads simply "Nature Center." It is an understatement; the nature center is only part of Hobcaw Barony, now a nature refuge and home of the Belle W. Baruch Science Institute devoted to marine biology and coastal research.

Its Bellefield Nature Center, just off the highway, is headquarters for public access to the 17,500 acres of beach, forest, and marshes that lie between Winyah Bay and the Atlantic Ocean. For more than a decade, naturalists have led pupils, teachers, and other groups through accessible portions of the refuge: the house where Baruch lived near old fields of the former rice plantation, a freshwater swamp with loblolly pine and cypress trees over a century old, a mixed pine and hardwood forest inhabited by deer, feral hogs, bobcat, wild turkey, fox squirrel, and numerous other species, and a salt marsh.

General public access is limited. Only the center's museum is open on a regular basis—10 a.m. to 5 p.m. Monday–Friday and 1 to 5 p.m. Saturday. Its tanks contain representative saltwater life of the region, including crabs, sea stars, turtles, and fish. Static exhibits explore such subjects as the estuaries and salt marshes, aquaculture of South Carolina, the impact of long-term ecological research, and Hobcaw Barony over the centuries. Once-a-week van tours highlight Hobcaw's history, education programs, and research projects; special programs deal with wildflowers and similar subjects. Short courses offered by the University of South Carolina cover subjects such as butterflies, winter birds, catching and cooking crabs and fish, and coastal fishing with light tackle.

The science institute was organized in 1969 jointly by the University of South Carolina and the Belle W. Baruch Foundation. Hobcaw Barony, owned by the Belle W. Baruch Foundation, serves as a field laboratory for the University of South Carolina and Clem-

Oceanfront, Pawley's Island. PHOTO BY JOHN BOWEN.

son University. Inaccessible Pumpkinseed Island is an important rookery for white ibis, great and snowy egrets, and herons.

Hobcaw is an Indian word meaning "between the waters." The first Spanish attempt at colonization of the region, in 1526, was made somewhere around Winyah Bay — perhaps at Hobcaw and perhaps in the Georgetown area. The colony, troubled by malaria and dissension, was short lived, but British attempts almost two centuries later were successful. Between 1790 and 1900, as many as ten rice plantations thrived on Hobcaw property, but these declined after the Civil War. In the early 20th century, New York financier Bernard Baruch acquired all of the property and later hosted Winston Churchill and President Franklin D. Roosevelt. Baruch's daughter Belle acquired part of Hobcaw from her father in 1936 and built a home there; in her will, she established a trust to maintain the tip of a peninsula between the bay and ocean and several marshy islands for education and research.

West of the Waccamaw River, which forms the western boundary of Waccamaw Neck, are more old plantation sites with impoundments and lowland forests. The Great Pee Dee River parallels the Waccamaw in this area, with 1,200 acres of bottomland east of U.S. Route 701 on county Road S–22–52 set aside for waterfowl hunting as the Samworth Wildlife Management Area.

Curving around to the north of Georgetown, the coffee-colored Black River is bordered by swamps with bald and pond cypress, tupelo, black gum, laurel oak, limestone bluffs, and a number of coastal plantation houses. The abundant wildlife includes alligators, deer, bobcat, wood duck, pileated woodpecker, herons, egrets, and owls.

The river is navigable for canoes most of its 90 miles, but has many obstacles and is considered dangerous at flood stage. Oxbows are confusing at times and may require backtracking and reading the currents. Canoe access points include those at county Route 35 west of Kingstree; at Scout Cabin Park in Kingstree; Turpentine Landing on a dirt road off county Route 142; county Route 30; Cantley Landing on a dirt road off county Route 527; Route 41 bridge and concrete ramps at Pear (Pea House) Landing; Brown's Ferry; and Rocky Point. Large pleasure craft can go about 18 miles inland.

Kingstree, a river port in the 18th century, retains some of its colonial ambience. Thorntree, a restored pre-Revolutionary house, is located at Fluitt Nelson Park, a few blocks from the waterfront.

Georgetown

Georgetown County Chamber of Commerce
P.O. Box 1776
Georgetown SC 29442
803/646-8436

Georgetown has a split personality. It has a superb, largely pre-Revolutionary historical district and an unattractive industrial side. Fortunately, the two are fairly well separated so that the former can be enjoyed.

The Georgetown Historic District has about 50 18th- and 19th-century buildings, some dating back to the early 1700s, as well as several historic graveyards. Four important structures — the Harold Kaminsky House (circa 1760), the Man-Doyle House (circa 1775), 1735 Prince George Winyah Episcopal Church, and the 1842 Old Market Building, now the Rice Museum — are open to visitors on regular schedules.

The Rice Museum provides an introduction to the history of Georgetown, the third oldest city in South Carolina. Dioramas, paintings, and photographs show how the city, founded in 1730 by the Reverand Elisha Screven and declared a port of entry in 1732, was dominated by indigo and rice cultivation until the 20th century.

Indigo profits in the 18th century financed the first public school in 1757. After the Revolutionary War, when Georgetown was a critical port after the fall of Charleston to the British, rice became the dominant crop along the five nearby rivers. This required clearing cypress swamps, digging canals, and building dikes fed by small floodgates called "trunk docks."

The museum is open 9:30 a.m. to 4:30 p.m. Monday–Saturday, except major holidays. Beside the museum is tiny Lafayette Park, which has a Braille trail identifying trees and plantings.

On the banks of the Sampit River behind the museum is the 1,000-foot Harborwalk. A stroll along this boardwalk is especially beautiful in the evening. Pleasure craft from the Intracoastal Waterway may anchor offshore and use a floating dock and piers.

The Kaminsky House, which stands on a tree-shaded bluff overlooking the Sampit River, is one of the oldest colonial townhouses in Georgetown. It was originally a "single house" — only one room wide and two rooms in length on three floors, with porches on all sides to shade the house — built by the Allston Family of Brookgreen Plantation. The Kaminskys, who purchased the house in 1931, enlarged it in 1947 but kept intact the orginal heart-of-pine floors, woodwork, mantels, and staircase.

The house, open from 10 a.m. to 5 p.m. Monday–Friday for guided tours, is furnished with American and European antiques. The oldest piece is an oak and walnut Spanish chest 300 to 500 years old. Among other outstanding pieces are a 16th-century English grandfather clock, four 18th-century blown-glass hurricane shades, six chairs of superb craftsmanship made in 1770 in Charleston, a 1760 American Chippendale bookcase/secretary made in Massachusetts, a 275-year-old English lady's side chair, an 18th-century Chippendale corner cupboard put together with pegs, an 1810 mahoghany Chippendale-style banquet table that seats 24, and an early American walnut slope-lid desk built by Thomas Elfe, a renowned Charleston cabinetmaker.

The Man–Doyle House (circa 1775), a rice planter's townhouse built with lumber cut on Mansfield Plantation, runs tours every hour from 10 a.m. to 3 p.m. Tuesday–Friday. The commentary covers architectural highlights and history; Theodosia, daughter of the ill-starred Aaron Burr, reportedly visited the house before she boarded a vessel in the harbor and sailed away, never to be heard of again.

Prince George Winyah Church at Broad and Highmarket streets is easily identifiable by its steeple with copper dome and clock. Inside are box pews modeled after those in the sanctuaries of British churches of the period and some ugly scars on the floor left by horses stabled there by British soldiers during the Revolutionary War. Since colonial churches did not have stained-glass windows, the ones in this church were placed later. The colorful English window behind the altar originally lighted a slave chapel at Hagley Plantation. Tinted side windows were installed early in this century, but four plain glass frames (some with their original glass) were kept.

The parish was founded by wealthy planters in 1721; the present building dates from about 1750. A gallery and chancel were added about 1809, and the handsome steeple was raised in 1824. The church is open to visitors in season.

Historic structures not regularly open to the public can be viewed from the outside by following a map obtained at a visitors center on U.S. Route 17 or the Chamber of Commerce office on Front Street. Tram tours, with stops at Prince George Episcopal and 1866 Bethel African Methodist Episcopal churches, also cover the historic district. Some private homes are opened to visitors during the Annual Plantation Tours in March or April, which also visit plantations near Georgetown.

Among the many interesting private homes are the Thomas Bolem House (circa 1739), believed to have been a pre-Revolutionary tavern; the Bedlam (circa 1740), whose unusual name is attributed to the penchant of five young sisters for music and frivolity at any hour; the Joseph Hayne Rainey House (circa 1760), the antebellum home of a black freed before the Civil War who served in the U.S. Senate during Reconstruction; the Henning House (circa 1770), whose owner, according to local legend, was sympathetic to the British during the Revolutionary War but whose daughter secretly kept the "Swamp Fox," General Francis Marion, informed; and the Heriot House (circa 1740), a large white structure near the river whose window lights allegedly guided blockade runners and bootleggers. A few historic structures serve as bed-and-breakfasts.

The 1824 Courthouse was designed by famous architect Robert Mills. The brick Winyah Indigo Society Schoolhouse dates from about 1854, and the Masonic Lodge was built about 1740.

Belle Isle Garden and Battery White

This historic plantation site, about three miles off U.S. Route 17 on South Island Road, was converted into residences and a yacht club in the 1970s. However, developers retained a number of historical and natural features that visitors may experience by telling the security guard at the gate where they are going.

Battery White on Winyah Drive is one of the best preserved Civil War earthworks in the state. Originally part of a much larger fort constructed to guard the entrance to Winyah Bay, it retains two 10-inch Columbiad cannon built in Raleigh that were considered too heavy to move when other artillery was sent to the defense of Charleston. Another Civil War relic, the mast of the Union sidewheeler *Harvest Moon,* can be seen offshore at low tide. The vessel was sunk by daring Confederates who rammed her hull with a torpedo. Relics such as minié balls and cannon shot are among the mix of artifacts found on the site that are shown in a mini-museum in the Belle Island Marina.

Other historical relics still visible include a rice canal dug by slave labor before the American Revolution and an old brick cooling hut that belonged to the original Belle Isle plantation. Belle Isle's history can be traced back more than 2,000 years to when the first Indians arrived. The site was explored by Spanish conquistadores and settled by the English in 1711. It was owned for a century by the pioneering Horry family, and there is some evidence that the parents of the legendary "Swamp Fox" lived for a time on part of the Horry tract. The last plantation home burned in the 1940s, but the garden and Battery White were open to tourists for a while thereafter.

An azalea trail, with numerous varieties and colors, extends several hundred yards from near the entry gate.

Wilderness and Plantations

GEORGETOWN'S PRETTY HISTORICAL FACE AND INDUSTRIAL HEART ARE supplemented by nearby wilderness areas. Much of the south shore of Winyah Bay and the two mouths of the Santee River are great marshy areas with limited access, and therefore a limited number of visitors. With a few exceptions, the wilderness area extends almost to the suburbs of Charleston. In this lush area, nature's creatures have little respect for the works of humans. For example, mud daubers build nests on the ceilings of porches whether they are attached to colonial mansions and churches or newer structures.

Tom Yawkey Wildlife Center

The wilderness area closest to the city, the Tom Yawkey Wildlife Center on North, South, and Cat islands, is also one of the most pristine. This 20,000-acre tract east of the Intracoastal Waterway is dedicated to wildlife and wilderness protection, research, and education and is especially noted for its waterfowl. It can be reached only by ferry and private boat and thus has limited public use.

Once a week, a three-hour guided field trip takes up to 14 passengers on a 21-mile circuit of Cat Island, the largest upland area on the reserve, and South Island. The tour covers the history and ecology of the islands and the adjacent Santee River, including Yawkey's association with the site. Cat Island is managed for wild turkey, and controlled burning improves the habitat for turkeys and the endangered red-cockaded woodpecker. The banks of the Santee River are a reminder of the ecological effects of the diversion of the river to the Cooper River and later re-diversion of the stream to its original bed. The tour passes ponds where research in marsh ecology is conducted.

The 2-mile causeway to South Island was constructed by rice planters who laid used cypress logs as a base and deposited fill material on top. Visitors are driven past an area where 12,000 ducks and a small number of Canada geese winter each year and along a 7-mile dike in the principal waterfowl refuge area where as many as 50,000 ducks winter. The managed wetlands provide food most favorable to the ducks but are also a major staging area for migrant shorebirds in the spring. Wading birds also use the area, and two bald eagle pairs are nesting. The devastating effect of Hurricane Hugo is still apparent, especially at the maritime forests at the southern end of South Island. There, surviving forested areas now feature live oak, palmetto, and yaupon, but young loblolly pine is slowly replacing virgin stands destroyed by Hugo that had been untouched since the previous storm. The trustees have determined to retain this virgin forest.

Tours are conducted on Tuesdays October–February and Wednesdays at other times. Each carries only 14 persons and is booked up well in advance but will accept walk-ons if cancellations occur. Tours begin at the ferry landing on the Intracoastal Waterway at the end of South Island Road.

The beaches on North and South islands are open to those with their own boats. North Island, a 4,500-acre wilderness area, has about 9 miles of oceanfront beach interrupted by tree trunks stripped and bleached by wind and waves. Dunes that rise to heights of about 20 to 30 feet extend 200 to 300 yards inland. The sizable maritime forest is undeveloped and closed to general use. This island, which adjoins Hobcaw Barony across Jones Creek, is stabilizing at the north end, eroding at the middle section of beach, and building at the south end. South Island is a sanctuary for waterfowl. The water off these beaches is shallow, and visitors should be careful not to be trapped by falling tides.

Formerly owned by Boston Red Sox owner Tom Yawkey, the site was bequeathed to the South Carolina Wildlife and Marine Resources Department in 1976. Indians lived on the present refuge when the first European settlers arrived. An Indian mound on North Island and a shell midden on Cat Island remain intact. Settlers created plantations to grow rice, many of them building handsome beach-front houses on the ocean side of the islands. In one of them, the Marquis de Lafayette reportedly swore to "conquer or die in the American cause." The 87-foot North Island Lighthouse completed in 1801 was one of the first to be built. The site is now on the National Register of Historic Places.

Confederate units set up defenses on all three islands during the Civil War; though now under natural growth, their earthworks are well preserved. Beginning in the 1890s, Northern industrialists used the islands for hunting. President Grover Cleveland was one of their prominent guests. Tom Yawkey's father obtained an interest in 1911.

Santee Coastal Reserve

The Santee Coastal Reserve and Game Management Area lies partly on the delta between the two forks of the Santee River and partly south of the river. The preserve is a sprawling collection of pine flats, cypress swamps (including a 200-year-old freshwater swamp), and savannahs, salt and brackish marshes, beaches, and mudflats. Boats may make landfalls between March 1 and November 1 at various points, including the beaches on Cedar and Murphy islands, where waterfowl and shorebirds are seen.

The delta is most noted for its large concentration of osprey and Southern species such as red-cockaded woodpecker, Bachman's sparrow, brown-headed nuthatch, swallow-tailed kite, and painted bunting. In all, more than 290 species of birds have been spotted. Permanent residents include the brown pelican, anhinga, mottled duck, wood duck, black-bellied plover, Carolina and long-billed marsh wrens, loggerhead shrike, pine and yellow-throated warblers.

Archery hunting for deer is permitted the first complete week and the last complete week in October. Bag limit is three, only one of which may be a buck.

Four self-guided trails begin about 5 miles east of U.S. Route 17 along Secondary Road 857 and Santee Club Road (turn off across from the road to Hampton Plantation State Park). Guide booklets are available at the kiosk near the Big Game Check Station. The 2.9-mile Marshlands Nature Trail goes around an old rice field and through a bottomland hardwood habitat, while the 1.1-mile Woodland Trail traverses pine flatwoods and mixed pine hardwoods. An 800-foot boardwalk extends into The Nature Conservancy's Washo Reserve, a large lake surrounded by a forested buffer especially noted for its birds. The nest of yellow crowned night heron, freshwater aquatic vegetation such as flowered blue flag and pondweed, bald cypress and tupelo trees, and the sunning place of a 13-foot alligator, the oldest resident of Washo, are nearby. The 7.2-mile bike-hike trail explores the range of habitats available in this region of the park and ends at the Intracoastal Waterway. In addition, a 4.25-mile canoe trail follows waterways in an impoundment area. The trails are open daily at varying hours March through October.

For canoers, the Santee River normally lives up to its Indian name — gentle. A trail extends more than 65 miles from Lake Marion to the coast, much of the southern bank bordering Francis Marion National Forest, where camping is permitted. The river, which forks and has shoals and mud flats, is deceptive, so a compass and map are essential. Scenery ranges from loblolly pine highland to freshwater and saltwater marshes. The diverse ecology supports alligators, deer, bobcat, feral hogs, and numerous birds. Access points on both forks include Wilson's Landing on country Route 31 below the dam, U.S. Route 52, several Forest Service roads, Britton Neck, and Route 17-701. A 12-mile trail explores Wambaw Creek but can be paddled only at high water.

Hopsewee Plantation, a colonial rice plantation, was the birthplace of Thomas Lynch, Jr., a signer of the Declaration of Independence. The mansion stands just off U.S. Route 17 on the banks of the Santee River at the end of a drive shaded by live oak hung with Spanish moss, magnolia, and other plants. Guided tours (10 a.m. to 4 p.m. Tuesday–Friday March through October) begin at a detached kitchen and continue to the white frame mansion, which is decorated with period furniture. Auxiliary buildings stand nearby.

Farther south, a short detour off U.S. Route 17 along Rutledge Road (state Route 857) leads to two colonial sites: St. James Santee Episcopal Church and Hampton Plantation State Park.

The 1768 church stands on a dirt road about 2 miles off Rutledge Road. In season, the visitor may pass a hunter patiently waiting beside his truck for his dogs to return. The early Georgian ecclesiastical-style church, sometimes known locally as the "Brick Church," has round brick columns, low-pitched hipped roof, shuttered windows, and box pews. It is listed on the National Register of Historic Places and used for worship only on special occasions.

The centerpiece of Hampton Plantation State Park is its mansion, open 10 a.m. to 3 p.m. Saturday and afternoons on other days. The original modest Georgian-style six-room frame farmhouse was built by French Huguenots around 1750; wings were added by 1785, and the Adams-style columned porch was placed in 1791. The house is displayed unfurnished, but illustrates the use of native materials in construction during the colonial period, including delicate woodwork. For example, in one downstairs room, a section of wall and ceiling has been cut away to show the frame and how the plaster was applied. In other rooms are heart-of-pine floorboards, a large cypress mantel panel, and delicate ornamental mouldings.

The presentation is being further developed as funds are available to include information on related subjects, including Dr. Archibald Rutledge, the last resident, who willed the plantation to the state in 1971. Rutledge, a celebrated poet, returned to his ancestral home after retiring from a teaching post in Pennsylvania and was poet laureate of South Carolina. It will remain a self-guided museum, however.

A mammoth live oak tree in the yard was never moved, as the owners had planned, because George Washington advised against it during a visit on May 1, 1791. A shrub and flower garden is maintained the way it was laid out 40 years ago by Dr. Rutledge.

Of the park's 322 acres, about 30 percent are developed for public use. Day-use facilities, not far from the mansion, were installed in 1982. Plans call for laying out a nature trail along old rice dikes — to traverse areas alive with deer, wild turkey, wild hogs, hawks, and wild flowers — and constructing a dock and creek overlook. In the interim, rangers usually advise against wandering off to some of the more spectacular natural phenomena — such as a heavily wooded cypress pond that is wet at times and dry at others — because of an abundance of snakes in the woods.

Francis Marion National Forest

Much of the coastal zone between the Santee River and the Charleston urban area is included in this forest, named for the "Swamp Fox" who gave the British so much trouble during the Revolutionary War because of his knowledge of the South Carolina terrain. The 250,000-acre wedge-shaped wilderness extends inland to the shores of Lake Moultrie.

A number of paved highways cross the forest, putting even the casual traveler in close proximity to tall pines, oaks hung with Spanish moss, and other flora. These include U.S. Route 17 near the coast, state Route 41 through the center of the forest, and U.S. Route 52 along its western edge.

The forest is divided into two districts, each with a ranger station. The Wambaw District office is just off Route 17 on the road to McClellanville and the Witherbee District Office is located off state Route 402 southeast of Moncks Corner. They are open Monday–Friday. (A joint visitors center for the forest and Cape Romain National Wildlife Refuge, planned for 1994, will be located on Route 17.)

Francis Marion Forest has just about everything a coastal wilderness could want and most of it is relatively easy to reach. However, visitors should make allowance for weather conditions — especially heat and flooding that occur after rains — and insects, especially in hot months.

A forest this extensive naturally includes a number of habitats. It embraces coastal sand and swamp areas, low flatlands, and extensive upland pine forests (predominantly loblolly but including longleaf) invaded by numerous creeks, "Carolina bays" (those small lakes that are either still wet or overgrown), and more. Streams, from the steady Santee River to dark-hued Wambaw and Huger creeks, are subject to tidal influence. Both saltwater and freshwater fishing are possible, mostly along Wambaw, Chicken, Echaw, Awendaw, Huger, Nicholson, and Turkey creeks; Guillard Lake; the Intracoastal Waterway; and the Santee River. Wildlife is plentiful and includes deer, rabbits, squirrels, alligators, foxes, bears, and bobcats. Poisonous rattlesnakes, water-moccasins, and copperheads are present. Both coastal and uplands species, such as bald eagle, swallow-tail kite, the endangered red-cockaded woodpecker, doves, quail, and the purest strain of Eastern wild turkey in the United States, are among more than 250 species of birds.

In all, more than 50 developed sites open up every section of the park. Gravel roads crisscross more isolated areas of the forest, leading to such natural attractions as Wambaw Swamp Wilderness, which at times is alive with wildflowers such as wild orchids, lizard's tail, and pickerel weeds; Little Wambaw Swamp Wilderness, which despite its name is the largest wilderness in the forest, with 5,223 acres of bottomland hardwood interrupted frequently by sloughs; and 2,200-acre Hellhole Bay Wilderness, where several miles of channels dug in the 1950s can be used at high water only, mostly in winter and spring. Water is normally 2 to 18 inches deep in low areas during the wet months.

The 20-mile-long Swamp Fox Hiking Trail extends from Route 17 to the Huger (pronounced Huge-ee) Recreation Area not far from the Witherbee station. It meanders along longleaf pine ridges where turkey and quail repose, skirts Ocean Bay, traverses a hardwood creek bottom frequented by deer and squirrels, and crosses boardwalks over creeks and through tupelo and cypress swamps. Camping is allowed at Halfway Creek trail camp. Parking lots on state Routes 98 and 599 divide the trail for those who prefer shorter segments.

The Buck Hall Recreation Area, with picnic facilities, campsites, and a boat ramp, overlooks the Intracoastal Waterway and a marsh only a few miles off Route 17. Crabbing is good and fishers take whiting, flounder, spot-tail bass, sea trout, mullet, spot, croaker, and other varieties.

The Honey Hill Recreation Area has a few day-use facilities, including water, but is visited mostly by hunters. Other hunting camps are located at Batty's Bridge, Elmwood, and Huger. Twenty to 40 percent of the forest is open to hunting for deer, feral hogs, migratory birds and waterfowl, and small game during seasons, except on Sundays.

A boat ramp at Still Landing, about 8.5 miles from McClellanville along state Routes 9 and 45 and forest roads, accesses Wambaw Creek Wilderness, a slender area of shallow water affected by tidal action and made hazardous in some places by logs. Two loop canoe trails on Wambaw Creek, whose banks are lined with maples, tupelo, bald cypress, and gums, total about 40 miles of paddling, with a campsite at Elmwood. Alligators are occasionally seen. Fishers in small boats take bream, catfish, striped bass, shad, crappie, and other species.

The 10-mile blazed Jericho Horse Trail loop, which begins at Jericho Swamp a few miles northeast of the Witherbee station on state Route 48, is located in a quiet area of the forest, which increases the chances of seeing wildlife such as deer and wild turkey. The trail traverses an old plantation site marked by live oak, cuts through woods, crosses bridges over creeks and marshy areas, and passes the Greentree Reservoir. Hikers also may use this trail. A two-loop, 40-mile motorcycle loop trail starts at Round Pond, about 15 miles from McClellanville along state Routes 45 and 654, and follows old logging railroad beds and narrow trails.

The Huger Recreation Area is known for its bass fishing and camping under moss-laden trees. The site has a boat landing that accesses the Cooper River, a .2-mile nature trail, picnic facilities, and one of the few remaining sheds built by the Depression-era Civilian Conservation Corps (CCC).

The 925-acre Guillard Lake Scenic Area is a visual delight that includes unusual limestone outcroppings on Stuart Creek and ancient cypress trees. A campground sits on a bluff overlooking an oxbow lake. Although there is no boat ramp, small boats can be carried to the water. During periods of high water, when some of the area floods, small boats can penetrate an old canal to the Santee River. The site is nearly 7 miles from Jamestown along state Route 45 and forest service roads.

Rifle ranges for shooting at stationary targets are located at Boggy Head, just off state Route 41, and at Twin Ponds, about 6 miles from U.S. Route 17 on state Route 133 West. At Bonneau, off state Route 52, the Rembert Dennis Wildlife Center, where wildlife is raised and studied, can be visited by reservation (803/825-3387).

The disastrous effects of Hurricane Hugo, which damaged about 100,000 acres of the forest, are demonstrated both formally and informally. Two sizable areas that were particularly hard hit, where fully grown trees were snapped like matchsticks and underbrush was virtually swept away, are marked with signboads that explain "in only five hours, this extremely powerful storm destroyed more timber in South Carolina than was ever recorded from any other natural disaster in the United States." One is situated just off Route 17 on the road to the Buck Hall Recreation Area and the other stands off the road to the Witherbee District office.

Vegetation recovering from the ravages of the hurricane, some aided by the planting of seed trees, also may be seen informally along Route 17 and other highways and the various trails through the forest, many of which were closed for a time because of the storm. Restoration efforts following the storm include artificial cavities for birds (87 percent of all colonies were harmed to some degree), establishment of about 150 acres of wildlife openings, placement of approximately 150 boxes for birds, squirrels, and wood duck, planting 200 acres of forage for wild turkey, and establishment of a 500-acre quail management area.

More than 2,000 Indian sites in the forest have been identified, about half of them prehistoric. Most date from about 1,000 B.C. to 1715 A.D. Much of the forest was converted to rice plantations in the 1700s. Dikes from the rice planting may still be seen in places. A strong French Huguenot influence is evident on the eastern branch of the Cooper River in the western section of the forest; there, along state Route 98, are Pompion (pronounced pumpkin) Hill Chapel, a National Historic Landmark noted for its superb workmanship, and St. Thomas and St. Denis Church, an 1819 Greek-Revival structure. At places, traces of the narrow tree-shaded colonial-era King's Highway (Old Georgetown Road) can still be seen.

Other historical relics include The Battery, the ruins of an L-shaped Civil War earthen fortification, and the Seewee Shell Mound, a 150-foot-wide circular mound of oyster shells on the edge of a salt marsh, which proves an Indian presence 3,500 years ago. Fossils and artifacts, including a 10-million-year-old clamshell and 2,000-year-old pottery shards, are displayed in the lobby of the Amoco Chemical Company off state Route 98. Middleburg Plantation mansion on the same highway is said to be the oldest frame house in South Carolina.

McClellanville, a water-oriented community, retains many of the picturesque qualities common to coastal villages a few generations ago, despite recent efforts to spruce it up for the tourist trade. A few buildings, such as the 1867 White Gables house, are marked by signs. A boat ramp and commercial fishing dock are near the Town Hall.

Francis Marion National Forest is flanked by two areas spectacular in their own right: Cape Romain National Wildlife Refuge to the east and the Sante-Cooper lakes area to the west.

Cape Romain National Wildlife Refuge

This beautiful neighbor to the national forest covers 64,000 acres of saltwater marshes and islands that are readily accessible to boaters. For others, Moore's Landing, a beautiful point at the end of sideroads through the forest, is the key to enjoying the beaches, marshes, and streams of the refuge. There, a pier used for fishing and crabbing is also the departure point for a boat that carries visitors to Bulls Island on Friday, Saturday, and Sunday between March 1 and mid-December (except the last week in August and first week in September) and on Saturday the rest of the year. There is a boat ramp at Moore's Landing, as well.

Visitors to Bulls Island should carry everything they will need for a day-long stay. They may walk on a dirt road from the dock on Summerhouse Creek across the island to the undeveloped Atlantic Ocean beach to engage in sunbathing, surf fishing, beachcombing, and exploring. From there, they may follow the beach and trails in both directions. In the northeast direction, a circular path follows Lighthouse Road past Moccasin Pond and Jack Creek Pool to the Boneyard Beach area, then to the ruins of an old fort on Jack Creek, then along Old Fort Road back to the boat dock. In the other direction, the walker arrives at the southwestern tip of the island. Shorter Sheepshead Ridge Trail runs through the island's interior. A 2-mile interpretive trail begins at the visitor contact point and picnic tables near the dock and crosses the island to a tower at the Summerhouse Ponds.

The isolated island is rich in wildlife, including more than 260 species of birds. Porpoises and sea turtles are sometimes seen en route to the island.

Fishing is allowed year-round during daylight hours at Bulls Island, Cape Island beaches, Lighthouse Island, and Raccoon Key. Some night fishing is permitted on Cape Island. Fishing is banned on other islands during nesting periods; these are open during daylight hours only between September 15 and February 15.

Capers Island

This state-owned isle west of Bulls Island is distinguished by waters favorable to intertidal oysters, shrimp, crabs, and many species of fish. The island's thick maritime forest, swamps, and marshes also teem with bird and land life — deer, raccoon, alligator, waterfowl, and osprey among them. Loggerhead turtles nest on the beaches.

The refuge can be reached only by boat, the closest landing being Moore's at Cape Romain. Overnight campers must obtain permits.

The Santee-Cooper Lakes

Lakes Moultrie and Marion, created in 1938 when the Santee River was dammed for a hydroelectric power project, have spectacular recreational opportunities for power and sail boaters, water skiers, birdwatchers, and others. Together, the lakes have more than 450 miles of shoreline and cover about 178,000 acres. They are connected by a diversion canal. Lake Moultrie has many ties to Francis Marion Forest and thus the coastal region; Lake Marion's coastal claim is marginal, but much of it lies east of Interstate 95.

The lakes are managed by a state-owned utility, which has planted 22,000 acres in slash and loblolly pine. The extensive natural area around the lakes — 70 percent of the shoreline is supposed to remain in a natural state — supports varied and plentiful wildlife. Present are deer, alligator, foxes, squirrels, bald eagle, osprey, ducks, doves, and wild turkeys.

Pinopolis, located at the end of a small peninsula jutting into pear-shaped Lake Moultrie a few miles from Moncks Corner, is one of numerous sites around the lake where recreational facilities for swimmers, campers, boaters, and others are located. Eleven fishing camps provide access to the bluegill, black crappie, largemouth bass, striped bass, white bass, blue and channel catfish, shell cracker, and other species in this lake. A 13,500-acre game management area is located along the southern shore just west of Pinopolis.

Elongated Lake Marion has similar attributes, plus more than 35 sites for boaters and fishers and swimming and camping facilities.

One of them is Santee State Park off state Route 6 just west of Interstate 95, which has 150 campsites and 30 cabins and two boat ramps, in addition to day-use facilities. The park also has four nature trails and a hike-bike trail. A 2.5-mile trail in the eastern section of the park follows the shoreline of Lake Marion before looping inland back to the starting point. An extension of this path explores Poplar Creek. The 1-mile Oak Pinolly Trail at the western end of the park makes an inland loop through a moss-draped forest of mixed pine and hardwoods. The ¾-mile Limestone Trail near the center of the park views part of a lake used for swimming and nearby woods. The 3.8-mile hike-bike path extends about half the length of the park, revealing a diversity of terrain, plants, and wildlife before terminating at the swimming lake.

A naturalist conducts organized programs such as nature walks, bird identification, and crafts that use natural materials found in the park. The park is open 6 a.m. to 9 p.m. during the peak months, 6 to 6 at other times.

Just off Interstate 95, on the north shore of Lake Marion, is the Santee National Wildlife Refuge. Three of the four units of this segmented 15,000-acre refuge are located east of the thruway, but many of the facilities are on its west side.

The site, which stretches intermittently for 18 miles along the lakeshore, encloses stands of mixed hardwood and pine trees, marshes, old fields, ponds, impoundments, and open water. Private farmers under contract plant corn, wheat, millet, and soybeans, a quarter of which are left for the wildlife. From November to February, about 50,000 ducks and 8,000 Canada geese winter on the refuge. The endangered red-cockaded woodpecker, osprey, red-tailed and red-shouldered hawks, and other birds are present throughout the year. Alligators laze in ponds and marshes, while white-tailed deer, bobcat, raccoon, rabbits, and other small game inhabit the forests.

Year-round boating is facilitated by boat ramps on both sides of Interstate 95. However, certain inlets are closed from November through February. Fishers may use boats and Scott's Lake Fishing Beach to catch largemouth bass, bream, catfish, and other varieties. Deer, doves, quail, waterfowl, and other small game are hunted during limited seasons.

A visitors center (open Monday–Friday) is located in the Bluff Unit off U.S. Route 301, west of Interstate 95. The site of old Fort Watson, an Indian mound, and a boat ramp are also in this unit. An observation tower on Wright's Bluff Nature Trail, which is open year-round, is a good place to view wintering waterfowl.

East of Interstate 95, boat ramps are found on service roads in the Pine Island and Cuddo units. The dikes around the Dingle Pond Unit near Exit 102 are excellent for birdwatching and waterfowl viewing. Trails are open to hikers and bikers from March through October.

Cypress Gardens

A 163-acre natural forested swamp was created to provide water for the rice fields of Dean Hall, a 3,000-acre antebellum plantation on the Cooper River. Brightly blooming flowers were planted in the late 1920s by Benjamin R. Kittredge to enhance the beauty of the site.

Hurricane Hugo swept through in 1989 and transformed the property. Recovery from the loss of about 12,000 trees has proceeded, with new growth illustrating nature's recuperative power and new plantings making the gardens even more beautiful.

The spectacular combination, located 24 miles from Charleston off U.S. Route 52 on Cypress Gardens Road, is viewable from either a flat-bottom boat or along 3 miles of walkways. In 1989, a small demonstration rice field was created; it is tended by 19th-century methods.

In 1963, the owners of the gardens gave them to the City of Charleston to ensure their perpetuation. The gardens are open from 9 a.m. to 5 p.m. daily.

Old Santee Canal State Park

In the feverish building period of the early 19th century, canals made streams navigable into the interiors of many states, including South Carolina. A remnant of one opened in 1800 to connect the Cooper and Santee rivers—which had three locks raising boats 34 feet and seven locks lowering them 60 feet—remains at this park, near a tail-race canal dug in the 1940s to handle runoff and navigation from the damming that created Moultrie and Marion lakes. Located on a Cooper River bluff a mile east of Moncks Corner, this special park combines outdoor and indoor history with above-average contact with nature.

A new interpretive center focuses on the canals and how they were built and used; unusual facets of the history of the site, including the construction of the Confederacy's first successful torpedo boat, *Little David,* during the Civil War; plantation life; archaeology in Biggin Creek; and the natural history of the region. One of the exhibits is an operating model of the old canal, said to be the first in America to facilitate river travel. The center also has two theaters for screening films, one of which is a reconstructed grotto.

This center opens onto an elongated natural area with interconnecting trails of various lengths. A swamp boardwalk is less than .2-mile long, the creek walk is slightly more than a mile in length, and the canal loop is almost 3 miles long. Deer and wild turkey are rare, but small mammals and birds such as osprey, great blue heron, and great chained owl are common. Rustic observation points are spotted around Biggin Creek. Blinds are available for photography. Fishing, mostly for bream, is permitted from boardwalks, from a floating dock on the Cooper River, and from the creek bank.

A house (circa 1840), furnished downstairs as it would have been at that time, is opened to the public at special times, such as Christmas.

Old Santee Canal State Park conducts a year-round interpretive program on natural and cultural history. Included are birdwalks and swampwalks and lectures on subjects such as animal adaptations, reptiles and amphibians, quilts, and square dancing. Hours are 9 a.m. to 5 p.m. year-round.

The park had been open only seven weeks in 1989 when it was struck by Hurricane Hugo. The storm did so much damage the park did not reopen until September 1991.

The Berkeley County Museum, emphasizing local history, is located at the entrance to the park. Moncks Corner was an important inland commercial center in the early 19th century because it stood at the head of navigable waters. The river carried farm products, lumber, and limestone from natural beds in the area downstream.

The Charleston Area: North

Charleston Trident Convention & Visitors Bureau
P.O. Box 975
Charleston SC 29402
803/723-7641

THE CHARLESTON INFLUENCE BEGINS LONG BEFORE ONE ARRIVES IN THE city. The land lying between the Ashley and Cooper rivers and the coastal region off U.S. Route 17 east of the city bears the unmistakable imprint of the relationship at places such as Mount Pleasant, Boone Hall, Patriot's Point, Sullivan's Island, and the Isle of Palms. In recent years, North Charleston has begun to emerge from the shadow of its more famous ancestor and assert itself.

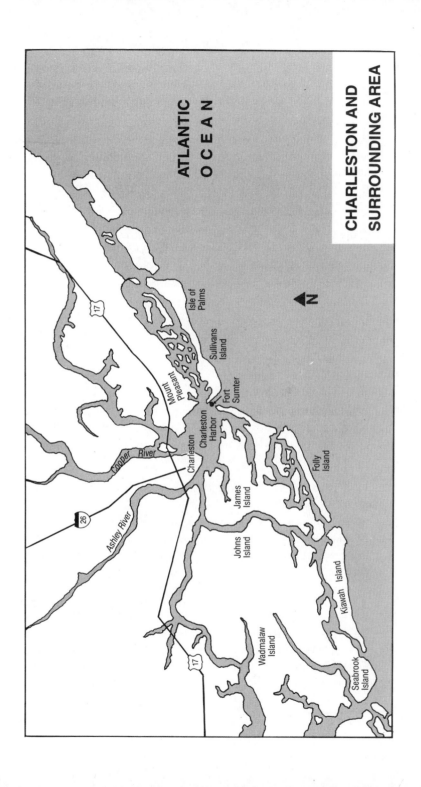

ATLANTIC
O C E A N

Isle of
Palms

Sullivans
Island

Fort
Sumter

Mount
Pleasant

Charleston
Harbor

Charleston

Cooper River

Ashley River

Folly
Island

James
Island

Johns
Island

Kiawah Island

Wadmalaw
Island

Seabrook
Island

N

CHARLESTON AND
SURROUNDING AREA

Mount Pleasant

This historic community properly describes itself as being "just across the bridge" from Charleston. It has much the same mindset, a history dating back to 1680, and a few of the attractions that Charleston treasures, such as Boone Hall and Patriot's Point.

It hosts a number of lowcountry-style events, including an oyster roast in February, blessing of the seafood fleet in April, a billfish tournament in June, and Scottish Highland Games Gathering in September.

The remains of the Old Pitt Street Bridge, until the mid-1940s the only link to Sullivan's Island, have been renovated to add a fishing pier. It is also a scenic outlook on the oceangoing vessels using the Charleston harbor, boats on the Intracoastal Waterway, Sullivan's Island, and the town's old waterfront homes.

Mount Pleasant has many private historic buildings, such as the Hibben House (circa 1755). These have well-maintained, handsome exteriors and even an occasional 18th century-style "joggling" board in the backyard. Boone Hall is the showpiece of the area.

Boone Hall

The handsome mansion and striking setting of this plantation, located on Long Point Road 9 miles north of Charleston off U.S. Route 17, have been featured in a number of American and European television movies and documentaries. The brick house with large white columns stands at the end of a ¾-mile-long avenue of oaks, first planted in 1743. Gardens around the mansion are brilliant when the azaleas and camellias are in bloom.

The plantation is one of the oldest in South Carolina, dating from 1681 when John Boone, one of the settlers in the "first fleet," received a land grant. As a rice and then a cotton plantation, it grew to cover more than 17,000 acres. The Boone family was intimately associated with much of South Carolina's early history. The plantation's founder was one of the most influential men in the colony. His daughter, Sarah, was the grandmother of a South Carolina signer of the Declaration of Independence and the state's first governor.

Boone Hall began raising pecans in 1815 and, by 1904, its groves were the largest in the world. About 140 acres are still producing. Brickmaking was another major occupation, and bricks made on the site were used in plantation structures, as well as a number of important buildings in Charleston. Some of them may have been used in the construction of Fort Sumter.

The present mansion is a virtual copy of the structure built by Major John Boone. Although it survived the Civil War, it was torn down in 1935 and rebuilt, using some of the original materials.

Guided tours explore the first floor of the handsome entrance hallway, the dining room, loggia, game room, and courtyard. The handsome hallway features a free-standing staircase. The loggia originally was open but is now closed in. From the courtyard, visitors can see along Wampacheone Creek a live oak that is 600 years old.

Furnishings are not original to the house but are mostly antiques. They include a maple bench made in the 1500s, a hunt board, an American-made dining table, and a mahogany Philadelphia high board made in the late 1700s.

Other historic plantation structures are the two-story cotton-gin house, which de-seeded its most important 1800s export crop; the tabby foundations of the old boat landing from the same period; nine 1743 slave cabins, the only intact brick slave street in the southeast; and a 1710 circular smokehouse.

Boone Hall, a working plantation producing primarily pecans and wheat, is open daily year-round: 9:30 a.m. to 6:30 p.m. Monday–Saturday, 1 to 6 p.m. Sunday April–August; 9 a.m. to 5 p.m. Monday–Saturday and 1 to 5 p.m. Sunday September–March.

Palmetto Islands County Park

A half-mile beyond Boone Hall on Long Point Road, this nature-oriented park has an unusual feature: a 350,000-gallon natural swimming hole that is five feet at its deepest point and has a sandy bottom. It also has a beach for sunning, a mile-long tidal canoe trail, fishing in Boone Hall Creek, a bike trail, self-guided Osprey Nature Trail, marsh boardwalk, 50-foot observation tower overlooking tidal creeks and salt marsh, a 2-acre pond, and other day-use facilities.

Patriots Point

Charleston's modern maritime side is visible at Patriot's Point, just off U.S. Route 17, where six historic vessels form what some claim is the world's largest naval and maritime museum.

The centerpiece is the 888-foot aircraft Carrier *USS Yorktown,* the

"Fighting Lady," still proudly wearing World War II battle stars on the side of her superstructure. The first carrier *Yorktown* (CV-5) was sunk during the Battle of Midway in June 1942 and was replaced by this ship (CV-10), which participated in a number of World War II naval battles and the Korean and Vietnam wars. In 1968, the *Yorktown* recovered the crew of *Apollo 8,* the first manned spacecraft to circle the moon.

Tours of the vessel begin on the hangar deck, where a collection of state flags overhangs mementoes and displays that depict the ship's past. Among them are a TBM Avenger, the type of plane in which President George Bush was shot down on September 2, 1944; an F6F Hellcat (for every one lost, F6Fs shot down an average of 19 Japanese aircraft); an A-4 Skyhawk; an F-9 Cougar; a B-25; and an open cockpit Curtiss trainer.

The "Arlington of Carrier Aviation" is a listing by ship of all naval pilots killed during World War II. Other displays cover such topics as the Battle of Midway, World War II carriers and later supercarriers, gun mounts, and shipbuilding and repair.

Tours then proceed in several directions, following color-coded routes. These move from deck to deck and cover everything from the engine room to living and working spaces. A major one goes through a pilot ready room and control centers to the superstructure bridge and the flight deck, where other combat craft are parked. The wartime record of the ship, including combat ribbons and enemy planes destroyed, is painted on the superstructure. Also displayed are photographs of famous naval aviators.

The view from the flight deck looks across the broad, calm Cooper River to the steeples of Charleston. It also looks down on the decks of the other ships in the museum: the experimental NS *Savannah,* the world's first nuclear-powered merchant vessel; the destroyer USS *Laffey,* which survived the impact of five *kamikaze* suicide planes and three bomb hits off Okinawa; the World War II submarine *Clamagore,* one of the last diesel-powered submarines to be decommissioned; the Coast Guard cutter *Inghan,* on active duty for 52 years, including three wars, and which was credited with sinking the German submarine *U-626* in 1942 with a single depth charge; and a river patrol boat developed for use in Vietnam. These vessels also may be toured.

Patriot's Point is open 9 a.m. to 6 p.m. daily April–October, 9 a.m. to 5 p.m. November–March.

Fort Moultrie

Fort Moultrie has seen it all. It has grown from a crude sand and log fort to a formal masonry fortification. It has languished in peacetime and stood resolutely in war. It has witnessed gunnery advances from smoothbore cannon to ever more powerful rifled artillery capable of hurling tons of metal seaward.

Fort Moultrie, which dates back to the Revolutionary War, is the oldest Charleston fortification. The first fort was built hastily in 1776 in anticipation of British attack by raising two palmetto log walls and filling the space between with sand. Ships entering the harbor had to pass under its guns. It repulsed a British fleet of nine warships on June 26, 1776 — the first decisive American victory over the British — as the soft palmetto logs absorbed the British cannon shot. Following this victory, South Carolina placed the palmetto tree on its flag and came to be known as the Palmetto State. Four years later, the British took the city anyway and used it as a base to invade the Carolinas and Virginia.

In 1794, a more ambitious structure was built as part of the new nation's coastal defense system. The five-sided earth and log installation deteriorated from disuse and was destroyed by a hurricane in 1804. The next Fort Moultrie, made of bricks, was completed in 1809. It later became part of a harbor defense system that included Fort Sumter. One of its pre-Civil War commanders was William Tecumseh Sherman, who later became one of the Union's most feared generals.

Major Robert Anderson's unit was situated there when South Carolina seceded but soon moved to Fort Sumter because Fort Moultrie was exposed to ground attack. Confederate batteries at Fort Moultrie helped bombard Fort Sumter and remained at the fort, piling sand on top of brick walls demolished by federal shells, until Charleston was declared an open city.

The fort was rebuilt in the 1870s to include bombproofs and magazines made of concrete, then covered with sand to absorb the impact of shells. It was strengthened again in the 1890s and used during World Wars I and II.

Today, the structure stands as a prime example of how forts were altered to conform to new periods and new weapons. Cannon representing the various wars are emplaced chronologically counterclockwise on the parapets, beginning with the small smoothbores of the infancy of the United States and advancing through the combination of smoothbores and rifled cannon of the Civil War to the long-range coastal batteries of the 20th century. Concrete battery positions and a fire-control tower added in World War II are apparent.

A series of displays outside the walls also trace the development of coastal artillery over the years. A Revolutionary War cannon stands on the site of the early sand and log fort. Artillery pieces from the Civil War and later are lined up on Cannon Walk. Nearby Battery Jaeger exemplifies the heavy coastal artillery that could throw huge shells 10 or more miles to sea.

Flanking the fort's entrance is the grave of the captured Florida Seminole Indian Chief Osceola, who died in 1838 while incarcerated there.

A visitors center across the street houses a small museum. The fort is open daily 9 a.m. to 6 p.m. May–September, 9 a.m. to 5 p.m. October–April, except December 25.

The broad, sandy beaches of Sullivan's Island long have attracted Charlestonians during the hot summer months. Isle of Palms may be better known for its resort complex, with golf and boating facilities, but it has public beaches. The island's vacation heritage dates back to the simpler days of 1898 when only boats and a railroad bridge accessed the island. Other public beaches are located at Folly Beach, Edisto Island, and Kiawah Island, south of the city.

Charleston

Charleston Trident Convention & Visitors Bureau
81 Mary Street
Charleston SC 29402
803/577-2510 or 800/868-8118

CHARLESTONIANS ARE "FULL OF THEMSELVES," AS A SOUTHERNER MIGHT say. When they refer to their community as the "holy city," they are not just referring to the numerous church spires that dominate the historic area. But who can blame them? To begin with, there is the nostalgia of a glorious past—a few streets still paved with cobble-stones that came as ballast on sailing ships, relics of plantation aristocracy and the historical imperatives of the Confederacy. No place better represents the Southern antebellum style of plantation living.

Nothing is ever fully forgotten. Tradition is an important factor in Charleston life. In antebellum days, December was a big social season, as plantation owners came to town for debutante balls, political events, and Christmas activities. December remains an important social period, with many black-tie events. The Christmas season is distinguished by candlelight and caroling, stories for children, and decorated antebellum mansions. Even everyday life offers examples of this congenital continuity. For example, basket-weaving techniques brought over by the first African slaves still are practiced by street peddlers.

Charleston is, as that indicates, a sensual place where languid, low-country ways still dominate. Horsedrawn carriages carry tourists through a semitropical landscape, along streets scented with fragrant wisteria, jasmine, and tea olive. April in Charleston, when the azaleas and flowers bloom, deserves a song just as much as Paris does. Charleston has very special aromas—steaming she-crab soup, for example—and very ordinary ones, such as fresh fruits, vegetables, and flowers at the open market. Visual perception is charmed by the city's architectural treasure trove and affronted by the jumble of traffic on narrow streets.

For all of their self-centeredness, Charlestonians can laugh at themselves. One of the stories told by guides concerns a visitor who lavishly praised the sunset and moonrise over the Battery, to which his hostess replied, "You should have seen it before The War." Another concerns a law that made hip pockets illegal—an attempt to eliminate the common practice of carrying flasks.

Charleston's life has been a schizoid sea-land split. The harbor, still the No. 1 industry, has given Charleston its commercial importance, while its people have lavished their attention on converting the land to comfortable living. In recent years, for both historical and commercial reasons (tourism is the second largest industry), a serious effort has been made to preserve and emphasize this lifestyle. A similar tug-of-war dating back to the earliest days persists between the more freewheeling coastal townspeople and the often strait-laced backcountry folks. Attempts to impose prohibition or moderation as inland areas grew in political power have been resisted by subterfuges such as the "blind tiger," where drinks came with admission to a nonexistent show.

Charlestonians are justifiably proud of their history, the way they have created a thriving and genteel city out of adversity. The city was founded in 1670 on the south shore of the Ashley River and, about ten years later, was moved to the more easily defended peninsula it since has occupied. Most of the first powerful settlers of Charleston, and of Carolina, were younger sons of wealthy plantation owners on Barbados. The original city was one of five in British North America fortified against pirates, Indians, and especially against the Spanish, who resented a British colony so close to their Florida base.

Charles Towne grew fairly rapidly. By 1690, after two decades of settlement, it was the fifth largest town in North America. Although the colony was controlled by the English proprietary government and later the crown, Charleston was a relatively open society. Beginning in the 1680s, large numbers of French Huguenot refugees settled there. Religious dissenters emigrated from New England. Charleston had the largest Jewish population in America prior to 1820. There was a sizable Afro-American population, primarily from Sierra Leone, as well.

Rice, and later indigo, were the staples that made Charleston the center of a rich plantation economy. Some of the wealthiest planters owned several plantations and built substantial homes on each of them. They also lavished attention on their houses in town, where they spent spring and summer months to avoid the diseases and mosquitos that followed the flooding of the rice fields. Many opulent townhouses were built. Visitors sometimes commented on the ostentation of Charlestonians after 1772, when Charleston was generally acknowledged as the wealthiest city in British North America. Charlestonians of that period used their wealth to try to transplant English fashion into the Carolina society, including a full theater season. In one season alone, more than 119 different plays, including about 25 Shakespeare productions, were performed. In the 1770s, some of the wealthiest Charlestonians also discovered the summer bliss of Newport, Rhode Island.

By the time of the Revolutionary War, Charleston had become one of the most important ports on the North American continent. British concentration in the northern states spared Charleston during the early stages of the war but, when Britain added a Southern option, the city became a focal point. It resisted two attacks but finally was taken after a two-month siege. It then became a base for invasion of the Carolinas and Virginia, a campaign that went well until Lord Cornwallis was cornered in 1781 at Yorktown, Virginia, and forced to surrender. The treatment he received there was influenced by the harsh terms he had imposed on the Charleston garrison. General Benjamin Lincoln, who had surrendered Charleston, was designated by General George Washington to receive the British surrender. When Cornwallis's troops marched out to a tune entitled "The World Turned Upside Down" and laid down their arms, the United States had won its independence.

After the war, Charles Town was reincorporated as Charleston. The motto on the seal—"She Guards Her Buildings, Customs and Laws"—reflected the Charleston character and was, some claim today, sort of a mandate for the preservation that would come more than a century and a half later.

Another golden age occurred as rice production reached a peak and plantations on the offshore islands began to market the prized sea island cotton for as much as six times the price of other varieties. The city expanded northward, as new suburbs of warm-weather villas were created by wealthy planters. One of the greatest of these, Ashley Hall, is today a school for girls. Barbara Bush is one of its alumna.

In the 1830s and 1840s, Charlestonians accepted some national trends but remained stubbornly addicted to classical revival architecture styles and to opulence that went along with Charleston's view of itself as an emerging Southern capital. In the first half of the 19th century, visitors often compared Charleston to the finest cities in England and France. For example, Fannie Kemble, noted English actress and abolitionist, wrote, "You seem in one street to be in an old town in Italy and, in the next street, to be in some seacoast town of England."

However, Charleston declined in stature and relative wealth as the century proceeded. While it was fifth in population in America in 1820, it was about thirtieth by the decade just before the War Between the States.

Charleston had a significant role in starting the Civil War by firing on the small federal garrison at Fort Sumter in the harbor. The commander of the Confederate forces, General Pierre Gustave Toutant Beauregard of Louisiana, was lionized by Charleston society and especially the women. He stayed first at the Mills House Hotel, but his presence created such commotion that the hotel owner offered his own home to the popular general. Both the rebuilt hotel and the Mills home are often shown on tours of the city.

The Civil War years were hard on Charleston. A great fire in 1861 destroyed many buildings and later Union bombardment took a toll. Since South Carolina passed the first ordinance of secession, Charleston was hated in the North as the center of secession. It was finally evacuated by Confederate forces early in 1865 as General William Tecumseh Sherman approached. As a result, most of the city's architectural treasures survived.

Charleston has a number of fine Victorian structures, but largely escaped the period because most Charlestonians did not have the money to invest in refurbishing their old houses or building new ones. For much the same reasons, Charlestonians did not begin to demolish old structures in any large numbers until well into the 20th century. And when they did, a conservation movement developed that became a guiding force in the restoration of the old city. Thus, few of the significant buildings from earlier centuries were torn down to make way for new structures. Artists and writers, including author Oscar Wilde, began to discover the city in the 1890s.

As a result, Charleston today appears much as it was depicted in a mid-18th-century engraved overview of the peninsula. There are no skyscrapers; the tallest structures are the spires of numerous churches. Charleston has one of the most handsome waterfronts on the East Coast. Palmettos and live oak grow in the sandy soil of White Point Gardens along the Battery (which got its name from the cannon placed there in the War of 1812). The wide sidewalks—to allow full-skirted ladies to pass—are made of crushed oyster shell, as most were in the early days.

Altogether, a hundred buildings predate the Revolutionary War and more than 2,000 predate the Civil War. Architectural styles are adapted from Anglo-Dutch traditions of the late 17th century and Caribbean interpretations of that style, with French and African infusions. The most distinctive architectural form is the "single house," a conventional Georgian house turned sideways on lots with little street frontage. The "false front doors" of these houses open onto a piazza or porch, rather than the house. This gave the families privacy when using the porches during hot weather. One visitor in the late 18th century observed that the race in Charleston was not to see who could have the most opulent house but who could have the coolest.

Charleston has a number of "double houses"—two rooms wide

facing the street. The staircases on these houses were called "opening arms" or "welcoming arms" stairs. The men would walk up the left side and the ladies up the right; this prevented men from seeing the ladies' ankles as they picked up their dresses to climb the stairs.

These buildings are so well constructed that they largely withstood the devastating winds of Hurricane Hugo, which uprooted about 10,000 trees. Damage was confined largely to roofs and flooding, which destroyed some priceless interiors and exteriors. Nearby fishing villages were badly hit.

Many architectural historians regard the 1769 Miles Brewton House as one of the finest Georgian townhouses in America. It descended in the family of Miles Brewton matrilinearly and is currently being re-restored as a private house. The oldest residence, dating from the earliest days of settlement, is a wooden structure on the corner of King and Broad streets. The great houses along East Battery (perhaps the most photographed section of the city) were finished after 1819 when the new sea wall was constructed.

Elliott Street is an example of the narrow streets laid out within the old walled city. It was considered one of the "most sinful" streets. While church steeples are visible from almost anywhere in Charleston, none can be seen from the street. Furthermore, at one time it was the red-light district.

Two outstanding examples of the Adams style of architecture are located in the 789-acre historic area, and both are open to visitors. The Joseph Manigault House, built in 1803 before cotton became king, has high ceilings, pine floors, cypress mantels, and decorative plaster. A hidden stairway connects the second and third floors of this house, which is open 10 a.m. to 5 p.m. Monday–Saturday and 1 to 5 p.m. Sunday. Among the unusual features of the 1808 Nathaniel Russell House are a three-story free-standing spiral staircase and incredible hand-carved woodwork, including a room on the second floor with gold leaf in the woodwork. The drawing room, brass fixtures, and garden are also outstanding. Russell, a merchant born in Rhode Island and also known as the "king of the Yankees," did not believe in slavery so he hired free blacks to build the house. The Russell House is open 10 a.m. to 5 p.m. Monday–Saturday, Sunday 2 to 5 p.m.

The long, narrow lot on which the Heyward-Washington House stands was laid out in 1680 within the old walled city of Charleston. The house (open 10 a.m. to 5 p.m. Monday–Saturday and 1 to 5 p.m. Sunday) is a typical Charleston "double" house, which essentially means that it has four rooms per floor divided by a central hall-way. A keystone arch divides the front half from the back half, a symbol well understood at the time: when a client or businessman entered the house, he knew he was not supposed to venture behind that arch and intrude on the personal life of the family.

A mahogany chest-on-chest-on-chest in the building illustrates how furniture could double as a traveling piece. Whenever one sees a three-tier chest like this, guides often say, there is a 99.7 percent chance it came from Charleston. The mahogany master bed (circa 1790) is the only piece original to the Heyward family, but all the furniture dates from the 1770s to 1810 and thus is similar to what the family would have had. Much of it was made by Thomas Elfe, a famous cabinetmaker of the period. One piece has a hole left by a bullet that came through a window during the Civil War.

The mansion was built by Daniel Heyward for his son, who was at the time studying law in London. Thomas Heyward returned with his law degree in 1771 and, in 1776, signed the Declaration of Independence. His father remained a Tory and, when war broke out, went to England and never returned to the United States. Thomas Heyward used the house as his summer and December home and law office. He also owned Whitehall, a rice plantation about 45 miles southwest of Charleston, where the family normally spent eight months of the year. George Washington stayed at the house during a visit in 1791.

The "single" house (circa 1740) that stood on the property before the present building was constructed as a mom-and-pop gunsmith-ing operation. It was common at the time for small merchants to live and work in the same building, operating shops on the first floors and living upstairs. The dependency buildings date from that period and, consequently, are about 30 years older than the mansion. The servants' quarters, carriage house, and detached kitchen provide in-sight into the early lifestyle of the city, as does the reproduction of an 18th-century formal English garden.

The Aiken-Rhett Mansion (circa 1817) retains some of the original furniture, paint, and wallpaper. It was the home of a pioneer rail-roader and governor, William Aiken, from 1833 to 1887. Confeder-ate General Beauregard established his headquarters in the building in 1864. Hours are 10 a.m. to 5 p.m. daily.

The Edmonston–Alston House, which fronts on East Battery Street, is a symbol of the American dream. Charles Edmonston ar-rived from Scotland at the age of 17 to work for a shipping company;

29 years later, in 1828, when he built the late Federal-style house, he owned his own shipping company. In 1837, he lost some of his fortune because of a depression and sold the house the following year to Charles Alston, a plantation owner from Georgetown who used it as his townhouse. At that time, Charleston was the fourth largest city and seaport in the United States in both population and wealth.

Alston altered the house to reflect the then more fashionable Greek-Revival style, adding a porch and altering the roof line, and personalized the house by putting his family coat of arms on the front. The house is privately owned by a descendant on Mrs. Alston's side of the family, but is open to public visitation 10 a.m. to 4:40 p.m. Tuesday–Saturday and 1:30 to 4:40 p.m. Sunday.

The sitting room on the first floor (sometimes called the morning room because it faced the morning light) was used by the family and by the gentlemen to receive business guests. On the second floor are the formal drawing rooms, one featuring late Federal-period furniture from 1800 to the 1820s, where most of the entertaining was done.

A few artifacts owned by the Edmonstons, including Spode china, which was a wedding gift to them in 1810, are on display. Ninety percent of the furnishings are original to the Alston family, some dating back as far as the 1760s but most from 1810 to 1840. One of the oldest pieces is a mid-18th century Queen Anne desk made in two sections so the top can be removed and carried as a chest. A few of the 700 Piranesi prints purchased by the Alstons during an 1856 tour of Europe are on the walls. Blue and white Cantonese china, popular in the 19th century and plentiful in seaport towns like Charleston where it could be purchased at the dock, is on display. Alston silverware was made by Hester Bateman, a famous 18th-century woman silversmith.

The 1850 brass light fixture in the first floor hallway signifies that the Alston family was one of the first in Charleston to have gas lighting.

The Calhoun Mansion on Meeting Street was the largest single family home in Charleston when it was built in 1876 by George Williams, Jr., at a cost of $200,000. He was considered something of a scoundrel by his contemporaries because he saved his money during the Civil War instead of giving it to the Confederate cause and emerged from the war with his fortune intact—and larger. Tour guides sometimes contend that Williams influenced the character of Rhett Butler in Margaret Mitchell's epic novel, *Gone with the Wind*. Though the house is privately owned, it is open to the public from 10 a.m. to 4 p.m. Wednesday–Saturday. Williams earlier lived in a

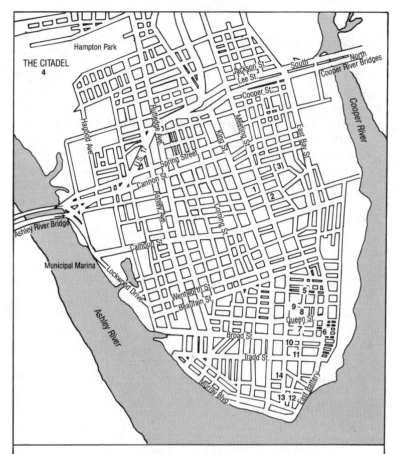

HISTORIC CHARLESTON

1. Visitor Reception and Transportation Center

2. Joseph Manigault House

3. Aiken-Rhett House

4. The Citadel

5. City Market

6. Old Exchange Building

7. Dock Street Theatre

8. St. Philip's Protestant Episcopal Church

9. Old Powder Magazine

10. St. Michael's Protestant Episcopal Church

11. Heyward-Washington House

12. Edmonston-Alston House

13. Calhoun Mansion

14. Nathaniel Russell House

house (circa 1797) that appears to be made of stone but is actually made of carved cypress wood.

The James Ladson home was built in 1792 by a Revolutionary War patriot. It originally had a Ladson Street address, but Ladson wanted a fashionable Meeting Street address so he purchased an intervening house and tore it down, creating the large lawn in front.

The summer home of the Drayton family on East Battery Street illustrates a side effect of plantation living. Many plantation owners had in-town summer homes to escape from the heat and mosquito-carried diseases of summer and to enjoy the city's active social life.

The Colonel William Washington House was the home of a cousin of George Washington. It has green shutters.

Historic Charleston was not all fine mansions. The breadth of the community's lifestyle comes alive along pastel-colored Rainbow Row on East Battery Street. Here, overlooking the colonial harbor, merchants had shops on first floors and lived on upper floors. A number of apocryphal stories explain the origin of the colors; one claims the merchants' wives selected the colors so their husbands could find the right house when they came home from the taverns. The pastels also reflect heat better than darker colors.

"Cabbage Row" on Church Street inspired the "Catfish Row" setting used in the musical *Porgy and Bess*. The authors, DuBose Heyward and George Gershwin, were major contributors to the cultural renaissance that occurred in Charleston in the 1920s.

Religion has been visible in Charleston from the town's beginnings. Today more than 138 different denominations are represented.

The steeple of St. Michael's Episcopal Church dominates the historic area the way cathedrals tower over some European cities. Similar in design to St. Martin's-in-the-Field in London, its Palladian Doric porch fronts on Market Street, a major route in the historic area. The church, begun in 1752 and the oldest in the city, contains old box pews and the original pulpit. St. Philip's has the oldest active Anglican congregration south of Virginia, dating back to 1670. The present building on Church Street dates from 1835–38. Tour guides may remark that the graveyard nearest the church was reserved for native Charlestonians and that visitors and transients were buried in one across the street. Even former Vice President John C. Calhoun, the story goes, was moved away from the church and his second wife when it was realized he was born elsewhere in South Carolina.

The less pretentious Gothic-style Huguenot Church, formed by

French Protestants who settled in Charleston, conducted services in French for more than 150 years. This church also is known as the "church of the tides" because services originally were scheduled around high tides so members going to church could use their boats. The present structure on Church Street, built in 1844–45, is the fourth on the site.

Other major religious structures include Second Presbyterian Church, which dates from 1809; First (Scots) Presbyterian Church, built in 1814 by a congregation organized in 1731; St. John's Lutheran Church, from 1815; First Baptist Church, built in 1822 to replace the original 1699 building; St. Mary's Roman Catholic Church, constructed in 1838; the 1847 Trinity Methodist Church, similar to the Church of the Madelaine in Paris but with a Tiffany stained-glass window; the 1852 Old Bethel Methodist Church; and the 1891 Circular Congregational Church, which was organized in 1681 (open 9 a.m. to 1 p.m. Monday–Friday).

Charleston also has the second oldest Jewish synagogue and the oldest in continuous use in the United States. Temple Beth Elohim, organized in 1749, was the birthplace in 1824 of American Reformed Judaism. The Greek-Revival structure on Hazel Street, built in 1840, is open to visits 10 a.m. to 2 p.m. Monday–Friday, Sunday by appointment.

Charleston was a vibrant port and market city, filled with the sounds and sights of seamen, artisans, traders, and slaves. The most famous relic is Market Hall, which often is described as a one-time slave market but was actually a farmers' market, as it partly is today. The main section, built in 1841, was used for the sale of steers, rams, sheep, and other animals, an activity that is not part of the present scene. Instead, it houses the Confederate Museum's excellent collection of swords, flags, uniforms, and other memorabilia that the United Daughters of Confederacy has been collecting since 1898. It was closed for a time for renovation; the museum normally is open Monday–Saturday at hours that vary according to season.

The Thomas Elfe Workshop, built prior to 1760, was the workplace of Charleston's most famous 18th-century cabinetmaker. Tours of the restored small "single house" and exhibits, which include excavated artifacts and period cabinetmaking tools, start at 10 a.m. Monday–Saturday, continue until 4:30 weekdays and noon on Saturday.

Old warehouses where cotton, lumber, and tar were stored now shelter restaurants, shops, and condos. Among the small inns occupying historic structures are the Battery Carriage House, built in the 1840s and enlarged in the 1870s; Meeting Street Inn, constructed as a residence, restaurant, and saloon; King's Courtyard Inn, which occupies an 1853 commercial row; Elliott House Inn, whose main building was a "single house"; and Sword Gate Inn, known for its Regency ballrooms and distinctive iron gate. Poinsett Tavern was established in 1734 by Elijah Poinsett, an ancestor of Joel Poinsett who brought the poinsettia to the United States from Mexico.

Charleston's version of a Revolutionary War "tea party" filled Provost Dungeon in the Old Exchange Building at East Bay and Broad streets with liberated tea. Instead of dumping the tea in the harbor, as was done in Boston, frugal Charlestonians stored it without paying taxes and dumped the casks in the harbor. Later, patriots were incarcerated in the Provost Dungeon. After the war, the South Carolina Assembly met in the Exchange Building to ratify the U.S. Constitution. The building and dungeon are open 9:30 a.m. to 5 p.m. Monday–Saturday, 1 to 4 p.m. Sunday.

The oldest public building, the Old Powder Magazine (circa 1713) with walls 32 inches thick, and the 1802 City Hall, designed by Gabriel Manigault, first used as a branch of the Bank of the United States, are now museums. The former is open 9:30 a.m. to 4 p.m. Monday–Friday, and the latter, in whose council chamber hangs a portrait of George Washington painted by John Trumbull, is open 9 a.m. to 5 p.m. Monday–Friday.

Dock Street Theatre on Church Street (tours noon to 6 p.m. Monday–Friday) stands on the site of the first building in America built specifically for theatrical performances and occupies the Old Planter's Hotel, built in 1809. The present main building of the College of Charleston, founded in 1770, dates from 1828. The Citadel, the state-operated military college, maintains long-standing traditions at its Friday dress parade. Its museum (9 a.m. to 5 p.m. Saturday, 2 to 5 p.m. Sunday–Friday) has an extensive collection of Civil War memorabilia, including two original Confederate flags, among the exhibits reflecting the role of the corps in American history. The Hibernian Hall, home of the early Irish society, dates from 1841.

The Charleston Museum, housed in a modern building on Meeting Street, has a full-scale replica of the Confederate submarine *Hunley,* which sank a Union warship off Charleston but unfortunately was carried down with it. Exhibits exploring lowcountry history, including a number of priceless silver pieces, may be viewed 9 a.m. to 5 p.m. Monday–Saturday, 1 to 5 p.m. Sunday.

Other attractions include the following:

1792 County Courthouse at the intersection of Broad and Meeting streets; used as offices, but at some point in the future may also house an interpretive center.

American Military Museum, 40 Pinckney Street: relics and uniforms from all American wars, including Vietnam. Open 10 a.m. to 6 p.m. Monday–Saturday, 1 to 6 Sunday.

The Old Slave Mart Museum on Chalmers Street: slave-trade artifacts and black arts and crafts at a site known to have been used in the slave trade. Formerly privately operated, the building has been acquired by the city with a view to operating it as a museum. Reopening date indefinite.

Gibbes Museum of Art, 135 Meeting Street: extensive collection from 17th century to the present includes views of Charleston and portraits of South Carolina leaders. Open 10 a.m. to 5 p.m. Tuesday–Saturday, 1 to 5 p.m. Sunday–Monday.

The first organized effort to preserve Charleston's historic district came in the 1920s when the Preservation Society of Charleston prevented demolition of the Joseph Manigault and Heyward-Washington houses. Other defensive moves prevented large out-of-state museums from stripping historic homes, including the Daniel Heyward House (circa 1770). A key leader was Charleston's and South Carolina's first woman realtor, Susan Pringle Frost, who for several decades almost singlehandedly saved many houses.

In 1928 and 1929, when an oil company began to buy significant corner lots and tear down the 18th- and 19th-century houses, the need for a broader-based, better financed effort became obvious. In 1931, the Charleston City Council formally established an "old and historic" district of about 400 buildings in a 23-block area. This was the first law of its kind in the United States. However, the district covered only the area of the original walled city and left many priceless structures unprotected. In the later 1930s, the Carolina Art Association was instrumental in obtaining money from wealthy Northerners who wintered in Charleston for the first architectural survey of any historic city. Later extensions of the historic district incorporated nearly half of the peninsula on which the heart of the city is located. Height restrictions are so strict that the tallest building is nine stories.

The Historic Charleston Foundation was created in 1947 to preserve and use the city's architectural and historic treasures. Before it could get rolling, however, two significant buildings were lost in the post-World War II construction euphoria: the old Charleston

Hotel and the 1790 Orphan House, the earliest in America. In 1958, America's first revolving fund to save historic buildings was created and was helpful in upgrading the 12-block Ansonborough area, an early 18th-century suburb, into middle-class residences. After rehabilitating about 60 houses, the foundation moved north of Calhoun Street into other early neighborhoods. A recent project rehabilitated small houses for low- and moderate-income resale.

In 1975, the foundation helped the National Trust acquire 1738 Drayton Hall, the Drayton family seat on the Ashley River, and more than 800 acres. A more recent foundation project is the acquisition and restoration of 50 acres of the McCloud Plantation on James Island, a sea island cotton plantation that has one of America's only surviving and intact slave streets, as well as numerous outbuildings related to sea island cotton. The site also has major cultural importance from the standpoint of prehistoric Indians and Afro-Americans of the Reconstruction period.

More than 100 commercial and residential properties in downtown Charleston are protected by easements obtained by the foundation. In addition, easements have been granted on five major plantations, including the earliest great plantation house in the Carolinas, Mulberry, built in 1711. Easements also are sought on more recent structures, such as a Beaufort structure designed by Frank Lloyd Wright in the late 1930s for a wealthy Savannah businessman.

In the 1970s and 1980s, the city government utilized federal funds to advance the restoration program. Charleston still has work to do. It has more than 1,000 unrestored historic buildings in the northern part of the city. There is a continuing tradeoff between the modern demands of auto traffic and historic interest.

Charleston naturally has a modern side. Spoleto Festival USA, a modern invention held in late May, also helps carry on Charleston's cultural tradition. The 2½-week program ranges from street concerts to opera and chamber music to avant garde theater and dance. Arts Line (803/723-2787) provides recorded information on programs. Riviera Theater on King Street is perhaps the best of a few examples of the art deco style of architecture in Charleston. (According to guide Sean Maddocks of Carolina Carriage Company, "Most of the younger generation, anyone younger than myself actually, don't know what these theaters were all about.") (The theaters once had community status long since lost to television.)

Shopping is a Charleston heritage, too. King Street, a main thoroughfare in the commercial district dating back to the 1800s, hosts rows of chic shops. Kerrison's Department Store was the first dry goods retail store in the South. The Omni Hotel also has a concourse featuring famous specialty shops such as Gucci and Godiva.

Fort Sumter

The most imposing symbol of the city's martial side is Fort Sumter, which stands on a manmade island in the bay. It is one of 29 forts authorized to protect the East Coast after British invasion during the War of 1812. Construction was started in 1829 and was being completed when the Civil War began. The fort dominates the entrance to the harbor. Not only was federal control an affront to the new sovereignty claimed by the Confederacy, but it made the harbor useless to a new nation dependent on foreign trade. The strategic importance of the five-sided fort was cited by Confederate General Robert E. Lee: "The loss of Charleston would cut us off from . . . the rest of the world." President Abraham Lincoln's determination to reinforce and resupply the garrison made the attack inevitable.

Thus, at 4:30 a.m., April 12, 1861, 43 Confederate batteries began firing from three sides. They hammered away for 34 hours while Sumter's 60 cannon and 85 men returned fire methodically. Ammunition and supplies low, its commander, Major Robert Anderson, surrendered the fort. The only casualty came as a battery fired a salute; a cartridge bag exploded, killing one of the men.

Confederates manned the fort for nearly four years despite persistent pounding from Union rifled artillery on warships and, after 1863, also from Morris Island. Confederates evacuated on February 17, 1865, as General Sherman approached Charleston.

Fort Sumter remained a military post until 1947. Post-Civil War coastal artillery additions include Battery Huger, added in 1898 for the Spanish-American War.

Accessible only by boat, Fort Sumter National Monument reflects the punishing bombardment it received during the Civil War. The fort is a reduced version of the three-story structure that stood at the start of the Civil War. Projectiles of the kind that destroyed the upper stories are imbedded in one wall. Near today's entry port are the ruins of the officer's quarters and barracks set afire during the Confederate bombardment. Period cannon on the parade ground and in place in casemates include a 15-inch Rodman, 9-inch Columbiad, 10-inch mortar, 100-pounder Parrott, and a Confederate mountain howitzer, the last used to defend against a surprise landing by Union forces.

The museum in a section of Battery Huger holds the flag that flew over the fort during the Confederate assault and numerous other wartime relics, including examples of projectiles. Pictorials describe the building of the fort, the advent of rifled artillery and its use against Fort Sumter and other subjects. The fort is open 9 a.m. to 6 p.m. in summer, 9 a.m. to 5 p.m. the rest of the year. Tour boats (2½ hours) leave from the city marina, 17 Lockwood Boulevard. Park Service rangers conduct tours of the fort itself.

From the parapet of even the reduced fort, watching today's ocean-going vessels sail past on the way upriver, the visitor can see clearly how thoroughly the fort commands the entrance to the harbor.

Next to history, Charleston's waterfront is its most impressive feature. The wealth of water makes it an ideal fishing and boating center. Boats leave the municipal dock and a number of private marinas for protected harbor waters and oceanic adventures. Offshore fishing is productive year-round, but is best in the summer when everything from king mackerel to hammerhead sharks are caught. Even in January, fishing can produce a bucketful of sea bass, however.

Tour boats offer a variety of trips year-round. Harbor tours leave from both the municipal marina and Patriot's Point. Each nonstop trip lasts about two hours and passes the historic forts, elegant waterfront homes, and the warships docked at Charleston's U.S. Navy Base.

Charles Towne Landing

Part of this multipurpose park on the south shore of the Ashley River recreates elements of the first permanent settlement in South Carolina. Visitors stroll past a modern Visitors Service Complex, geodesic dome meeting area, and open-air interpretive center housing historic artifacts to enter a forested area that illustrates what life was like for the hardy band of men and women who settled there in 1670.

A reconstructed house-print shop, woodworkers shop, and smithery in the Settlers Life Area illustrate the simple but surprisingly comfortable lifestyle the first 150 pioneers were able to quickly carve from the wilderness of live oak, pine, magnolia, and dogwood. Not far away is a demonstration garden of crops that have been staples of South Carolina's economy over the years — the rice and indigo of the early settlers and the cotton and sugar cane that came later are planted in season. Down another path is a garden that has some form of plant in bloom year-round. Azaleas and camellias are among its 78 varieties of shrubs and trees.

A simple log palisade and earthworks in a forested area demonstrate how settlers countered the ever-present dangers from Indians and Spanish marauders. When the settlement existed, homes would have stood inside a substantial palisade.

Animals the settlers may have seen when they arrived more than 200 years ago, including puma, bear, elk, alligator, and buffalo, are housed in a 22-acre zoo that recreates their natural habitat.

Docked along the riverbank is the *Adventure,* a 53-foot replica of a 17th-century trading vessel of the type built then to serve the river and coastal trade. Visitors may go on board to talk with costumed interpreters — who in the off-season may even make a spare part for the vessel.

The Old Towne House, a former plantation residence, can be viewed from the outside but is presently not open to the public.

A 30-minute movie introduces the recreated settlement site. In addition, tram tours are available at a fee for those who prefer it. Bikes can be rented. An annual arts and crafts show is held in late March.

Charles Towne Landing, located on Route 171 south of the Ashley River, is open 9 a.m. to 6 p.m. June–August, 9 a.m. to 5 p.m. the rest of the year.

Ashley River Plantations

Charleston still has a symbiotic relationship with the old plantations around it. No visit to Charleston is complete without visiting some of the plantations that helped give the city its vitality in former years.

Three that are open to the public — Drayton Hall, Magnolia Plantation, and Middleton Place — are located within five miles of each other on state Route 61, sometimes called "River Road."

Drayton Hall. After John Drayton, a member of the planter aristocracy who was born at Magnolia Plantation in 1713, failed to inherit it, he acquired an adjacent tract of land at age 22 and built Drayton Hall. Begun in 1738 and completed in 1742, the Georgian Palladian structure, contemporaneously admired as a "grand palace," survives today largely in its original form. The mansion has solid, 18-inch-thick brick walls, wide loblolly pine floorboards, and bald cypress wall panels. Eighty percent of the woodwork is original and,

Drayton Hall. PHOTO BY JOHN BOWEN.

remarkably, two rooms still have the original coats of buff-colored paint. The porch railings also are largely original.

Today, Drayton Hall is considered the finest building of its kind in the United States. The visitor approaches the rear or "land front" of the mansion, built at a time when houses normally fronted on streams because they were the easiest means of transportation. The two "fronts" emphasize the sophistication of the house at the time it was built. The "land front" has a handsome Palladian porch reminiscent of what was in vogue in Italy at the time. The "river front" is more functional and less impressive.

Shown unfurnished, the mansion is a study in the symmetric architecture of the period. For example, in the drawing room is the fake door often used in Georgian architecture to achieve balance. The patterns in the 17th-century ceiling in this room were carved freehand in wet plaster — one of only five of the type in the United States documented as intact and in their original place. The overmantle in the Great Hall is an interpretation of the fashionable patterns of the period in England and other European countries. The mantle features Greek and Roman motifs. Among recent additions is some "Montgomery Guards" graffiti scribbled on a wall in 1874.

The outbuildings that were attached to the main house by curved, covered walkways were lost to Charleston's two natural nemeses: storms and earthquakes (Charleston stands astride the second largest fault in the United States). For example, a two-story storage building at the left rear of the mansion was felled by the largest earthquake ever to strike the United States, on August 31, 1886. Drayton Hall, on the banks of the Ashley River, is now owned by the National Trust for Historic Preservation. It is open daily, except Thanksgiving, Christmas, and New Year's. Tours are conducted hourly from 10 a.m. to 4 p.m. March–October, twice a day the remainder of the year.

Magnolia Plantation. The gardens at Magnolia Plantation were opened to the public in 1870 and, in the last decades of the century, horticulturalists and tourists rode steamers up the Ashley River in spring and summer to view the effusion of color. In a 1900 British travel guide, the garden was listed as one of the three greatest attractions in the United States.

Today's multifaceted plantation is still spectacular, with more than 900 types of camellias and 250 kinds of azaleas. The original 1680s formal garden, "flowerdale," now incorporated inconspicuously into more than 50 acres of plantings, supports Magnolia's claim to be the oldest gardens in the United States. Some flowers are blooming in every season of the year. Even in January, such species as evergreen euonymus, ornamental kale, Japanese anemone, holly, common camellia, kaffir lily, narcissus, garden pansy, Japanese quince, scotch marigold, rosemary, and acuba brighten the trails.

Walkways also pass ancient live oak trees (including the one where John Drayton, a minister, meditated and composed his sermons), sabal palmetto, roses, hibiscus, daffodils, jessamine, bougainvillea, dogwood, hollies, lantana, narcissus, day lilies, hydrangea, tea olive, rhododendron, wisteria, dwarf iris, deutzia, and numerous other varieties; cross swamps growing bald cypress and ponds on white bridges; enter a plot that grows plants identified in the Bible; and overlook an old 125-acre rice field that is now a wildlife pond. A sign details the damage done to the natural habitat in the post-Civil War era, when owners were forced to mine the phosphate rock underlying much of the plantation to make ends meet.

A ¼-mile maze and an herb garden framed by boxwoods recreate 18th-century plantation escapes. A schoolhouse (circa 1825) for the plantation's slaves and a petting zoo stand near the parking lot.

The 500-acre plantation, open 8 a.m. to 5:30 p.m. daily, is now listed as a wildlife sanctuary and is especially known for waterfowl, water birds, and small land birds. An observation tower provides a vantage point for viewing the avians and surrounding terrain. A 3½-mile walking and biking trail circumvents the wildlife pond; walkers can cut it in half if they wish. Canoeists follow white markers on poles along a circular trail that takes about two hours to paddle. Fishing also is permitted.

Audubon Swamp Garden, opened in 1988 as a separate section, features a rustic boardwalk, bridge, and causeway trail that takes about 45 minutes to complete through 60 acres of cypress and tupelo swamp; growths of ferns, wisteria, azaleas, and daffodils; and a wildflower field. Complimentary binoculars at a number of strategic locations enhance viewing of American alligator, bald eagle, anhinga, great blue heron, wood duck, otters, turtles, and other animals common to the swamp. Signs identify many trees, such as magnolia, yaupon, black gum, sweetgum, and eastern red cedar. A sculpture, *Music of the Swamp,* is located near the head of the trail. Optional extensions along a lake cover more than 30 acres of a hardwood forest.

Walks are conducted on Saturdays in the area where James J. Audubon may have obtained anhinga specimens during a visit as a guest of the Reverand Mr. Drayton. In all, more than 200 species of birds frequent Magnolia Plantation.

Magnolia Plantation was founded by one of the early English transplants to Barbados who moved on to more promising prospects in the American colonies. Stephen Fox, who acquired the tract of land on the Ashley River that became Magnolia Plantation when the Carolina colony was largely untamed wilderness, married the daughter of Thomas Drayton, Jr., who had arrived with his father in the 1670s. Members of the family have owned the site since.

The present mansion, the third, replaced houses that burned. Moved to the site from Summerville after destruction of the second mansion during the Civil War, it retains a pre-Revolutionary section, with additions from the early 1800s and Victorian period. Furniture, art, and silver in the seven rooms open to tours date from the late 18th and early 19th centuries. Former bedrooms now display original ornithological paintings by Edward Von Seibold Dingle, often called "the Carolina Audubon," and the works of local artists.

Three miles from Magnolia Gardens on Ashley River Road is Old St. Andrew's Parish Episcopal Church, where the Reverend John

Drayton preached. The church is the oldest active church in South Carolina. The present building was erected in 1706 and enlarged in 1746, but much of the original interior is preserved. Open 10 a.m. to 4 p.m. weekdays; a tearoom and gift shop run by church ladies offers lowcountry specialties and homemade desserts from 11:30 am. to 2 p.m. daily (except Sunday) in late March and early April.

Middleton Place. The gardens at Middleton Place, laid out around 1741, have classic formality with allees and parterres. Started by Henry Middleton, later president of the First Continental Congress, the gardens are said to have taken ten years to complete. Today's plantings of azaleas, magnolias, roses, camellias, crepe myrtle, and perennials bloom year-round.

A self-guided walk around the gardens begins at the Reflecting Pool, where swans swim to the edge in anticipation of food from visitors. The complete walk laid out by the gardens moves to the ruins of the mansion and the 1755 house, the guest wing of the mansion that burned in 1865. The trail then loops around the house and between the parterres and butterfly lakes to wind through the handsome Octagonal Sunken Garden, along camellia-bordered allees, past a giant crepe myrtle and a series of beds and forested areas holding plants such as lilies, China and tea roses, bamboo, partridge berry, trillium, violets, laurel, and the Middleton Oak, which marked an Indian trail centuries before Europeans settled the area. The final leg is a waterfront trail known as the Lower Walk that overlooks flooded rice fields and a rice mill pond where anhinga, swans, wood duck, geese, and mallards mingle; crosses the pond on a footbridge; and then tours the barns and crafts buildings before crossing the greensward in front of the 1755 house to the Reflecting Pool. Visitors also may wander, map in hand, to those areas that interest them most.

The gardens lay untended for many years after the Civil War but were restored early in this century by a direct descendant of the founder. Middleton Place became a National Historic Landmark in the 1970s.

Among relics on display in the house are a silk copy of the Declaration of Independence, owned by the plantation founder's son, Arthur, a signer of the document; portraits and books; silver; and antique furniture.

Interpreters are on hand year-round in a restored stable and yard to demonstrate everyday colonial crafts, but are especially active at blacksmithing, corn grinding, pottery making, candle dipping, syrup making, spinning, weaving, and wool dyeing during Plantation Days in November. Christmas at Middleton Place demonstrates how early Americans celebrated the holiday.

Middleton Place is open 9 a.m. to 5 p.m. daily.

Summerville-Harleyville Area

Farther along state Route 61 is the historic town of Summerville, whose Old Town Hall predates 1860; Givhans Ferry State Park, more than 1,200 acres on a bluff overlooking the Edisto River; and Colleton State Park. Each park has 25 campsites, a nature trail, picnic facilities, and fishing; Givhans also has four cabins. Colleton is only a few minutes from Interstate 95.

The state's first designated canoe and kayak trail follows the meandering Edisto River between the two parks and beyond in both directions. There are at least eight put-in/take-out points (seven free) along the 56-mile trail, as well as two on the intersecting Four Hole Swamp. The trip traverses an area that is still largely wild, with overhanging live oak boughs heavy with Spanish moss, forests of pine, black willow, cypress, tupelo, gum, and red swamp maple, numerous alligators, snakes, and other wildlife, as well as fields. The water level on the otherwise gentle river changes markedly from season to season, and canoeists should check on the current situation (803/538-3659). Guided trips are available (803/549-9595). Fishers, mainly for redbreast sunfish, and tube floaters share the river in places.

Old Dorchester State Park, 4 miles south of Summerville on state Route 642, preserves the ruins of a 1757 tabby fort guarding a powder magazine and the tower of old St. George's Church as adjuncts to an interpretive center explaining the history of South Carolina's first inland settlement. The town was founded by settlers from Dorchester, Massachusetts, and the fort was reinforced during the Revolutionary War.

Francis Beidler Forest. From Summerville, U.S. Routes 78 and 178 and Beidler Forest Road access the almost primeval Francis Beidler Forest, where trees 1,000 years old stand in what is said to be the largest virgin blackwater-bald cypress-tupelo gum swamp forest in the world. The forest, near Harleyville, also can be reached from Interstate 26 via State Route 27 (Exit 187), U.S. Routes 78 and 178, and the forest road.

The National Audubon Society and The Nature Conservancy own

5,819 acres deep in the expansive Four Holes Swamp, an inland phenomenon that stretches for 60 miles. Seven of these miles are in the Beidler Forest, and the remainder are in the hands of lumber companies, hunting clubs, and individuals.

The drive into the Audubon/Conservancy property along a dirt road, which winds through a forest featuring dogwood, sassafras, pine, blueberries, wild azaleas, and sweetleaf and past open fields, provides a tame introduction to the wilds that lie in the swamp. The fringes of the Beidler Forest were ravaged by Hurricane Hugo in 1989, but the ancient core of the swamp sustained only light damage.

A 1.5-mile boardwalk, which starts at a visitors center raised off the ground to allow the flow of water beneath it, passes pine hills, hardwood flats, cypress creeks, bluffs underlaid by marl deposited when the Atlantic Ocean extended into the region, and a blackwater lake. The trail shows the swamp forest in its natural state: ramrod-straight bald cypress with gnarled knees, misshapen tupelo trunks, stands of loblolly pine and oaks, American elm, Carolina ash, water hickory, lichen growing on tree trunks, fern clusters, wildflowers such as greenfly orchid, dwarf trillium, and lilies and dead trees. These provide habitat for more than 300 species of animals: white-tailed deer, foxes, rabbits, squirrels, raccoon, mink, river otters, bobcats, bats, owls, wood ducks, red-shouldered hawks, songbirds, and others. Eastern cottonmouth and copperhead are among 50 species of reptiles. While most of the mammals are nocturnal, a few sometimes are seen in daylight along the route. Insects are present most of the year. Guided walks, including night and bird-spotting outings, are held on a regular schedule.

Unremoved brush and debris created by Hurricane Hugo, including a huge uprooted cypress, are visible at a number of places along the walkway. Nearly half of the 6,500 feet of boardwalk had to be replaced after the hurricane.

Naturalist-guided half-day canoe trips are held weekdays in February and early March and on Friday, Saturday, and Sunday from mid-March through May. Advance phone reservations are required. The water level is highly variable, fluctuating an average of 3.5 feet. It is highest after winter and summer rains.

Four Holes Swamp drains southeast through the rolling terrain of the Beidler Forest, then turns to the southwest to enter the Edisto River. The switch apparently results from a pre-Pleistocene sandhill. The swamp was frequented by the Yemasee Indians, who apparently named it for four fishing lakes, and was well known to

Francis Marion. It was, for a time, a haven for runaway slaves. The land was acquired in the late 19th century by the Beidler family of Chicago, but it was not cut over. Francis Beidler, inspired by a trip as a young man to Old Faithful and other western natural wonders, was a devoted conservationist. Though he continued cutting, he left large tracts like this one untouched.

The forest is open 9 a.m. to 5 p.m. Tuesday–Sunday, except Thanksgiving Day, December 22–25 and 31, and January 1.

Charleston Area: South

James Island

THE FIRST SHOT AGAINST FORT SUMTER WAS FIRED FROM FORT JOHNSON at 4:30 a.m. on April 12, 1861. It burst almost directly over the island fortification and was a signal for other Confederate batteries to open fire. Fort Johnson today is owned jointly by the South Carolina Wildlife and Marine Resources Commission and the College of Charleston. A new complex houses an oceanographic center and marine biology laboratory.

County and city parks are adjacent on James Island. In the approximately 600 acres on Riverland Drive are a pier for crabbing and fishing on a tidal creek of the Stono River, walking trails, a paved bike trail, lagoons, 12 acres of open meadows, a 125-space RV campground, and ten cottages. The parks are open year-round.

Island Beaches

While the broad sandy beaches on Sullivans Island and Isle of Palms long have attracted Charlestonians during the hot summer months, the most extensive facilities lie south of the city. Public beaches are located at Folly Beach County Park, Beachwalker Park on Kiawah Island, and Edisto Island. Folly Beach Park has 4,000 feet of oceanfront with four beach walkovers and lifeguards along 600 feet of it, plus 2,000 feet of riverfront. The park is open daily year-round. Kiawah and Seabrook are better known to outsiders as upscale resorts, but 30 acres of beachfront on the west end of Kiawah Island have been set aside for public use by the Charleston County Parks and Recreation Commission. The site is open daily May–September, weekends April and October, and closed November–March.

Edisto Island

One of the first highway signs on this island identifies that stretch of state Route 174 as a scenic highway. The reason is obvious: for much of the way, gnarled live oak trees border the road, their huge limbs decorated with Spanish moss sometimes overhanging the road. Otherwise, the highway proceeds through a typical South Carolina low-country rural area, with small low houses set back from the road among scrub trees and grasses that grow well in sandy soil.

Shell mounds prove that Indians feasted on the bounty of the surrounding waters at least 4,000 years before Europeans arrived around 1690. Some of the old plantation homes and pre-Revolutionary War churches created by the English remain, but the island is now best known as a resort. Edisto Beach, dominated by privately owned summer cottages, stretches out along the southern tip of the island almost at the end of the highway. A number of public beach-access points are available.

The best public access to both the beach and coastal terrain is 1,255-acre Edisto Beach State Park, located at the entrance to the resort strip. During the warm months, the 1½-mile strip of sandy beach pounded by Atlantic Ocean surf is crowded with sun worshippers, beachcombers, and surf fishers angling for sea trout, spottail bass, drum, whiting, and other species. Many use the 100-site camping areas and five cabins. A boat ramp at Live Oak Boat Landing accesses Big Bay Creek.

The park is divided between maritime forest, including a dense live oak tract and some of the tallest palmettos in South Carolina, and salt marsh. A level 4-mile nature trail winds through a section of maritime forest, visits ancient Indian shell mounds six to eight feet high on a cliff, and traverses a marsh on a boardwalk. The woods host numerous wild animals, including white-tailed deer and bobcat, which are seen occasionally by walkers. Nesters include the threatened small tern and loggerhead turtles, which visit the beach between May and September.

The park is open year-round.

Jacksonboro

The Edisto Nature Trail, on property owned by Westvaco along U.S. Route 17 south of Jacksonboro, combines forest and a view of the purposes to which the land has been put over the centuries. Fifty or so plants grow in the forest. Species such as yellow jessamine, beautyberry, wax myrtle, dwarf palmetto, southern catalpa, and persimmon are marked along a mile-long trail that also crosses old fields and abandoned canals and follows an old logging road and logging-train railbed and part of the original King's Highway. The trail can be cut to ½ mile by those who wish to do so and still see more than ten varieties of plants, such as spruce pine, water hickory, red mulberry, dogwood, muscadine grape, and dahoon.

Trail maps are located just inside the trail entrance on Route 17. A parking lot is provided and the trail is open during daylight hours.

Bear Island Wildlife Refuge

These 12,000 acres of forested hammocks and marshland have been open more than 30 years, but are mainly known by hunters. White-tailed deer, dove, ducks and geese, quail, rabbits, squirrels, and coots are taken by permit during short seasons: one week with bows and one week with guns for deer; five short periods for dove; and small game on designated dates in January and February. Deer normally weigh 130 to 160 pounds, but may reach 180 pounds. Among the birds harvested in recent years are blue-winged and green-winged teal, wigeon, merganser, gadwall, mallard, shoveler, pintail, black duck, bufflehead, scaup, wood duck, and snow goose.

Fishers may use designated areas of the refuge, whose main purpose is wildlife restoration, during daylight hours from April through September. Birdwatching, photography, and tours are possible from late January to the first of November. Nesting pairs of bald eagles reside on the property. Swans, herons, egrets, wood storks, cranes, ibises, gallinules, red-winged blackbirds, and a few songbirds also are present.

The refuge, about 13 miles off U.S. 17 on Bennett Point Road, is closed on Sundays year-round.

The refuge is located in the ACE Basin, where the Ashepoo, Cumbahee, and South Edisto rivers flow into St. Helena Sound. There, a major effort is being made by a coalition of government agencies and private organizations and individuals to conserve the rich resources of about 350,000 acres of pine and hardwood upland, tidal marshes, barrier islands, and beaches that support abundant wildlife, including at least four endangered or threatened species. Most of the land is privately owned, and the ACE Basin Plan contemplates no change in this except for protection in the form of voluntary easements. Limited areas are being acquired by conservation groups. Ducks Unlimited has a refuge on Mary's Island and organizations such as The Nature Conservancy and the U.S. Fish and Wildlife Service are encouraging easements and organizing estuarine research projects. Protection of the old rice fields in the area is being encouraged by the North American Waterfowl Management Plan.

Beaufort

The view from the intersection of Federal and Pincaney streets is strictly early 18th century. Big, handsome Marshlands mansion framed by live oak trees disdains its historic neighbors to face the Beaufort River. The mood is reinforced by the sound of horses' hooves in the distance and then a horsedrawn carriage follows. Only the realization that it carries tourists in shorts and T-shirts breaks the mood.

The second oldest city in South Carolina has many places along oak shaded streets where such moods are possible. At the John Mark Verdier House on Bay Street, one can almost see the Marquis de Lafayette speaking from the small second-floor columned porch during his tour of the United States in 1825. The building (circa 1790) was constructed by a shipbuilder when Beaufort was one of Georgia's principal ports, successively for rice, indigo, and cotton. The house, open 11 a.m. to 4 p.m. Tuesday–Saturday, has been restored and furnished with antiques to recreate its appearance around the turn of the 18th century.

The George Parsons Elliott House on Bay Street, built about 1840 and used during the Civil War as a federal hospital, is also an exhibition building. It is open 11 a.m. to 3 p.m. weekdays.

A self-guided walking tour (maps available at the Chamber of Commerce building) passes 23 structures older than the Civil War, many going back to the Revolutionary period. Even a short walk along the first few streets back from the waterfront passes historic houses from several periods. The oldest is the 1717 Thomas Hepworth House, a white frame structure that no longer faces the street.

The 1785 Edward Barnwell House, built by the grandson of South Carolina's most famous Indian fighter, "Tuscarora Jack," was used as headquarters by occupying federal forces during the Civil War. "The Castle" (the origin of the nickname is not readily apparent) or the Joseph F. Johnson House (circa 1850) is an impressive building with an oak 20 feet thick and a garden overlooking an inlet. Its wide center hall and dual stairways provided access to rooms housing sick Union soliders during the Civil War. Across from Marshlands, a.k.a. the James Robert Verdier House and handsome enough to have been the setting of a novel, is the smaller Federal house named Tidewater, built as a summer home about 1830 by a planter who owned 20 plantations totaling 12,000 acres.

On Craven Street, two blocks from the waterfront, stands the Arsenal Museum. Built in 1795 for one of the oldest military units in the nation, the Beaufort Artillery, and rebuilt in 1852 as a crenelated structure, it now houses Indian artifacts, war relics including cannon, and a variety of other mementoes discovered locally. The Milton Maxey House, also on Craven, is known as the "Secession House"; there, the first meeting to consider taking South Carolina out of the national union was held. In the 800 block of Craven is the studio of W. Jackson Causey, who advertises himself as the "realist painter of the South."

St. Helena's Episcopal Church, one block farther inland, was built in 1724 with brick brought from Great Britain as ballast in ships and enlarged in 1819 and 1842. Its communion silver commemorates a woman kidnapped by the Yemassee Indians in 1715.

Among other key structures are 1720 Riverview, built with hearts of pine on tabby foundations; the Tabby Manse or Thomas Fuller House with walls more than a foot thick, dating from 1786; the Elizabeth Barnwell Gough House (circa 1789), a tabby home with stucco exterior, in the Adams style; Petit Point (circa 1820), a beautifully proportioned small house with an impressive garden; the 1844 Greek Revival-style Baptist Church of Beaufort; the 1852 Berners Barnwell Sams House, a classic Greek-Revival mansion with Doric columns and outbuildings made of tabby; the Edward Means House (circa 1853) with a double verandah and flanked by a walled formal garden; and the 1856 The Oaks, which has a widow's walk. Some of the historic homes that still are private residences are included in the annual spring tours of homes and gardens.

The community's water orientation is commemorated at a waterfront park near the Chamber of Commerce building. Near period cannon, a plaque honors Confederate Brigadier General Stephen Elliott, who defended the city before it was taken by federal forces. Plays and concerts are held in the park on a regular schedule. A marina serves skippers on the inland waterway and other boaters.

Beaufort, despite the activity around it, retains a leisurely atmosphere appropriate to its antiquity and its new role as a tourist center, after more than 270 years as a port and farm center. It kicks up its heels the weekend prior to Labor Day at the Gullah Festival of South Carolina. The festival reflects the mixing of cultures that developed as slaves brought their native languages and customs to their new homes; this situation eventually produced a dialect spoken by many whites as well as blacks. The language was basically English and included a number of Elizabethan words and other modifications in pronunciation, plus the addition of African words, construction, and speaking rhythm. It still can be heard in some areas.

Spanish and French Huguenot explorers tried separately for more than half a century to settle the area, but nothing stuck until the British arrived in 1711 to grow rice and indigo, crops that utilized its fine natural harbor. Occupied by federal forces much of the Civil War, after the war it continued as a market for nearby cotton farms and a harbor for shrimp boats and crabbers. The former was replaced by truck farming in this century, but tourism is now the number one industry.

Parris Island Marine Recruit Depot

Since 1915, the U.S. Marine Corps has turned civilians into Marines in times of war and peace at this base—more than 40,000 in World War I and five times that number in World War II. The story of this enormous task is told in a museum occupying the War Memorial Building on Boulevard de France. Displays also depict the history of Parris Island, settled in 1562 by French Huguenots. The Spanish built a fortified village, Santa Elena, four years later, but eventually abandoned the island to the British, who turned it into cotton plantations. The island is named for its owner in the 1730s, Alexander Parris. Plantation owners fled when Union forces captured Port Royal Bay during the Civil War. Later, the plantations were broken up and the land given to ex-slaves. A Navy yard was constructed there in 1885, but it was abandoned in 1911 and the island was used as a prison before being converted to a Marine recruit center.

The main gate is located on state Route 802 south of Beaufort. Civilians are permitted free access to the base and may also take a driving tour of its training facilities. The museum is open from 10 a.m. to 4:30 p.m. daily, except Thanksgiving, Christmas, and New Year's Day. Tours may be arranged by calling 803/525-1951.

Parris Island was a focal point for historical research in connection with the 500th anniversary of Columbus's arrival in the New World. Santa Elena, founded in 1566 by Pedro Menendez de Aviles, served for almost a decade as capital of Spanish "La Florida," which extended from the Florida Keys to Newfoundland. The settlement thrived briefly, with as many as 100 to 300 men manning four forts at times. Indian attacks led to abandonment of the settlement in 1576; an attempt to revive the settlement was unsuccessful, and it was abandoned for good in 1587.

Excavations by the South Carolina Institute of Archaeology and Anthropology, started in 1979, located the exact site of the settlement, now on the fringe of a golf course overlooking Port Royal Sound. Pottery shards and other artifacts have been recovered and work is continuing in an effort to plot the layout of the town and the location of its major buildings.

Hunting Island

The approach to this island state park is across other islands that are hardly recognizable as islands, including St. Helena, famous for its early plantation and 1855 Baptist Church. The 50-acre Penns School Historic District includes a museum (open 8:30 a.m. to 5 p.m. Monday–Friday) where handicrafts, photographs, rare books, and other artifacts relate the history and lifestyle of black people on the sea islands.

U.S. Route 21 cuts through farmlands and scrub forests typical of this semitropical coastline. Once across Johnson's Creek, the setting changes abruptly to one of wilderness with recreational facilities fitting unobtrusively into diverse habitats: maritime forest, lagoon, salt marsh, freshwater wetlands, dunes, and beach.

The main road runs through one of the best developed forests of palmetto and slash pine in the region. Live oak, wax myrtle, water oak, red cedar, and holly also are prominent among the more than 100 species of plants on the island. More than 125 species of birds use their branches. The stunted white-tailed deer that have become a subspecies on this and a few other islands are plentiful, as are raccoon and other small animals.

The most prominent feature of the 5,000-acre park is an 1875 striped lighthouse and three original ancillary buildings at the end of a road near the visitors center. An 1859 lighthouse was threatened by serious erosion but actually was demolished by Confederate troops during the Civil War. The new one was made of cast iron and designed to be dismantled and moved if necessary. It was relocated to the present site in 1889 and was deactivated in 1933.

Other principal features of one of South Carolina's most frequented parks include more than 4 miles of beaches, two short nature trails and a short boardwalk across a saltwater marsh, a lagoon where herons and egrets maintain a wary distance and gulls are less concerned, camping sites, cabins, and a boat ramp. A pier provides access to shallow water for fishers for drum, flounder, and other types and for crabbers. Offshore catches include sailfish, barracuda, tarpon, black grouper, king mackerel, bluefish, and albacore.

Displays in the visitors center show how sparse human use left the island largely in a wilderness state throughout its history. Indians made mounds; unsuccessful Spanish and French settlements in the early 1600s left little trace. Since the island was not considered a prime agricultural area, it was never cleared as a plantation. Its unusual name comes from the practice of using it as a hunting preserve.

Park naturalists lead guided walks covering the diversity of habitats and wildlife, including a few resident alligators, and history. Hunting Island State Park was founded in 1938, but the site was used informally for hunting and other forms of recreation for many years prior to that. In the 1850s, wealthy sportsmen engaged in "devil fishing" or harpooning large members of the ray family.

The visitors center is open 9 a.m. to 5 p.m. weekdays and 11 a.m. to noon and 4 to 5 p.m. Saturday and Sunday.

The Hunting Island Road also accesses Fripp Island, a private development where vacation homes and villas may be rented. The relaxed vacation pace is obvious, with many people using bikes and golf carts for transportation. The island retains much of its natural beauty along jogging and bike paths, near the marina and 18-hole oceanside golf course.

Pritchard's Island, southeast of Fripp Island, is used mainly by the

University of South Carolina for education and research purposes. The public has limited public access by boat only May through August.

Bluffton and Other Sites

A number of historic sites stand in Beaufort's hinterland, many of them near U.S. Route 17. In Grahamsville, for example, is the 1855 Church of the Holy Trinity, used briefly by General Sherman as a headquarters during his march northward. East of the town off U.S. Route 278 occurred the Civil War Battle of Honey Hill, one of the few Confederate victories in the last months of the war.

The Church of the Cross on Calhoun Street in Bluffton dates from 1857.

Visitors hankering for information on fish and shellfish farming may visit the Waddell Mariculture Center located just off U.S. Route 278 en route to Hilton Head. The center, opened about eight years ago by the state Wildlife and Marine Resources Department, is one of the largest of its type in the nation. It has 35 ponds ranging in size up to 1.5 acres, in which depths and degree of salinity can be controlled, and a number of buildings housing hatcheries, spawning facilities, and laboratories. An hour-long tour, offered two days a week by appointment, covers facilities doing research into all phases of mariculture, from beginning to the growout and harvest phases. For appointments call 803/757-3975; information is available 24 hours a day at 803/837-7174.

Deer and small game hunting is allowed at times on approximately 1,100 of the 1,255 acres at Victoria Bluff Wildlife Management Area, an elongated strip between U.S. Route 278 and the Colleton River near Bluffton. Archery hunting for deer takes place for slightly more than a week in early November and early December. Small-game seasons follow those for this section of the state, except that no hunting is allowed before mid-October and after February 1. The site was acquired by South Carolina in 1978, primarily to preserve "Florida scrub" and wet-depression plant communities.

Pinckney Island National Wildlife Preserve

Pinckney Island National Wildlife Preserve, at the land end of the bridge to Hilton Head Island, occupies about 4,000 acres of typical lowcountry terrain. More than 65 percent of the refuge is salt marsh dominated by cordgrass, marsh elder, black grass, saltgrass, glasswort, sea oxeye, and small tidal hammocks. It also has five large freshwater ponds, forests and brushland and fallow fields.

Five islands and a number of unnamed hammocks are included within the boundaries of the park, whose principal waterways are Port Royal Sound, Skull Creek (part of the Intracoastal Waterway), Mackay Creek, and the Chechesse River. Protected from storms, the refuge is a safe haven for many forms of wildlife. Four species on the endangered list—Southern bald eagle, wood stork, peregrine falcon, and American alligator—are found there, along with deer, raccoon, otter, mink, snakes, turtles, egrets, tricolored (Louisiana) herons, night herons, little blue herons, ibis, and 19 kinds of ducks.

Public use is concentrated on Pinckney Island. A short circular drive crosses a marshy inlet to meander past ponds and through a lowland forest. In addition, the island has more than 14 miles of gravel roads and grassy trails, some dating back to the plantation era, for hiking, bicycling, and wildlife viewing. These visit various habitats, including pine forests, thickets, and ponds. A roundtrip along gravel road and grassy trail to White Point, at the northern tip of the island, covers almost 8 miles. The roundtrip walk to Ibis Pond, the first major feature, is 1.2 miles. Various intermediate trips are possible.

A boat ramp and fishing pier are located on Mackay Creek south of U.S. Route 278. Fishing from boats is permitted. Managed hunts for white-tail deer thin the herds.

Pinckney Island Refuge, established in 1975, stands on ground that was inhabited by prehistoric Indians, but is named for the family that owned it after 1796. Charles Cotesworth Pinckney, son of the first owner, served in the Continental Congress, signed the U.S. Constitution, and was a candidate for president in 1804. His home at White Point, from which he managed a cotton plantation, was destroyed in 1824.

Hilton Head

HILTON HEAD ISLAND IS SHAPED LIKE A HUMAN FOOT, THE TOE POINTING in a southwesterly direction. Some people feel that a well-turned ankle would be a more appropriate symbol, but the island makes the most of the shape and qualities that nature has given it.

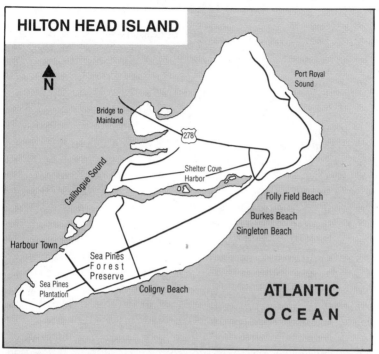

HILTON HEAD ISLAND

N

Bridge to Mainland

278

Calibogue Sound

Shelter Cove Harbor

Port Royal Sound

Folly Field Beach

Burkes Beach

Singleton Beach

Harbour Town

Sea Pines Forest Preserve

Sea Pines Plantation

Coligny Beach

ATLANTIC OCEAN

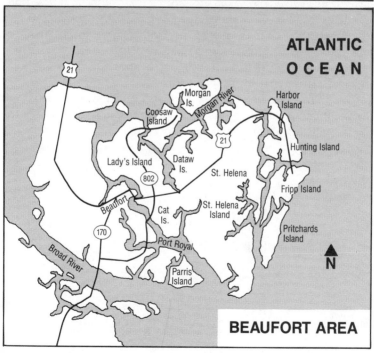

ATLANTIC OCEAN

21

Morgan Is.

Morgan River

Coosaw Island

21

Harbor Island

Hunting Island

Lady's Island

Dataw Is.

St. Helena

Fripp Island

802

Beaufort

Cat Is.

St. Helena Island

Pritchards Island

170

Broad River

Port Royal

N

Parris Island

BEAUFORT AREA

The wide beaches on which its reputation is built are made of shell particles and quartz, reduced to microscopic size, which sparkle at times in the sun. They are packed hard enough to support automobiles—but these are forbidden. The incoming tide is rapid.

Indeed, the resort aspect of the island is readily apparent long before the visitor reaches the beach. A drive along William Hilton Parkway (U.S. Route 278), which extends virtually from one end of the island to the other, is a succession of large signs identifying mammoth beach resort hotels and complexes that include private homes and condos.

The 11 planned resorts and residential communities, for the most part called "plantations" in keeping with the historic agricultural role of the island, are one of the major attractions of Hilton Head whether one patronizes them or not. Some, like Port Royal Plantation, preserve historic names, while others—even some that sound historical—are modern inventions. The major resorts are huge. Sea Pines Plantation, for example, occupies the entire western tip of the 42-square-mile island. It was the first resort developed, in 1956, and is the one most open to casual visitors.

Most residential areas are reserved for residents and guests, but prospective patrons are taken on escorted tours of the facilities. Nonresidents also can view some aspects of the "plantations" en route to restaurants open to the public. Sea Pines, one of the most interesting, issues an inexpensive day pass to all comers because it has numerous commercial establishments on the grounds, as well as a variety of natural and scenic attractions.

Sea Pines' Harbour Town is the oldest resort area on the island. Its yacht basin and shopping mall are dominated by a 96-foot lighthouse, which was built in 1969 to serve as a focal point of the development. Visitors may climb the steel structure with masonry stucco, built to withstand 160-mph storm winds, and look out over the harbor.

South Beach, also part of Sea Pines, was designed to resemble a New England village. Million-dollar yachts, as well as more modest vessels, tie up at a marina noted for its shops. Charter fishing boats and excursion boats also operate from the area. The latter include 1½-hour tours to view the playful dolphins in Calibogue Sound and the soaring osprey and herons and to inspect Harbour Town and Daufuskie Island from the water side.

In all, Hilton Head Island has nine marinas with more than 1,000 slips. Charter boats operate primarily from April through October, fishing the hundreds of miles of inlets and channels around the island and the Gulf Stream, about 60 miles offshore. Catches include cobia, grouper, snapper, bluefish, swordfish, shark, flounder, sea trout, and croaker.

Hilton Head is youthful in atmosphere, as well as appearance. The average age of the residents is in the mid-thirties. Sports is a way of life, if not a passion, among the residents and visitors. More than 20 golf courses accommodate approximately 800,000 rounds of golf each year. Tennis is played at more than 200 grass, clay, and hard courts. Bike riding is another favorite pastime, especially at Sea Pines, where more than 15 miles of paved paths take bikers to almost every part of the plantation and along the hard-packed sand beaches. A large windsurfing school is located at South Beach. Other sports include jogging, kite flying, horeseback riding, swimming, scuba diving, fishing, crabbing, and walking.

The island comes by its fondness for sports naturally. The lobby of the Harbour Town Golf Club at Sea Pines explains one reason golf has become a Hilton Head passion. There, a diorama shows a section of the course of the first golf club in America—the South Carolina Golf Club at Charleston, organized in 1786—with the steeple of St. Michael's Church appropriately in the background. Its minister, the Reverand Henry Purcell, was the club's first president. The MCI Heritage Classic tournament is held annually on the Harbour Town course, and the winner receives a tartan jacket.

Despite the general resort glitter, Hilton Head maintains a strong sense of history. The Indians settled the island perhaps 3,800 years ago. Their presence, and the depredations of pirates, discouraged European settlement in the late 17th century when the British, French, and Spanish were fighting for control of the region between South Carolina and the Spanish stronghold at St. Augustine, Florida. The Spanish visited the island as early as 1521, but Great Britain laid claim after Captain William Hilton marked a good stand of pines on the island on his charts. Sailors afterward commonly referred to the place as Hilton Head.

The island was part of a 1698 grant by the British crown to John Bayley, and was known at that time as Bayley's Barony. The first settler on Trench's Island, as it was later known, was John Barnwell, who arrived in 1717, but the island economy did not blossom until William Elliott planted the first crop of long-stem sea island cotton in 1790, a type that became popular in European markets.

At the outbreak of the Civil War, 24 plantations were producing a variety of valuable commodities — cotton, indigo, sugar, rice, and other crops. The island's strategic location made it an early Union target, and on November 7, 1862, an amphibious operation mounted by a task force of 15 warships and 31 transports and supply vessels landed more than 12,000 troops. They easily overran small Confederate garrisons at Fort Walker on Hilton Head and Fort Beauregard on the mainland. Plantation owners fled to the mainland.

Hilton Head remained in Union hands for the remainder of the war and was the headquarters of the Union Department of the South, commanded by Brigadier General Thomas W. Sherman (sometimes known as the "other" Sherman). It was a key coaling and supply depot for the ships blockading the Confederate coast and an important staging area for amphibious operations against South Carolina and Georgia. At times, as many as 30,000 Union troops were quartered on the island.

The island's plantation economy never recovered from the Civil War hiatus, and much of the land came into the hands of former slaves after the war. Small farms, hunting, and small-scale seafood harvesting sustained them until the island's tall loblolly pines attracted loggers in the 1940s. Hilton Head's modern affluence dates from 1956 when Charles Fraser started constructing the Sea Pines resort community and the state built a bridge to the mainland. Hilton Head was incorporated as a town in 1983 and has a population of about 23,000.

Historic relics are often incorporated into modern development. The late 18th-century ruins of buildings at Stoney-Baynard Plantation, now on the grounds of Sea Pines resort, are a good example of tabby construction. Portions of the walls of the main house and the foundations of the kitchen, a storeroom, and other ancillary buildings remain. An effort is being made to place the ruins on the National Register of Historic Places.

A few Civil War sites are partially preserved. Near the Old Pub Restaurant at Hilton Head Plantation, a concrete walkway and steps lead around and over the preserved earthworks of Fort Mitchell, one of a series of fortifications raised by the Union in 1862. The ruins of Confederate Fort Walker and Union-built Fort Sherman (named for the "other" Sherman) are on the grounds of Port Royal Plantation.

Hilton Head has a kinder, gentler side, too. It is, first of all, better landscaped than nature ever intended; that seems to be one of the benefits of upscale resort development along the sandy barrier islands off the southern Atlantic coast. The resorts are handsomely landscaped with trees, bushes, and flowers, including native palmettos, pines, and magnolias. In addition, a conscious effort has been made to preserve small areas in their natural state. For example, about one-fourth of the land area of Sea Pines is forests, wetlands, and open space. This openness helps sustain a substantial animal population. The Audubon Society counts about 200 species of birds. Blue heron, egrets, white ibis, osprey, and other birds regularly visit the numerous waterways on the grounds of the resorts and planned communities. Alligators are so common that the South Carolina Department of Wildlife and Marine Resources thins here to repopulate less productive areas in state parks and preserves. Bobcat and wild boar have been spotted infrequently; raccoon, deer, otter, and mink are easily seen. Hunting is not permitted, and fines are levied for feeding wildlife.

The largest reserved natural area is Sea Pines' 605-acre forest preserve. There, 7 miles of unpaved paths and boardwalks meander through uplands dominated by live oak and pines and lowlands thick with red maple, black gum, and water lilies. Near the west entrance, a trail crosses a dike constructed in the 18th century to create rice fields (now attractive to wading birds) and passes 200-year-old grape vines. An Indian shell ring, whose purpose is not known, is at least 3,500 years old. The trails also are used for horseback riding. Four ponds are stocked with bream and catfish.

Trails at the Audubon-Newhall Nature Preserve also explore varied terrain, including a pocosin filled with mats of sphagnum moss, sawgrass, maidencane grass, Virginia chainfern, and tupelo. Woods recovering from fires in 1963 and 1971 feature longleaf and pond vines, live oak, Southern magnolia, American holly, mockernut hickory, saw palmetto, Florida scrub, fetterbush, and common bracken and cinnamon ferns. Also present is the unusual Chinese tallowtree whose white seed (resembling popcorn) is favored by woodpeckers and songbirds.

Plants along the trails include elephant's foot, jessamine, lantana, coreopsis, baptissa, prickly locust, hound's ear, sassafras, virgin bower, Cherokee rose, azalea, blackroot, buckthorn, cherry laurel tree, and devil's walkingstick.

Insects and arachnids are thick in the preserve, especially during warm months. These include mosquitos, ticks, golden silk spiders, beetles, and dragonflies.

A 137-acre Whooping Crane Conservancy on the grounds of Hilton Head Plantation has none of the rare birds, but plenty of other birds, small mammals, and reptiles. One-hour bird walks are conducted on Saturdays from September to March. In addition, the

1,500-foot Nancy Cathcart Trail leads to 1,000-foot Beany Newhall Boardwalk through pine flatlands and swamp.

Hilton Head's 12 miles of beaches are naturally an active place for sandpipers, gulls, and terns. Huge loggerhead turtles, an endangered species, can be spotted at numerous places — late at night when they come ashore. Hermit crabs and the delicious blue crab are common. The bottlenose dolphin feed on small fish close inshore during the summer months.

All beach areas are public, even those in front of resorts. However, access is available only at certain points. Public facilities are available at Folly Field Beach, the primary public beach. Burke's Beach is also an interesting study in nature. Other access points are Coligny Beach, the first public-access beach to be developed by Hilton Head (favored by the spring break crowd) and Singleton Beach. Burke's and Singleton beaches are named for the black families that received land on the island as a result of the Civil War.

The Museum of Hilton Head conducts beach walks, usually at Burke's Beach. Docents like Dr. George Skidworthy explain that the beach is blessed by its diversity. It has remnants of the kind of pine forest used for lumbering until resorts began to take over, nuts from live oak trees, and cones from pine trees and saw palmetto.

The live oak is so-named because it is always green; at Hilton Head, the new leaves usually push off the old leaves in March. The live oak tree was important in colonial times to shipbuilders because its long, naturally bent branches were used for the ribs of ships. Live oak damaged in Hurricane Hugo in 1989 are being used to provide new ribs for the *USS Constitution* in Boston. Live oak can survive close to the water because its hard-surfaced leaves keep the sand off. Trees on the seaward side are stunted because the prevailing winds come from the northeast and become permanently bent, in the fashion of the more famous divi-divi trees in Aruba. Underbrush includes greenbrier and wild bamboo.

The beach is an example of tidal action at work. At high tide, low areas are filled with water, which flushes nourishment out of the marsh bed and carries it out into the ocean. The water is deep enough that even dolphins invade the inlets in pursuit of fish at high tide.

Also, a miniature decaying salt-marsh area, which soon may become a swale, and then develop into a lagoon — in effect, turning from saltwater to freshwater — is part of the pattern on the island. According to Dr. Skidworthy, "If you look at the island in cross-section, you can see it's a series of dunes and swales. The high land, low land combination is characteristic of how a barrier island is formed. The sand dune forms, the sand dune blocks off the sea, the marshy area in between turns from a saltwater area to a freshwater area, the dunes extend on out and you get the next line."

Sea oats, a beautiful spire with nice head, give the dunes internal stability by sending a network of roots deep into the sand. The stem catches windblown sand and keeps it piling up on the dunes. The dune in turn protects the land from the sea; it absorbs like a sponge and gives a little when the waves hit it. Among other plants along the beach are camphorweed, which has a yellow flower, and croton, which survives in the sand by having a hairy sort of leaf that keeps the sand away from the moist areas. Salt-tolerant cordgrass can excrete visible amounts of salt that it absorbs as crystals, which are washed away by the next high tide. The black mud seen on the beach results from decayed cordgrass and silt carried down by streams. This rich mud, mixed with oyster shells and spread over the soil, was the fertilizer that produced the sea island cotton on which many lowcountry fortunes were based from colonial days to the Civil War.

Oysters grow in abundance in marshes there. They often occur as beds mixing old oysters—the white shells indicating dead oysters and greenish shells live ones. The water is a murky pea-green color, the result of detritus of salt marsh, plankton, and other microscopic life forms that are food for oysters. An oyster can siphon about 7 gallons of water an hour to obtain nutrition.

Also on the beaches are good examples of shells such as spiral staircase, sharkeye and other snails, horseshoe crab, channeled and lightning whelk, coral, incongruous ark, shark's tooth, baby's ear, and sand dollar (sea urchin).

Hilton Head is in the process of developing public-access parks, and the public beaches ultimately will include parks, restrooms, boardwalk, picnic tables, concessions, and lifeguards. Burke's, a long sloping beach without a strong undertow, is ideal for kids and senior citizens.

The well-balanced mixture of quartz and calcium carbonate at Hilton Head creates what is popularly known as "brown sugar" sand, which packs hard and provides a firm base that is great for walking, jogging, and biking—even horse racing and vehicle racing, if they were allowed (which they are not). Farther south, the whiter sand contains more calcium carbonate; farther north, the sand is coarser because it contains more quartz. Black streaks in the sand result from the iron in cordgrass, not from oil residue or other pollution.

Barrier islands such as Hilton Head are dynamic, not static, displaying a constant contest between the ocean and the land. Burke's Beach is an accreting or building beach, thanks primarily to the protection of Joyner's Bank, a sand spit on the heel of the island. A short distance westward, the Atlantic strikes the beach at a 45-degree angle, moving the sand toward the toe of the island. Consequently, in general the toe is growing and the heel is receding. Consequently, a beach replenishment program is maintained.

Daufuskie Island

Daufuskie Island, across Calibogue Sound from Hilton Head, is reminiscent of the way Hilton Head was 35 years ago. Boats provide the only access to the island, which has been inhabited for more than 200 years. The "gullah" dialect that developed in the region still can be heard among the approximately 90 permanent residents, most of them black. Houses are dispersed along dirt roads, which for the most part are bordered by forests of lowland vegetation such as live oak. Traditionally, the economy was based on farming and seafood harvesting, but tourism is increasingly making an impact. Electricity reached the island in the mid-1950s and telephone service was added in 1971.

The largest wild animal on the island is the stunted white-tail deer common to this coastal area. It is regarded as a subspecies and seldom exceeds 100 pounds. Herds as large as 25 have been seen on Daufuskie, although hunting in season is permitted. Other animals include rabbits, squirrels, raccoon, and opossum.

The first imprint of resort development is being made by Haig Point and Melrose. Boats make regular runs between Haig Point's handsome dock and Hilton Head. These developers own about 70 percent of the island.

Daufuskie — according to one source, the name results from being "de first key" after the entrance to the Savannah River, but others claim it is an Indian word — also can be visited on a half-day outing from Palmetto Bay Marina or Harbour Town Marina March through November. The *Daufuskie Queen* and the *Vagabond* cruise down the Broad River — whose shore is lined with beautiful homes — then head straight across Calibogue Sound for small (3 by 5 miles square) Daufuskie Island. Along the way, porpoises play and pelicans cautiously rise as the boat creates turbulence in the water. A commentary points out significant places and the history of the area.

On Daufuskie, a guided bus tour covers the simple, rustic way of life and history of the people and includes examples of the unique "gullah" language and explanation of "haints" or "hags" (spirits). The drive along roads bordered by loblolly pine, live oak, sweetgum, and Carolina jessamine passes the 1884 Union Baptist Church, which still has straight-back, handmade pews; a late 19th-century winery, no longer functioning; Bloody Point, the scene of two battles between Indians and settlers; a small post office; and a two-room school, where students may come on board to sell items that raise money for their activities. The tour skirts the two developments already underway before making a 15-minute stop on broad, hard-sand Front Beach to allow time for walking and hunting for sand dollars, which are plentiful at times, and other shells. Before visitors reboard the boat to return to Hilton Head, they have an opportunity to taste homemade deviled crab prepared the "gullah" way.

Turtle Island, southwest of Daufuskie and touched by the Intracoastal Waterway, has about 1,700 acres of marshland, maritime forest, and beaches. It is a game-management area, where waterfowl hunting is allowed before noon on Wednesday and Saturday mornings in season. Access is by boat only. The site was donated to the state by Union Camp Corporation.

Savannah National Wildlife Refuge

This 25,600-acre refuge, created in 1927, stretches out along the Savannah River a few miles south of Hardeeville and 13 miles north of Savannah. It straddles the South Carolina-Georgia border, but most of it is located in South Carolina.

About half the Savannah National Wildlife Refuge is hardwood bottomlands, but the tract also encompasses significant tidal streams and freshwater marshes. To sustain waterfowl, the water levels of about 3,000 acres of impoundments made by former rice plantations are manipulated by gated culverts of the very efficient kind dating back to the 1700s and a modern diversion canal. The refuge also is populated by alligators up to 12 feet in length, deer, feral hogs, otters, butterflies, reptiles, and 260 species of birds, including rare swallowtail kite and bald eagle, as well as wood stork, herons, ibis, purple gallinule, common moorhen, red-winged blackbird, and bobolink.

Much of the refuge is accessible only by boat. From the Millstone, Beck's Ferry, Abercorn, and Front River landings (the last is adjacent to U.S. Route 17) on the Savannah River, canoeists may explore tidal creeks bordered by bottomland hardwood forests. Freshwater canals and pools attract fishers from mid-March to late October; tidal creeks are active from February 1 to late October. A few areas can be visited by land. The refuge's 39 miles of rice dikes provide an insight into the coastal plantation economy that existed in the 19th century, but now are primarily observation points for nature viewing. Unless posted, all the dikes are open to hiking and biking during daylight hours. In addition, the Tupelo Swamp Walk, which starts 2 miles north of U.S. Route 17, borders a major paddy and skirts Vernezobre Creek. Certain areas are closed November through mid-March to protect wintering waterfowl.

The easiest way to experience the refuge is the circular 4-mile Laurel Hill Wildlife Drive. It starts at the live oak-shaded visitor contact point on U.S. Route 17 and winds along dikes and across wooded hammocks. As the trail moves south to the edge of the property, then turns north and wends its way back to Route 17, it provides clear views of many aspects of the refuge. These include numerous dikes perpendicular to the drive; gated water-control culverts; large stands of cypress and tupelo, as well as mulberry, hackberry, cherry laurel, and greenbrier; ponds coated with water lilies or bordered by a profuse bush and wildflower growth; a VORTAC station, a navigational guide for aircraft; industrial plants in the distance on the other side of the Front River, an arm of the Savannah; an access road to Fife Plantation (private); and a 5.5-mile diversion canal dug by the U.S. Army Corps of Engineers to preserve a freshwater habitat for wildfowl and wading birds. The canal is also a popular fishing spot.

A narrated tour of the drive operates from Savannah (912/233-7770). Laurel Hill Drive also may be used by hikers and bikers, who will have more time to appreciate the profusion of wildflowers and details of the management of the site.

The Cistern boardwalk and trail loop on Recess Island, which begins at an old brick cistern in a maritime forest, skirts a marsh and provides a quick look at the terrain and life forms, including numerous migratory songbirds in spring and fall. Principal features are identified on interpretive signs.

Managed hunts for deer, feral hogs, and squirrel are conducted in autumn and winter.

Other Border Features

The Houlihan drawbridge across the Savannah River on U.S. Route 17, constructed in 1925, was the first fixed crossing of the river.

Tiny Tybee Island National Wildlife Refuge, not open to the public except for use of offshore waters, was established in 1933 as a sanctuary for wildfowl that nest and feed on the beaches at low tide. The endangered brown pelican, herons, egrets, cormorants, and gulls are among them. The stable sections of the 100-acre island, partly created by sand dumping by the Corps of Engineers, are covered with eastern red cedar, wax myrtle, and groundsel thickets. Currents near the island are sometimes tricky. This island at the mouth of the Savannah River is managed by the Savannah National Wildlife Refuge.

These traits of southern South Carolina provide a good introduction to the natural wealth, much of it unspoiled, of the Georgia coastline.

PART FOUR

Georgia

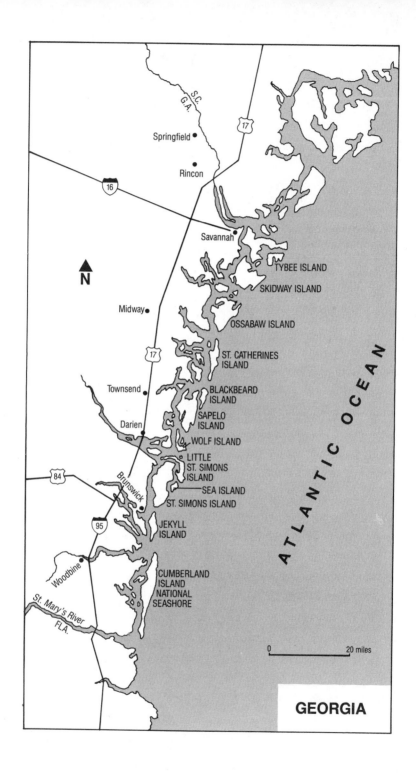

S.C.
G.A.

17

Springfield

Rincon

16

Savannah

TYBEE ISLAND

SKIDWAY ISLAND

N

Midway

OSSABAW ISLAND

17

ST. CATHERINES
ISLAND

Townsend

BLACKBEARD
ISLAND

Darien

SAPELO
ISLAND

WOLF ISLAND

84

LITTLE
ST. SIMONS
ISLAND

Brunswick

SEA ISLAND

ST. SIMONS ISLAND

95

JEKYLL
ISLAND

Woodbine

CUMBERLAND
ISLAND
NATIONAL
SEASHORE

St. Mary's River
FLA.

0   20 miles

ATLANTIC OCEAN

GEORGIA

Georgia's Colonial Coast

LONDON ADVOCATES OF AMERICAN COLONIAL SETTLEMENT IN THE 17TH and 18th centuries were not noted for their modesty. Promoters claimed the beaches at Jamestown, Virginia, the first permanent colony, were strewn with semi-precious stones. They lied. A century later, handbills circulating in London lauded the Georgia coastline and its barrier islands as a "future Eden." Attaining such lofty status would require more time than the handbills indicated.

Born of the colonizing fervor of 17th- and 18th-century Europe, Georgia was the last of the British outposts along the Southeast Coast. In 1721, provincial forces from South Carolina built a fort on the Savannah River to serve as a barrier against Spanish and French incursions. In 1733, Britain formalized its claim by founding the colony of Georgia, both as a buffer and an escape valve for the increasing numbers of unemployed and debtors in Great Britain. It was also hoped the land could produce silk, spices, and wine.

The soil was rich enough but wealth lay in other directions and was some time in coming. The cultivation of rice and the discovery of sea island cotton finally turned the region into one of the richest of the English colonies.

Human life may have reached the area 10,000 or so years ago; sites as old as 4,500 years of age have been identified. Tribes of the Creek nation were spotted throughout the region when the first whites arrived. The first Native Americans encountered were the Guale. Some believe the Vikings were the first Europeans in the area, but the French and Spanish have a documented claim. A French artist who visited the area in the 1500s depicted the Indians as hunters, fishers, farmers, and foragers who lived in small mud and wattle huts. Among the animals they hunted were alligators, which they killed by driving pointed poles down their throats, then turning them over and finishing them off with arrows, spears, and clubs. They planted gardens of beans, squash, and corn. They traveled the numerous waterways of the area in dugout boats.

French colonists, headed by Jean Ribault, described the Georgia coast as "the fairest, fruitfullest and pleasantest in all the world," but they settled just across the border in Florida, where they came to grief. Though disappointed by the absence of gold, the Spanish were the first Europeans to stay. In 1540, Hernando deSoto passed through Georgia on his epic westward journey; four years later, the Spanish began establishing a chain of small forts and missions on the islands, but did not attempt to colonize the area in large numbers. They called the area Guale, after the Indian inhabitants.

The site of Santa Catalina de Guale, one of the oldest missions in the region, may have been identified by recent excavations on St. Catherines Island by archaeologists from the Museum of Natural History in New York. An Indian uprising in 1597 ended with many priests' severed heads being impaled on stakes at prominent points as a warning. Nevertheless, some Spanish missions operated until 1702. Increasing pressure from other Indian tribes in South Carolina made the Guale abandon the area in the late 17th century.

The British put down permanent roots when 125 hopefuls led by General James Oglethorpe founded Savannah on a bluff about 20 miles from the mouth of the Savannah River. The new colony was a social and business venture, organized by an assortment of trustees who were either philanthropists or investors. From the beginning, the Georgia colony was a ray of hope for the destitute and the oppressed from many places in Europe, especially debtors from English prisons and religious dissenters from Britain and the continent. In addition, a small group of Jewish families, including Dr. Samuel Nunis, arrived on their own ship without the knowledge of the trustees. Nunis's arrival was timely; the colony's only doctor had died of the fever then infesting the settlement. Nunis's dedicated treatment of the patients persuaded Oglethorpe to ignore orders to send the unauthorized families back to England.

Oglethorpe quickly began to create small fortified settlements as far south as Cumberland Island, which were expected more to sound an alarm than to deter an advance of Spanish military forces. On a trip to Europe, Oglethorpe enlisted a polyglot army of a few hundred men to serve as a core for defending the colony. He also made a point of cultivating good relations with the Indians, but the ability of the English colony to survive a Spanish assault remained in doubt. The issue was resolved in 1742 when a Spanish invasion force was defeated at the Battle of Bloody Marsh. (A more detailed account of this battle is related in the section on St. Simons Island.)

In the colony's formative years, Oglethorpe ruled supreme as the representative of the trustees. His retirement to England was followed by limited self-rule for the colony, formalized in 1751 by the creation of a colonial assembly. This brief period of semi-independent government created an atmosphere that made more difficult the transition to crown control in 1752. From the start, the legislature and the king's first appointed governor, John Reynolds, a harsh, dictatorial former sea captain, were in conflict. The legislature even rejected his proposal to raise units to fight in the French and Indian War. The popularity of Reynolds's successors depended largely on their attitude toward local sensibilities. Nevertheless, this royal era witnessed substantial new immigration and the foundation of the great plantations.

Time after time, the Georgia coast has been assaulted and ravaged. During the Revolutionary War, the British attacked coastal settlements, especially ports supplying the new country. During the Civil War, many of the islands were occupied and used as Union bases to attack the Confederate mainland. However, Fort Pulaski and others designed to protect Savannah and other coastal points remained in Confederate hands until late in the war when General Sherman burned his way to the sea at Savannah. Later, he wanted to give land confiscated from Confederates to freed slaves and to turn the coastal islands from Charleston, South Carolina, to the St. John's River in Florida into an independent state for freed slaves. St. Catherines Island was to be the "capital." Congress, however, disapproved Sherman's directive.

Through all of this, Georgia coasters have exhibited an appealing mixture of lustiness and gentility. The wilderness bent people that way, just as Indians bent saplings to mark their trails, and the hardiness of plantation living and seafaring kept them that way. The sharp angles of lowcountry architecture virtually ooze with vigor, while the curves of Greek-Revival and Georgian houses project refinement — both produced, sometimes at different periods of their careers, by persistent planters and shrewd traders whose symbiosis created viable communities and sired poet Sidney Lanier's rhapsodic appreciation of the rhythms of nature. These men did not alter the land as much as they thought; British actress Fanny Kemble, married to an antebellum Georgia planter on St. Simons Island, marveled at the "fairy tale" scenery around her.

Antebellum Georgia, led by Savannah's openness to the world, struggled to recover from the ravages of the Civil War. The city's freewheeling style and ready access to a farming hinterland whose growing season included about 300 frost-free days, helped make Georgia cotton, tobacco, and naval stores important again and facilitated a turn to new crops like pecans, peaches, peanuts, and apples. Editor Henry W. Grady of Atlanta became a spokesman for the revived state, even lauding Abraham Lincoln in 1886 as the "first typical American." After World War II, an industrialization policy revived the port of Savannah and created new industries. Tourism has become one of the state's largest industries.

Despite its colorful history, the Georgia coast may be better known for its physical attributes—a combination of rivers, sand ridges, wooded uplands, estuaries, sounds, tidal marshes, and barrier islands. The coast extends 120 miles as the crow flies, but has more than 800 miles of shoreline. It is exceptionally dynamic, even for the volatile East Coast.

The geographical coastal plain is deeper than the psychological and historical coastal region—the "wide, silent spaces" observed by conservationist Rachel Carson. While the fall line reaches as far inland as Augusta, founded by Oglethorpe himself 150 miles up the Savannah River only a few years after he started Savannah, much of this land generally is not regarded as being coastal in nature, appearance, or attitude. Historically, the coastal region never extended far inland, either. In his bicentennial history of the state, Howard H. Martin explains this mental dichotomy thus: Augusta quickly became "more Carolina than Georgia in its orientation as the Charleston traders flocked there to barter with the Indians."

The Altamaha and Savannah, the state's most significant rivers, originate in the Appalachian Mountains and scour sediment from the rich Piedmont region, which they deposit along the way and in deltas at their mouths.

The Altamaha, formed by the union of the Ocmulgee and Oconee rivers about 140 miles from the coast, is one of the most important ecosystems in the southeastern region. No dams block its largely unimpeded flow through pine and hardwood forests and past river islands and cypress swamps. It is rich in wildlife. The river's flood plain is 3 to 12 miles wide; its delta is a major ecological feature. The tidal influence extends about 40 miles inland. Two-thirds of the state's shad come from this river, and eel are netted in commercial quantities. The Altamaha has been an important commercial stream throughout modern history, especially to the rice plantations near its mouth and to the logging industry that made Darien an important port. Lumbering has gone on since the early 1800s, but the construction of railroads after the Civil War reduced the commercial value of the river. At various times since then, proposed electric power plants, flood-control schemes, barges, and water-use plans have threatened to interrupt the free flow of the Altamaha River, but so far have not been successful.

The Savannah, likewise an alluvial river, forms the boundary between Georgia and South Carolina. Browned by the sediments it carries, it is bordered at different places by both bottomland and high bluffs, but has been considerably altered over the years by construction of dams and development of sizable factories. Eighteenth-century naturalist William Bartram described the river's soothing vistas, many of which today are restricted by limited accessibility. In a general way, this appealing landscape forms a dividing line between more northern animals and plants and more southern ones, although a few Deep South species such as the saw palmetto, Ogeechee tupelo, and gopher tortoise have breached the line.

The Ogeechee River extends inland about 245 miles. This length allows different characteristics at various sections of the stream. The twisted coastal portion, meandering past bluffs and sandbars and sometimes widening to lake-like proportions, supports an extensive birdlife, large variety of insects, and abundant flora, including the Ogeechee lime tree. A major Indian trail crossed the river at the time the Georgia colony was established. Later, General Oglethorpe built small Fort Argyle, whose site is now on the grounds of Fort Stewart.

Blackwater rivers such as the 260-mile Satilla and the 125-mile-long St. Marys originate in the coastal plain and are colored by a high level of organic deposits leached from neighboring land and lowland areas. The tea color of the surface is even darker at greater depths. Sand scoured by these rivers may collect in sandbars. Small tidal rivers such as the Jerico, Crooked, and Medway are mostly inlets, except in periods of heavy rainfall. In these rivers, the water is salty at the mouth and becomes less brackish farther upstream. The exchange of fresh and salt water is complicated and varying, but productive.

Boating is not as popular on Georgia's rivers as it is on some others in the region, but the streams and many of their tributaries have their advocates. For example, motorboating dominates the section of the St. Marys east of U.S. Route 301. Motorboaters should be alert to changes in water depths and obstacles such as trees and other vegetation toppled from riverbanks; curves where they may collect can be especially dangerous. That also is good advice for canoeists, who also should be aware that normally placid-looking steamflows can be deceptive, especially after heavy rains in winter and early spring and because of tidal conditions near river mouths. In addition, multiple channels can develop.

Canoeists may explore deep into the wilderness along all the rivers and many of their tributaries, such as Briar Creek off the Savannah River and the Oconee River, which empties into the Altamaha. The streams seem designed to be divided into convenient one- and two-day segments of 10 to 15 miles or 30 to 35 miles. Forests are thicker the farther upstream one goes. The Altamaha has limited access, with Doctortown near U.S. Route 85/25 and Bethlehem Church convenient inland starting places. The river is most diverse in the delta area, where Lewis Island has one of the state's largest virgin stands of bald cypress. Ebenezer Creek, only an hour's drive from Savannah and usuable year-round, has been designated a wild and scenic river by the Georgia legislature; the section between highways 119 and 21 passes some of the high bluffs along the stream. The Savannah River still seems relatively wild at places below Augusta, and can be a delightful challenge near the coast where it is broad and strong. The Savannah National Wildlife Refuge has a number of places accessible only by boat. Another good put-in place is Tuckassee King Landing near the historic church. The St. Marys River is most scenic west of U.S. 301, where the banks are lined with bald cypress and tupelo tinseled with Spanish moss. Suitable primitive camping sites can be found, but canoers should obtain permission before using private land.

The material transported to the coast by the rivers is continually reworked by wind and wave actions. The concave shape of the coastline between Cape Hatteras and central Florida creates unusual conditions. The tidal surge builds in height as it rolls up the continental shelf. Tides thus are lower (averaging 3 feet) at the ends and increase at depth at the center, averaging 7 to 8 feet on the Georgia coast. They break on the beaches at an angle, depositing or moving grains of sand up the beaches and then back on the receding wave. Storms, predominantly from the northeast in the winter, sculpt the region in a north-to-south direction. Hurricanes may quickly alter this normal pattern and effect changes that might otherwise require years of steady normal activity.

Sand ridges are important coastal structures, in part because they protect the land against natural violence. In addition, the ancient Trail Ridge blocks the natural drainage in the southeastern corner of the state and is in part responsible for one of the region's most unique features, the Okefenokee Swamp. The Suwannee River drains part of the swamp southwestward, instead of to the Atlantic. Tannin from the swamp gives the Suwannee a brownish color. That from other sources does much the same thing to the Satilla and St. Marys rivers, which do flow to the Atlantic coast.

Georgia has about 5.2 million acres of wetlands, 90 percent of them in the coastal region. But that is considerably less than the 6.8 million acres it had in 1790. In recent years, the state has been losing an additional estimated 7,300 acres per year. Even more deleterious is the damage caused by pollution, sedimentation, intensive timber cutting, and falling groundwater tables. Pollution of streams is more a periodic than a chronic problem. Since the 1960s, attention has increasingly focused on the situation. However, the murkiness of coastal waters is more likely to result from rich sediments than pollution.

A band of salt marshes extends the 120-mile length of the Georgia coast, from Tybee Island in the north to Cumberland Island near the Florida border. It varies in width, measuring about 10 miles at Tybee Island and narrowing as it moves southward. "Bald spots" or barren sand flats high in salt content sometimes occur in the higher marsh elevations. The nearly 475,000 acres of salt marsh in Georgia account for a third of all such marshes on the East Coast. The salt marshes and intertidal creeks are incredibly rich and productive. For example, an acre of cordgrass produces about 17.8 tons of biomass each year.

The marshes make a commercial impact in several ways. They are a nursery for fish and shellfish, supporting both an extensive sportfishing habit and a multimillion dollar commercial seafood industry. Nearby waters also receive from the marshes nutrients that are consumed by a variety of species. Coastal waters team with "spat" or embryo oysters that attach to any suitable surface. More than 30,000 acres of bottom are dedicated to oysters, including public areas set aside by each coastal county. Blue crab also are taken commercially and individually. The more than 9 million pounds harvested annually are the state's second most important seafood crop.

In addition, the marshes deter human use of the coastline and serve as a treatment facility for the effects of human activities. Famous systems, such as the Marshes of Glynn, praised in verse as "nothing-withholding" and magnificent at sunset, attract tourists and birdwatchers because of their natural beauty and substantial and varied aviary, including the endangered wood stork. The salt marshes on Sapelo and Cumberland islands and at Fort Pulaski also are easy to inspect—the latter even casually from highways. Others can be approached with varying degrees of difficulty.

Georgia was among the first states to enact laws limiting encroachment on its vital marshes, beaches, and dunes and conducts an active program of research and inspections. While some sections of the Georgia coastline are fully developed, others remain virtually pristine. Future development is being controlled.

The barrier islands that extend the length of the state—the Golden Isles—are the most notable feature of the Georgia coastal region. Thirteen major coastal islands and numerous smaller ones hug the coastline—more than any other state. Like other such islands, they are constantly changing form—eroding at one end and building up at the other. They have been forming for about 40,000 years. Sapelo, St. Simons, and parts of Jekyll and Cumberland islands are the oldest— an estimated 25,000 to 35,000 years old. Tybee, Wassaw, Blackbeard, and Sea islands are younger, some of them barely 5,000 years old. Williamson Island has appeared above water since World War II and now measures approximately 250 acres. It is still forming. In other places, sedimentation has turned some piles of ballast discarded in recent centuries by sailing vessels into small river islands.

The barrier islands have both fresh and brackish ponds that host migratory and wintering waterfowl, herons, and egrets and provide a habitat for frogs, small fish, and grass shrimp. The best examples are found on Little St. Simons Island, the northern end of Cumberland Island, and the interiors of Wassaw and Blackbeard islands.

The Georgia islands more or less share a common history with other islands north and south of them, but each has a character of its own. The oldest islands have well-developed soil. Some, like Sea Island, harbor prestigious resort areas; others, like wild Blackbeard Island, are more or less left to the vagaries of nature. St. Simons is most noted for its historical impact on the fate of the British colonies, and thus what is now the United States.

Shifting sandbars build up at tidal inlets and often develop parallel to the beaches. Terns and skimmers use them for nesting between March and July. Those that extend above water at low tide are attractive sources of shells; however, visitors should preplan a means of escape because the tides are strong and the currents tricky. Unseen sandbars pose a problem at times for boaters.

There is a direct relationship between the sandbars and the onshore dunes that protect the barrier islands. Sand moves from the beaches and dunes to the sandbars during winter storms and is gradually washed back ashore during calmer periods. The most extensive dunes are located at Nannygoat Beach on Sapelo, Cumberland Island, and the South Beach area of Jekyll Island.

The Continental Shelf slopes gradually eastward to a depth of about 300 feet about 70 miles offshore.

Vegetation is abundant throughout the region—and has a certain wild quality, especially on the Wassaw Island National Wildlife Refuge and Cumberland Island National Seashore. Forests are well developed on most Georgia islands and the mainland. Among the species growing there, sometimes hung with Spanish moss, muscadine grape, and resurrection fern, are live oak, cypress, tupelo, cabbage and saw palmettos, Southern magnolia, redbay, holly, white and laurel oak, American beech, dogwood, holly, pignut hickory, witch hazel, pawpaw, American elm, red maple, and sparkleberry. Six species of pine—slash, spruce, loblolly, pond, longleaf, and shortleaf—are native to the area. In logging zones, the fast-growing slash pine is replacing varied forests. Undergrowth frequently includes wild azalea and plants such as blueberry and hackleberry. Dunes are held together by the roots of sea oats, sandspur, pennywort, wax myrtle, and broomsedge.

Nearly 70 species of plants on either federal or state protection lists grow in Georgia, most of them in the coastal region, including two varieties of trillium, yellow flytrap, six kinds of pitcher plants, plumleaf azalea, four varieties of sedge, two kinds of quillwort, harperella, Oglethorpe oak, and Michaux sumac.

Logging is a major industry in the coastal area today—just as it has been throughout the state's history. (Lumber is a leading export of the port of Savannah.) However, Georgia also is a leader in reforestation, restoring more than 2.5 million acres of forests since the 1920s.

Marine species—everything from sharks to delicious blue crab—are significant in the offshore ecosystem. Playful bottlenose dolphin swim alongside boats traversing some of the waterways. The large right whale, an endangered species, migrates into these waters during the winter months. Five species of sea turtles—loggerhead, leatherback, Kemp's ridley, hawksbill, and green—frequent Georgia's offshore waters. In some instances, laws limit beachfront lights so newly hatched turtles can identify the horizon and move toward it. Ghost crab burrow in the sand.

The West Indian manatee (*trichechus manatus*), an endangered species, is seen occasionally. It is most often spotted between Sapelo Island and Cumberland Sound from May through October. A subspecies, the Florida manatee, also appears from time to time. These gentle giants normally grow to about 10 feet long and weigh 1,000 to 2,000 pounds, but may be larger. They are vegetarians and, in this area, may eat as much as 100 pounds of cordgrass daily. They are slow swimmers, but have a surprising range. Studies show they may swim hundreds of miles in a single summer, making several trips between Georgia and southern Florida.

Their 2- to 6-mph speed makes them vulnerable to the steel propellers of speedboats and the size and weight of barges and larger boats. Many are killed annually in this manner. Although federal law prohibits touching or approaching them, scuba divers and boats may wait for the ponderous mammals to approach them.

Throughout the region, terns, gulls, and shorebirds in large numbers share the sustenance of beaches at low tides. Osprey and bald eagle wheel overhead; also present are parula and yellow-throated warblers and painted bunting. Counts in recent years have turned up the rare rufous and black-chinned hummingbirds, as well as the more common ruby-throated variety.

Four islands are regarded as having their own animal subspecies — the Blackbeard Island deer, Sapelo Island raccoon, Cumberland Island pocket gopher, and the Anastasia Island cotton mouse. Among more than 30 protected animals in the region are the American alligator, five kinds of whales, ivory-billed woodpecker, Southern bald eagle, American and Arctic peregrine falcons, piping plover, red-cockaded woodpecker, and wood stork.

Hunting

An abundance of game animals makes hunting a popular sport. White-tailed deer thrive in the extensive forests, as do squirrels, raccoon, rabbits, and even feral hogs. Georgia is fourth in the number of deer shot per year — about 325,000 from a herd estimated to be in excess of 1.1 million statewide — and a large percentage of these are coastal animals.

Seasons for bow and gun hunts vary somewhat from region to region, even county to county. Dogs may be used in some instances. Generally in the coastal area, the seasons are as follows: deer, bucks may be taken late October to mid-January, and either sex late

November and late December (seasonal limit is five); feral hogs, during deer hunts on public lands, no season on private lands; bobcat, early December to mid-February; rabbits, mid-November to late-February; squirrels, mid-August to end of February; raccoon, mid-October to late November; fox, first of December to middle of February; and opossum, mid-October to mid-February. There is limited bear hunting in some areas near the coast, generally in late September–early October.

Patient coastal hunters bag their share of the 45,000 wild turkey taken from late March through mid-May each year across the state by up to 93,000 hunters. The eastern wild turkey (*meleagris gallopavo silvestris*), a native of North America, existed in large numbers when the first Europeans arrived and was an important element in the diet of Native Americans. It also became a staple on the tables of the first colonists in Georgia, as it was in other colonies. Despite its uncanny ability to detect anything unusual in the surrounding terrain, by the early 1900s the numbers had shrunk to an estimated 30,000 in the United States. Conservation measures, including relocation, have facilitated a remarkable comeback, with an estimated 350,000 gobblers now roosting in Georgia alone.

Other game birds include ducks (late November–early December and mid-December–early January); sea ducks (late November–early January); Canada geese (two four-day periods in January); doves (late September–late October, late November–early December and mid-December–mid-January); quail (mid-November–end of February); coots (late November–early December and mid-December–early January); woodcock (late November–mid-January); common snipe (mid-November–end of February); gallinules (late November–early December and mid-December–early January); rails (late September–early December); quail (mid-November–end of February); and grouse (mid-October–end of February).

The state has initiated a program named Preservation 2000, which will over time add 100,000 acres of land to those dedicated to wildlife, natural areas, and parks. At least three-quarters of these lands should be available for hunting and fishing under original guidelines.

Fishing

Saltwater fishing, both a major commercial enterprise and a popular sport, has more than tripled in the last decade. Shrimping is a major seafood industry. Shrimp boats also harvest whelk when shrimping is slow; about 670,000 pounds of whelk meat, which often ends up as "fritters" on restaurant menus, was taken in 1990.

More than 200,000 sports anglers make in excess of 750,000 fishing trips annually. Inshore and offshore sportfishing is practiced year-round, but the main season extends from spring, when bluefish, king and Spanish mackerel, and cobia begin showing up, through late autumn. Autumn usually is best for catching red drum and black drum. Largemouth bass is another important species. Spotted sea trout, a good fighter on a light line, is a coastal favorite. Other catches include amberjack, barracuda, dolphin, sailfish, tuna, black sea bass, red and vermillion snapper, grouper, sheepshead, weakfish, and red drum. Sharks, now considered a gamefish by some, range from 2 to 4 feet in length inshore and 6 to 12 feet offshore. Even in February, fishing with fiddler crab bait attracts black sea bass and sheepshead. Live shrimp or pieces of shrimp or squid also are used as bait. Many experienced fishers avoid days around a full moon and after storms because the water is usually muddy; they claim the most successful days are those with tides of less than 8 feet.

Seasons are in effect for some species, such as bluefish, cobia, tarpon, and amberjack. Georgia does not require a saltwater fishing license, but imposes minimum length restrictions and catch limits on some kinds of fish.

Gray's Reef, 17.5 miles off Sapelo Island and about 60 nautical miles west of the Gulf Stream, is a natural 17-square-mile underwater phenomenon also known as Sapelo Live Bottom. There, about 65 feet below the surface, a generally sandy ocean floor is broken by patches of limestone outcroppings and ledges up to 8 feet high. The transitional character of the reef gives it both resident and migratory fish populations. Among the recreational fish are snapper, grouper, king mackerel, bluefish, black sea bass, porgy, sheepshead, and cobia. Mixing with these are numerous tropical reef fish such as cardinalfish and angelfish. Amberjack and barracuda also are present. Eels hide in caves and crevasses and loggerhead turtles use the reef year-round. Trapping and collecting are prohibited.

Named for Dr. Milton B. Gray, the marine scientist who discovered it about 25 years ago, it was designated a national marine sanctuary in 1980. The wonderland of underwater shapes and life also attracts divers and photographers, as well as scientists who study such subjects as the effects of weather on marine life.

The state is engaged in a major program to create underwater barriers as a long-term aid to sportfishing and scuba diving. Since the

1930s, periodic dumping of old cars, refrigerators, and similar objects has improved fishing conditions off the coast. In October 1990, Georgia sank the 80-foot ferry/deck barge *Modena* about 7 nautical miles off Blackbeard Island. Next, the state sank other ships and dumped concrete rubble from Reidsville Women's Prison and demolished bridges, worn-out tires, and fiberglass boat molds at this and other sites.

Eight of 14 planned artificial reefs have been formed 7 to 23 miles off the coast between the Savannah River delta and Cumberland Island. Four of the first reefs, each covering about 4 square miles, are located off Cumberland and Jekyll islands. Seven nearshore reefs that avoid shrimp beds but are readily accessible to 16- to 20-foot boats are part of the program. The reefs are marked by yellow or orange-and-white buoys with 6-foot towers and radar reflectors.

The project is funded by the Sportfish Restoration Program, a federal project financed by taxes on fishing equipment and motorboat fuels. The Georgia Department of Natural Resources (GDNR) provides brochures giving map coordinates of the reefs and showing general areas where various kinds of materials were sunk.

Piers and other facilities for non-boating saltwater fishers are sprinkled along the coastline. Of 27 listed on a recent GDNR brochure, eight are in the Savannah area, two are near Darien, and eight are in the Brunswick area.

Nature plays tricks on the unwary. During late fall and winter, the mildness of the climate can be deceiving, especially on the water where spray and wind can create chills. Storms with rain and high winds may come up suddenly on the water.

Biking

Bicycling is comfortable in the Georgia coastal region most of the year, the terrain is handsome and easy, and many natural and historic sites are nearby. Major roads have heavy volumes of traffic but byroads are often lightly traveled. Accommodations, ranging from lodges and cottages at Georgia's state parks to primitive tent and platform campsites, are plentiful.

A network of designated trails criss-crosses the state. For example, the Savannah River run begins at Dillard in the Piedmont region and runs 272 miles down the Savannah River Valley, past Toccoa Falls, three lakes created by the U.S. Corps of Engineers, and a number of state parks to Savannah. The 112-mile Coastal Route starts in Savannah and utilizes for the most part heavily traveled U.S. Route 17 to the Florida border near Kingsland. Short detours visit many islands and historic sites. The cross-state Southern Crossing route passes the Okefenokee Swamp en route to Brunswick.

A trail map that includes information on accommodations is distributed by the Georgia Tourism Division.

General

In the wilderness areas of coastal Georgia, danger is never very far away. Alligators are present wherever water exists, even in some of the ponds of residential communities. Though usually shy, they should always be given a wide berth. Six species of poisonous snakes are present, too, including the eastern diamondback rattlesnake and the cottonmouth, but not in large numbers. Only two of them are normally found on the barrier islands.

Swarms of insects, especially mosquitos, are prevalent, and chiggers and ticks lurk in high grass and heavily wooded areas. The former may be present all year, but are most prevalent during the hottest months. Ticks and chiggers normally are a problem from April through October.

The Bartram Trail has been mapped out to commemorate, and partly trace, the routes of naturalist William Bartram in the 1760s and 1770s. Savannah was a base for trips to areas in Georgia and nearby states, largely using paths already made by Indians or colonists. The trail begins in Charleston, South Carolina, where Bartram landed by boat, and traverses coastal Georgia and the Gulf states. A Georgia coastal auto route begins on state Route 21 at Rincon northwest of Savannah and follows state Routes 21, 275, 307, and 308 to Clyo, Georgia 119 to Tuckassee King Landing, then to Savannah, where it generally follows U.S. Route 17, with diversions as desired to Kings Ferry Park, Sunbury, Midway, Colonels Island, LeConte-Woodmanston Plantation and other sites, to Kingsland. It can be shortened by beginning in Savannah. The Bartram Trail Conference, c/o Elliott O. Edwards, Jr., 431 East 63rd Street, Savannah, GA 31405 (912/354-5014) provides maps.

Bartram accompanied his father to Georgia in 1765 to collect specimens for botanical gardens in England and colonial America. He discovered the *Franklinia alatamaha,* a flowering shrub no longer growing wild, and named it after his friend, Benjamin Franklin. The *Franklinia* is grown successfully by nurseries, thanks to the seeds collected by Bartram. He also discovered the Georgia fever tree, which still grows wild along creek banks. Bartram returned to Georgia in 1773 for a four-year horseback trip through the Southeast and Gulf states, which provided material for one of the earliest books about the southeastern environment.

Savannah
Poetry of Nature

Savannah Area Convention & Visitors Bureau
222 West Oglethorpe Avenue
Savannah, GA 31499
912/944-0456 or 800/444-2427

SAVANNAH IS THE SUBSTANCE THAT POEMS ARE MADE OF, THE LYRICISM of nature that Georgia poet Sidney Lanier observed and understood so well. "Affable live oak, leaning low," in the words of Lanier, undergirded by aromatic flowers, lesser trees, and azaleas turn the city's 22 squares into restful oases. Around the squares, the shadows of trailing vines on lattices shackle the doorways of many historic homes.

The shaded garden squares are only one reason the shapes of Savannah leave a lasting impression. Intricate iron grillwork, decorative handrails, and iron dogs cast lengthened shadows on steps and walls. Angular shadows walk the streets near the sharp corners of typical lowcountry buildings. Even Factors Walk, rebuilt after a disastrous fire in the 1880s, has plenty of right angles. So does the old City Market, where restaurants entertaining in traditional fashion or in shaded patio settings mingle comfortably with artists, artisans, and shopkeepers.

Savannah began as a British outpost against Spanish expansion from Florida. On February 12, 1733, 144 English men and women disembarked from the ship *Ann* in what is now the historic area of the city and began building a community carefully planned by General James Edward Oglethorpe around easily defensible squares.

Spanish military reaction was not long in coming, but the British gained permanent control of this section of coastline on the battlefield at nearby St. Simons Island.

Savannah was an early trendsetter. Oglethorpe's Trustees Gardens, a 10-acre plot growing trees, herbs, and other plants from around the world, was the first agricultural experiment station in the colonies. Among the plantings were cotton and peaches, consistent contributors to Georgia's economy in the intervening years. Oglethorpe's decision to lay out the city in large symmetrical lots around twenty-four squares made it America's first planned city. The first newspaper in the colony, the *Georgia Gazette,* was founded there in 1763. Savannah quickly became an active and prosperous port along classical British colonial lines, exporting rice grown in diked paddies around the city, providing supplies for ships from bountiful forests, and importing manufactured goods for Georgia's growing population.

However, its misfortunes were far from over. Taken by colonial insurgents at the start of the Revolutionary War, it was occupied by the British and then unsuccessfully besieged by an American army. Devastating fires in 1796 and 1820 destroyed most of its colonial structures, but Savannah arose from the ashes as one of the leading commercial centers of the South. Construction of the Central of Georgia Railroad and harbor dredging kept Georgia's agricultural products flowing to foreign markets. A branch of the Second Bank of the United States (it occupied the 1790 structure now known as the Pink House) provided ready access to capital. Construction of Old Fort Jackson and then Fort Pulaski certified the port's value to the South and the new nation.

By the 1850s, Savannah's 15,000 inhabitants prospered as a market town and on the export of cotton, which had replaced rice as the principal crop in the early decades of the century. The Civil War brought an end to the idea that cotton was "king" as a tightening Union blockade strangled port activity. Although the federal navy bombarded Fort Pulaski continually, Savannah held out until Union General Sherman completed his "march to the sea." The city surrendered on December 22, 1864, and Sherman sent a telegram to President Abraham Lincoln tendering the city as a "Christmas present."

Gradual recovery after the war ended abruptly when cotton prices collapsed in 1895. Savannah went into decline that lasted for half a century. The metropolitan area now has about 500,000 people. The port remains the largest industry, with tourism second and paper manufacturing ("When people ask about the smell, we say that's payroll perfume") third.

Saving Historical Places

Preservation got an early tentative start when, in 1875, Mary Telfair willed her William Jay-designed home and furnishings to the Georgia Historical Society. The 1820 house was opened in 1886 as an art museum, the original mantels, molding, cornices, and many innovations providing an artistic backdrop for the paintings and antique furniture. Today, it is open 10 a.m. to 5 p.m. Tuesday–Saturday and 2 to 5 p.m. Sunday.

Organized preservation efforts did not begin until 1921 when a campaign was launched to save the city's most distinctive feature, the handsome squares, from destruction intended to facilitate the flow of automobile traffic. Even that did not arouse the city to other threats to 2,300 architecturally and historically significant buildings. Like other communities, Savannah looked on complacently as historic structures disappeared one by one. Elegant homes in its core area, constructed in the boom periods of the 19th century, were torn down to make way for gasoline stations and parking lots. The migration to the suburbs left rows of vacant structures, many of which were vandalized.

In 1954, the impending destruction of red-brick Isaiah Davenport House, considered the city's most outstanding Federal-style building, energized conservationists and history lovers. The Historic Savannah Foundation (HSF) was formed to spearhead revival, house by house and step by step, of the glory and grandeur of the historic area. In 1959, Marshall Row, four old rowhouses dating from about 1859 and built of soft Savannah gray brick with marble steps, was saved from demolition. The Oliver Sturgis House, built in 1813 and scheduled to be demolished to make room for a bank parking lot, was saved in 1963.

Not all projects were instant successes; HSF held the house at 15 West Perry Street, acquired in 1967, for five years until a buyer could be found. The purchaser not only restored the building, but later purchased and restored others as an investment. Franklin Square, one of the squares eliminated to facilitate traffic, was restored in 1985.

To date, more than 1,700 historic structures have been saved and restored through a combination of individual and collective initiative. Now, from Chippewa Square, a statue of General Oglethorpe sculpted by Daniel Chester French perpetually surveys the largest historic district in the United States, covering 2½ square miles. The most startling change, however, has been the transformation in attitude; preservation is now a recognized imperative.

Squares and Fountains

Five Bull Street garden squares, stretching inland from City Hall to Forsyth Park, anchor the heart of the downtown historic district. Johnson, Wright, Chippewa, Madison, and Monterey squares, each quickly identified by a statue of Oglethorpe or Pulaski or some other notable feature, are often called the "Sisters." Savannah's twenty-two squares are classed as a National Civil Engineering Landmark.

When the sun shines on the handsome white fountain in Forsyth Park, it glistens like icing—perhaps symbolic of the permanent luster of the city. It resembles one in the Place de la Concorde in Paris. Though not in the Historic District, Forsyth may be the best known of the Savannah open areas. The handsome entrance on Gaston Street features a live oak alley leading to the famous fountain, which is so much a part of the city's psyche that people bought memorial bricks to refurbish it.

Today, much of the city's largest park remains in a managed natural state, symbolic of the wilderness area set aside by William Hodgson at his own expense for "public pleasures in the forest." Its public status became official in 1851 when the park was created as part of Forsyth Ward, named after former Governor and U.S. Secretary of State John Forsyth. A Bavarian landscape architect, William Bischoff, was chosen to create the design. The spectacular fountain was added in 1858. The park was enlarged after the Civil War by incorporating property used for musters and camps during and before the war years.

Forsyth Park also continues its historic role as a place for all kinds of neighborhood and community activities. For example, the city's annual public arts program is held there in July. The Savannah Symphony sometimes offers concerts, and even puppet shows may be seen. A jog around the park measures about 1 mile. Confederate, Spanish-American War, and a few civilian monuments identify some of Savannah's heroes. The park is especially beautiful in the spring when the azaleas bloom.

Savannah is fountain rich, but the other 15 fountains are overshadowed by the one in Forsyth Park. A handsome griffon fountain enhances the approach to the Cotton Exchange on Bay Street. Three others are spotted along nearby River Street and one is inside City Hall. Water flows from two sources in Johnson Square. A new fountain was dedicated in Orleans Square recently by the German Heritage Society, while the Lafayette Square water memorial was placed earlier by the Colonial Dames of Georgia. The Columbia Square fountain was donated by the Wormsloe Plantation. Two fountains are located at the Civic Center bounded by Barnard, Montgomery, Oglethorpe, and Liberty streets. The peripatetic Cohen Fountain, only recently turned on again, presently stands at the intersection of Bull Street and Victory Drive. Over the years, it has graced a number of locations.

Not all of Savannah's fountains are decorative; in Troup Square are two drinking fountains for dogs, copies of originals placed there in 1897. "UGA," the University of Georgia mascot, was the first to drink at these fountains when they were restored in recent years.

Historic District

Savannah's architectural lineage is chronicled at the Massie Heritage Interpretation Center at 207 East Gordon Street, whose central section was the first public school building in Georgia. The 1855 building, enlarged in the late 19th century, is filled with architectural relics and a model representing the original city and preserves a 19th-century classroom. It is open from 9 a.m. to 3 p.m. Monday–Friday.

Historic Savannah is compact enough to be handled on a self-composed walk. A good place to start is the Central of Georgia Railway Station (circa 1861) at 301 Martin Luther King Boulevard, which reminds Savannahians they spearheaded the construction of a railroad to Macon and the farmlands of middle Georgia in the 1840s and 1850s. The station now houses a visitors center and the Savannah History Museum. The museum, located in the area where trains stopped to discharge and load passengers, explores key people, events, and periods in the city's history. Audiovisuals include a holographic presentation of the Revolutionary War siege of the city.

Parking is available there and near Factors Walk, among other places. For RVers, several main streets are broad and accommodating and traffic is relatively light.

From the visitors center, Martin Luther King Boulevard leads past historic Scarbrough House to Factors Walk. The restored Riverfront

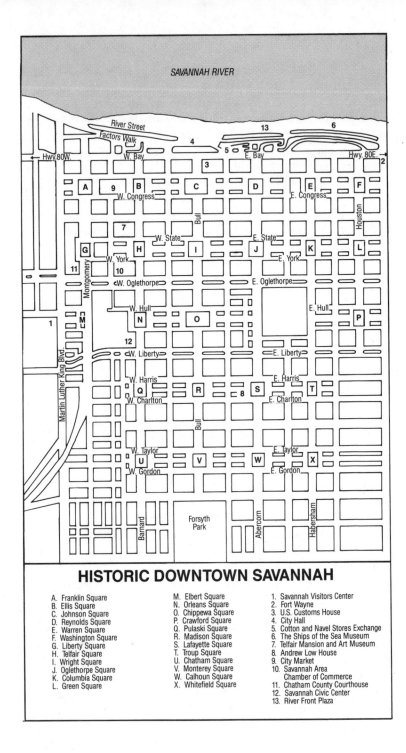

HISTORIC DOWNTOWN SAVANNAH

A. Franklin Square
B. Ellis Square
C. Johnson Square
D. Reynolds Square
E. Warren Square
F. Washington Square
G. Liberty Square
H. Telfair Square
I. Wright Square
J. Oglethorpe Square
K. Columbia Square
L. Green Square

M. Elbert Square
N. Orleans Square
O. Chippewa Square
P. Crawford Square
Q. Pulaski Square
R. Madison Square
S. Lafayette Square
T. Troup Square
U. Chatham Square
V. Monterey Square
W. Calhoun Square
X. Whitefield Square

1. Savannah Visitors Center
2. Fort Wayne
3. U.S. Customs House
4. City Hall
5. Cotton and Navel Stores Exchange
6. The Ships of the Sea Museum
7. Telfair Mansion and Art Museum
8. Andrew Low House
9. City Market
10. Savannah Area
    Chamber of Commerce
11. Chatham County Courthouse
12. Savannah Civic Center
13. River Front Plaza

district vividly recalls the noisy, bustling port whose imaginative merchants normally exported cotton, rice, naval stores, and lumber and occasionally became involved in visionary schemes, such as sending the first commercial steamship—the first ship to bear the name of the city—across the Atlantic. The first ship named *Savannah* is believed to have taken on cotton and resin from warehouses at 121 and 123 West River Street (now part of the River House) before heading for Europe.

Named for the cotton factors (brokers), the warehouses whose walls are formed of oyster shells, ballast, and brick stand in an unusual position between the river and a high bluff. This permits entrance to specialty shops, restaurants, and the Ships of the Sea Museum from two levels—at River Street and Factors Walk. Ramps leading down to the River Street and the handsome waterfront plaza overlooking the river are paved with cobblestones that arrived as ballast on early sailing ships.

The Ships of the Sea Museum, designed to resemble the interior of a ship, reflects the colorful maritime history of the city and seafaring in general. Among the artifacts is a porcelain cat that stood outside a British house of ill repute to signal prospective customers—the origin of the term "cat house." Green eyes in the cat meant the house was open and red eyes meant it was full; when the cat's back was turned toward the street, the house was closed. Scrimshaw objects carried less obtrusive messages, but sailors at sea carved whale's teeth, ostrich eggs, and other mediums to create everything from decorated whalebone corsets to chess sets. The symbols on tavern signs also were messages; they told unlettered seamen what to expect inside.

A set of nine pins recalls that sailors were so obsessed with the game that it was outlawed. However, the sailors simply added a tenth pin, the reason the modern game of bowling has that number. A collection of ship models includes those to carry the city's name, starting with the steamship and including the first nuclear-powered cargo vessel, as well as Civil War ironclads. A complete ship chandlery and ship's carpenter shop also are among the extensive displays.

The museum is open from 10 a.m. to 3 p.m. daily, except on St. Patrick's Day, Thanksgiving, Christmas Day, and New Year's Day.

Nearby, in Emmett Park, is the Vietnam War Memorial, in part built with memorial bricks.

In 1791, George Washington made a visit to the city. The cannons captured at Yorktown, Virginia, which he presented to the Chatham Artillery, are emplaced on Bay Street across the street from the 1852 Customs House, which monitored commerce through the port for many years.

This waterfront was a place for personal dreams, too. The Waving Girl Statue by Felix De Weldon memorializes the constancy of Florence Martus, who waited in vain for her loved one to return. For more than 40 years, she waved a white scarf by day and lantern by night at every passing ship, hoping it carried her sailor lover. He never returned, but her story touched the hearts of other sailors, who lined the railings of passing ships to wave back and often brought her gifts. Her statue still waves at oceangoing vessels moving upstream to the modern port area, the largest handler of foreign commerce on the South Atlantic coast.

Continue walking to Washington Square and along St. Julian Street, where many 18th- and 19th-century homes with attractive porches have been restored as private residences. From Warren Square, head for two early 19th-century exhibition buildings: Haberham Street leads south to the Isaiah Davenport House, then west along East State Street to the Owens-Thomas House.

The Isaiah Davenport house at 324 East State Street, built in 1820 by a Rhode Island master builder who migrated to Savannah, is especially known for its interior, with an elliptical staircase, interior hallway arch, and delicate plaster work. It is furnished with antiques, including rich carpets. The garden also has been restored. Open 10 a.m. to 4:30 p.m. Tuesday–Saturday, 1:30 to 4:30 Sunday, except major holidays.

The 1818 Owens-Thomas House, 124 Abercorn Street, is sometimes described by tour guides as "the finest Regency-house museum in the United States." The Marquis de Lafayette spoke from a side porch during an 1824–25 tour of the United States. Designed by William Jay for cotton merchant Richard Richardson, the house has a columned porch, double entrance stairway, and arched second-story window. Interior features include curved walls and doors, recessed arches, Carrara marble mantel with Swedish steel fireplace insert, amber inside glass on some windows to make it appear like the sun was always shining, hearts-of-pine boards painted to look like walnut and mahogany, and a bridge in the upstairs hallway. Furnishings date from about 1820 and include a Duncan Phyfe sofa, sewing table, and card table. One of the paintings is a typical product of the period—a child's head painted by an itinerant painter on a generic body. Open 10 a.m. to 5 p.m. Tuesday–Saturday, 2 to 5 p.m. Sunday–Monday.

At Oglethorpe Square, turn north to Reynolds Square, easily identified by a statue of John Wesley, founder of Methodism; facing the square are the Pink House (circa 1790, now a restaurant) and the 1813 Oliver Sturges House. St. Julian Street leads to Johnson Square, the first square planned, and then to the City Market area. The walk can be extended or modified or other routes can be planned using a map available at the visitors center.

Other historic exhibition houses, many with high porches to avoid the mud and dust of the streets, are sprinkled throughout the historic area. Among them are the following:

The white Wayne-Gordon Mansion, 142 Bull Street. Built around 1820, it has elaborate plaster work and a mixture of Egyptian and classical patterns but is better known as the birthplace in 1860 of Juliette Gordon Low who, in 1912, founded the Girl Scouts in the United States. Open 10 a.m. to 4 p.m. Monday–Tuesday and Thursday–Saturday, 12:30 to 4:30 p.m. Sunday, except major holidays.

The Andrew Low House (circa 1848), 329 Abercorn Street. Now the headquarters of the National Society of the Colonial Dames of America in Georgia, this building features a stuccoed brick exterior with iron railings and a handsome interior that includes carved woodwork, elaborate cornices, and crystal chandeliers. It was built by a wealthy cotton merchant, Andrew Low. Robert E. Lee stayed there in 1870 and British author William Makepeace Thackeray was twice a guest. Low's daughter-in-law, Juliette Gordon Low, was living in the house at the time she organized the first Girl Scout troop. Open 10 a.m. to 4 p.m. weekdays and noon to 4 p.m. Sundays, except December 13–27 and holidays.

Flannery O'Connor House. The birthplace of the modern author, located on Lafayette Square, is open 1 to 4 p.m. Friday–Sunday.

English Regency-style William Scarbrough House, regarded as the "ultimate in townhouse design," is used as an events house but is generally not open to the public. Erected in 1819 following a design by English architect William Jay for a wealthy cotton prince, the house contains an atrium with Doric columns and a third-floor skylight. Scarbrough lost his fortune when he helped finance the unprofitable inaugural voyage of the transocean steamship *Savannah*. For about 90 years, starting in 1872, the house was the West Broad Street School.

Many privately owned structures have interesting features. For example, the entrance hall of the Greek Revival-style Champion-

McAlpin-Fowlkes House, built in 1844, has a black marble floor and an oval rotunda skylight that lights three stories of hall space. The house at 18 East Oglethorpe Avenue, two doors from the Low birthplace, is an early 18th-century wooden home.

West Jones Street and nearby Monterey Square (with its statue of General Casimir Pulaski, who died liberating Savannah in the Revolutionary War), the Washington Square area, and Trustees Gardens stand as models of 19th-century grandeur. The 1854 William Remshart rowhouses, like others in Savannah, mimic those in London; one Savannah businessman who visited London liked them so much that he copied them when he returned home. Townhouses built in the 1850s, when Savannah had matured and had considerable street traffic, have high porches to escape the mud of the streets. The small Foley House has oriental windows and beige burned brick.

The 1850s home of musician-singer Johnny Mercer's mother is built back from the street; she put a fence around her yard to keep cows that in those days grazed freely from eating her flowers. ("You could have all the cows you wanted as long as they were belled and brought in at 6 o'clock.")

Colonial Park Cemetery, consecrated in 1750 as the city's second, is the final resting place of many of Georgia's colonial stalwarts, including Button Gwinnett, one of the signers of the Declaration of Independence.

From its early days, Savannah was a diverse city, with many of its prominent citizens in the 18th century coming from elsewhere. They founded churches of many denominations — Episcopalian, Baptist, Methodist, Presbyterian, Roman Catholic, and others. The present Gothic-Revival St. John's Episcopal Church was constructed in 1852–53. The adjacent Green–Meldrim parish house was built in 1853 as the home of Charles Green, who arrived in Savannah with only a few dollars and made a fortune as a cotton broker; a decade later, General Sherman lived there at the invitation of the owner after accepting surrender of the city. The house is open from 10 a.m. to 3 p.m. Tuesday and Thursday–Saturday.

President James Monroe came to participate in the dedication of the Independent Presbyterian Church in 1819 and danced in the ballroom of the Scarbrough House (the only one in a Savannah home at the time). The Lutheran Church of the Ascension was founded by Salzburgers who escaped persecution in Austria in 1734–36 and the Moravians who came about the same time. First Baptist Church is said to be the only church that kept its doors open throughout the Civil War. During the occupation period, Union soldiers and civilians worshipped on one Sunday and the Southerners the next. The first African Baptist Church was formed in 1861 by the oldest black congregation in the United States, dating from 1788 at Brampton Plantation. Gothic Mickve Israel Synagogue on Monterey Square was built in 1878, but the Reformed Jewish congregation is the third oldest in the United States. A small heritage museum and the handsome sanctuary are open to the public.

Savannah celebrates its diverse heritage virtually year-round. Georgia Day on February 12, the date of the founding of the thirteenth colony, features historical programs, costume contests, crafts demonstrations, tours, carriage and riverboat rides, and a pageant. Scarlett O'Hara would have been at home at the candlelight dinners and evenings of chamber music. The St. Patrick's Day parade is one of the largest in the nation. In early May, tartan-clad Scots have a turn at highland games and a "Piping on the Green." A Christmas in Savannah reflects the 19th-century tradition and includes trees from around the world, in keeping with Savannah's tradition as a multiethnic city.

A variety of guided tours cover many aspects of the city. A ride in a horsedrawn carriage awakens nostalgic escape from the automobile age. Walking and bus tours cover the major sites. Specialized tours range from a champagne reception at the 1819 William Scarbrough House to a walking examination of the various architectural styles. Riverboats provide a perspective from the water. One-hour harbor tours leave daily from River Street. The boats also conduct moonlight and special-interest cruises, as well as trips to Fort Jackson.

Historical Living

Savannah is one of the best cities in the United States to experience the ambience of the mid-19th century at bed-and-breakfasts occupying historic buildings. The Eliza Thompson House, for example, was built about 1847 and enlarged later to house the owner's visiting relatives and friends. Sitting in the parlor, surrounded by antique furniture and wall paintings of pale, well-proportioned belles of bygone years, one can feel a little of Rhett Butler stirring in the veins. The bedrooms, while modernized, are otherwise furnished as they would have been when our ancestors came to visit. In the coolness of the evening, the smell of wisteria growing on the iron stairway wafts over the small courtyard where evening gatherings were held 140 or more years ago.

Numerous other bed-and-breakfasts in buildings dating from the 1800s are operated with the same tender, loving care. Among them are the East Bay Inn (circa 1800), Liberty Inn (circa 1834), Ballastone Inn (circa 1853), River Street Inn (circa 1853), Pulaski Square Inn (circa 1853), Remshart–Brooke House (circa 1853–54), Jesse Mount House (circa 1854), Presidents' Quarters (circa 1855), Gastonian (circa 1868), and Victoria Barie House (circa 1868). The fourstar, three-story Mulberry Hotel occupies a building built in 1860 as a livery stable and surrounds a courtyard with gas light, fountains, trees, and flowers. Antebellum antiques and objets d'art are used in furnishings.

Savannah also is a delightful place for historic dining. Bakers Cafe and Bistro serves in a converted 1853 cotton warehouse. At Mrs. Wilkes' Dining Room (it was once a boarding house), people willingly stand in line until she is ready to open, then wait until grace is said in order to enjoy her homestyle meals and carry their plates to the kitchen when finished.

A relic of the great American railroad era is one of Savannah's newest major attractions. Because the Roundhouse Complex near the visitors center was altered in successive railroading periods, it is considered the "most significant complex of antebellum railroad structures to survive in the United States." It reflects to some degree the history of railroading from 1833, when the Central of Georgia Railroad was founded, to the first half of the 20th century. The main feature, the engine roundhouse, was built in 1926, but some other features of the complex date back to the 1850s. The complex is located in a 5.5-acre park. Guided tours are held at 2 p.m. Friday–Tuesday; special events are held on Memorial Day, July 4, Labor Day weekend, and the first weekend in October.

A small monument on Louisville Road between the Roundhouse and the train station marks the site of the bloodiest fighting of the American effort on October 9, 1779, to free Savannah from British occupation. The American attack centered on Spring Hill Redoubt, which anchored the British line; several hundred men fell in an hour of fighting, including Pulaski, who was mortally wounded while leading his cavalry unit, and French Comte d'Estaing. The site has been considerably altered and no remnant of the redoubt remains.

Savannah history is not limited to the antebellum period. Savannah has other districts that also are protected. The Victorian era produced another boom in construction. The Historic Savannah Foundation maintains a revolving fund to facilitate the preservation process. Hamilton-Turner House is an elegant Victorian mansion, built in 1873. King-Tisdell Cottage, built in 1896, houses a museum on the culture of blacks in Savannah and the nearby coastal islands. Part of an African-American heritage trail that also includes the Beach Institute at 502 East Harris Street, it is open daily from noon to 4:30 p.m. Ardsley Park was one of the first planned post-World War I developments.

Like Lanier, who equivocated about his chosen profession, Savannah has a second secular side. The Victorian element came along after a huge fire in the 1880s and includes such extreme styles as 1890s steamboat Gothic at the Cord-Asendorf house, also known as the "Gingerbread House," which some say is the most photographed home in Savannah and is popular for wedding receptions and similar events. Light and tasteful interiors from that period reflect the gentility that Lanier sought and seldom found.

The broad avenue to Ardsley Park, now called Victory Drive, originally had a bridle and bike path on the median strip. Later, a palm tree was planted as a memorial to the 150 men from Chatham County who were killed in World War I; now more than 700 palms and azaleas brighten the highway.

Science Museum

At the Savannah Science Museum, 4405 Paulsen Street, a pendulum appears to be swinging and knocking down pegs. It is standing still and the pegs are being knocked down because the earth is rotating. This is just one of the innovative displays at the museum. Visitors also may walk into a human heart or a mouth and watch bees at work in a hive. The five poisonous snakes of the region, including rattlesnakes, cottonmouth, and copperhead, are regularly on exhibit in tanks, as are parts of the museum's extensive insect, rock, and mineral collections. Skeletons of a 14-foot-tall prehistoric ground sloth, now extinct but once common in the Georgia coastal area, and a whale have been reconstructed. A ramp provides a vantage point for viewing work in the laboratory, which enables visitors to see live reptiles such as an alligator, salamanders, and turtles and amphibians such as greater siren and anthiuma.

In addition to floor displays, the museum houses more than 30,000 specimens of reptiles and amphibians and more than 2,000 pressed plants in its collection, many of them used in student programs. The museum is open from 10 a.m. to 5 p.m. Tuesday–Saturday and 2 to

5 p.m. Sunday, except major holidays. The planetarium holds a public program at 3 p.m. on Sundays.

Although Lanier wrote about specific sights such as the Marshes of Glynn, even those works are often a summation of his total experiences. In the end, the visitor to Savannah has a similar feeling, that "somehow my soul seems suddenly free." It means he (or she) is absorbing a little of Lanier's philosophy—that love and beauty redeem us from materialism.

Savannah's Surrounds

GREATER SAVANNAH, IF THERE WERE ONE, WOULD RADIATE FOR MILES— up and down river and up and down coast—because much of the historical development around Savannah resulted from the city's existence and influence. These include historic forts, great plantations, old houses and churches, and Civil War battle sites. However, the tone of the area also has been set by nature: the numerous waterways, marshlands, coastal forests, and, above all, the barrier islands.

The 1996 Summer Olympic Games, scheduled for Atlanta, will spill over into the Savannah area. Ten classes of yachting races will be held in July off Skidaway Island. The Olympic marina will be located at Priest Landing on the Wilmington River. Many competitors will train at the site. A series of events, including a tall ships parade, are leading up to that event. Pre-Olympic regattas are planned each year, starting in 1993. Check with state or Savannah tourism offices for schedules.

Bonaventure Cemetery

This old burial ground occupies such a beautiful site on the banks of the Wilmington River that tour buses often stop to allow people to wander among its alleys of 200-year-old live oak draped with Spanish moss, magnolias, dogwood, azaleas, wisteria, camellias, yellow jessamine, and other flowers. The scene is reminiscent of that witnessed by conservationist John Muir, a founder and first president of the Sierra Club, when he camped there in 1867 during his

"Thousand Mile Walk to the Gulf." He recalled seeing "one of the most impressive assemblages of animal and plant creatures I have ever met."

The site originally was part of Bonaventure Plantation, founded in the 18th century by Colonel Mulryne. His daughter, Mary, and her husband, Josiah Tattnall, are interred there, as is Noble Jones, one of Georgia's earliest pioneers and founder of Wormsloe Plantation. The life-size statue of Gracie, the young daughter of hoteliers in Savannah, who died in the late 1800s, is popular.

The cemetery, open from dawn to dusk, is located on Bonaventure Road south of Savannah. Turn off U.S. Route 80 (Victory Drive) onto Mechanics Avenue to reach Bonaventure Road.

Thunderbolt

This community, first an Indian village and then a military outpost and station for trading with Indians, has reverted to a martial tradition on a number of occasions. During the Revolutionary War, it was defended by an outpost manned by French allied troops. The Civil War witnessed the construction of a coastal battery there. During World War II, a crash boat rescue unit took over a yacht basin constructed in 1939.

Early attempts to start potash and candlemaking industries were unsuccessful, but in the 1850s the town found its calling—the seafood industry. It has been a shrimp and fishing center ever since and is now the focal point of the shrimp fleet in the Savannah area. On June 1, the fleet is blessed by the Bishop of Savannah as it sails in line down the river. At other times, visitors may hike to the water's edge in late afternoon to watch the boats return from a day's fishing.

Thunderbolt has been a tourist destination off and on since the mid-1800s. After the Civil War, it was a regional center for yacht and harness racing until the 1865 Park House, a grand hotel, burned. Near the turn of the century, streetcars carried venturesome Savannahians to a casino. A Wheelman's Park for bicyclers opened in 1893. Today, Thunderbolt is a stop on the Intracoastal Waterway and is known for picturesque seafood restaurants such as River's End, which is built on pilings overlooking the harbor.

The restful campus of Savannah State University began to take shape in 1890. Some of its buildings date from those formative years. Today, approximately 3,000 students attend. Another historic building is a town jail erected in 1863.

The bluff on which the town is built is clearly visible from just across the bridge over the Wilmington River and near the fish house to the left at the water's edge.

The town was incorporated in 1865 as Warsaw, but the name was changed in 1921 to recognize a legend: that a bolt of lightning striking the ground brought forth a spring.

Isle of Hope

Wormsloe, one of Georgia's first plantations, was carved from the wilderness on this island by Noble Jones, a physician and carpenter who also served as a soldier, surveyor, rum agent, constable, and member of the Royal Council of Georgia for 18 years. The name is believed to have come from the silk industry, one of the crops with which Jones experimented.

The introduction to Wormsloe State Historic Site, a memorable stone archway and 1½-mile avenue of live oak, is relatively modern. The alley of trees was planted in the 1890s. It passes the modern museum and the start of a nature trail and points directly to the tabby ruins of the fortified mansion that Jones constructed between 1739 and 1745.

Exhibits and audiovisuals in the museum focus on early Georgia history, including the colonization of Savannah, the state's first families, and life in the royal colony, and spotlight later events at Wormsloe, such as archaeological excavations conducted in the 1960s. Sketches by Philip Georg Frederick von Reck, one of the early settlers, are among the exhibits.

A model of the Noble Jones home makes the nearby ruins of a fortified house easier to understand. The tabby walls reveal a star-shaped fort with four bastions that incorporated a tabby-and-frame house in the southern wall. The house had five rooms, only one of which had a wooden floor.

A mile-long nature trail traverses a coastal forest featuring Georgia pine, dogwood, magnolia, azalea, and ferns and crosses tidal creeks that host deer, opossum, raccoon, and a variety of birds. It passes an area where living history demonstrations depicting crafts and skills essential to survival of the early settlers are presented on a regular basis year-round, and then circles the tabby ruins and monument marking the Jones family cemetery.

The Isle of Hope has been integrated into Georgia life since the Spanish conquistador Hernando DeSoto explored the area more than

400 years ago in search of gold. It guarded the Skidaway Narrows for the embryo Georgia colony and later became a place of refuge for royalists escaping the French Revolution. Many residents fled to the island hoping to escape a yellow-fever epidemic in Savannah in 1876. The name is believed to have come from an English site associated with the plantation founder, however.

Descendants of Noble Jones live on a 65-acre tract of the original land grant. Their house, built in the 1840s and since modified, it not open to the public.

The state park is open from 9 a.m. to 5 p.m. Tuesday–Saturday and 2 to 5:30 p.m. Sunday.

Savannah's Forts

Defense has been a number one priority ever since the Georgia colony was founded in 1733. As a result, a ring of forts stands guard over the water approaches to the city.

Old Fort Jackson. Started in 1809 3 miles east of Savannah, Old Fort Jackson is Georgia's oldest standing fort. The well-preserved example of the coastal fortifications built in the formative decades by the new American nation guarded the approach to the city during the War of 1812 and again during the Civil War.

The fort is now a museum, part of an 8-acre site operated by the Colonial Heritage Society. It is open daily from 9 a.m. to 5 p.m., until 7 p.m. from July 1 to August 15.

Visitors may walk ramparts that command the Savannah River and its adjacent flatlands and watch oceangoing ships pass en route to the Savannah harbor. Guardrooms, storerooms, and cells in the wall of the fort house a small but interesting museum displaying flags, the South's largest antique cannon, and other weapons, uniforms, information on construction of the fort, and the nation's oldest known portable steam engine.

More than 200 interpretive events are held each year. "The Military through the Ages" in late May at Old Fort Jackson recalls 200 years of Savannah's martial side. On Memorial Day weekend, uniformed Civil War troops fire salutes to honor the war dead. At other times, interpreters in period costume discuss the fort's role in Georgia history; demonstrate blacksmithing, brickmaking, and military-related trades; fire cannon and play patriotic music (Fourth of July); and dramatize the evacuation of Savannah before its capture by Union forces.

Fort Pulaski. Fort Pulaski on marshy Cockspur Island 15 miles east of Savannah is part of a string of forts built after the War of 1812 to defend strategic points on the East Coast from naval incursions of the type that resulted in the burning of the White House in Washington, D.C. Savannah, as a leading port, was entitled to this protection. In 1829, a young second lieutenant and engineer named Robert E. Lee, who later would become the Confederacy's most revered general, designed and built the dikes and drainage system, the first step in construction of the fort. Over the next two decades, more than 25 million bricks were laid to create a wall 7.5-feet thick on piles driven into the soggy soil of the island. The fort was considered so strong that U.S. Chief of Engineers Joseph C. Totten declared an opponent "might as well bombard the Rocky Mountains."

Fort Pulaski was a Confederate stronghold at the start of the Civil War, guarding the city from Union warships and protecting an important route for blockade runners. After the Union seized Hilton Head Island, the Confederacy considered Tybee Island vulnerable and withdrew. That was a mistake. Early in 1862, artillery batteries hauled ashore on Tybee Island bombarded the fort for 30 hours, breaching the wall at the southeast angle. The Confederate surrender marked the end of the era; the successful use of rifled artillery against a land fortification signaled the end of large, fixed coastal forts. Within six weeks of capture, Pulaski was repaired as a base for federal forces, and it was used briefly after the war to house political prisoners, then abandoned.

Fort Pulaski was designated a national monument in 1924 while still under military ownership. Restoration by the National Park Service was begun in 1933. In the late 1930s, Civilian Conservation Corps members started showing visitors through the grounds while restoration work was still underway. The fort opened as a national monument in 1942 but closed during World War II because small defense installations were established nearby. It reopened after the war.

The moated fort is shown today basically as it was after repair by federal units during the Civil War, with audio stations at strategic locations. A considerable number of shellholes remain on the south and southeast walls and parapet area. Eight projectiles are imbedded in the southeast wall and one remains in the south wall. A sizable museum is located in casements. On entering through the sally port, the visitor turns left to enter rooms in the gorge wall restored to their appearance during Confederate and Union use. Farther along is a restored enlisted man's quarters, an exhibit on the sling cart (the prime quartermaster's mover of the era), and historical exhibits, including the use of rifled cannon. A few cannon are placed in the northwest bastion and on the parapet.

Visitors may walk on the ramparts to look out over the marshy terrain, which now includes a wooded area that would have been cut away when the fort was operational to preserve the fields of fire. Paved trails run through those woods. In addition, visitors may walk along a flood-control dike around the island, which is a good place to observe the approximately 200 species of birds spotted at the fort, especially shorebirds and songbirds. Alligators are present and one occasionally will even invade the moat of the fort. Many snakes live in and around the fort, but only the eastern diamondback rattlesnake is poisonous. Other wildlife includes marsh rabbits, raccoon, mink, and opossum. Northwest of the fort is a monument to John Wesley, founder of the Methodist Church, who landed in America at Cockspur Island in 1736.

Demonstrations on military garrison life and martial arts are part of the living history program. The fort is open year-round from 8:30 a.m. to 5:15 p.m. (6:45 during the summer), except Christmas Day. The gate to the grounds closes a quarter-hour later.

Oatland Island Education Center

The entry fee to this 175-acre public school-operated site is unusual—a can of cat or dog food per person. For that, visitors may feast upon a number of features. They may follow a 1.5-mile nature trail through woods with 12 habitats that sustain animals indigenous to Georgia, including alligator, panther, bobcat, fox, deer, bear, wolf, and bison; past a barn animals area with a cow, sheep, goat, bunnies, chickens, and a pig; and by an aviary with birds of prey such as hawks, eagles, pelicans, and owls. All are outdoors in large fenced-in habitats. The nature trail also leads to a 6-acre freshwater pond, featuring ferns, crayfish, fish, hawks, owls, woodpeckers, and waterfowl. A 520-foot wooden walkway extends over Richardson Creek marsh, which is covered with salt-tolerant plants and mudflats that sustain fiddler crab, periwinkle snail, marsh hens, egrets, herons, and other species.

In addition, visitors may view log cabins about 150 years old— from outside on weekdays when they are used by school groups and inside on Saturday. One cabin was moved from Gum Branch and the other from Jesup. Cane-processing equipment also is on display.

The center's Marine Monitoring Station utilizes a solar heating panel. Fifty acres of the tract are in plants of various ages, including some mature stands. Laurel oak and magnolia typical of native upland vegetation are included. An amphitheater is located in a hardwood area. Once a month from October to May, at a special Saturday at Oatland, children are allowed under supervision to pet the barn animals. At the same time, cane-processing equipment is demonstrated. Four times a year at these Saturday programs, telescopes are used for astronomy programs, but the dates vary from year to year.

Once a year, on the second Saturday in November, the cane mill is used for grinding. Three or four cane boilings are held that day and the previous Friday night. A crafts festival is held at the same time. Other set programs include these: February, Georgia Week and Black History Month; March, "Sheep to Shawl" demonstrations during which two sheep are sheared and the Handweavers Guild of Savannah demonstrates the steps required to turn the wool into a shawl; May, Nature Fair; in odd-numbered years in January, a program is given on birds of prey, including the eagle.

The center, operated by the Savannah–Chatham County public schools, is open from 8:30 a.m. to 5 p.m. Monday–Friday and from 11 a.m. to 5 p.m. the second Saturday of each month October–May. Although primarily an educational facility, it is open to the public. Insect repellent is recommended during warm months.

Tybee Island

While all of Georgia's barrier islands are nominally included in the Golden Isles designation, some are so closely tied to Savannah that they are regarded as local. Tybee Island, east of the city, is one of them.

Tybee is part of a complex of mostly residential islands, including White Marsh, Talahi, and Wilmington, linked by the Islands Expressway (U.S. 80/Georgia 24). En route, the highway also crosses the Intracoastal Waterway and other streams, including Lazaretto Creek, which hosts a public boat ramp and fishing pier on one side and a commercial fishing dock on the other. The road passes Fort Pulaski and cuts across mile after mile of some of the richest saltwater marshland on the South Atlantic coast. Since 1970, the marsh, a nursery for bluefish, crabs, flounder, and numerous other species, has been protected by law because of its ecological value.

On Tybee Island, Butler Avenue (sometimes called the Strand), which parallels the beach, is lined with houses, motels, and condos. More than a dozen walkways, bearing signs warning against "underwater hazards, strong currents," provide public access to the beach. Fences are used in places to keep people off dunes. Kite flyers join sunworshippers, joggers, and surfcasters on the windy beach. Bike riders use Butler Avenue and the lanes connecting public parking lots 1 and 2.

Tybee Island Marine Science Center, on the beach at 16th Street, has an aquarium populated with aquatic species found offshore, a profile of the beach and dune system, examples of shells found in the area, and a room devoted to displays on sharks. In addition, video programs explore the marine environment.

It is open to the public from 9 a.m. to 5 p.m. daily from Memorial Day to Labor Day. At 10 a.m. and 2 p.m. during that period, interns lead beach walks that examine coastal habitats, beach seining, invertebrates, and plankton carried back to the center and examined on microscopes. A Saturday evening lecture series covers topics such as Gray's Reef, coastal fishing, beach processes, shrimping in Georgia, archaeology, safe boating, and the Fish and Wildlife Service refuge system.

The center—developed jointly by the National Oceanic and Atmospheric Administration, University of Georgia Marine Science Extension Service, City of Tybee Island, and the Tybee Island Marine Science Foundation—opened in 1988 in a building used earlier as a police station. During the school year, teachers use the facility to take students on field trips.

Fort Screven on the northeast edge of Tybee Island represents the type of coastal fortifications that resulted from the experience of the Civil War. The series of batteries built in 1898 had concrete walls 20 feet thick, fronted by 30 feet of sand. These guardians of the approach to Savannah thus were virtually indistinguishable from the surrounding landscape. The fort originally was a coast artillery station, but also became a training center in World Wars I and II.

Both the Tybee Museum, whose collection of Civil War memorabilia is supplemented by a wide range of historical objects such as Japanese swords and seashells, and the Tybee Lighthouse across the street, which incorporates the base of the original 1773 structure, are located on the site of the fort. Visitors may climb the 300-odd-step spiral staircase of the lighthouse. Hours are 10 a.m. to 6 p.m. Wednesday–Monday April–September and 12 to 4 p.m. weekdays except Tuesday and 10 to 4 p.m. Saturday and Sunday October–March.

The top of the museum also provides a vantage point for viewing the coastline and the inlet that forms the South Carolina border. Tybee Island has changed little in total size—a 3 percent decrease in this century—but has gradually changed shape, eroding at the northeast corner and building up at the southern end. Massive shoaling and sedimentation shifts also are occurring.

On the Atlantic side, Tybee has a broad, sandy, low-energy beach with a steady breeze from the ocean, backed by a line of tufted dunes. Under the water offshore are the remnants of numerous frustrated efforts to prevent erosion of the land when it was occupied by a fort. The jetties once installed to prevent beach erosion have been covered by pumped sand and fences at the back of the beach that help stabilize dunes. The strong winter waves take some of the sand off the beach, lowering the level several feet, but the gentle waves that return in the summer bring sand back.

Tidal action supports an abundance of plant and animal life: live oak, wax myrtle, salt meadow hay, spike grass, sea oxeye, glasswort, cordgrass, and sea lettuce; shrimp, crabs, silver-side minnow, oysters, clams, periwinkle, ribbed mussel, fiddlers, several types of crabs and snails; raccoon, clapper rail, and marsh rat. Sandpipers and gulls roam the beaches.

Chimney Creek, just off the Islands Expressway on the sound side, has a marina that sends charter boats out about 35 miles to Snapper Banks in search of snapper, Spanish and king mackerel, cobia, grouper, dolphin, sea bass, barracuda, bluefish, redfish, spotted sea trout, and shark or farther to the Gulf Stream for billfish. Fishers also try inshore waterways.

Skidaway Island

For someone with only a half-day to spare who is interested in the Georgia coastline, there is 12-mile-square Skidaway Island. Only 5 miles southeast of Savannah across the Diamond Causeway, it combines private and public uses and provides a diverse ecological and historical experience.

The island lies between the mainland and a wide marshy area and Wassaw Island on the ocean side. Skidaway Narrows, once a creek, is now part of the Intracoastal Waterway, due to dredging by the Army Corps of Engineers.

In 500-acre Skidaway Island State Park are many of the features found along the Georgia coast: tidal creek, salt marsh and salt flats, freshwater wetlands, hammocks, and maritime forests. The Cherokee rose, the state flower, grows in forests that include cabbage palmetto, saw palmetto, and yaupon holly, from which ancient Indians extracted a black drink used in ceremonies. Deer, raccoon, red fox, feral hogs, and other small animals thrive, as do painted bunting, pileated woodpecker, screech owl, and other birds, including shorebirds and wading birds.

The 1-mile-long self-guided Sandpiper Nature Trail uncovers most of these features, as well as the remains of earthen fortifications raised by Confederates during the Civil War and an old whiskey still. Along the way are signboards noting some of nature's ways: the hardiness of black rush, the balls of sand left by fiddler crabs, the importance of tidal action in the food chain, the contributions of plants such as cordgrass, and the tracks left in the earth by small animals.

The Big Ferry Nature Trail off the Big Ferry Causeway is a more thorough immersion in much the same terrain. Its two loops combined total 5 miles, with a shorter loop just short of half that distance. The trail leaves a forested area, crosses a small marsh on a boardwalk, and traverses a mature hardwood forest before skirting a salt marsh to the still and Confederate earthworks. It then follows the marsh and crosses a salt marsh back to the starting point.

Interpretive programs and exhibits explain the features of the island. Annual events explore birding (April) and wild game cooking (winter). Guided tours may be arranged in advance. Facilities include tent and trailer campsites and a swimming pool.

The park is open year-round. Office hours are 8 a.m. to 5 p.m.

Not far away is an unheralded but important attraction—the aquarium of the University of Georgia Marine Extension Service at the Skidaway Oceanographic Institute. In the aquarium are tanks holding dozens of coastal species: gray triggerfish, scrawled cowfish, barbfish, cobia, spotfin butterfly fish, vermillion and gray snapper, bigeye, tomtate, squirrelfish, sea catfish, Atlantic spadefish, sharksucker, striped bass, pompano, nurse shark, Atlantic croaker, black sea bass, longnose gar, bluefish, spotted sea trout, oscillated moray, lined sea horse, and loggerhead and green turtles.

A large collection of shells—from the enormous horseshoe crab to the handsome lettered olive and the delicate angel wing—also is displayed, as are the bones of a pygmy sperm whale that beached itself on Wassaw Island in 1951 and models of sharks and dolphins.

The aquarium has an especially fine display on Gray's Reef, including a relief model of the Pleistocene rock ledges rising from a sandy ocean floor undercut by caverns created during the Ice Age. A thick carpet of seaweed, sponges, and other life attracts so many fish to the site it is often called a "live bottom."

The aquarium is open daily year-round (afternoons on weekends). Interpretive programs, including movies on coastal habitats, are held on a regular basis.

The oceanographic institute and aquarium occupy historic ground. One of Savannah's earliest outposts was located there and visited by theologian John Wesley in 1736. Later, John Milledge founded a plantation named Modena, apparently named after the seat of Italian silk culture. His son, John Jr., was active in the Revolutionary War and afterward was named state attorney general at the age of 23. He later served in the U.S. House of Representatives and U.S. Senate and helped found the University of Georgia.

Sea kayakers paddle the Wilmington River, putting in at Skidaway Island and sometimes going as far as the north end of Wassaw Island.

Wassaw Island National Wildlife Refuge

Wassaw and Pine islands, which protect Skidaway Island from the vagaries of the Atlantic Ocean, form one of Georgia's most pristine refuges. Little development mars the natural state of more than 10,000 acres of beaches, dunes, ponds, marshes, and woodlands.

Wassaw Island, which has 7 miles of gently sloping hard-packed beach, is open to daytime recreational use such as sunbathing, beachcombing for sand dollars, whelks, and other varieties of shells, surfcasting, and nature study. However, the only access is by boat. Boaters may put in at various places, including Lazaretto Creek public ramp at Skidaway Island and marinas. The U.S. Fish & Wildlife Service maintains a landing on Wassaw Creek near the southern end of the island.

The beautiful Wassaw Island beach has many surprises. The appearance is different in winter than it is in summer because high waves pushed by northeasterly winds remove sand from the dunes and beach. Much of it is returned the following summer. Piles of bleached trees uprooted and broken by natural force, including storms, create an unusual sight at the northern end. Nearby are the ruins of a Spanish-American War fort constructed in 1898 and still being reduced by waves. High sand dunes back up the beach at the southern end. Blackwater sloughs are seen in places.

Between mid-May and mid-September, after daytime beachgoers depart, loggerhead turtles laboriously make their way ashore to lay their eggs. Two months later, the offspring hatch and crawl to the water. A scientific project monitors the results.

Migratory birds, including many songbirds, pass through. Bird-watching for parasitic jaeger, roseate spoonbill, yellow-throated warbler, painted bunting, and other species is best during migration periods. Egrets and herons have rookeries on the island, some only a short distance from dunes. Terns, gulls, and other shorebirds feed on the beach, scampering away from incoming waves and then following them out to peck at deposits.

More than 20 miles of interior dirt roads dissect a maritime forest dominated by live oak, palmettos, and slash pine in the north and smaller plants such as yucca and young pines in the south. The routes generally parallel the beach but are connected by much shorter crossroads, including one known as The Avenue that extends inland from the ocean beach to near Wassaw Creek. Despite a problem with insects in the interior, especially during warm months, a combination inland road-beach roundtrip of about 10 miles reveals the diversity of this primitive island to its best advantage.

Deer are plentiful. Gun and bow hunts are held in the fall and winter. Among other animals on the refuge are alligators, turtles, frogs, otters, rabbits, and cottonmouth snakes.

Fishing is excellent in nearby waters—trout, bass, and flounder inshore and Spanish and king mackerel, marlin, and dolphin at Snapper Banks or farther out.

A Wilmington Island charter boat, *Miss Judy IV*, takes birdwatchers, surfcasters, beachcombers, photographers, and others to the beach at the north end of Wassaw Sound. A firm on Skidaway Island takes visitors on a boat tour around the island but will land them on the beach or at the park dock if they wish (see Appendices).

Williamson Island

A sandbar only a quarter century ago, this "new" island is a fascinating study in natural dynamics. It probably was created with sand extracted from nearby Tybee Island. Some scientists wonder whether it can last, but for the time being it is a full-fledged island with a white, sandy beach strewn with seashells and developing sand dunes. The ever-present shorebirds do not question the stability of the island. Neither do other life forms such as ghost and hermit crabs. Offshore waters are shallow and tricky, making it difficult for boaters. Owned by the state, the island is named for a former Darien mayor, Jimmy Williamson.

Fort McAllister/Richmond Hill State Park

These side-by-side state parks bring together the natural finery of the Georgia coastal region and the violent history that so often intruded into the sylvan beauty.

At Fort McAllister Historic Park, a self-guided tour explores the restored massive earthworks that were raised among the pines and cabbage palmettos on the south bank of the Ogeechee River in 1861 under the direction of Captain John McCrady of Charleston, South Carolina. "Bombproofs" whose interiors are fitted out with sparse furniture, strategically placed cannon, and a hot-shot oven imbedded in the earthworks provide insight into the way the garrison lived and fought. Signboards pinpoint some of the unusual aspects of the fighting, including sending Confederate sharpshooters into the marshes to shoot at sailors on attacking Union ironclads.

Restoration of the earthworks was begun in the 1930s by private interests; the earthworks and "bombproofs" were restored to approximately their 1864 condition after the property was transferred to the state.

The fort proved to be one of the most enduring fortifications in the Savannah area. Frequently pounded by Union warships during 1862 and 1863, the sandy earthen walls sustained little damage and were repaired under cover of darkness by Confederate defenders and slaves. During a furious bombardment by ironclad monitors on March 3, 1863, the only casualty was the garrison mascot, Tom Cat. His death was listed in the official report.

In December 1864, General Sherman's army finally subdued the fort in fierce hand-to-hand combat. A period cannon fortifies the angle where the final assault took place. Memorial Day and July 4 interpretive programs sometimes include mock battles; the two-day early December "Winter Muster" recreates the life of soldiers of the period.

An outdoor museum near the park office includes three pieces of rotating machinery from the *CSS Nashville,* which was sunk in the Ogeechee River in February 1863. A boat ramp is nearby.

Adjoining Richmond Hill Park has tent and trailer campsites in an isolated natural setting conducive to birdwatching and other outdoor activities. A nature trail winds about 1.3 miles through woods featuring live oak, palms, cedar, hickory, and a few pines and along the edge of a marsh and creek. A boat ramp and dock provide access to Redbird Creek, whose 4.2-mile canoe trail ascends an ever-narrowing waterway bordered by mature forests and marshes.

The parks, located off U.S. Route 17 along Georgia Route 144 and 144 Spur, are open year-round. However, Fort McAllister is closed Mondays that are not legal holidays and on Thanksgiving and Christmas.

Fort Stewart

Southeast of the town of Richmond Hill along state Route 144 is Fort Stewart, an Army base opened in 1940. A museum features the 24th Infantry Division (Mechanized), which was organized at the outbreak of World War II using units of the old Hawaii Division and which subsequently served in Korea and other overseas posts. The museum displays arms such as a "super bazooka" improvised during the Korean War, equipment, clothing, and photographs of the division and the enemies it faced, as well as the history of Fort Stewart and its Hunter Air Field.

The museum is open from noon to 4 p.m. Tuesday–Friday, 11 a.m. to 3 p.m. Saturday and Sunday, except federal holidays.

Midway

Midway, founded in 1752 by South Carolina Calvinists as a center for missionary work among the Indians of the region, is a quiet, attractive community. It soon also became a market for the rice and indigo farmers in the area and is sometimes recognized as the "cradle of Revolutionary spirit in Georgia."

An 18th-century house on U.S. Route 17 has been turned into a museum housing antique furniture, implements, and documents, open Tuesday–Saturday. Clapboard Midway Church, constructed in 1792, retains its original high pulpit and slave gallery. The live oak in the churchyard predates the building.

LeConte-Woodmanston Plantation

A few miles west of Riceboro, the internationally famous 1810 garden of the LeConte-Woodmanston Plantation is slowly being restored by a dedicated committee. The plantation was used for logging for many years so little remained of the garden or mansion when restoration was started. A mile-long nature walk and an avenue of oaks have been created.

A two-day LeConte-Woodmonston Plantation Rice Festival is held each year at mid-April. Visitors may go there at other times (on Sandy Run Road off U.S. 17), but it is not easy to locate. Those interested should ask for directions at the Midway Museum (912/ 884-5837).

Woodmanston Plantation was developed between 1760 and 1774 by William and John Eatton LeConte. John's son, Louis, took over in 1809 and planted a widely acclaimed botanical and floral garden. One of his sons, Joseph, was a founder of the Sierra Club.

Sunbury

Sunbury State Historic Site on the Medway River preserves the memory of a colonial town described by 18th-century naturalist William Bartram as "beautifully situated." In the mid-18th century, Sunbury was a bustling, fortified port whose future seemed so bright that prominent Georgians invested heavily in land, including that on St. Catherines Island. One of the residents, Dr. Lyman Hall, was a signer of the Declaration of Independence.

At the start of the Revolutionary War, Fort Morris, a quadrangular earth fortification with a moat and 25 cannon, was constructed. When British forces demanded its surrender, the stalwart defenders replied, "Come and take it." The British failed that time, but captured the fort and burned the town the following year. During the War of 1812, Fort Defiance was constructed to protect the town, but it was already in decline by that time. After yellow-fever epidemics, destructive storms, and the Civil War added their havoc, few families remained.

A museum and visitors center with displays and audiovisuals on the history and the ecological importance of the area, stand near the site of the forts. As presented, the first fort was larger than that represented by the surviving earthworks of the second. Some historians argue they were essentially the same size, however. At any rate, despite a profusion of live oak trees hung with Spanish moss where none stood in 1776, the surviving moated earthworks indicate what forts of the period were like.

A trail identifies the presumed boundary of the 1776 fort and enters the walls of the later fort, then circles to a wooded area and boardwalk that overlook the marsh near the town of Sunbury, the naturally deep river, and, in the distance, St. Catherines Sound, which was a major route for sailing vessels. Signs along the path identify plants such as hickory, pecan, black walnut, holly, and wax myrtle.

Living history programs cover such subjects as St. Catherines Island, the War of 1812 in Georgia, Sunbury's Afro-American heritage, the state's poisonous plants, 18th-century women, 18th-century trade, Thanksgiving in Colonial Sunbury, and a colonial Christmas. Annual events include a flintlock, musket, and rifle competition and Revolutionary War battle reenactment in January and Revolutionary War encampments on the Memorial Day and July weekends. Colonial Sunbury Cemetery is about a mile from the historic park.

The fort, about 7 miles off Interstate 95 on an extension of U.S. Route 84/Georgia 38, is open Tuesday–Sunday year-round (except Thanksgiving and Christmas) and on holiday Mondays.

The surrounding area, generally referred to as Dorchester, is a quail hunting area—as hunt club signs indicate. Dorchester Presbyterian Church, 6 miles from Sunbury, was built in 1854 and is one of the original structures of the settlement.

Ebenezer Church

Inland from Savannah, where state Route 275 ends at the river, stands brick Jerusalem Lutheran Church, built in 1767–69 to serve the community of Ebenezer, founded in 1736 by Salzburger exiles. The church, which has held regular services for more than 200 years, proved to be more durable than the community. A nearby restored house is the only other surviving structure from the colonial town, which at its peak had 500 inhabitants, a flour mill, and a pulp plant. The Georgia Salzburger Society maintains a small museum in the church.

Ogeechee River Tract

The Savannah Science Museum owns a 172-acre tract of land off state Route 204 about 1 mile from I-95 and 2 miles from U.S. Route

17 about 10 miles from the mouth of the Ogeechee River. The tract stretches out along the riverbank, and a sandhill ridge apparently created by the ebb and flow of waters in geologic history covers about 22 acres. This puts riverfront and sandhill environments in close proximity.

The last logs were cut more than 30 years ago, and the forest and underbrush have reverted to a natural state. Mixed hardwood trees grow in the river swamp, but longleaf pine, palmetto, scrub oak, and reindeer lichen grow on and along the sandhill ridge and in other areas. Large numbers of wildflowers, such as wild azalea, and dense understory that includes sparkleberry make the tract especially beautiful in the spring. Wild animals, including rare ones like the gopher tortoise, frequent the tract.

No trails have been cut, but an old L-shaped logging road can be used. Finding it is difficult; access lies through the driveway of one of the adjacent landowners and should not be used without consent. Those who want to inspect the property should contact the museum (912/355-6705) for directions. An old canoe landing exists on a creek about half a mile into the property from the river.

A paper company and hunting club own adjoining property along the river.

Tuckasee King Landing

This high bluff on Georgia Highway 119 west of I-95 is an uncommon phenomenon in many regards. Not many bluffs of this height (75 to 100 feet) exist in coastal Georgia. Within the site are a number of plants normally associated with more northern climates, such as mosses, wild ginger, and liverworts.

A boat ramp provides access to the river.

An historical marker on Route 119 records the area's significance to Baptists. Not far away is a replica of the first Baptist church built in Georgia.

Tuckahoe Wildlife Management Area

This 10,950-acre site on the Savannah River and Brier Creek, 66 percent of which is wetlands, is a prime hunting area for deer, wild turkey, feral hogs, and squirrels, with smaller populations of ducks, rabbits, and quail. The river, creek, and 69 acres of oxbow lakes also are favorable to fishing.

Located in Screven County about 50 miles west of Savannah, the refuge extends nearly 12 miles along the Savannah River. Hardwood forests dominate the high ground, with natural and planted pines covering about 22 percent of the land. Nature viewing includes fur-bearing animals, alligators, Mississippi and swallow-tail kites, wading birds, and songbirds. Two Indian mounds and a Revolutionary War battlefield are on the site, which is crisscrossed by old logging roads.

Tuckahoe Wildlife Management Area lies east of Sylvania and off Georgia Route 24 on County Road 243 (Brannen Bridges Road) and County Road 127.

Golden Isles
Green Land

SOUTH OF SAVANNAH, HUGGING THE MAINLAND, IS A STRING OF BARRIER islands that are now known collectively as "The Golden Isles." Spanish conquistadors, disappointed they did not find gold metal, nevertheless recognized the substantial beauty and gave them the name. The term now is revived as a promotional tool, but these are, indeed, special islands. And there is nothing collective about them. The islands are as diverse as their mixed heritage would indicate. Some have long been playgrounds for the rich and famous; others are so remote or barren they have been left to the forces of nature and the animals that can contend with them. They range from posh resorts like Sea Island to the undisturbed wilderness of Wolf Island and the organized wilderness of Cumberland Island.

The adjacent mainland has much the same diversity. A number of coastal rivers and bays are dotted with fishing villages and historic sites. The silt-laden Altamaha River, the principal stream of Georgia's largest drainage system, combines two inland rivers and then flows 135 miles through coastal plain that includes extensive areas of hardwood and cypress swamps broken by hammocks. This habitat sustains an extensive animal population and is an excellent area for canoeing, boating, fishing, and camping. It empties near the center of the island chain.

Brunswick, after Savannah the largest community in the region, combines both an industrial base and an extensive collection of historical buildings. It is the second oldest town in the state.

Ossabaw Island

The charm of Ossabaw Island is obvious to the few who get to visit it. It has 25,000 acres of high ground and freshwater and saltwater marshes. The terrain is flat, the highest elevation being 18 feet. Forests are mainly hardwood, with some stands of pine. Underbrush is light. Nine miles of sandy beaches where loggerhead turtles nest are constantly being molded by waves, winds, and storms, sometimes on a daily or weekly basis.

Feral hogs, descendants of those released on the island in the early decades of this century to increase hunting potential, and donkeys taken to the island as pets in the 1960s roam at will. Alligators lie in the sun on the banks of ponds. Beaver, mink, otter, and raccoon share the ponds and marshes with them. The substantial bird population includes a large number of wood stork and Eastern brown pelican, a few bald eagle and wild turkey, numerous herons, egrets, terns, doves, black ducks, mallards, green-winged teals, Canadian geese, and gadwalls. Bluebirds are aided by boxes spotted at various places.

Ossabaw was designated in 1976 as Georgia's first Heritage Preserve for natural, cultural, and scientific purposes. Consequently, public use is restricted. Controlled deer hunts the first weekend in November, Thanksgiving weekend, the first weekend in December, and the weekend before Christmas have in recent years had the highest success rate in the state. Bags average about 80 to 90 pounds, with 134 pounds being the island record. About 285 are taken each year from a herd estimated at more than 50 per square mile. Small game hunts — rabbits, squirrels, ducks, geese, and rail — are held the last weekend in December and the first two weekends in January.

Boaters can land and use beaches to the high-water mark on both sides of the island without permits, but should be careful not to get stranded by falling tides. While many boaters land at Bradley Point on Ossabaw Sound, most of the palm tree-lined ocean shore may also be used. Indeed, fishing and crabbing are especially good at Bradley and Big sloughs at Middle Beach.

The Georgia Department of Natural Resources, which manages the island, has a dock at Torrey Landing for its own use and that

Wild hog, Ossabaw Island. PHOTO BY JOHN BOWEN.

of the Ossabaw Foundation, which sponsors educational and artistic programs. Several shelter sites are used by educational groups for field trips or research programs. Rustic camps are available to hunters. Occasionally, groups are permitted to visit the interior of the island.

The island retains many signs of its uses over the centuries since the Indians hunted there before the Spanish came to look and British colonists cleared the forests and dug canals to develop a plantation economy. A few tabby buildings, originally slave quarters, survive from the plantation era. Old bottles, china, and charred wood have been discovered near the site of an old port. A hunting lodge recalls the early part of this century when it became a recreation site for wealthy businessmen. A wrecked helicopter lies forlornly in a marsh near the southern end of the island.

The island was purchased in 1924 by Dr. N. H. Torrey as a winter homesite. His daughter, Mrs. Eleanor Torrey West, made it her permanent home and retained a life right when the state acquired the property. She founded the Ossabaw Foundation in the 1960s.

Harris Neck Wildlife Refuge

The Harris Neck National Wildlife Refuge, 7 miles off U.S. Route 17 on Georgia Route 131, occupies a 1750s plantation site on the banks of the South Newport River that in the 1890s provided a retreat for the wealthy P. Lorillard family, then was used as an Air Force training center during World War II. More than 60 percent of the approximately 2,700 acres in the refuge is saltwater marsh. The remainder is open fields, where remnants of the World War II runways remain, and mixed deciduous forests.

More than 225 species of birds have been identified, including tricolored and night herons, great egret, wigeon, teal, and gadwall. At least ten species of ducks and nine of wading birds nest there.

The refuge has more than 15 miles of paved roads open to hiking, biking, and driving. The principal feature is an 8-mile marked trail that begins at the visitor contact point on Route 131, proceeds through alternating sections of forest and field, crosses the abandoned airstrip, visits more forests (a detour leads to the South Newport River Recreation Area) and fields, and exits on Route 131. A right turn takes the visitor back to the refuge entrance. A left turn leads to Barbour Point Landing, which has a boat ramp for general use that provides access to tidal waters and nearby islands and a dock that is restricted to permit holders (fishers use the bank, too).

Fishing piers at the visitor contact point provide access to Harris Neck Creek. Managed archery and gun hunts for white-tailed deer are held in autumn and winter.

The refuge, created in 1962, is open daily year-round. Controlled burning and flooding are part of the conservation program. Some areas may be closed at times to protect wildlife.

St. Catherines Island

An anomaly—it was formed in two distinct geologic periods—gives this 14,000-acre barrier island unusual attributes. The most striking is a 22-foot bluff overlooking a broad sand beach at the northern tip. Eleven miles of beach face the Atlantic Ocean.

The varied terrain and lush subtropical vegetation have proved to be amenable to experimental breeding of exotic animals, ranging from lemurs to hartebeests and Madagascar turtles, under a program established in 1968 in cooperation with the New York Zoological Society. The St. Catherine Island Foundation, which owns and manages the island, also cooperates with the Georgia Department of Natural Resources, University of the South, Georgia Southern University, and other organizations on research regarding more than 300 endangered species and supervises a sea turtle monitoring and nest protection program.

The Guale Indians, the last of a series of tribes to inhabit the island, regarded St. Catherines as their capital. One of the original Spanish missions, Santa Catalina de Guale, was founded about 1566. (The foundations were excavated in 1982 by the American Museum of Natural History, in association with the Edward J. Noble Foundation.) Between 1765 and 1777, it was a plantation owned by Button Gwinnett, a Georgia signer of the Declaration of Independence and member of the Continental Congress before he was killed in a duel. A mansion and slave cabins built around 1800 remain.

Public access to the island is limited. Since Georgia beaches to the high water mark are public property, these are open to boaters. In addition, organizations such as The Nature Conservancy and schools run group field trips. Certain areas are posted during the nesting periods of pelicans, Wilson's plover, terns and other birds.

Altamaha River Sites

The Altamaha River is one of the principal rivers of Georgia, dumping about 3.2 trillion gallons of water into the Atlantic Ocean each year. Near the coast, it broadens out into a flood delta about 5 miles wide that is enriched by alluvial sediments. Islands, oxbow lakes, sloughs, and sand ridges show how river channels have changed from time to time. Tidal action is apparent in many ways.

The 21,000-acre Altamaha State Waterfowl Management Area straddles the river and a number of other streams and encompasses eight large islands with flooded fields and forests. While much of the area was cleared for rice farming and logging in the 18th and 19th centuries, Lewis Island, added to the refuge in 1973, has a 300-acre stand of virgin cypress over 1,000 years old, one of which is estimated to have been standing 1,300 years.

Rare flora include cork tree, *spartina acori,* and rosemary. The varied habitats of the refuge produce typical growth, including birch, ash, sycamore, red maple, tupelo, red bay, oaks, water elm, sweetgum, spruce pine, hackberry, palmetto, hornbeam, American beautybush, trumpet vine, greenbrier, holly, lizard tail, poison ivy, pickerel weed, wild rice, arrow arum, false dragonhead, spider lily, pond weed, wigeon grass, panic grass, wild millet, cordgrass, bullrush, and needle rush.

The Altamaha River complex is a prime waterfowl area, with a high concentration of ducks. Other game animals include white-tailed deer, squirrels, rabbits, wild turkey, and doves. Also present are alligators, bobcat, raccoon, bald eagle, osprey, herons, hawks, owls, kites, and other species.

The refuge provides recreational opportunities primarily for hunters, fishers, boaters, canoers, and campers. Normally, about a dozen hunting periods, most of them short, are set for deer, waterfowl, snipe, doves, squirrels, rabbits, fox, bobcat, raccoons, and opossum. Feral hogs may be taken during some deer-hunting seasons. Canoeists and boaters can reach into a sylvan wilderness area for fishing and nature viewing. Ramp access includes one at the site of Fort Barrington, a frontier fort built about 1750 that accesses Lewis Island.

The refuge also can be used to good advantage by naturalists, birdwatchers, and photographers. Just south of the Champney River Bridge on U.S. Route 17 is the James Allen Williamson Park, which has a boat ramp, a pier, and a short footbridge alongside the highway crossing. On the opposite side of Route 17, an inconspicuous dirt road leads to the Ashley/Hodges Memorial Deck for wildfowl viewing over a pond and marsh (with Interstate 95 in the distance).

Butler Island, now within the refuge, was owned by Pierce Butler, who is credited with introducing the rice culture into Georgia.

Farther upstream, a 1,330-acre scenic buffer preserves a 300-foot-wide strip at The Narrows, which includes swamps and upland hammocks. A number of public boat ramps permit canoeing, boating, fishing, and camping.

The Big Hammock Wildlife Management Area straddles state Route 144 about 20 miles west of Jesup along state Route 169. The 6,400-acre tract on the north shore of the Altamaha River also contains a public fishing area. Big Hammock Natural Area is adjacent; it abuts county road 441. The site is mostly lowlands stretching 11 miles along the river and Watermelon Creek, with adjacent uplands dominated by hardwoods. A number of lakes are reachable by primitive roads or on foot. A sign-in box is located on Route 144.

Turkey, squirrel, and raccoon hunting is rated as good, while deer, hog, and duck populations are considered only fair. Quail and rabbit numbers are low. Wildlife viewing — osprey, Mississippi and swallow-tail kites, wood duck, white ibis, anhinga, great blue heron, common egret, gopher tortoise, and indigo snake included — is excellent.

Eight paths suitable for walking leave unpaved roads. A Tattnall County boat landing is located on the river at the western end of the refuge, but there are no camping facilities.

Sapelo Island

Sapelo Island has a number of masters — state, federal, and private — but they seem to work well together in preserving the island as nature intended.

The R.J. Reynolds State Wildlife Refuge covers about 8,240 acres of maritime forest, fields, and marshland. Oaks and pines dominate the forests, which also have hollies, magnolia, blackgum, red bay, and red maple and understories featuring wax myrtle and palmettos. Tidal streams in the tract include Cabretta Creek and Mud River.

The refuge, home to moderate herds of white-tailed deer and flocks of turkeys, is managed by the Georgia Department of Natural Resources, Game and Fish Division. Normally, three archery and firearms hunts are held each year for conservation purposes. Doves and ducks are scarcer. Wading and shore birds are numerous, while

Sand drifts and boardwalk, Sapelo Island. PHOTO BY JOHN BOWEN.

osprey, southern bald eagle, eastern brown pelican, and peregrine falcon are there in small numbers.

At the southern tip of Sapelo, the University of Georgia operates a marine institute in a tabby house built during the first half of the 19th century and later structures originally used as dairy barns. It does not cater to visitors, but does not turn them away, either.

More than 5,900 acres of unspoiled forest and nearby salt marshes on the inland side of the island have been designated as the Sapelo Island National Estuarine Research Reserve, founded in 1976 by the National Oceanic and Atmospheric Administration (NOAA) and administered by the Georgia Department of Natural Resources, Game and Fish Division. The tidal currents on Duplin River and Doboy Sound are typical of estuaries found along the coast from North Carolina to northern Florida.

Flora in the reserve include live and laurel oaks, slash and lob-lolly pines, cordgrass, glasswort, needlerush, and sea oxeye.

Visitors arrive aboard the 145-passenger boat *Sapelo Queen* after a 30-minute cruise from Meridian down Hudson Creek and along other tidal streams and marshes where playful dolphin sometimes may be seen. Groups may tour the island March through October on Saturdays and the last Tuesday of each month, and Wednesdays and Fridays June through Labor Day by prior arrangement. The basic tour is a three-hour morning visit to the south end of the island; once a month (the last Tuesday), a five-hour all-island trip is conducted. Primitive camping is permitted.

Narrow roads wind through pines, oaks, red cedar, marsh elder, camphorweed, wax myrtle, and yucca. Wildflowers are rampant in the March–October period. The roads pass a manmade freshwater duck pond also inhabited by alligators, the "Big House" (the former Reynolds home) now used for educational conferences, and the small 1820 lighthouse, tabby ruins, and an artillery range marker from the World War II era. Picnic shelters overlook a broad sandy beach alive with shorebirds. Fishers may seek bluefish, menhaden, mullet, sea trout, red drum, flounder, and other species from beach, pier, and tidal creek vantage points.

The intracoastal waterway snakes through landward streams also visited by many species of birds, including ducks, geese, osprey, little blue, great blue, and green herons, snowy egret, white ibis, red-winged blackbird, black-bellied plover, least sandpiper, eastern brown pelican, willet, and clapper rail. Even a few piping plover, an endangered species, have been seen.

Among other species found on the island and its waterways are river otter, feral cows, mink, raccoon, diamondback terrapin, marsh periwinkle, sand fiddler, blue crab, purple marsh crab, ribbed mussel, white shrimp, wasps, grasshoppers, flies, mosquitos, sea turtle, starfish, sand dollar, and manatees.

Hog Hammock, a 434-acre enclave created in the early 19th century, has a permanent population of about 90 and two noteworthy structures: St. Luke's Baptist Church and a store that sells T-shirts and other souvenirs. Rental units are available. The island has a 6,000-foot airstrip that can accommodate small planes.

Indian settlement of the fourth largest of Georgia's barrier islands dates back at least 3,400 years. A ceremonial ring 60 yards in diameter and 12 feet high and shell middens indicate a lifestyle 3,000 years ago dependent on indigenous seafood and game. Pottery believed to be 4,500 years old has been discovered on the island. Guale Indian villages existed in the 1520s when the first Europeans arrived and began to fight over the island. The British solidified their claim by purchasing the island from Indian Princess Mary Musgrove. It was a thriving plantation growing sea island cotton, sugar cane, and corn at the outbreak of the Civil War, but declined afterward.

In 1927, aviation pioneer Charles A. Lindbergh flew from Sapelo. Tobacco heir Richard J. Reynolds, Jr., purchased the island in 1934 and was instrumental in having the University of Georgia establish a research institute there. In 1969, the state purchased three-quarters of the island from Reynolds's widow for a wildlife refuge. It acquired the southern end of the island in 1976.

Like other barrier islands, Sapelo is dynamic, constantly eroding in places and building up in others according to wind, wave, tidal, and hurricane conditions. The island began as a series of shoreline dunes and ridges created by sand carried downriver. Rising sea levels during the "Great Ice Age" (Pleistocene Epoch) flooded the island behind the dunes. The land side of the island apparently was formed 25,000 to 36,000 years ago, while the seaward side was added as recently as 4,000 to 5,000 years ago.

Managed deer hunts are held five times between September and December, three of them open. Conventional firearms, primitive firearms, and bows are permitted. In addition, several turkey shoots are held in the March–May season and hunting for opossum, squirrels, and other small game is allowed. Hunters also may bag marsh hens in the spring.

Blackbeard Island National Wildlife Refuge

Isolation has given this refuge northeast of Sapelo a bye in the tourist tournament. While the elongated, 5,600-acre island has been minimally developed, motor vehicles are not permitted and few tourists make the effort to go there. This means the island is a special treat for nature lovers.

Forests featuring slash pine, live oak, cabbage palmetto, Southern magnolia, and American holly shelter deer, small animals, hummingbirds, owls, and numerous kinds of songbirds. The annual avian migrations make the island an excellent place for birdwatching. Even a bald eagle is spotted occasionally. Loggerhead turtles nest on the beaches at night during the warm months. A few deer hunts are held in autumn and winter, but the herd is not large.

A thick jumble of broken and dead trees covers the beach at the northern end—so-called Boneyard Beach. Otherwise, a broad, hard-packed sandy oceanside beach extends the length of the island and curves around both tips—a distance of about 7 miles. It is lightly visited, except by shorebirds and wading birds, making it ideal for day-use sunbathers, swimmers, surf fishers, or shell seekers (plenty of shells) who prefer isolation.

More than 20 miles of roads and hiking trails extend almost the length of the island, passing parallel sand dunes separated by narrow grassy plains, the oceanfront beach, and saltwater and freshwater ponds.

Tidal creeks and docks permit saltwater fishing year-round; freshwater fishing is permitted in North and Flag ponds near Sapelo Sound from mid-March to late October. A public dock is located near Bay Hammock at the north end. Another dock stands at the refuge headquarters farther south on Blackbeard Creek. Mainland public and private put-in places are not far away; Barbour Point Landing at Harris Creek National Wildlife Refuge is one.

Those without boats can arrange for a visit at Shellman's Bluff, at the end of Shellman's Bluff Road on the Julienton River. Captain Suzanne Forsyth carries hunters, photographers, and naturalists who want to do their own thing, as well as visitors interested in history and short nature walks. She usually takes the groupies to both docks, conducting a 2.5-mile walk in the dense hardwood forest at the northern end of the island, where an 1890s crematorium marks the site of an old quarantine station, and a 1-mile walk through young-growth woods to Nelson's Bluff and the sand dunes and beach at the south end.

Although there is no recorded association with Blackbeard, legend persists that the infamous pirate anchored his ship, *Queen Anne's Revenge,* and rowed ashore here to bury a chest full of treasure. Whatever the reality, the island's thick woods and ready creeks provided the kind of refuge that attracted pirates when they raided the sea lanes along the Atlantic coastline. Actually, the island has been in federal hands since 1800, when the U.S. Navy purchased it as a source of oak timber for shipbuilding. It was transferred to the U.S. Fish and Wildlife Service in 1924 and made a national refuge in 1940 by presidential proclamation. Three thousand acres were declared national wilderness in 1975.

Darien and Fort King George

A good time to visit Darien is early April when the shrimp fleet is being blessed. This annual event turns a normally idle nearby street into a flea market selling everything from homemade crafts and food to manufactured oddities. The traffic jam includes an occasional motor home almost too big to negotiate the narrow street.

The harbor, the cause of this pleasant unrest, lies on the banks of the North Branch of the Altamaha River (often shown as the

The shrimp fleet at Darien. PHOTO BY JOHN BOWEN.

Darien River on local maps) at the end of downhill paths. It is small, but the docks are crowded with boats, some of them large and impressive. Drying nets hang from masts.

This riverfront has kept Darien on the cutting edge of Georgia history. It was the reason General Oglethorpe placed a fortified settlement here, populating it with Scottish Highlanders. These fierce fighting men on several occasions rallied to the defense of Georgia; in 1742, they were instrumental in the defeat of the Spanish in the Battle of Bloody Marsh on St. Simons Island. A monument to these pioneers stands where U.S. 17 and state Route 99 cross in the historic section of town. Another monument of sorts is First Presbyterian Church, started by the Scots in 1739 as the first congregation of the denomination in Georgia. The present Gothic-Victorian building was raised in 1900.

Darien was heavily damaged by a Union raid in 1863, but revived faster than many other communities. In the latter part of the 19th century, when lumber and rice were major Georgia exports, Darien was the largest port in the state. At that time, the Darien Bank (the two-story structure on West Broad Street, built about 1820) was the state's most important financial institution. Since the 1920s, shrimp fishing has been a foundation of the town's economy.

Darien is a pleasant community with a low-key outlook. A self-guided walking tour covers the principal historic sites, including pre-Civil War tabby ruins. The James Grant House, dating from the 1840s, was the only home to survive Civil War destruction. The handsome Methodist Church raised in 1884, 1878 St. Andrew's Episcopal Church, 1868 First African Baptist Church, and 1876 St. Cyprian's Episcopal Church, a tabby structure, stand among houses with pleasure boats on trailers and clusters of gourd birdhouses in their yards.

The principal tourist attraction at Darien is reconstructed Fort King George, whose ancestor antedates the official settlement of Georgia. A log outpost on the Altamaha River was built in 1722 by provincial forces from South Carolina worried about Spanish and French incursions from Florida.

Gunports of the three-story, 26-foot-square cypress blockhouse, faithfully reconstructed by the Georgia Department of Natural Resources, overlook a branch in the river's marshy delta (the river has changed course since the original fort was built). Part of the log palisade and most of the short-lived fort, which was abandoned in 1727 (except for two lookouts) in favor of Port Royal, also have been reconstructed.

Interpreters in the familiar red British uniform of the period demonstrate drilling, load and discharge the awkward muskets of the era, and discuss the strategic importance of the small fort, as well as the day-to-day woodworking and other household activities of the garrison. They also describe the uniforms and life of the garrison—members of the 41st Regiment of the South Carolina Independents, known as the "Invalid" Regiment because it was formed of battle-scarred veterans of British wars.

Exhibits in the modern brick museum cover the British-Spanish rivalry along the Georgia coast, the construction of the fort, and personal details about the British garrison, as well as the Indian and Spanish presence. Fort King George is open 9 a.m. to 5 p.m. Tuesday–Saturday, 2 to 5 p.m. Sunday year-round except Monday and major holidays.

Nature harmonizes with history in this state historic site. An abundance of wildflowers, aquatic birds, lizards, snakes, and alligators give the forested area much the same appearance as when the fort was founded. These may be experienced on a walk along a 1-mile marsh trail.

Boaters may visit small nearby islands formed by nature around ballast stones thrown overboard by schooners before they continued upriver to load longleaf pine at Darien.

The site of the fort (just off U.S. 17 and I-95) earlier held a Guale Indian village, the earliest recorded settlement of coastal Georgia, and a Spanish mission. The Indians hunted alligators and wild game, fished and collected shellfish in dugout canoes, and cultivated beans, squash, and corn. They lived in small mud and wattle huts. The Spanish mission was part of a chain established on the islands and waterways of Georgia, but an Indian uprising in 1597 destroyed many of them. Priests' severed heads were impaled on stakes at prominent points along the riverbank as a warning. However, pressure from tribes in south Carolina caused the Guale to abandon the area in the late 17th century.

Around Darien

A driving tour extending in various directions from Darien covers a number of other coastal sites. South along U.S. 17 are remnants of the dikes and canals, designed by engineers from Holland, which made Butler Island famous for rice through the mid-19th century. The state-managed Altamaha Waterfowl Area is headquartered on the island.

A mile north of Darien, on state Route 99, is Ashantilly, a restored 1820s mansion. Now privately owned, it is the headquarters of a publishing company. Adjacent is St. Andrew's Cemetery, established in 1818.

Farther along Route 99, in the quiet community of Ridgeville (known locally as "The Ridge"), lived many of the lumber barons and harbor pilots who helped make Darien Georgia's second largest port. The Downey House dates from 1880, and the cypress Tyson House from about 1890; both are now privately owned. In South Newport, off U.S. 17, is tiny Christ Chapel, which seats 12 people and is reputed to be the smallest church in Georgia. The chapel was designed as a place of meditation and worship for travelers when U.S. Route 17 was the major artery through the area.

Wolf Island National Wildlife Refuge. Actually, three islands (Wolf, Egg, and Little Egg) are included in this soggy, isolated preserve at the mouth of the Altamaha River off Darien. About 4,000 acres of tidal marshland and 135 acres of stunted forests and beaches provide habitat for numerous shorebirds, water fowl, wading birds, loggerhead turtles, and other species. Forests feature pines, red cedar, oak, dewberry, and wax myrtle, while marshes are dotted with cord-grass and needlerush.

The narrow beach on Wolf Island is usable during the daytime.

Hofwyl-Broadfield Plantation. Hofwyl-Broadfield Plantation Historic Site interprets the rice-growing culture prominent along the Georgia coastline in the early 19th century and serves as a wildlife sanctuary. Some of the dikes that created rice paddies remain.

All visitors are exposed to the coastal countryside by a quarter-mile walk to the L-shaped white-frame "big house," which was a modest structure when it was built in the affluent 1850s. The structure, modified over the years, is furnished as it was when the state acquired it in 1973. Original furnishings, including those made by craftsmen in Philadelphia and South Carolina, date from several periods. The oldest was made in 1790.

Ancillary buildings, including a shed built to pay workers after the Civil War freed the slaves, also may be visited. Most of them, including the ice house, milking barn, and bottling house, date from the 1915–1940s period when the site was a dairy farm.

Those who want to study the terrain more closely may approach the house along a 1-mile path that starts at the visitors center. It goes to a freshwater marsh near the ruins of a pre-Civil War rice mill, then follows a dike along paddies that date back almost 170 years before turning to reach the main house. Animals such as raccoons and feral hogs, snakes, and fire ants in hills may be seen along the way.

The visitors center contains a fine introduction to the rice culture of coastal Georgia. Despite the title, "The Aristocracy of Rice," it covers the methods of planting, growing, and harvesting rice.

Broadfield Plantation, created in 1806 by William Brailsford, was ruined by the Civil War but replanted afterward. After the rice market collapsed late in the 19th century, the land was used for dairy farming. Hofwyl-Broadfield Plantation is open Tuesday–Sunday year-round (afternoons on Sundays) and a few Monday holidays. It is closed Thanksgiving and Christmas Day.

Brunswick

The second largest community on Georgia's coastline is also one of the state's commercial centers. The odor from the paper mills is often obvious as soon as the city comes into view. It is also the self-proclaimed "Shrimp Capital of the World"; visitors may watch the vessels unload at the docks on Bay Street (U.S. Route 341) between Gloucester and Price streets on most weekday afternoons. Laid out in 1771 as a seaport, Brunswick has always had a commercial and industrial heart. It managed to survive Revolutionary and Civil Wars and their aftermaths and boomed during the Resort Era that began in the late 19th century. Today, it is best known as the approach to the prestigious St. Simons and Sea Island resorts offshore.

.Brunswick's extensive historic district, bounded by Reynolds, Union, Egmont, London, and Prince streets, makes it a legitimate stop in itself, however. Thirty-six structures are cited by the Old Town Brunswick Preservation Association as having historical significance. The oldest dates from 1819; many, like the Dart-Brown residence (circa 1887) that houses the Chamber of Commerce are striking Victorian houses. The city is intimately associated with Georgia's greatest poet, Sidney Lanier. He visited the home on Albany Street, just off George Street, on numerous occasions during the 1870s when it was owned by his brother-in-law, Henry C. Day.

A self-guided driving or walking tour covers these and other features such as the Lovers Oak at the intersection of Prince and Albany streets. The 900-year-old tree, a favorite subject of artists, reputedly was the meeting place of a young Indian couple. A map can be obtained at Old City Hall or a visitors center on Route 17.

The impressive 1907 Glynn County Courthouse, with large columns and a cupola clock, stands in a four-acre park shaded by live oak decorated with Spanish moss, swamp holly, and tung and Chinese pistachio trees. The Mary Miller Doll House at 1523 Glynn Avenue holds more than 3,000 dolls, some of them three centuries old, from 90 countries. The museum is open 11 a.m. to 5 p.m. Monday–Saturday.

The live oak tree under which Lanier sat while looking out over "a world of marshes that borders a world of sea," which he described beautifully in his famous poem, "The Marshes of Glynn," stands near U.S. Route 17 about a mile north of the city and less than half a mile south of the road to St. Simons Island.

Visitors may view tidal action (". . . all is still, and the currents cease to run, And the sea and the marsh are one," in the words of Lanier) on a short boardwalk at the Marshes of Glynn Overlook Park. It crosses a salt marsh and tidal creek and ends at another creek where crabbing, fishing, and shrimping are allowed. An exhibit room adjacent to the department office houses three saltwater aquariums stocked with local marine life and a "petting" tank.

The picnic area also overlooks the famous Marshes of Glynn. Boating facilities include a dock and ramp. The park is managed by the Georgia Department of Natural Resources.

Brunswick was surrounded by many historic plantations, of which some remnants remain today. Hopeton on the Altamaha was the home of a pioneer agriculturalist, James Hamilton Couper. Part of the old Elizafield Plantation is now Boys Estate, a state boys' home.

Brunswick is also the gateway to some of the most prestigious resorts on the East Coast.

The Triumvirate

In the center of the Georgia coastline, three islands cluster together like a unit, almost heart-shaped. Someone with only a one-shot chance to visit the islands will be able to see something of the diversity of use and habitat that characterizes the entire barrier chain.

St. Simons. The largest of Georgia's barrier islands is also perhaps the most accessible to the casual visitor. It is also arguably the most historic. Despite extensive development, it retains much of its quiet charm. One can still commune with nature along live oak-bordered roads, view swamps filled with cordgrass and a few alligators, and follow trails through maritime forests to the edge of marshes.

The most significant colonial battle on the Georgia coast, which kept the colony under the English crown, took place on St. Simons Island. In 1734, General Oglethorpe chose the bluff at Devil's Elbow, a sharp bend in the South Branch of the Altamaha River, as the site of a fort to defend settlements at Savannah and Darien. When the fortified town was ready two years later, he named it after Frederick, Prince of Wales, the only son of King George II. The strategic importance of the fort was proved less than a decade later when a Spanish invasion force landed on the coast of St. Simons Island. However, Oglethorpe did not wait behind prepared defenses, as the Spanish apparently expected him to do. On July 7, 1742, soldiers from the fort, reinforced by a few hundred Highlanders largely from Darien, surprised and defeated more than 2,000 Spanish soldiers in the confused Battle of Bloody Marsh. The defeat ended Spanish hopes of asserting claims to the Georgia colony.

The site, on the southern end of the island, off Old Military Road, is a detached part of Fort Frederica National Monument, which also preserves the ruins of a fortified town established by Oglethorpe to protect the embryonic Georgia colony. In the park visitors center at the town site, a movie describes the life of the settlers. At its peak more than 1,500 people lived there, frequenting five taverns and surreptitiously engaging in smuggling. The town had plenty of tradesmen, but no lawyers because General Oglethorpe regarded them as "scalawags and thieves."

A model of the tabby fort and brick-and-tabby military town provides a good introduction to the ruins outside. From the visitors center, a path called Broad Street leads past the remnants of a burial ground, vestiges of the military road General Oglethorpe used to reach Bloody Marsh, and ruins of several buildings. Signboards and audio stations explain the remains of structures such as the foundations of houses, the ruins of the soldiers' barracks, and the turreted remnants of the King's Magazine, where arms were stored. The fort has been described as the "largest, most regular, and perhaps most costly" British fortification in the U.S. Near the magazine are several cannon, one of which was excavated on the site and, therefore, must have been one of Oglethorpe's.

Signboards also explain everyday artifacts discovered at the townsite such as fishhooks, tools, a pewter spoon, and a section of chain. The route is flanked at times by live oak hung with Spanish moss and planted pecan trees.

The community withered after Oglethorpe withdrew his troops. A fire in 1758 caused major damage. The town lasted only 25 years, but served its purpose well. In later years, the old buildings were cannibalized by residents and used to build new structures.

Rangers conduct guided tours and demonstrate such activities as musketball manufacture, mixing tabby, and women's chores and diversions. The park is open 8:30 a.m. to 5:30 p.m. in summer, 8 a.m. to 5 p.m. at other times, except Christmas Day.

Bikes are often used on St. Simons Island to visit historic places such as Christ Church, which stands on the site of a giant oak tree where John and Charles Wesley preached their first sermon to the Indians. The brothers, who founded the Methodist movement, were serving at the time as chaplain and secretary to General Oglethorpe. The square first church built by planters was severely damaged during the Civil War by Union soldiers who used it as a barracks. The present handsome brick building, raised in 1884 by Anson Green

Phelps Dodge, Jr., as a memorial to his wife, is in the form of a cross. The wide sanctuary has many qualities seen in the interior of a ship. One of the stained-glass windows depicts John and Charles Wesley preaching under the oak tree; another shows Oglethorpe negotiating with an Indian chief.

The church is open for three afternoon hours starting at 2 p.m. in the summer and shoulder months and 1 p.m. at other times.

Roads also pass the sites of some of the 12 historic plantations that existed on the island. A driving tour marked by Five Flag signs that starts in Brunswick can be shortened by starting at Overlook Park at the entrance to the causeway to St. Simons Island. It passes the well-known historic and natural attractions and some of the less-known ones, including Retreat Plantation (now a golf course), Massengale Park ocean beach, the Bloody Point battle site, Fort Frederica, Christ Church, and Gascogne Bluff, whose live oak timbers were used in construction of *Old Ironsides* and the Brooklyn Bridge.

Epworth-by-the-Sea, a Methodist Church center, stands on the site of Hamilton Plantation, one of the largest and most important antebellum farms. Old slave cabins remain from that era. A museum displays historic relics. Two fishing piers are on the grounds.

A lighthouse has stood on a site at Couper's Point, purchased for $1 by the U.S. government, since 1811. During the Civil War, Confederate troops at first fortified the site; when they moved out in 1862, they dynamited the lighthouse to prevent its use by Union forces. The present lighthouse and keeper's house were erected in 1872. The Fresnel lens, visible 18 miles at sea, continues to serve as a navigational beacon, but visitors may climb the 129 steps to the top for a splendid view over the island and nearby waters.

The lighthouse complex on the southern end of the island is now the Museum of Coastal History. Regional history displays are housed in the lightkeeper's house, while coastal artifacts, illustrations, and other objects are displayed in an 1890 brick oil house. An early 20th-century gazebo also is on the site. The museum is open 10 a.m. to 5 p.m. Tuesday–Saturday, 1:30 to 4 p.m. Sunday between Memorial and Labor Days, Tuesday–Sunday afternoons in other months. It is closed on major holidays.

A fishing pier also is located at the southern end of the island.

St. Simons became a popular summer resort during the last decade of the 19th century when the to-the-beach movement was in full swing. Boats took families from the mainland to island docks, where carriages met them and carried them to fashionable hotels and boarding houses. The soft breezes of a semitropical climate, historical explorations, and unhurried atmosphere regenerated them. The movement accelerated after World War II with the construction of elegant new resort facilities and luxury condominiums. Today, St. Simons is a prestigious vacation island, with an extensive sports capability, especially golf, in addition to traditional pursuits.

Little St. Simons. Resort living and nature complement each other on this 10,000-acre island, to the ocean side of large St. Simons. Reachable only by boat, the island has the feel of a secluded personal retreat.

Today's small upscale resort is centered around the comfortable Hunting Lodge, built in 1917. The early 1920s Michael Cottage also dates back to the period when the island was a private family sanctuary. Roads reach the most important points on the ocean end of the island, including the main beach. Historic ruins of an old rice plantation and Indian middens are located at various places.

Visitor activities are oriented toward the outdoors, such as horseback riding and hiking through stands of virgin pine and maritime oak; canoeing in Mitchell Marsh; trout fishing in Mosquito Creek and surfcasting for redfish; outdoor photography expeditions; and beachcombing on 7 miles of private beach, including Rainbow Beach. Hunting for European fallow deer begins in November.

Most of the wilderness has been retained. A large herd of deer feeds on the sparse coastal vegetation, which also sustains raccoon, opossum, armadillo, alligator, snakes, and frogs. More than 200 species of birds change with the seasons, including ducks, peregrine falcon, bald eagle, Northern harrier, cormorants, tree swallow, whimbrel, royal and Caspian terns, rails, loons, wood stork, Wilson's and semipalmated plovers, and a few of the endangered piping plover.

Day trips lasting about six hours begin at the Hampton River Club Marina between June and September. After a 20-minute boat tour to the Little St. Simon Island dock, visitors are taken on a truck tour of the north end of the island, followed by lunch. The feature of the afternoon is a beach walk led by a naturalist. Small groups can arrange horseback riding or other day trips.

The Guale Indians lived on the island when Europeans arrived and began to cultivate the island. English Actress Fanny Kemble was impressed by the island's "wild savage loneliness." It was for more than a century part of Hampton Plantation, but was sold in 1908 to Eagle Pencil Company as a source of red cedar. Only selective cutting took place, however, before Philip Berolzheimer decided to make it a private retreat for his family.

Sea Island. Today, Sea Island is a recognized example of luxurious living, probably the most prestigious in the region. The neat island, seaward of St. Simons Island, is noted for the Cloister resort and upscale cottages of permanent and part-time residents. The rich and famous, from presidents to jetsetters, avail themselves of its recreational and recuperative attributes.

The Cloister's rise to fame was anticipated when the first section of the Spanish Mediterranean-style resort, sheltered among palm, magnolia, and live oak trees, opened in 1928. Since the days of its founder, Howard Earle Coffin, an auto executive, the resort has suggested a dress code. Now, the complex covers a large area between the oceanfront and the Black Banks River. It includes docks for boaters and fishers, golf course, tennis courts, gun club, bridle riding, and facilities for other activities. Its 27-hole golf course is located on the site of Retreat Plantation on St. Simons Island. The lakes, ponds, and some of the ruins of the old plantation mansion have been incorporated into the course.

Since all of the property on Sea Island is privately owned, day visitors have limited access — essentially the waterways and roads. Sea Island Drive is often called "Millionaire's Row."

Sea Island is lush and green year-round, but it gives the impression of being carefully manicured, as most of it is. However, there are areas where live oak hung with Spanish moss and resurrection ferns grow naturally.

Birdwatching is easy on the waterways and at Pelican Spit at the north end of the island. Among the species regularly frequenting the island are pelicans, terns, cormorants, and migratory shorebirds. The saltwater waterways are noted for bass, trout, drum, flounder, whiting, croaker, and sheepshead.

Sea Island's earlier history reads much like that of the other Georgia islands. Indians lived there when Europeans — the first reputed to include Norsemen — began poking about the area. Through strategic moves and a military victory at nearby St. Simons Island, the British finally succeeded in asserting their claim to Georgia.

Plantations worked by slaves brought nearly a century of prosperity to the island, whose name identifies the long staple cotton that became famous. In the aftermath of the Civil War, loggers cut down great forests and then left the land fallow for many decades. Wealthy industrialists acquired plots for hunting and escape from the cares of the world before Howard Coffin appeared in 1925 with a vision of a "place to charm" and purchased the old Retreat Plantation and 5 miles of beach. The Depression intervened and brought Coffin's nephew, Alfred Jones, into the business. His family has continued in the business ever since.

Jekyll Island

Jekyll Island's tenderloin period began in 1886 when it was purchased for $125,000 by a group of 50 wealthy Northern businessmen attracted by its isolation. They wanted a retreat where they could relax in a less formal atmosphere than that at Newport, Rhode Island, where "cottages" compared with the mansions of the European nobility.

The exclusive Jekyll Island Club, designed by Charles A. Alexander, was their first project. It opened in 1888 with 53 members who together ostensibly owned a sixth of the world's wealth. To them, "simplicity" was hardly what the word means today. Many arrived on their own yachts. Families brought 18 to 20 trunks packed

The clubhouse at Jekyll Island. PHOTO BY JOHN BOWEN.

with formal dinner wear for the men and enough evening gowns so the women could wear a different one every night. They were attended by personal maids, butlers, and chauffeurs.

Soon, "cottages" began to rise, some more elegant than the others and all substantial in size. Indeed, a few had as many as 25 to 31 rooms and one had 17 bathrooms. In all, fifteen houses were built. An apartment complex was added to the club in 1901.

Hunting was the first sport, but it was soon followed by golf (the course, opened in 1898, was one of the world's finest), swimming, tennis, horseback and carriage riding, and bicycling. A steam launch operated coastal excursions and a ferry made regular runs to the mainland. The club operated oyster beds and terrapin pens to provide delicacies for the dining-room menu.

Among the inhabitants in the early years were industrialists whose names were household words all over the world: William Rockefeller, J. P. Morgan, Gordon McKay, Pierre Lorillard, Marshall Field, and Joseph Pulitzer.

Despite the emphasis on relaxation, business was not ignored. For example, the clandestine meetings that resulted in the Federal Reserve Act of 1915 took place there. An historical marker recalls that the first experimental transcontinental telephone call originated there in 1915 while AT&T President Theodore N. Vail was recuperating from an injury.

The island declined during the Depression years and, by the outbreak of World War II, was nearly deserted. The Jekyll Island Club remained open until 1942; promoters in 1936 described it as "the ingenious solution of a difficult problem of finding profound seclusion and congenial companionship in one and the same spot."

Prior to the millionaires era, Jekyll Island's history more or less paralleled that of other Georgia coastal islands. It was inhabited by Guale Indians, who called the island Ospo, when the Spanish soldiers and missionaries arrived in the late 16th century. The mission, San Diego de Ocone, could not withstand Indian attacks and had disappeared by the time the British began farming the island in the early 18th century. Crops of hops and grain may have supplied Georgia's first brewery — to supply Savannah — which according to legend was established here.

In 1792, the island was purchased by a group of emigrés fleeing the French Revolution. One of them was Christophe Poulain du Bignon, whose family eventually purchased all of the island and raised sea island cotton until it sold the property to the New York millionaires.

The State of Georgia acquired the entire island in 1947 for $675,000 and turned it into a state park. It is managed by the Jekyll Island Authority. The oceanfront is extensively developed with hotels, restaurants, and shopping centers, as well as a convention center and other public facilities. Golf courses, a campground, and businesses cover most of the center of the island. However, historic sites are preserved and numerous outdoor areas remain.

Thus, Jekyll Island remains unabashedly what it was intended to be: a resort. The aura of the gaslight era survives. The Club, now a hotel, retains the large public rooms where gentlemen and their ladies relaxed, the fancy dining room, and some of the traditions, such as croquet on the lawn.

The Club is part of a Millionaire's Village Historic District beside the Marshes of Glynn. Four of the eight homes built during the first decade also remain; "cottage" construction began in 1888 and continued through 1928. The wharf on Jekyll Creek, where the millionaires parked their yachts, was one of the first structures to be built, in 1886.

A tram tour starts at the Macy Cottage Reception Center on Riverview Drive and passes more than a dozen homes. Guided visits are made to some, such as 1892 Indian Mound, built by shoe manufacturer Gordon McKay and purchased by William Rockefeller after McKay's death. According to tradition, the Victorian-style house received its name from a mound that once existed on the site. The house is shown as it was after remodeling by Rockefeller added a handsome porte-cochere, verandah, and additional upstairs rooms.

Hollybourne is a handsome tabby house built in 1890 by bridge builder Charles Stewart Maurice. He employed many bridge-building techniques in the design of the house, making it exceptionally sturdy. The Maurice family lived on the island from the formation of the Jekyll Island Club until the state acquired the island in 1947.

The 1890 Walter Rogers Furness "cottage" later was occupied by Pulitzer and eventually moved and turned into a hospital. The elegant Sans Souci Apartments were constructed in 1896 by a five-man syndicate for themselves and other millionaires. J. P. Morgan became the sixth member of the association, started by William Rockefeller, Henry B. Hyde, James A. Scrymser, Joseph Stickney, and William P. Anderson.

The ruins of Chicota—foundations, two decorative lions, and swimming pool—illustrate the way original and subsequent owners upgraded their properties. The pool, installed by Edwin Gould after he became the owner in 1900, was the only one at a private cottage on the island.

The frame 1884 du Bignon house, relocated to its present site, is a transitional house with some elements of stick-style architecture and some of Queen Anne. It was acquired by the Jekyll Island Club when it bought the island and was used primarily as the residence of the club superintendent. The house, including original oak and mahogany woodwork and marble fireplaces, has been restored to its early condition.

Cherokee, built in 1904 by George F. Shrady and later purchased by Dr. Walter B. James, and Henry Kirke Porter's 1900 Mistletoe show the diversity of the houses built in the 1900–1917 period.

When Richard T. Crane, Jr., decided to build the largest "cottage" on the island in 1917, he brought in architects, contractors, and workers from Chicago to handle the job. The handsome structure, with a formal garden, now houses the headquarters and offices of the Jekyll Island Authority.

The first building on the site, Solterra, built by warehouse magnate Frederick Baker in 1890, burned in 1914. The Bakers hosted President William McKinley in 1899 during his visit to the island as guest of Secretary of the Interior Cornelius Bliss.

Brick Faith Chapel, built in 1904, is small but beautiful. The stained-glass window over the altar, "The Adoration of the Christ Child," was part of the original structure. It was designed by Maitland and Helen Armstrong, who had worked with the Tiffany company. The Tiffany stained-glass window in the north end was added in 1921; Louis Comfort Tiffany visited the island to either oversee the installation or attend the dedication. Earlier Union Chapel was moved to the servants' compound at that time.

A few relics of the island's colonial heritage remain. Near the north end of the island are the ruins of the 1742 tabby house built by General Oglethorpe's chief aide, William Horton, who received a 500-acre land grant. His original 1735 home was burned by the Spanish as they retreated after losing the Battle of Bloody Marsh on St. Simons Island. The ruins of the first brewery stand across the road, not far from the du Bignon cemetery.

Like many areas in this region, Jekyll Island has inspired a few legends. One of them involves a great white stallion, the leader of a herd of wild horses in the colonization era. A massive effort to capture the stallion cornered him on the north end of the island, but he jumped off the dunes into the sea rather than be captured. Now, the legend goes, sometimes at night, the luminous figure of the stallion can be seen.

Jekyll has about 20 miles of paved trails, only a few of them on the roads. A bicycle trail that can be divided into segments of a few miles circles and crosses the island. It cuts through the golf course, traverses the historic district, passes the Horton house and old brewery ruins, circles through a wilderness area on Clam Creek and a marsh featuring oak, cabbage palmetto, pine, and cedar and runs the length of the ocean beachfront strip of resorts, restaurants, and shopping centers to St. Andrew Beach to the southern tip of the island. The trail also is a jogging path.

Jekyll doubles as a wildlife reserve. A boardwalk crosses sand dunes from a picnic area to St. Andrew Beach. A quarter-mile footpath follows the Jekyll River. Near South Dunes picnic area, a pathway connects two small ponds and winds through dunes to the beach. In season, bird songs are ever present in the historic area. However, a path special to birdwatchers starts at Old Village Boulevard near the historic area and traverses the marsh, tidal creek, and forest between Shell Road and the Ben Fortson Parkway near the causeway to the mainland. Also present are alligators, a few marsh deer, and mink. Alligators that occasionally invade a yard or the beach are trapped by the Jekyll Island Authority's wildlife branch and transported.

A free fishing pier fronts on St. Simons Sound at the northern end of the island, near Driftwood Beach and Claim Creek. The prospect from this point is a spectacular combination of water, beach, dunes, and marshes. St. Simons Island lies to the north in the distance. A path that starts at the main road traverses much of this area. During the loggerhead turtle nesting season, mid-June to mid-August, naturalists conduct nocturnal walks of 2 to 3 miles. Nature programs, including beach and marsh exploration and films, are scheduled year-round (912/635-2232).

Hazzard's Neck Wildlife Management Area

A 5,187-acre tract of paper company land between the Little Satilla River and White Oak Creek near Waverly a few miles off I-95 and U.S. Route 17 is managed by the Georgia Department of Natural Resources. About 40 percent of the flat terrain is covered by young planted pines, while 18 percent hosts older stands of loblolly and slash pines with understories of palmetto, gallberry, and wax myrtle. The remainder is cypress ponds and bottomland hardwoods such as water oak, blackgum, bay, live oak, and swamp chestnut oak with understories featuring palmetto and ironwood.

Deer, turkey, small game, quail, and dove populations are low, but most are slowly increasing.

Woodbine

Named for a nearby plantation, the seat of Camden County was organized in 1894 when the railroad was constructed. It was incorporated in 1908. The 1928 courthouse is listed on the National Register of Historic Places. The Bryan-Lang Historical Library is a repository of documents, maps, books, photographs, and genealogical records.

Rice was grown at Woodbine Plantation, founded in 1787 about 25 miles north of St. Marys. Many of the dikes and paddies remain and are now used to raise commercial crayfish. Visitors are taken on tours of the farm to see the method of raising crawfish in the brackish water and how the river's tidal action creates ponds. The last Saturday in April every year, Woodbine holds a crayfish festival at which visitors may consume crayfish in many forms.

The farm also is a good place for birdwatching because the birds are attracted to the crayfish.

Kingsland

The site where Kingsland now stands was part of a vast plantation dating back to the earliest days of the colony when John King acquired the land. The plantation, known as The Longwood, was still in the hands of his descendants in the late 19th century. In 1893, the Florida Central and Peninsular Railroad invaded the cotton, sugar cane, corn, and sweet potato fields near the plantation house to build a station. It was named King's Land to honor the plantation owner at that time, William Henry King. As a town developed around the station, the streets were named after members of his family. Soon, the town's name was contracted to a single word. In 1908, when the community was incorporated, William Henry King became the first mayor. A later railroad spur to St. Marys linked the two communities.

Kingsland has been a crossroads ever since, adjusting to the automobile era by ferrying vehicles across the St. Marys River to Florida before the old Dixie Highway was paved and became U.S. Route

17 in 1927. Though bypassed by I-95 in the post World War II-era, the community is only 2 miles west of the throughway.

Kingsland's annual Labor Day Catfish Festival lives up to the town's "Get the Royal Treatment" slogan. It features a fishing tournament, live entertainment, arts and crafts, a frog race, races, clogging, and sports events, in addition to feasts of Southern fried and Cajun-style catfish and Kingsland catfish stew.

Crooked River State Park

So many outdoor opportunities exist along the Georgia coast that this state park on Georgia Route 40 about 10 miles off I-95 does not get the respect it deserves. The serious birdwatcher may see as many as 80 species, including ducks, hawks, egrets, herons, sandpipers, woodpeckers, doves, flycatchers, swallows, crows, and buntings. Fishers may use boats or share a dock with crabbers and shrimpers. Water skiing is permitted.

A 1.5-mile trail that starts near the campground traverses a mature forest dominated by longleaf pine and live oak and passes a tupelo pond. A ¾-mile nature trail parallels the Crooked River through a maritime forest and over bridges and boardwalk at a marshy area.

The 500-acre park has cabins (these have a long lead time on reservations) and a swimming pool. The office is open 8 a.m. to 5 p.m. Monday–Friday. The gates are open 7 a.m. to 10 p.m. daily.

St. Marys and Its Neighbors

WHEN IRON MEN SAILED WOODEN SAILING VESSELS, SAILORS PRIZED THE water of the St. Marys River. The tannic acid that darkened the stream, in part because of its headwaters in the Okefenokee Swamp, made it pure and kept it from spoiling on long ocean voyages, as some other water did.

Thus, St. Marys was well known as a site even before the town was laid out in 1787 by a group of 20 men headed by Jacob Weed, who had received a land grant from the state of Georgia. Since its founding, commercial activity has been the core of its existence. A natural port, it became a leading exporter of timber for naval stores or commercial uses. It also served inland plantations, where fields of cotton and sugar cane stretched for miles and miles. It was the site of a major customs house. After the town ceased to be a major seaport, it subsisted for a while on shrimping and fishing. Joseph S. Arnow, who built a home in 1834, is said to have planted the first pecan trees in Georgia—now a major industry in the state.

The 10-mile-long St. Marys Railroad, constructed around the turn of the century as a spur off the main north-south coastal railway, gave a new boost to port activity. Then, the decision by Gilman Paper Co. in 1939 to build a plant close to its source of raw materials produced another renaissance. The plant stands along the banks of the North River near the town's historic area.

Nature has always been close to St. Marys residents in other ways, as well. The original plan incorporated a commons and other public areas and two cemeteries—one for persons of means and another for paupers and prisoners. The river continues to serve commercial and recreational users—and provide access to the national seashore on Cumberland Island. Local residents swear that, even in today's polluted society, the river is one of the "purest in the world."

Today, St. Marys is a laid-back, often overlooked community whose commercial heart does not overpower its wealth of historic structures.

The Jackson-Archibald Clark-Bessent Home is the oldest documented house in St. Marys. The oldest section was constructed in 1802 by Revolutionary War soldier Charles Jackson. On Conyers Street is an unpretentious lowcountry home where one of the town's richest early citizens, John Wood, lived. John Wood maintained a modest lifestyle for himself, but when his daughter, Jane, decided to marry the handsome young Presbyterian minister, the Reverend Horace Pratt, he built Orange Hall mansion for them.

Orange Hall gets its name from the trees that once bordered the yard and stood in a nearby grove. The Greek Revival-style house is not well documented, but construction was started prior to 1829 because both John Wood and his daughter died that year. The minister remained in the house with two children and eventually remarried. His new bride, Jane's cousin, Isabelle Drysdale, supervised the furnishing of the house and the beautiful landscaping of the lawns.

Orange Hall. PHOTO BY JOHN BOWEN.

By 1835, the house was regarded by some as the center of the town's social life.

Orange Hall, on Conyer Street, is now an exhibition building. Visitors enter the ground-floor kitchen and proceed through the high-ceilinged parlors, wide hallway, and dining and music rooms on the next floor and the bedrooms on the top floor. The structure retains many original features, including heart-of-pine floors and window shades that fold back into the walls. A turn-of-the-century chandelier was made by Tiffany. (Other Tiffany crafts in town include a window in the Long House and a lamp in the Riverview Hotel, which opened in 1914–15.) Orange Hall is open 9 a.m. to 5 p.m. Monday–Saturday and 1 to 5 p.m. Sunday.

First Presbyterian Church, across from Orange Hall, was built by town conscription in 1808 as an interdenominational church. It became a Presbyterian Church in 1822 and is cited as the oldest church of that denomination still in constant use in Georgia. The structure has been modified; originally, the main door faced Osborne Street and the steeple was at the rear of the church.

The handsome sanctuary has plain glass windows, which church members say bring the natural surroundings of cedar and dogwood trees, blue sky, and birds into the services.

In the late 1820s, the church became part of the smuggling folklore of coastal Georgia when a shipowner used it to create a diversion while he illegally unloaded a cargo of rum. He stole the minister's horse, coaxed it up the steps to the rear steeple of the church, and tied it to the bell. Naturally, the fidgety horse rang the bell (at that time a near-universal signal of alarm) and townspeople came running. While they discussed how the horse had gotten there and how to extricate it, the shipowner quickly unloaded the rum into a water-front warehouse and sailed away.

Christ Episcopal Church, which dates from 1888, is the second church on the site. The first was constructed in 1812; its initial minister, the Reverend Anson Phelps Dodge, inspired one of the characters in Eugenia Price's *St. Simons Trilogy*. St. Marys United Methodist Church, organized in 1799, was the community's first church; the present structure dates from 1858. The 1837 brick St. Marys Roman Catholic Church originally housed the town bank; the church acquired it in 1843.

Many street names—Weed, Osborne, Conyers, Dillingham, Ready, Wheeler, and others—honor the town's founders.

Some of the historic structures have been converted into bed-and-breakfasts. Among them are the Victorian Goodbread House (circa 1883) and the 1882 Spencer House Inn.

Oak Grove Cemetery, one of the graveyards laid out in the original 1788 plan, is known for its extensive plantings of many varieties of camellias. It also is heavily planted with live oak, cedars, magnolias, gums, walnut, and pecan trees. Brick and rock walls are formed of ballast material discarded by sailing ships. The earliest marked tombstone is 1801, but a Revolutionary War soldier is known to be buried there. One section with many inscriptions in French is devoted to the Acadians who settled in St. Marys in 1799 after leaving Canada. One of the headstones identifies a friend of Evangeline.

In modern times, St. Marys claims, a visit by artist Roy Crane provided material for his "Wash Tubs and Easy" comic strip. The unusual car-train that operated between St. Marys and Kingsland was locally called the "Toonerville Trolley," "hinky-dink," "doodle bug" and various other affectionate names. The train was saved and restored in the 1970s by the Kiwanis Club and is now on display.

In early October, the normally quiet streets of the town fill with people attending the annual one-day Rock Shrimp Festival. Gorging on fried and boiled shrimp is supplemented by arts and crafts, live entertainment, Toonerville-Trolley rides, and other activities.

Cumberland Island

"Don't miss the 4:45 return boat," the ranger in St. Marys warns visitors waiting to embark for Cumberland Island, the largest of Georgia's barrier islands. "If you do, you'll have to stay overnight and fend for youself." The statement comes at the end of a short lecture on the history and facilities of the island.

The 45-minute ride on the ferryboat *Cumberland Queen*—it operates twice daily year-round (outgoing at 9 a.m. and 11:45 a.m.) except on Tuesdays and Wednesdays in the off months, reservations required—is a pleasant excursion down the mouth of the St. Marys River and across Cumberland Sound to the southern end of the island. The boat stops first at the Dungeness Dock, near the Ice House Museum that explores the cultural history of the area, and then at the Sea Camp Dock, less than a mile away on the sound side. On Sundays from April through September and the first Sunday of other months, the boat continues from the Sea Camp area to Plum Orchard Dock near the center of the island; there the 30-room mansion constructed by Lucy Carnegie in 1898 as a wedding present for her son, George Lauder Carnegie, and his wife, Margaret Thaw, has been restored by the National Park Service. Interpretive tours of the mansion, including the dining room, are guided by rangers.

Four managed hunts for deer and feral hogs are conducted three days in mid-November, four days in late November–early December, three days in mid-December, three days in early January. A three-day hunt for hogs is held in mid-January. The national seashore park is closed to other visitors during those times.

Parts of the 36,000-acre island remain private. On one parcel is Greyfield Inn, a private commercial hotel with nine rooms and columned porches about 1½ miles north of the visitors center. The inn, owned by descendants of Thomas Carnegie—younger brother of financier Andrew Carnegie—who built the house soon after the turn of the century, is furnished in period furniture. Rates are seasonal and include all meals. It is open year-round, except in late August when it closes for refurbishing and repairs. (The inn caters primarily to guests but will accept campers and visitors for meals if space is available and arrangements are made a week ahead of time.)

A tour guide/naturalist on the hotel staff offers tours of about 4 hours that cover the human history of the island, natural history, and similar subjects.

The inn operates its own boat from Fernandina Beach, Florida.

The barge ferry, which also carries supplies for the hotel, leaves Fernandina Beach at 3:30 p.m. on Monday, Tuesday, and Thursday, at 5 p.m. Friday–Sunday for the 1½-hour trip to the island. The ferry leaves the island at 9:30 a.m. Monday, Tuesday, Thursday, and Friday, Saturday at 12:30 p.m., and Sunday at 3:30 p.m.

For those with time, campgrounds — developed and primitive — allow stays up to seven days. All campsites are near the complex of hiking trails. Yankee Paradise and Brickhill Bluff campgrounds are behind the little-visited beach on the northern half of the island. Hikers should be wary of the heat and humidity and carry water in summer. Campers should take what they will need since there are no supply sources on the island. Campfires are allowed at developed sites, but not elsewhere, so campers in those areas will need portable stoves. Backcountry camping permits are required. Swimming is permitted, but dunes may be crossed only at designated points. Sunrise over the ocean sometimes is spectacular.

A narrow road, Grand Avenue, runs almost the length of the island, from the Dungeness area to the remnants of an old dock at Terrapin Point, used by those visiting in the 1870–1920 period. On the northern part of the island, a number of connecting trails with names like Tar Kiln, Bunkley, Oyster, and Roller Coaster reveal varied ecosystems, including the largest freshwater pond, Lake Whitney, and a sandy bluff. Diamondback rattlers and cottonmouth moccasins are the most dangerous snakes. Alligators are present.

The Duck House Trail follows an old hunter's path through the Sweetwater Lake area and a marsh alive with ibis, ducks, and herons. Deer and small animals are often seen. Wildflowers such as the violet wood sorrel, lupine, Virginia spiderwort, and salt-marsh pink bloom in all seasons. The gulf fritillary, cloudless sulphur, and swallowtail are among the most frequently seen butterflies. A wooden hunting lodge named Duck House is deteriorating from decay and encroaching dunes.

A small white-frame chapel at Halfmoon Bluff is seldom, if ever, used, but the basic sanctuary furniture — podium, table, and pews — are still in place. The building normally is not locked.

Even those not remaining overnight can get a good impression of the island by a walk between ferry trips. One of the best (about 1½ hours) follows the Dungeness Trail from the first dock across the narrow island to wide, sandy Nightingale Beach on the oceanfront, then proceeds to Sea Camp Beach and recrosses the island to the Sea Camp dock and visitors center.

The Dungeness Trail is shaded much of the way by limbs of trees in a maritime forest—live oak, cabbage palm, American holly, magnolia, red cedar, and pine. Saw palmetto, muscadine vines, Spanish moss, and resurrection fern help create a jungle effect. The bright colors of pileated woodpecker, prothonotary warbler, Carolina wren, and other birds liven the shadows. Wild turkeys may be seen. Feral horses wander this area, unconcerned about visitors. White-tailed deer and smaller animals, such as gray squirrel and raccoon, also may be seen. Bobcats were reintroduced to the island a few years ago and are monitored by naturalists but seldom seen.

Nearing the oceanfront, the trail breaks into an open area dominated by the ruins of Dungeness, a mansion constructed in the 1880s by Thomas Carnegie. The house burned in 1959. Nearby tabby ruins are all that remain of the Dungeness house begun by Revolutionary War General Nathaniel Greene in 1786 and finished by his wife after his death.

The trail then passes an extensive salt marsh dominated by fields of *spartina alterniflora* (golden in fall and winter) and other types of cordgrass waving in the breeze and crosses the large sand dunes at the back of Dungeness Beach. It proceeds northward along a beach strewn with shells, starfish, and debris (sometimes even fossilized sharks teeth) cast up by waves and alive with sanderling, ruddy turnstone, American oystercatcher, and other shorebirds pecking at the wet sand left by retreating waves. Shrimp boats work offshore, while surf fishers (no license required) cast for red bass, spotted trout, and bluefish and offshore boats haul in red bass, trout, croaker, and drum. Loggerhead turtles lay their eggs on the beach in late August; these hatch and immediately head to sea about 60 days later.

The cross-island trail to Sea Camp Dock passes a bathhouse, exhibits on nature, and, for lucky hikers, an armadillo hiding in the lush underbrush of the maritime forest. A small museum at Sea Camp Dock includes a large number of shells obtainable on the island; a nature lecture explains the dune system and the interaction of the various kinds of life observed on the beach and upland. A ranger meets the ferry each morning to conduct a river walk. Other ranger-directed activities include a footsteps program to the Dungeness area, explanation of the Ice Museum on the island, and a dockside program at 4 p.m. each day.

Birds are a constant companion throughout the walk—osprey, pelican, marsh hawk, seaside sparrow, marsh wren, wood stork, great egret, yellow-crested night heron, red-winged blackbird, and many other species.

Late in the day, the returning ferry is accompanied by shrimp boats headed for harbor after a day's work.

Indians, who arrived on the island perhaps 4,000 years ago, called it Missoe. It was populated by the Timucuan tribe in the mid-1500s when Spanish explorers and missionaries arrived. In the early 1700s, the British fortified the island, renamed it, and built a hunting lodge named Dungeness. In its early period, Cumberland was prized mostly for forests of live oak that could provide timber for shipbuilding. Among the famous people to visit the island in the early period were Revolutionary War hero Henry "Light-horse Harry" Lee of Virginia, who died there, and inventor Eli Whitney.

The island's population was evacuated by federal troops during the Civil War, and only a few returned afterward. Greene's Dungeness burned after the war. Carnegie purchased the property in 1881.

Cumberland Island was set aside as a national seashore in 1972. It is 16 miles long and 3 miles wide at the widest point.

Little Cumberland Island, which sits like a cap on Cumberland Island, is privately owned and under development.

Okefenokee Swamp

The name conjures up images of isolation and mystery. And rightly so. The "Land of Trembling Earth" is a geologic phenomenon created about 6,000 years ago when the Trail Ridge trapped receding ocean waters. What is left is a peat-bottomed, shallow lake with forests of pine, cypress, tupelo, and bay trees, vast prairies vivid with vegetation and escaping methane gas, a few natural open waterways and ponds, and 70 islands, 60 of them named.

The complex, at 438,000 acres the largest swamp on the East Coast, is about 38 miles in length from north to south and 18 miles wide at its broadest point. It varies from about 103 feet above sea level in the southern end to 128 feet above in the northern section. More than 75 percent of the land area is covered by water in one way or another, including thickets of water-loving plants. About 20 percent features cypress or cypress mixed with other trees. Pond cypress predominates and bald cypress is relatively rare. The vast prairies, or marshes filled with aquatic plants, are covered with two to three feet of water except after long drought periods. The largest prairies—Chase (6,000 acres) and Chesser and Grand (slightly smaller)—are located on the eastern side of the swamp. Nearly 20 others are large enough to have names.

The phenomenon of methane gas bubbling up and sometimes pushing mats or chunks of peat to the surface led the Indians to describe the site as "the land of trembling earth." The phenomenon does not follow an established pattern, however, and there is considerable debate as to the reasons for its irregularity.

The swamp is the source of two rivers: the Suwannee, which starts in the west center section and flows lazily to the Gulf of Mexico, and the St. Marys, which meanders from the southern edge of the swamp southward, then northward past Folkston and finally eastward to the Atlantic Ocean. However, they drain only slightly more than 20 percent of the water in the swamp, split almost evenly between the two. Much greater quantities are lost through evaporation and absorption by plants.

The swamp may at one time have been a freshwater marsh with oak forests. Decaying vegetation was changed to peat, which accumulated and reduced the depth of the lake. As dry land appeared, the marsh was replaced by swampland growing cypress and similar trees. Periodic natural fires kept the swamp from filling completely but left unpredictable patterns of water and land.

All of this makes the Okefenokee Swamp one of the most striking natural features on the southeastern coast.

More than 388,000 acres of wetland, plus about 8,000 acres of upland, are preserved in a national wildlife refuge that remains relatively pristine despite the intrusion of thousands of visitors annually. Life in the park is luxuriant. Some areas are virtually impenetrable. Year-round, navigable waterways mirror the bright colors of tall trees, lily pads, wildflowers, and numerous other plants. Tannic acid released by decaying vegetation turns the water a dark tea color.

Despite its semitropical appearance, the swamp changes to a degree with the seasons, sweetgum leaves turning red and cypress needles brightening to gold in November. The wide variety of trees—southern bayberry, southern catalpa, Allegheny chinquapin, live oak, white oak, water oak, black tupelo, American holly, flowering dogwood, eastern redwood, swamp bay, red bay, southern magnolia, sweet bay, chinaberry, loblolly pine, pond pine, long leaf pine, slash pine, bald cypress, pond cypress, black cherry, sycamore, pecan, and sweetgum among them—flower at various times from February through August. The insect-eating pitcher plant is there. Also among the approximately 300 types of wildflowers flowering from April into October are arrow arum, lady lupine, partridge pea, yellow stargrass, dwarf butterwort, yellow and purple butterwort, floating bladderwort, prickly pear, Barbara's button, bitterweed, blackeyed Susan, daisy fleabane, dandelion, deer tongue, whitetop aster, yellow thistle, blue iris, pine lily, swamp rose mallow, Osceola's plume, pineland hibiscus, meadow beauty, pale meadow beauty, butterfly weed, drumhead, orange milkwort, false dragonhead, nightleaved skullcap, grass pink, rose orchid, rose pogonia, snow orchid, yellow-fringed orchid, rattlesnake master, passion flower, hooded pitcher plant, dayflower, Florida violet, and lanceleaved violet.

The varied habitat supports most of the mammals present in the southeastern coastal plan and numerous other animals. The higher elevations harbor deer, black bear, Florida wildcat, foxes, rabbits, round-tailed muskrat, wild pigs, Florida striped skunk, Virginia opossum, raccoon, southern flying squirrel and other squirrels, Georgia pocket gopher, armadillo, moles, shrews, rats, and mice. At least eight species of bats have been identified.

Water-lovers include the Florida river otter, beaver, and mink. The watery environment also sustains more than 60 kinds of reptiles and amphibians, including 21 species of frogs and toads, 16 of salamander, 11 of lizards, and 15 of turtles, including the alligator snapping turtle. Alligators laze on dead tree trunks along the banks of the canals and in the water. Water snakes naturally are commonplace. The most abundant is the banded water snake, but the Florida green, red-bellied, brown, and eastern glossy also are numerous. Of the five venomous species, the Florida cottonmouth is aquatic and numerous. On land, canebrake and diamondback rattlesnakes are fairly common, while dusky pigmy rattlesnake and Eastern coral are rare. Among more than 30 nonpoisonous snakes are the Eastern garter and Southern black racer.

Controlled hunts are conducted. Indians hunted the land for almost 4,500 years before Europeans arrived.

April is the best month for bass fishing. Other catches include bream, warmouth perch, catfish, redfin and chain pickerel, bluegill, black crappie. More than 40 species of fish have been tabulated.

The Okefenokee is one of the most active bird areas on the East Coast and the wide-open prairies make the flocks that arrive, nest, and depart all year long highly visible. Greater sandhill crane, osprey, wild turkey, herons, egrets, ibis, red-tailed hawk, brown-headed nuthatch, parula and prothonotary warblers, eastern kingbird, purple martin, swallow-tailed kite, cedar waxwing, phoebes, robins, swallows, the endangered red-cockaded woodpecker and even a few bald eagle, wood duck, green-winged teal, and hooded mergansers are among the species that may be seen along the waterways in season.

About 120 miles of water trails traverse all kinds of features. A 100-mile self-guided canoe trail has partially covered platforms alongside where canoeists may stop at night. Reservations must be made for 2- to 5-day trips. Rangers teach a commonsense approach to the park, such as watching where the pines grow to locate islands. Water depths are deceptive.

Okefenokee Swamp National Wildlife Refuge has three sections open to visitors, each managed by a different entity and each suited to a different type of visitor. A combination of U.S. Routes 1, 84, and 441 and Georgia highways 2/94 and 121 circumnavigate the park, making travel from one section to another easy.

On the eastern side, about 8 miles from Folkston along state Route 121/23, the Suwannee Canal Recreation Area opens up one of the most beautiful areas of the swamp. It has an excellent interpretive center, restored swamp homestead on Chesser Island, photo blinds, a 4.5-mile wildlife drive, more than 4 miles of hiking trails, and a 4,000-foot boardwalk to a tower that overlooks the vast prairie, broken by stands of cypress, scrub forest, and open water, prevalent in this section of the swamp.

The canal dug in the 1890s to facilitate logging operations reaches 11.5 miles into the swamp and makes this area of the swamp one of the most accessible. The lakes that dot the prairies provide good fishing (boats are available). The recreation area is one of the starting points for the canoe trail that crosses the park and winds through the northeastern section of the refuge. Another canoe put in place is Kingfisher Landing.

Okefenokee Swamp Park on the northern tip of the refuge provides a capsule view for the short-time visitor: alligators, bear, deer, and butterflies; wildlife lectures; a 20-minute boat ride along the narrow waterways of Cowhouse Island and into a prairie; a long boardwalk through the same terrain with a 90-foot tower; an aquarium; and a pioneer exhibit commemorating an 1838 Indian massacre. This 1,600-acre section of the park is operated by a nonprofit organization created in 1945 by the Tourist Bureau and the Chamber of Commerce of nearby Waycross.

Stephen C. Foster State Park, whose entrance is on Jones Island off State Highway 2/94 on the western side of the swamp, is designed more for the longer-term visitor. Its comfortable cabins are within walking distance of the landing where rental boats and guided tours provide easy access to many of the swamp's most intimate secrets. Private boats may be used, but are limited to a 10-hp motor. Fishing normally is permitted year-round for brim, shiners, crappie, perch, chain pickerel, redfin pickerel, bluegill, warmouth, bowfin, and largemouth bass, but is stopped in periods of severe drought.

A short circular nature walk near the park headquarters provides a sampling of the attributes of the refuge. It follows an inlet through a mature pine forest, crosses a boardwalk over a coffee-colored wetland supporting cypress and other vegetation, and then proceeds onto a forested hammock.

March–May and September–October are good times to visit the 84-acre park. Guided tours explore open waterways bounded by pond cypress and luxuriant vegetation and stop at Billy's Island, about 5 miles long and 1¼ miles in width, where a logging village with 600 to 800 inhabitants stood until 1926. At the time, 500 miles of railroad track hauled felled trees from the swamp. Among the town's facilities were hotels, an elementary school, baseball diamond, barber shop, and commissary — all destroyed by fire. As a result, only a few rusted metal relics of the cypress logging era remain in woods dominated by pine, live oak, saw palmetto, and hackberry. Nearby are two ancient Indian burial mounds and a modern cemetery. Billy's Island also is noted for its rattlesnakes.

Elsewhere in this section of the park is a small earthen dam, constructed after a natural fire in 1954 to maintain the water at a safer level.

Stephen C. Foster Park is so well known for its profusion of wildflowers that an annual Wildflower Weekend is held in late April (912/637-5274).

Insects, especially mosquitos and yellow flies, can be a problem almost year-round throughout the Okefenokee Swamp.

Native Americans lived in the swamp at least 4,500 years ago, based on the disclosures of ancient mounds. Indian legends mentioned islands where lived beautiful women who disappeared when men approached, and who taunted the men by reappearing and disappearing in their paths. A few white explorers visited the swamp in the 18th century, including William Bartram, who recorded seeing a large lake nearly 300 miles in circumference and islands in the "Great Swamp." White settlement began in the 1850s when the Lee family built a residence and cleared a farm on Billy's Island on the western side and the Chesser family occupied the island on the eastern rim that now bears its name. The farmers were plagued by wild animals and sometimes had to fight off bears with any weapon that may have been at hand. Pigs were sometimes snared by lurking alligators.

Plans to cut timber began to develop about the same time and, by 1890, the swamp had been thoroughly explored. A logging invasion began in 1891 when the Suwannee Canal Company acquired 238,000 acres, set up Camp Cornelia near Chesser Island, and attempted unsuccessfully to dig an outlet canal through the Trail Ridge. It exploited a large cypress stand by floating logs to a sawmill at Camp Cornelia and persisted for three years despite the hardships imposed by "trembling earth," tormenting swarms of mosquitos and flies, and attacks by wild animals such as bears, alligators, cougars, and snakes.

Suwannee's successor, Hebard Cypress Company, built railroad lines on pilings from the swamp to a new sawmill in Waycross and, at the peak of operations, employed up to 2,000 men. Logging operations began on Billy's Island in 1917 and soon produced a sizable community complete with normal amenities. Other companies operated on smaller scales in other areas of the swamp, but by 1927 large operations had ceased because the great stands had been cut.

An organized effort to save the site began in the early decades of the 20th century and was aided by printed accounts describing the beauties of the swamp. The effort enrolled such diverse personalities as scientists from Cornell University in New York state, Georgia Assemblyman J. L. Sweat, and the Okefenokee Preservation Society, founded in 1919 with headquarters in Waycross. The effort resulted in 1936 in an executive order signed by President Franklin D. Roosevelt establishing a national refuge.

Nine miles north of the Okefenokee refuge on state Route 177 is Laura S. Walker State Park, located in Dixon Memorial Forest and named after a pioneer conservationist. Created during the Depression era, the 306-acre park has camping facilities and permits swimming, boating (ramp available), fishing, and hunting.

One of the annual interpretive events is an old-fashioned gospel sing in late April featuring local groups (912/287-4900).

Jacksonville, Florida

Behind its bustling business facade, Jacksonville has a tourist heart. The nostalgia that seasons the modern overlay makes it an interesting city to visit. Furthermore, some special sights, ranging from Fernandina Beach to the inland wilds of St. John's River, are located just outside the city. However, these are beyond the scope of this book.

Not so the airport, which serves the south Georgia coast in a major way. It shares access to Sea Island and nearby resorts with Savannah and is the closest approach to St. Marys and Cumberland Island.

The airport, located 18 miles northwest of the city near Interstate 95, is part of a larger entity known as Jaxport, which includes the Port of Jacksonville. American, Continental, Delta, TWA, United, and USAir serve about 2.7 million passengers each year. Nearby general aviation airports are 1,100-acre Fernandina Beach Municipal Airpark and 30-acre Hilliard Airpark on U.S. Route 1 in Nassau County.

Appendices

A. Recommended Reading

Books

Abbott, Shirley, *Historic Charleston*. Birmingham: Oxmoor House, 1988.

Baldwin, William P., *Plantations of the Low Country: South Carolina 1697–1865*. Greensboro, NC: Legacy Publications, 1985.

Ballance, Alton, *Ocracokers*. Chapel Hill: University of North Carolina Press, 1989.

Biggs, Walter C., Jr., and James F. Parnell, *The State Parks of North Carolina*. Winston-Salem: John F. Blair Publishers, 1989.

Cheatham, James T., *The Atlantic Turkey Shoot*. Greenville, NC: Williams and Simpson Inc., Publishers, 1990.

Corey, Jane, *Exploring the Seacoast of North Carolina*. Chapel Hill: The Provincial Press, 1984.

DeBlieu, Jan, *Hatteras Journal*. Golden, CO: Fulcrum Inc., 1987.

Dennis, John V., *The Great Cypress Swamps*. Baton Rouge: Louisiana State University Press, 1988.

Ferguson, Sonny Bubba, *Southern-Fried, Semi-Low Calorie Cookbook*. Nashville: Rutledge Hill Press, 1989.

Fox, William T., *At The Sea's Edge*. Englewood Cliffs, NJ: Prentice-Hall, 1983.

The Georgia Conservancy, *A Guide to the Georgia Coast*. Jacksonville, FL: Miller Press, 1989.

Gragg, Rod, *Pirates, Planters and Patriots: Historical Tales from the South Carolina Grand Strand*. Winston-Salem, NC: Peace Hall Press, 1985.

Jones, Lewis P., *South Carolina: A Synoptic History for Laymen*. Orangeburg, SC: Sandlapper Publishing, 1971.

Joyner, Charles, *Down by the Riverside: A South Carolina Slave Community*. Champlain: University of Illinois Press, 1984.

Lefler, Hugh T., and William S. Powell, *Colonial North Carolina*. New York: Charles Scribner's Sons, 1973.

Martin, Harold H., *Georgia: A History*. New York: Norton, 1977.

— *This Happy Isle: The Story of Sea Island and The Cloister,* Sea Island: Sea Island Co., 1978.

Messner, Catherine Campant, *South Carolina's Low Country: A Past Preserved*. Orangeburg, SC: Sandlapper Publishing, 1988.

Meyer, Peter, *Nature Guide to the Carolina Coast*. Wilmington, NC: Avian Cetacean Press, 1991.

Ockershausen, Jane, *The North Carolina One-day Trip Book*. McLean, VA: EPM Publications, 1990.

Osborne, Anne Riggs, *The South Carolina Story*. Orangeburg, SC: Sandlapper Publishing, 1988.

Pilkey, Orrin H., Jr., et al., *From Currituck to Calabash*. Durham, NC: Duke University Press, 1982.

Pirtle, Caleb, III, *Georgia Through a Looking Glass*. Atlanta: Travelink Publishing Co., 1988.

Powell, William S., *North Carolina Through Four Centuries*. Chapel Hill: University of North Carolina Press, 1989.

Poyer, Dave, and Chris Kidder, *Insider's Guide to North Carolina's Outer Banks*. Manteo, NC: Storie/McOwen Publishers, 1989.

Rankin, Hugh F., *The Golden Age of Piracy*. Williamsburg, VA: Colonial Williamsburg, 1969.

Reiter, Beth Lattimore, *Coastal Georgia*. Savannah: Golden Coast Publishing Co., 1985.

Rhyne, Nancy, *Coastal Ghosts*. Orangeburg, SC: Sandlapper Publishing, 1985.

Rights, Douglas L., *The Indian in North Carolina*. Winston-Salem: John F. Blair Publishers, 1957.

Rosen, Robert, *A Short History of Charleston*. San Francisco: Lexicos, 1982.

Russell, Francis, *The Okefenokee Swamp*. New York: Time-Life Books, 1973.

Rutledge, Archibald, *Home by the River*. Orangeburg, SC: Sandlapper Publishing, 1987.

Schwartz, Frank J., *Sharks of the Carolinas*. Morehead City, NC: University of North Carolina Press, 1989.

South Carolina Wildlife and Marine Resources Department, *Wildlife Facilities Atlas*. Columbia: 1988.

Stick, David, *Graveyard of the Atlantic*. Chapel Hill: University of North Carolina Press, 1952.

Stick, David, *North Carolina Lighthouse.* Raleigh: North Carolina Department of Cultural Resources, 1991.

Twining, May A., and Keith G. Baird, editors, *Sea Island Roots: African Presence in the Carolinas and Georgia.* Trenton, NJ: African World Press, 1991.

Whedee, Charles Harry, *Legends of the Outer Banks.* Winston-Salem: John F. Blair Publishers, 1966.

Wheeler, Mary Bray, and Genon Hickerson Neblett, *Hidden Glory.* Nashville, TN: Rutledge Hill Press, 1983.

Wright, Louis B., *South Carolina: A Bicentennial History.* New York: W. W. Norton and Co., 1976.

U.S. Department of Interior, Fish and Wildlife Service, *National Wildlife Refuges of the Georgia Coastal Complex.* Washington, D.C.: 1983.

Periodicals

Coast, Myrtle Beach, SC.
Coastal Cruising, Beaufort, NC.
Georgia Sportsman, Marietta, GA.
Islander, Hilton Head, SC.
Mailboat, Harker's Island, NC.
South Carolina Public Beach and Coastal Access Guide, Charleston, SC.
South Carolina Wildlife, Columbia, SC.
The State, Raleigh, NC.
Travel Report, Raleigh, NC.
Wildlife in North Carolina, Raleigh, NC.

Newspapers

Charleston, SC, *News & Courier.*
Fayetteville, NC, *Times.*
Georgetown, SC, *Times.*
Savannah, GA, *News.*
Wilmington, NC, *Star-News.*

Maps/Charts

Marine Sciences Program, Ecology Building, University of Georgia, Atlanta, GA 30602 (404/542-2112).

Raleigh Blue Printers, 313 West Martin Street, Raleigh, NC 27601 (919/832-2841).

B. Climate

The Southeast coastal area extends into two climatic zones. Most of the North Carolina coast lies in the temperate zone. South Carolina and Georgia coasts are subtropical.

Weather conditions naturally vary along this diverse 600-mile coastline. The North Carolina coastal waters are far rougher and less predictable than those farther south, especially when winds are from the northeast. But there are certain constants. For example, humidity is high year-round and is especially oppressive if temperatures are high during the summer months. The shoulder seasons are often the most pleasant time for travel. Resorts in the southern sector of the region can be very pleasant in mild winters.

Precipitation is moderate. The northern part of the area may experience light snow at times. Rain conditions generally approach from the west or southwest, but hurricanes that form in the Caribbean often move toward the coast. At those times, all bets on rain and wind are off. Storm conditions sometimes form off the North Carolina coast.

Daily mean temperatures (Fahrenheit) on the North Carolina Outer Banks near the northern end of the region are as follows:

	MINIMUM	MAXIMUM
January	38	52
February	38	53
March	43	58
April	51	66
May	60	74
June	68	80
July	72	84
August	72	83
September	68	79
October	59	71
November	49	63
December	40	55

Daily mean temperatures (Fahrenheit) at Sea Island near the southern end of the region are as follows:

	MINIMUM	MAXIMUM
January	43	62
February	45	64
March	50	69

	MINIMUM	MAXIMUM
April	58	76
May	66	83
June	72	88
July	74	89
August	74	89
September	71	85
October	61	77
November	51	70
December	43	62

C. Flora and Fauna

Conditions in the Southeast coastal area create an incredible abundance and diversity of flora and fauna. Two climatic zones — moderate and subtropical — meet almost in the center of the area. The Gulf Stream sails by 30 to 70 miles offshore. Outcroppings at places such as Gray's Reef attract microscopic animals that feed swarms of finfish and shellfish. Artificial reefs have been created with the same idea in mind. Shoreline habitats are diverse and include barrier islands, saltwater and freshwater marshes, maritime forests, bottomlands, swamps, upland forests, river deltas, and more. The isolation of some of these islands has produced a few subspecies of familiar animals. A considerable number of feral animals still roam the barrier islands. The area is on the Atlantic flyway for wildfowl and shorebirds, as well as hummingbirds. The area long has been a prime hunting and fishing area — and continues to be. A special gleam comes into the eyes of sportsmen in the area when they talk about getting out the gun or rod. Wildlife-viewing possibilities are excellent, ranging from butterflies and bumblebees to deer, but vary from place to place and according to changes in habitat. Mosquitos and flies are an almost year-round problem. In some places, birdwatchers may outnumber beachcombers. The beaches of the region are strewn with pretty shells. Because of this situation, a single definitive list is impractical in a work of this kind. The following general list includes other species typical of the area.

Flora

PINE FAMILY
Loblolly pine
Longleaf pine
Pitch pine
Pond pine
Shortleaf pine
Slash pine
Virginia pine
Dwarf pine pond

CEDAR OR CYPRESS FAMILY
Atlantic white cedar
Bald cypress
Eastern red cedar
Pond cypress
Southern red cedar

POPLAR AND ASPEN FAMILY
Eastern cottonwood
Swamp cottonwood

WILLOW FAMILY
Swamp willow
Coastal plainwillow
Eastern cottonwood
Black willow

WAX MYRTLE FAMILY
Evergreen bayberry
Southern bayberry

WALNUT FAMILY
Bitternut hickory
Black walnut
Mockernut hickory
Pignut hickory
Sand hickory
Water hickory
Pecan

HORSECHESTNUT FAMILY
Red buckeye

BIRCH FAMILY
American hornbeam
Eastern hornbeam

Hazel alder
River birch
Roundlead birch

BEECH FAMILY
Allegheny chinkapin
American beech
Bastard oak
Black oak
Blackjack oak
Bluejack oak
Chapman oak
Chestnut oak
Cherrybark oak
Florida chinkapin
Laurel oak
Live oak
Myrtle oak
Northern red oak
Oglethorpe oak
Overcup oak
Post oak
Shumard oak
Southern red oak
Swamp chestnut oak
Turkey oak
Water oak
White oak
Willow oak

ELM FAMILY
American elm
Georgia hackberry
Slippery elm
Sugarberry
Water elm
Winged elm

MULBERRY FAMILY
Osage-orange
Red mulberry

CORKWOOD FAMILY
Corkwood

MAGNOLIA FAMILY
Pyramid magnolia
Southern magnolia
Umbrella magnolia
Sweetbay
Yellow poplar

CUSTARD-APPLE FAMILY
Paw-paw

LAUREL FAMILY
Red bay
Sassafras
Swamp bay

ROSE FAMILY
Swamp rose
American plum
Blackberry
Black cherry
Carolina laurelcherry
Chickasaw plum
Cockspur hawthorne
Fanleaf hawthorne
Flatwood plum
Green hawthorne
Littlehip hawthorne
May hawthorne
One-flowered hawthorne
Parsley hawthorne
Raspberry
Southern crabapple
Serviceberry

WITCH-HAZEL FAMILY
Sweetgum
Witch-hazel

SYCAMORE FAMILY
American sycamore

LEGUME FAMILY
Black locust
Eastern coral bean
Eastern redbud
Honeylocust
Waterlocust

CASHEW FAMILY
Poison ivy
Poison oak
Poison sumac
Shining sumac
Smooth sumac

HOLLY FAMILY
American holly
Carolina holly
Dahoon
Large gallberry
Myrtle dahoon
Yaupon
Winterberry holly

MAPLE FAMILY
Box elder
Florida maple
Red maple

DOGWOOD FAMILY
Flowering dogwood
Stiffcornel dogwood

TUPELO FAMILY
Black gum
Black tupelo
Ogeechee tupelo
Water tupelo

STORAX FAMILY
Two-winged silverbell
Bigleaf snowball

EBONY FAMILY
Common persimmon

SAPOTE FAMILY
Tough brumelia
Buckthorn brumelia

CITRUS FAMILY
Common hoptree
Hercules-club

BUCKTHORN FAMILY
Carolina buckthorn

HEATH FAMILY
Dwarf azalea
Sourwood
Staggerbush
Sparkleberry
Trailing arbutus
Checkerberry

SWEETLEAF FAMILY
Common sweetleaf

OLIVE FAMILY
Carolina ash
Devilwood
Fringetree
Green ash
Pumpkin ash
Swamp privet
White ash

HONEYSUCKLE FAMILY
American elder
Elderberry
Wild honeysuckle
Japanese honeysuckle
Coral honeysuckle
Possumhaw viburnum
Rusty blackhaw
Walter viburnum

MADDER FAMILY
Northern bedstraw
Partridge berry
Common buttonbush
Pinckneya

CYRILLA FAMILY
Swamp cyrilla
Buckwheat tree

YUCCA FAMILY
Aloe yucca
Moundlily yucca
Spoonleaf yucca
Adam's needle

PALM FAMILY
Bush palmetto
Cabbage palmetto
Saw palmetto
Dwarf palmetto
Cabbage palm

GINSENG FAMILY
Devil's walkingstick

RUE FAMILY
Common hoptree
Toothache tree

TITI FAMILY
Ironwood

MULBERRY FAMILY
Red mulberry

GRAPE FAMILY
Wild grape

TEA FAMILY
Loblolly bay
Virginia stewartia

ASH FAMILY
Carolina ash
Ocean ash
Pumpkin ash
White ash

BASSWOOD/LINDEN FAMILY
Carolina basswood

Florida basswood
White basswood

FERN FAMILY
Bay-scented fern
Christmas fern
Cinnamon fern
Climbing fern
Marsh fern
New York fern
Rattlesnake fern
Resurrection fern
Royal fern
Southern lady fern
Virginia chain fern
Bracken
Tree polypody
Giant chainfern
Deep swamp fern
Ebony spleenwort
Sensitive fern
Lowland brittle fern
Water fern
Fox-tail club moss
Carolina club moss

CATTAIL FAMILY
Narrowleaf cattail
Common cattail

GRASSES
Reed grass
Smooth cordgrass
Saltmeadow cordgrass
Big cordgrass
Saltgrass
Sawgrass
Maidencane grass
American beach grass
Wigeon grass
Wild rice
Wild celery
Eelgrass
Spike grass
Sea oats

Autumn bentgrass
Mannagrass
Wild rye
Carpetgrass
Cupgrass
Vaseygrass
Bull paspalum
Panicgrass
Plumegrass

SEDGE FAMILY
Sedge
Biltmore sedge
Purple sedge
Whitetop sedge
Brownsedge

PINEAPPLE FAMILY
Spanish moss

PONDWEED FAMILY
Curled pondweed
Sago pondweed

WATER-NYMPH FAMILY
Bushy pondweed
Curled pondweed

RUSH FAMILY
Black needlerush
Soft rush
Spikerush
Great bulrush

SEAWEEDS
Banded
Brown fuzz
Coarse red weed
Graceful red weed
Green-tufted
Hollow tube
Sea lettuce

PITCHER-PLANT FAMILY
Parrot pitcher-plant
Trumpet pitcher-plant

SUNDEW FAMILY
Venus fly-trap
Round-leaved sundew

BLADDERWORT FAMILY
Floating bladderwort
Horned bladderwort
Purple bladderwort
Two-flowered bladderwort
Dwarf bladderwort

ARROWHEAD FAMILY
Broad-leaf arrowhead

ARUM FAMILY
Arrow arum
Jack-in-the-pulpit

PICKERELWEED FAMILY
Pickerelweed
Water hyacinth
Water plantain

LILY FAMILY
Tiger lily
Turk's cap lily
Greenbriar
Day-lily
Onion
Swamp pink
Trillium
Yellow pond lily
False Solomon's seal

ASTER FAMILY
Duney aster
Groundsel-tree
Rabbit tobacco
Sea oxeye
Seaside goldenrod
Calliopsis
Saltmarsh fleabane
Common fleabane
False dandelion

COMPOSITE FAMILY
Black-eyed Susan
Common groundsel
Cornflower
Climbing hempweed
Dusty miller
Goldenrod
Groundsel-tree
Ironweed
Marsh fleabane
Oxeye daisy
Salt-marsh fleabane
Sunflower
Yarrow

IRIS FAMILY
Blue-eyed grass
Vernal iris
Dwarf blue flag
Southern blue flag
Red flag
Yellow flag
Blue-eyed grass

BARBERRY FAMILY
Mayapple

BUTTERCUP FAMILY
Marsh marigold
Swamp buttercup
Tall buttercup
Meetinghouse
Blue jessamine
Wild columbine
Liverwort

POPPY FAMILY
Celandine
Bloodroot

BEDSTRAW FAMILY
Bluet
Quaker ladies

PEA FAMILY
Clover
False indigo
Partridge pea

MALLOW FAMILY
Marsh hibiscus
Saltmarsh mallow
Seashore mallow
Scarlet hibiscus

ST. JOHN'S-WORT FAMILY
St. John's-wort
St. Andrew's-wort
Pineweed

EVENING PRIMROSE FAMILY
Common evening primrose
Seaside evening primrose
Primrose willow

ORCHID FAMILY
Pink lady's slipper
Yellow lady's slipper
Showy orchid
Orange-fringed orchid
Purple-fringed orchid
Round-leaved rein orchid
Rose pogonia
Ladies tresses
Rattlesnake plantain
Cranefly orchid

BLUEBELL FAMILY
Marsh bluebell
Southern harebell
Chicken spike
Indian tobacco
Cardinal flower
Vernus looking-glass
Long-leaf lobelia

PURSLANE FAMILY
Spring beauty

Common purslane
Rose moss

FIGWORT FAMILY
False pimpernel
Wood-betony
Pondberry

MILKWEED FAMILY
Common milkweed
Marsh milkweed
Butterfly weed
Swamp milkweed
Sand milkweed
Whorled milkweed

FLAX FAMILY
Common flax

WOOD SORREL FAMILY
Pink-wood sorrel

GERANIUM FAMILY
Crane's-bill
Wild geranium

PARSLEY FAMILY
Queen Anne's lace
Water pennywort
Spotted water hemlock
Wild carrot
Sea holly

GENTIAN FAMILY
Downy gentian
Fringed gentian
Bottle gentian
Large marsh pink

MUSTARD FAMILY
Bittercress
Cut-leaved toothwort
Wild radish

PINK FAMILY
Carolina wild pink
Starry campion
Bladder campion
Common pink
Round-leaved catchfly

PRIMROSE FAMILY
Scarlet pimpernel
Shooting star
Rough-leaf loosestrife

SEA LAVENDER FAMILY
Sea lavender

TOUCH-ME-NOT FAMILY
Jewelweed

JESSAMINES
Carolina jessamine

NIGHTSHADE FAMILY
Bittersweet nightshade
Horse nettle
Black nightshade

GROUND CHERRIES
Virginia ground cherry

MORNING-GLORY FAMILY
Beach morning glory
Arrowleaf morning glory
Wild morning glory
Common morning glory
Ivey-leaf morning glory
Wild potato vine

PHLOX FAMILY
Blue phlox
Downy phlox

Creeping phlox
Jacob's ladder

BORAGE FAMILY
Virginia cowslip

DOGBANE FAMILY
Periwinkle

TOMATO FAMILY
Jimsonweed

VIOLET FAMILY
Common blue violet
Birdfoot violet
White violet
Lanceleaf violet
Canada violet
Downy yellow violet
Wild pansy

WATER-LILY FAMILY
Lizard's tail
Wild ginger
White waterlily
Yellow waterlily
Yellow pond lily

LOTUSES
Sacred lotus
Yellow lotus
Marsh marigold
Leather flower

WINTERGREEN FAMILY
Indian pipe
Pipsissewa

GOOSEFOOT FAMILY
Lamb's quarters

Fauna

Representative Bird Sightings

LOONS AND GREBES
Common loon
Red-throated loon
Red-necked loon
Horned grebe
Pied-billed grebe
Eared grebe

SHEARWATERS AND STORM-
PETREL
Audubon's shearwater
Cory's shearwater
Greater shearwater
Manx shearwater
Sooty shearwater
Band-rumped petrel
Black-capped petrel
Leah's storm petrel
Northern fulmer
Wilson's storm-petrel

TROPICBIRDS
White-tailed tropicbird
Mashed booby

GANNET, PELICANS, AND
CORMORANTS
Northern gannet
American white pelican
Brown pelican
Great cormorant
Double-crested cormorant
Anhinga

FRIGATE BIRDS
Magnificent frigate bird

BITTERNS, HERONS, AND IBISES
American bittern
Least bittern

Great blue heron
Green heron
Little blue heron
Great egret
Snowy egret
Cattle egret
Louisiana heron
Black-crowned night heron
Yellow-crowned night heron
Glossy ibis
White ibis
Wood stork

SWANS, GEESE, AND DUCKS
Fulvous whistling duck
Tundra swan
Greater white-fronted goose
Snow goose
Blue goose
Ross goose
Brant
Canada goose
Wood duck
Blue-winged teal
Green-winged teal
Eurasian teal
American black duck
Mallard
Northern pintail
Northern shoveler
Gadwall
Eurasian wigeon
American wigeon
Canvasback
Redhead
Ring-necked duck
Greater scaup
Lesser scaup
Common goldeneye
Oldsquaw

Harlequin duck
Black scoter
Surf scoter
White-winged scoter
Common goldeneye
Bufflehead
Hooded mergenser
Common merganser
Red-breasted merganser
Ruddy duck
Harlequin duck
Common eider

VULTURES, HAWKS, AND
FALCONS
Black vulture
Turkey vulture
Osprey
Bald eagle
Golden eagle
American swallow-tailed kite
Mississippi kite
Northern harrier
Sharp-skinned hawk
Cooper's hawk
Red-shouldered hawk
Broad-winged hawk
Red-tailed hawk
Red-shouldered hawk
Rough-legged hawk
American kestrel
Merlin
American peregrine falcon
Arctic peregrine falcon

GROUSE, QUAIL, AND TURKEY
Wild turkey
Northern bobwhite

RAILS AND COOTS
Black rail
Clapper rail
King rail
Virginia rail

Yellow rail
Sora
Common gallinule
Purple gallinule
Common moorhen
American coot

PLOVERS, SNIPES, AND
SANDPIPERS
Semipalmated plover
Black-bellied plover
Lesser golden plover
Wilson's plover
Piping plover
Kildeer
American golden plover
Common snipe
American oystercatcher
Long-billed curlew
American avocet
American woodcock
Black-necked stilt
Greater yellowlegs
Lesser yellowlegs
Solitary sandpiper
Spotted sandpiper
Upland sandpiper
Willet
Whimbrel
Hudsonian godwit
Marble godwit
Ruddy turnstone
Red knot
Sanderling
Semipalpated sandpiper
Western sandpiper
Least sandpiper
White-rumped sandpiper
Baird's sandpiper
Purple sandpiper
Pectoral sandpiper
Dunlin
Curlew sandpiper
Stilt sandpiper

Buff-breasted sandpiper
Ruff
Short-billed dowitcher
Long-billed dowitcher
American woodcock
Wilson's phalarope
Red-necked phalarope
Red phalarope

JAEGERS, GULLS, AND TERNS
Long-billed jaeger
Pomarine jaeger
Parasitic jaeger
Great skua
South polar skua
Great black-backed gull
Laughing gull
Little gull
Common black-headed gull
Bonaparte's gull
Ring-billed gull
Herring gull
Iceland gull
Lesser black-billed gull
Glaucous gull
Great black-backed gull
Sabine's gull
Black-legged kittiwake
Gull-billed tern
Caspian tern
Royal tern
Sandwich tern
Roseate tern
Common tern
Arctic tern
Forster's tern
Least tern
Bridled tern
Black tern
Black skimmer

ALCIDS
Dovekie
Razorbill

DOVES, CUCKOOS, OWLS,
SWIFTS, AND HUMMINGBIRDS
Rock dove
Mourning dove
Common ground dove
Black-billed cuckoo
Yellow-billed cuckoo
Common barn owl
Eastern screech owl
Great horned owl
Snowy owl
Barred owl
Short-eared owl
Burrowing owl
Northern saw-whet owl
Chuck-will's-widow
Whippoorwill
Common nighthawk
Chimney swift
Belted kingfisher
Ruby-throated hummingbird

WOODPECKERS AND
FLYCATCHERS
Red-cockaded woodpecker
Ivory-billed woodpecker
Red-headed woodpecker
Red-bellied woodpecker
Yellow-bellied sapsucker
Downy woodpecker
Hairy woodpecker
Common flicker
Northern flicker
Pileated woodpecker
Eastern wood-peewee
Yellow-bellied flycatcher
Acadian flycatcher
Least flycatcher
Eastern phoebe
Acadian flycatcher
Great crested flycatcher
Western kingbird
Eastern kingbird
Gray kingbird
Scissor-tailed kingbird

LARKS AND SWALLOWS, JAYS,
AND CROWS
Horned lark
Purple martin
Northern rough-winged
  swallow
Tree swallow
Bank swallow
Barn swallow
Cliff swallow
Purple martin
Blue jay
American crow
Fish crow

TITMICE, NUTHATCHES, AND
WRENS
Carolina chickadee
Tufted titmouse
White-breasted nuthatch
Red-breasted nuthatch
Brown creeper
Carolina wren
House wren
Winter wren
Sedge wren
Marsh wren

KINGLETS, THRUSHES, AND
THRASHERS
Mockingbird
Golden-crowned kinglet
Ruby-crowned kinglet
Blue-gray gnatsnatcher
Veery
Gray-chested thrush
Swainson's thrush
Hermit thrush
Wood thrush
American robin
Gray catbird
Northern mockingbird
Brown thrasher
Eastern bluebird

WAXWINGS, SHRIKES, AND
STARLINGS
Water pipit
Cedar waxwing
Loggerheaded shrike
European starling

VIREOS AND WOOD WARBLERS
White-eyed vireo
Solitary vireo
Yellow-throated vireo
Philadelphia vireo
Red-eyed vireo
Blue-winged warbler
Golden-winged warbler
Tennessee warbler
Orange-crowned warbler
Nashville warbler
Northern parula
Yellow warbler
Chestnut-sided warbler
Magnolia warbler
Cape May warbler
Black-throated blue warbler
Yellow-rumped warbler
Black-throated green warbler
Blackburnian warbler
Yellow-throated warbler
Pine warbler
Prairie warbler
Palm warbler
Bay-breasted warbler
Blackpoll warbler
Black-and-white warbler
American redstart
Prothonotary warbler
Worm-eating warbler
Ovenbird
Northern waterthrush
Connecticut warbler
Louisiana waterthrush
Kentucky warbler
Common yellowthroat
Hooded warbler

Wilson's warbler
Canada warbler
Yellow-breasted chat

TANAGERS AND SPARROWS
Summer tanager
Scarlet tanager
Northern cardinal
Rose-breasted grosbeak
Blue grosbeak
Indigo bunting
Painted bunting
Dickcissel
Rufous-sided towhee
American tree sparrow
Chipping sparrow
Clay-colored sparrow
Field sparrow
Vesper sparrow
Lark sparrow
Savannah sparrow
Grasshopper sparrow
Sharp-tailed sparrow
Seaside sparrow
Fox sparrow
Song sparrow
Lincoln's sparrow
Swamp sparrow
White-throated sparrow
White-crowned sparrow
Dark-eyed junco
Lapland longspur
Snow bunting

BLACKBIRDS AND FINCHES
Bobolink

Red-winged blackbird
Eastern meadowlark
Yellow-headed blackbird
Rusty blackbird
Boat-tailed grackle
Common grackle
Brown-headed cowbird
Orchard oriole
Northern oriole
Purple finch
House finch
Pine siskin
American goldfinch
Evening grosbeak
House sparrow

ACCIDENTAL SPECIES
Pacific loon
Western grebe
Herald petrel
Red-billed tropicbird
Reddish egret
Roseate spoonbill
Sandhill crane
Mute swan
Mississippi kite
Swainson's hawk
Spotted red hawk
Black-tailed godwit
Bar-tailed godwit
Little stint
Franklin's gull
Thayer's gull
White-winged owl
Snow bunting

Mammals

DEER
White-tailed

MARSUPIALS
Virginia opossum

CARNIVORES
Black bear
Bobcat
Red wolf
Beaver

Gray fox
Red fox
Long-tailed weasel
Mink
Muskrat
Raccoon
River otter
Florida striped skunk

RABBITS
Eastern cottontail rabbit
Marsh rabbit

SQUIRRELS
Gray squirrel
Southern flying squirrel
Southern fox squirrel
Woodchuck
Eastern chipmunk

GOPHERS
Georgia pocket gopher
Southeastern pocket gopher

SHREWS AND MOLES
Southeastern shrew
Least shrew
Southern shorttail shrew
Eastern mole
Star-nosed mole

NUTRIA AND VOLES
Nutria

MICE AND RATS
Cotton mouse
Eastern harvest mouse
Golden mouse

House mouse
Oldfield mouse
Black rat
Hispid cotton rat
Norway rat
Marsh rice rat
Roof rat

BATS
Big brown bat
Eastern pipistrel
Evening bat
Hoary bat
Red bat
Seminole red bat
Northern yellow bat
Rafinesque's big-eared bat
Free-tailed bat

FERAL ANIMALS
Feral hog
Feral horse
Feral donkey
Feral cattle

ARMADILLOS
Armadillo

AQUATIC
West Indian manatee
Bottle-nosed dolphin
Goose-beaked whale
Finback whale
Sei whale
Black right whale
Sperm whale
Humpback whale

Fish

DEEPSEA GAME
Blue marlin
White marlin
Sailfish

Bluefin tuna
Dolphin
Wahoo

SNAPPERS
Yellowtail
Gray
Vermillion

GROUPER
Black
Nassau
Red

BASSES
Black sea bass
Striped bass
White perch

SUNFISHES
Bluegill
Pumpkinseed
Largemouth bass
Black crappie
Dollar sunfish
Spotted sunfish
Warmouth

PERCHES
Yellow perch

BLUEFISH
Bluefish

COBIA
Cobia

JACKS AND POMPANOS
Florida pompano
Round scad

TARPON
Atlantic tarpon

DRUMS
Black drum
Red drum
Atlantic croaker

Southern kingfish
Northern kingfish
Gulf kingfish
Spot
Spotted sea trout

MACKEREL
King
Spanish
Bonito

WRASSES
Tautog

MULLETS
Sea mullet
Striped mullet

PORGIES
Porgy
Sheepshead
Scup

FLOUNDER
Flounder

GAR
Longnose gar
Florida gar

STURGEONS
Atlantic sturgeon
Shortnose sturgeon

HERRINGS
Shad
Menhaden

PIKES
Chain pickerel
Redfin pickerel

GRUNTS
Tomtate

CATFISHES
Sea catfish
Channel catfish
Brown bullhead
Yellow bullhead
Blue catfish

SUCKERS
Sharksucker
Lake chubsucker

KILLIFISHES
Least killifish

FLOUNDERS
Summer flounder
Southern flounder

SMALL TROPICAL REEF FISH
Cardinalfish
Damsel fish
Angelfish
Purple reef fish
Yellowtail reef fish

SHARKS
Scalloped hammerhead sharks
Whale shark
Bonnethead shark
Tiger shark
Finetooth shark
Bull shark
Sand tiger shark
Atlantic sharpnose shark
Sandbar shark
Lemon shark
Nurse shark
Blacktip shark

EELS
American eel
Oscellated moray
Moray eel

STINGRAYS
Southern stingray

JELLYFISHES
Stinging jellyfish

Invertebrates

CRABS
Atlantic horseshoe crab
Blue crab
Ghost crab
Hermit crab
Horseshoe crab
Marsh crab
Marsh fiddler crab
Sand fiddler crab
Calico fiddler crab

CRAYFISHES
River crayfish

SCALLOPS
Ravenel's scallop
Zigzag scallop

Miniature smooth scallop
Lion's paw
Calico scallop
Bay scallop
Fragile scallop
Rough scallop

CLAMS
Atlantic ribbed mussel
Black clam
Carolina marsh clam
Small ring clam
Channeled duck clam
Atlantic surf clam
Dwarf surf clam
Common rangia
Quahog

Mottled chione
Broad-rimmed chione
Checkerboard
Sunray shell
Concentric ervilia
Atlantic razor clam
Atlantic jackknife clam
Green jackknife clam
Lightning Venus
Queen Venus
Disk dosina

COCKLES
Giant Atlantic cockle
China cockle
Common cockle
Great heart cockle
Atlantic strawberry cockle
Eastern microcockle
Little cockle
Egg cockle
Morton's egg cockle
Spiny paper cockle
Yellow cockle

OLIVES
Lettered olive
Dwarf olive
Rice dwarf olive
Jasper dwarf olive

GARIS
Stout tagelus

OTHER BIVALVES
Common oyster
Jingle shell
Saw-toothed pen shell
Stiff pen shell
Incongruous ark
Angel wing

SNAILS
Black triphora
Saltmarch snail
Violet snail

HORNS
Florida hornshell
Alternate bittium
Variable bittium

SLIPPERS
Thorny slipper
Convex slipper
Common slipper
Flat slipper

MOONS
Lobed moon
Northern moon
Spotted moon
Colorful moon
Spotted ear

DOVES
Greedy dove
Fat dove
Well-ribbed dove
Crescent mitrella

DOG WHELKS
Variable dog whelk
Mud dog whelk
New England dog whelk
Mottled dog whelk

WHELKS
Channeled whelk
Marsh periwinkle
Knobbed whelk
Deep-sea whelk
Hairy whelk
Lightning whelk
Perverse whelk
Fig whelk
Arrow triton

BARREL BUBBLES
Channeled
Ivory
Gould's

SHRIMPS
Brown shrimp
Grass shrimp
Pink shrimp
White shrimp

SEA STARS, SEA URCHINS
Starfish

Common sea star
Sand dollar

Seahorses
Lined seahorse

CORAL
Soft coral

Butterflies

HESPERIDAE FAMILY
Silver-spotted skipper
Gold-banded skipper
Hoary edge
Confused cloudy wing
Northern cloudy wing
Southern cloudy wing
Common sooty wing
Southern sooty wing
Horace's dusky wing
Juvenal's dusky wing
Mottled dusky wing
Sleepy dusky wing
Wild indigo dusky wing
Checkered skipper
Clouded skipper
European skipper
Least skipper
Swarthy skipper
Cobweb skipper
Cross line skipper
Fiery skipper
Leonard's skipper
Peck's skipper
Tawny edged skipper
Aaron's skipper
Delaware skipper
Mulberry wing
Southern golden skipper
Yehl skipper
Northern broken dash
Broken dash
Little glassy wing
Satchem

Broad-winged skipper
Sawgrass skipper
Dion skipper
Duke's skipper
Black dash
Two-spotted skipper
Dun skipper
Dusted skipper
Carolina roadside skipper
Reversed roadside skipper
Roadside skipper
Salt marsh skipper
Giant yucca skipper

LYCAENIDAE FAMILY
Coral hairstreak
Northern hairstreak
Gray hairstreak
White hairstreak
Spring azure
Eastern tailed blue
Little metalmark
American copper
Bronze copper
Harvester
Great purple hairstreak
Banded hairstreak
Red-banded hairstreak
Edward's hairstreak
King's hairstreak
Olive hairstreak
Striped hairstreak
Hessel's hairstreak
Brown elfin

Frosted elfin
Henry's elfin
Pine elfin

LIBYTHEIDAE FAMILY
Eastern snout

PAPILIONIDAE FAMILY
Pipe vine swallowtail
Zebra swallowtail
Black swallowtail
Giant swallowtail
Spicebush swallowtail
Tiger swallowtail
Palamedes swallowtail

PIERIDAE FAMILY
Checkered white
European cabbage
Falcate orange tip
Clouded sulphur
Orange sulphur
Dog face
Cloudless sulphur
Little sulphur
Sleepy orange

NYMPHALIDAE FAMILY
Great spangled fritillary
Meadow fritillary
Regal fritillary
Silver-bordered fritillary
Variegated fritillary
Pearl crescent
Baltimore checkerspot
Comma merchant
Red admiral
Question mark
Mourning cloak
American painted lady
Viceroy
Tawny emperor
Hackberry
Pearly eye
Creole pearly eye
Gemmed satyr
Appalachian-eyed brown
Carolina satyr
Georgia satyr
Little wood satyr
Common wood nymph
Monarch

Reptiles and Amphibians

TURTLES
Atlantic green
Atlantic loggerhead
Hawksbill
Kemp's ridley
Leatherback
Loggerhead musk turtle
Eastern box
Eastern mud
Eastern painted
Eastern musk
Diamondback terrapin
Red-bellied
Florida red-bellied
Eastern chicken turtle
Common snapping

Alligator snapping
Spotted
River cooter
Florida cooter
Red-eared pond sider
Yellow-bellied pond sider
Florida box turtle
Striped mud turtle
Stinkpot
Gopher tortoise
Florida softshell

LIZARDS AND SKINKS
Eastern glass lizard
Slender glass lizard
Island glass lizard

Mimic glass lizard
Carolina anole
Green anole
Eastern fence lizard
Southern fence lizard
Five-lined lizard
Broad-headed skink
Northern mole skink
Southeastern five-lined skink
Six-lined racerunner
Ground skink

SALAMANDERS
Dwarf siren
Lesser siren
Greater siren
Eastern newt
Striped newt
Central newt
Common mudpuppy
Dwarf mudpuppy
Neuse River waterdog
One-toed amphiuma
Two-sided amphiuma
Marbee's salamander
Flatwoods salamander
Spotted salamander
Marbled salamander
Mole salamander
Tiger salamander
Talpid salamander
Long-tailed salamander
Eastern mud salamander
Southern dusky salamander
Blackbelly salamander
Two-lined salamander
Three-lined salamander
Red-backed salamander
Slimy salamander
Mud salamander
Many-lined salamander
Cave salamander
Zigzag salamander
Gulf Coast mud salamander

TOADS AND FROGS
Eastern spadefoot toad
Oak toad
Southern toad
Fowler's toad
Eastern narrow-mouth toad
Southern cricket toad
Gray treefrog
Green treefrog
Spring peeper
Pine barrens treefrog
Barking tree frog
Squirrel tree frog
Brimley's chorus frog
Southern chorus frog
Ornate chorus frog
Little grass frog
Southern cricket frog
Crayfish frog
Bullfrog
Green frog
Pickerel frog
River frog
Southern leopard frog
Carpenter frog
Florida gopher frog
Bronze frog
Pig frog

SNAKES: POISONOUS
Diamondback rattlesnake
Canebrake rattlesnake
Timber rattlesnake
Pygmy rattlesnake
Southern copperhead
Eastern cottonmouth
Coral

SNAKES: NON-POISONOUS
Worm snake
Scarlet snake
Black racer
Southern ringneck
Corn snake

Greenish rat snake
Mud snake
Rainbow snake
Eastern hognose snake
Southern hognose snake
Common kingsnake
Mole kingsnake
Eastern kingsnake
Scarlet kingsnake
Red-bellied water snake
Banded water snake
Northern water snake
Brown water snake
Green water snake
Plainbelly water snake
Florida green water snake

Glossy crayfish snake
Striped crayfish snake
Rough green snake
Glossy crayfish snake
Black swamp snake
Brown snake
Red-bellied snake
Eastern ribbon snake
Eastern garter snake
Smooth earth snake
Queen snake
Coachwhip
Southeastern crowned snake
Milk snake
Indigo snake

D. Additional Information

North Carolina

Accommodations

HISTORIC HOTELS, B&Bs, AND INNS

Albemarle Area: Bed & Breakfast in the Albemarle, Everetts 27825
(919/792-4584)

Beaufort: Captain's Quarters, 315 Ann St. 28516 (919/728-7711).
Delamar Inn, 217 Turner St. 28516 (919/728-4300). Shotgun
House, P.O. Box 833, 406 Ann St., 28516 (919/728-6246).

Edenton: Governor Eden Inn, 304 North Broad St. 27932 (919/482-
2072). Lords Proprietors Inn, 300 North Broad St. 27932 (919/
482-3641). Trestle House Inn, Rt. 4, Box 370, Soundside Rd.
27932 (919/482-2282).

Elizabeth City: Elizabeth City B&B, 108 East Fearing St. 27909
(919/338-2177).

Goldsboro: Miss Betty's, 600 West Nash St. 27893 (919/243-4447).

New Bern: The Aerie, 509 Pollock St. 28660 (919/636-5553). Harmony House Inn, 215 Pollock St. 28560 (919/636-3810). New
Berne House, 708 Broad St. 28560 (800/842-7688).

Pollockville: Trent River Plantation, P.O. Box 369, 28583 (800/ 541-7915).
Tarboro: Little Warren, 304 East Park Ave. 27886 (919/823-1314). The Main Street Inn, 912 Main St. 27886 (919/823-2560).
Washington: Five Star, 14 North 7th St. 28401 (919/763-7581). James Place, 9 South 4th St. 28401 (919/251-0999). Pamlico House, 400 East Main St. 27889 (919/946-7184). Worth House, 412 South 3rd St. 24801 (919/762-8562).
Wilmington: Catherine's Inn on Orange, 410 Orange St. 28401 (919/ 476-0723).

RESORTS
Atlantic Beach: Ocean Resorts Inc. 28512 (919/247-3600).
Outer Banks: The Sanderling Inn Resort, S.R. Box 319Y, Duck 27949 (919/261-4111).
South Brunswick: The Winds, 310 E. First St., Ocean Isle Beach 28429 (919/579-6275 or 800/334-3581).
Topsail Beach: Queens Grant 28445 (919/328-0511 or 800/334-7842). St. Regis, North Topsail Shores 28460 (919/328-0778 or 800/ 257-3444).

RESORT RENTALS
Atlantic Beach: Cartaret Rental Agency 28512 (800/334-2727).
Emerald Isle: Sun-Surf Realty, 3103 Emerald Dr. 28594 (919/354-2958).
Sunset Beach: Sunset Vacations, 401 S. Sunset Blvd. 28459 (919/ 579-1000).

CAMPGROUNDS
Bath: Krek-Vue, Rt. 1, Box 107 27808 (919/923-5211).
Belhaven: Riverside, Rt. 1, Box 101 27810 (919/943-2849).
Engelhard: Big Trout, Hill Top Rd. 27824 (919/925-3471). White Plains, Hill Top Road 27824 (919/925-4651).
Holden Beach: Campgrounds by the Sea, 1113 Ocean Blvd. W. 28462 (919/842-6306).
Manteo: Cypress Cove, Rt. 1, Box 1675 27954 (919/473-5231). Sandpiper's Trace, P.O. Box 370 27954 (919/473-3471). Shallowbag Bay 27954 (919/473-3588).
Newport: Pender, #1 Pender Park Trading Post 28570 (919/726-4902).
Shallotte: S&W RV Park, Rt. 2, Box 686 28459 (919/754-8576). Sea Mist, P.O. Box 1481 28459 (919/754-8916).
Southport: Woodside Trailer Park, Rt. 5, Box 52 28461 (919/457-6854).
Swan Quarter: Fisherman's Wharf, Oyster Creek Rd. 27885 (919/ 926-1221).

Washington: Goose Creek State Park, Rt. 2, Box 382 27889 (919/ 923-2191).
Wilson: Kampers Lodge of America, Rt. 4, Box 519A 27893 (919/ 237-0905).

Biking
North Carolina Dept. of Transportation
P.O. Box 25201, Raleigh 27611 (919/733-2804).

BIKE TOURING
Four Seasons Cycling, P.O. Box 203, Williamsburg, VA 23187 (804/253-2958).

DEDICATED ROUTES
Ports of Call (approximately 300 miles): From the Virginia border at Corapeake follow Routes 1002, 1316, and 32 to Edenton; U.S. 17 and Routes 32 and 308 to Plymouth, Routes 1100, 1508, 1528, 1343, and 1334 to Bath; Route 92, Pamlico River Ferry; Routes 306, 1003, 1611, 1615, 1600, and 55 to New Bern; Routes 1004, 58, 1119, 1115, 1434, 1432, 172, 210-17, 1318, and 117 to Wilmington; Routes 1140, 1100, 1571, 421 and Cape Fear River Ferry to Southport; Routes 211, 1115, 1129, 1130, 1132, 130, 17, and 179 to Calabash and South Carolina border.
Queen Anne's Revenge (approximately 135-mile segment of statewide Mountainst-to-sea route): From Washington on Routes 43 and 92 to Bath and Belhaven; U.S. 264 past Mattamuskeet National Wildlife Refuge and through Lake Landing to Manteo.

Boating

MARINAS
Atlantic Beach: Bailey's, Atlantic Beach Causeway 28512 (919/247-4148). Capt. Stacy Fishing Center, Atlantic Beach Causeway 28512 (800/533-9417). Jim Bailey's Crows Nest Marina, Atlantic Beach Causeway 28512 (919/726-4048). Sea Water Marina, Atlantic Beach Causeway 28512 (919/725-1637).
Beaufort: Airport (919/728-2010). Beaufort Docks (919/728-2503). Lane's (919/728-4473). Town Creek (919/728-6111).
Calabash: Marsh Harbour, 10155 Beach Rd. 28459 (919/579-3500).
Carolina Beach: Carolina Beach Docks—Batson's Charter Boats (919/ 458-8671).
Cedar Point: Dudley's (919/393-2204).
Duck: Station Bay Marina, 27949 (919/261-3267). TWs Bait & Tackle, Loblolly Pines Shopping Center 27949 (919/261-8300).

Elizabeth City: The Pelican, Camden Causeway 27909 (919/335-5108).

Emerald Isle: Island Harbor, 28594 (919/354-3106).

Engelhard: Big Trout, Hill Top Rd. 27824 (919/925-3471). White Plains, Hill Top Rd. 27824 (919/925-4651).

Harkers Island: Barbour's 28531 (919/728-6181). Calico Jack's 28531 (919/728-3575). Harkers Island Fishing Center, P.O. Box 400 28531 (919/728-3907).

Hatteras: Albatross Fleet, P.O. Box 85 27943 (919/986-2515). Hatteras Harbor, P.O. Box 537 27943 (919/986-2166). Oden's Dock, P.O. Box 477 27943 (919/986-2555). Teach's Lair 27943 (919/966-2532). Village 27943 (919/986-2522).

Holden Beach: Holden Beach Marina, Rt. 1, Box 565-A, Supply 28462 (919/842-5447).

Holly Ridge: Monk's, Highway 50 & 210 28445 (919/329-7351).

Kitty Hawk: TWs Bait & Tackle, Milepost 4, 158 Bypass 27949 (919/261-7848).

Manteo: Pirate's Cove Yacht Club, P.O. Box 1997 27954 (919/473-3906). Manteo Town Dock, Waterfront 27954 (919/473-3320). Oregon Inlet Fishing Center, P.O. Box 533 27954 (919/441-6301). Salty Dawg Marina Inc., P.O. Box 489 27954 (919/473-3405).

Morehead City: Coral Bay (919/247-4231). Gould's Charter Boats, P.O. Box 174 28557 (919/726-3821 or 800/833-4080). Island Marina, Radio Island 28557 (919/726-5706). Morehead City Yacht Basin, 208 Arendell St. 28557 (919/726-6862). Radio Island Marina 28557 (919/726-3773).

New Bern: Tailwater, P.O. Box 1656 28563 (919/633-1404).

Ocracoke: O'Neal's Dockside 27960 (919/928-1111). Park Service Dock 27960 (919/928-5111).

Ocean Isle Beach: Ocean Isle, P.O. Box 5352 28459 (919/579-2702).

Shallotte: Pelican Pointe, Rt. 6, Box 48 28459 (919/579-6440).

Snead's Ferry: New River, Swan Point Rd. 28460 (919/327-9691). Swan Point, P.O. Box 10 28460 (919/327-1081). S&L, P.O. Box 96 28460 (919/327-2831).

Southport: Bald Head Island, 820 Indigo Plantation 28461 (919/457-5000). Indigo Plantation, W. 9th St., Southport 28461 (919/457-4551). Southport Marina, P.O. Box 10578 28461 (919/457-9900).

Swan Quarter: Fisherman's, Oyster Creek Rd. 27885 (919/926-1212).

Swansboro: Caper's Marine Service, 102 Broad St., Swansboro 28584 (919/327-2258).

Topsail Beach: Annamarina, 904 S. Anderson Blvd. 28445 (919/328-5681).

Wrightsville Beach: Bridge Tender, Airlie Rd. 28480 (919/256-6550). Caribbean Trading Co., 602 Causeway Dr. 28480 (919/256-

2112). Hanover Fishing Center, Airlie Rd. 28480 (919/256-3665). Wrightsville Beach Sportfishing Center, Highway 76 28480 (919/256-9610).

A Few Ramps

Albemarle Area: Belhaven, Riverside Campground and River Forest Manor. Chockowinity, Twin Lakes Campground & Yacht Basin. Goose Creek State Park. Hertford, Hertford Campground. Mattamuskeet, State Route 94. Merchants Millpond State Park. Pettigrew State Park.

Atlantic Beach: Sundowner Motel, 8½ Marina Village.

Cape Fear Area: Carolina Beach State Park. Jones Lake State Park. Waccamaw Lake, Wildlife Resources Commission site on road to state park.

Crystal Coast: Beaufort, Coastal Riverside Campground. Cedar Island, Driftwood Campground. Harker's Island, Fisherman's Inn. Morehead City, Arrowhead Campsites. Emerald Isle, Bridgeview Campground. Holden Beach, Holden Beach Campground. Indian Beach, Salter Path Campground.

Knotts Island: Mackay Island Causeway can be used for small boats.

New Bern: Yogi Bear's Yellowstone Park.

Outer Banks: 22 on National Park Service land, including Pea Island Refuge, Coquino Beach and Oregon Inlet, and four on Ocracoke, including Ocracoke Village and Beachcomber Campground. Cape Hatteras KOA. Frisco, Scotch Bonnet Marina, and Frisco Woods Campground. Kill Devil Hills, Durham St. Kitty Hawk, Colington Park Campground. Nags Head, Fin 'n Feather Motel.

Swanquarter, Oyster Creek Rd.

Topsail Beach: Queen's Grant Condos.

Washington: Tar River.

Windsor: Cashie Park.

Sailing

Delta Lady, P.O. Box 131, Beaufort 28616 (919/728-5088). Dreamkeeper Sailing Charters, P.O. Box 2266, Manteo 27954 (919/473-3515). Joseph W. Bach Ent. Inc., 5109 Springwood Dr., New Bern 28562 (919/638-4729). Nor'Banks Sailing Center, P.O. Box 1113, Kitty Hawk 27949 (919/261-2900). The Waterworks, P.O. Box 1134, Nags Head 27959 (919/441-8875). Kitty Hawk Sailing Charters, M.P. 8, Kitty Hawk 27949 (919/441-1195).

Scuba Diving & Snorkeling

Carolina Cape Divers, Old Yacht Basin, Southport 28461, or 5422 Oak Island Dr., Long Beach 28465 (919/278-5611). Nags Head

Pro Dive Center Inc., P.O. Box 665, Nags Head 27959 (919/441-7594). Capt. Kris Klingerberger, Towles Rd., Wrightsville Beach 28480 (919/350-0039).

WINDSURFING
Cape Hatteras Boardsailing School, P.O. Box 896, Buxton 27920 (919/995-4795). Hatteras Outdoors, P.O. Box 947, Buxton 27920 (919/995-5815). Kitty Hawk Sports, P.O. Box 340, Nags Head 27959 (919/441-2756). Nor'Banks Windsurfing, S.R. Box 328 N. Duck Road, Kitty Hawk 27949 (919/261-2900). The Waterworks, P.O. Box 1134, Nags Head 27959 (919/441-8875). Windsurfing Hatteras, Box 539, Avon 27915 (919/995-4970).

Civic Organizations

Ocracoke Civil Club, P.O. Box 456, Ocracoke 27960 (919/928-6711).

Conservation Organizations

Coastal Wildlife Refuge Society, P.O. Box 1808, Manteo 27954 (919/473-1101).
Corolla Wild Horse Fund, Box 361-PMM, Corolla 27927.
Friends of Nags Head Woods, 701 West Ocean Acres Drive, Kill Devil Hills 27948 (919/441-2525).
National Estuarine Research Reserve, Center for Marine Science Research, 7205 Wrightsville Ave., Wilmington 28403 (919/256-3721).
The Nature Conservancy Field Office, Carrmill Mall, Suite 223, Carrboro 27510 (919/967-7007).

Cultural Attractions

AQUARIUMS
North Carolina Aquarium, Kure Beach 28449 (919/458-8257). Roanoke Island, P.O. Box 967, Manteo 27954 (919/458-8257). Pine Knoll Shores, Atlantic Beach 28512 (919/247-4003).

ART MUSEUMS
St. John's Museum of Art, 114 Orange St., Wilmington 28401 (919/763-0281).

EVENTS
Albemarle Area: Christmas at Hope Plantation, P.O. Box 601, Wind-

sor 27983 (919/794-3140). Edenton Tea Party Anniversary Celebration (October), P.O. Box 474, Edenton 27932 (919/482-2637).
Cape Fear Area: Christmas by the Sea Festival, Southport-Oak Island, (919/457-6964). Holiday Flotilla (November), Wrightsville Beach, Greater Wilmington Chamber of Commerce, 514 Market St., Wilmington 28401 (919/762-2611). North Carolina Azalea Festival (April), Wilmington area, Wilmington 28402 (919/783-0905 or 800/922-7117 in state or 800/222-4757 out of state). North Carolina Fourth of July Festival, 113 W. Moore St., Southport 28461 (919/457-5578).
Crystal Coast: Emerald Isle Beach Music Festival (May) (919/354-2872). North Carolina Seafood Festival, P.O. Drawer M, Morehead City 28557 (919/726-6848). Annual Sea Turtle Release (May), Pine Knoll Shores (919/247-4004). Snead's Ferry Shrimp Festival (August) (800/786-6962).
Kinston: M-150 Two-Day Bike Tour (September) (919/781-0676).
New Bern: Spring Historic and Garden Tour, P.O. Box 119, New Bern 28560 (919/638-8558). Chrysanthemum Festival (October) (919/638-5781).
Outer Banks: Annual Hang-Gliding Spectacular (May) (919/441-4124). Coastweeks (September), Manteo (919/473-3494). Ft. Fisher Celebration (May) (919/458-5538). Nags Head Rogallo Kite Festival (June) and Rogallo Wing Invention Anniversary (August) (919/441-4124). National Aviation Day (August), Kill Devil Hills (919/441-3761).
Topsail Island: Onslow County Museum Kite Festival (April) (919/324-5008).

MUSEUMS
Aurora Fossil Museum, Aurora 27806 (919/322-4238).
Belhaven Memorial Museum, P.O. Box 220, Belhaven 27810 (919/943-3055).
Blount-Bridgers House, 130 Briders St., Tarboro 27886 (919/823-4159).
Museum of the Albemarle, 1116 U.S. Highway 17 S., Elizabeth City 27909 (919/335-1453).
Native American Museum & Natural History Center, P.O. Box 399, Frisco 27936 (919/995-4440).
New Bern Civil War Museum, 301 Metcalf St., New Bern 28560 (919/633-2818).
North Carolina Maritime Museum, 315 Front St., Beaufort 28516 (919/728-7317).
Port O' Plymouth Roanoke River Museum, P.O. Box 296, Plymouth 27962 (919/793-1377).

Tobacco Museum of North Carolina, P.O. Box 88, Kenly 27542 (919/284-3431).
USS North Carolina Battleship Memorial, P.O. Box 417, Wilmington 28402 (919/762-1829).
Wayne County Museum, 116 North William St., Goldsboro 27530 (919/734-5023).
Wilmington Railroad Museum Foundation, 501 Nutt St., Wilmington 28401 (919/763-2634).

OUTDOOR DRAMA
The Lost Colony, nightly early June–late August, P.O. Drawer 40, Manteo 27954 (919/473-2127; tickets 919/473-3414).
Worthy Is the Lamb, Crystal Coast Amphitheatre, P.O. Box 1004, Swansboro 28584 (919/393-8373 or 800/662-5960).

Ferries

Bald Head Island Ferry Dock, 704 East Monroe St., Southport 28461 (919/457-5000 or in NC 800/722-6450).
North Carolina Department of Transportation Ferry Division, 113 Arendell Street, Morehead City 28557 (departures from Ocracoke 919/938-3841; from Cedar Island 919/225-3551; from Swan Quarter 919/926-1111).

Fishing

REGULATIONS
North Carolina Division of Marine Fisheries, P.O. Box 769, Morehead City 28557 (919/728-7021 or 800/682-2623); P.O. Box 1507, Washington 27889 (919/946-6481 or 800/338-7804); 127 Cardinal Dr. Ext., Wilmington 28405 (919/395-3900 or 800/248-4536); 1367 U.S. 17 South, Elizabeth City 27909 (919/264-3911 or 800/338-7805); P.O. Box 1550, Manteo 27954 (919/473-5734).

PIERS
Avon: Avon Pier (919/995-5480).
Frisco: Cape Hatteras (919/995-5480).
Holden Beach: Holden Beach Fishing Pier, 441 Ocean Blvd. West 28462 (919/842-6483).
Kill Devil Hills: Avalon Pier, Milepost 6 27948 (919/441-7494).
Nags Head: Jennette's (919/441-6116). Nags Head Fishing Pier, P.O. Box 7 27959 (919/441-5141). Outer Banks Pier, Milepost 18½, South Nags Head 27959 (919/441-5028).

Ocean Isle: Ocean Isle Beach 28469 (919/579-0873).
Rodanthe: Hatteras Island 27982 (919/987-2323).
Sunset Beach: Sunset Beach, 101 Main St. 28459 (919/579-6630).
Topsail Beach: Topsail Sound, 1520 Carolina Rd. 28445 (919/328-3641).
Wrightsville Beach: Johnny Mercer's 28480 (919/256-9610).

GUIDES

Atlantic Beach: Capt. Stacy Fishing Center, Atlantic Beach Causeway 28512: Calcutta Charters (Capt. Dew Forbes) (919/393-8560). *Fine Line,* Capt. Sonny Rains (800/445-2055). *Purrsuasion,* Capt. Dan Leone (919/247-7877). *Capt. Stacy VII,* P.O. Box 3013 28512 (919/247-7501 or 919/726-4675). *Laura J.* (Capt. Leonard Rigsbee), Sea Water Marina 28512 (919/726-2533). *Sea Hawk,* (Capt. Fred Willis), P.O. Box 512 28512 (919/726-3818). *Ultimate Joy* (Capt. Bob Stiehl), Anchorage Marine 28512 (919/726-8758).
Beaufort: Sea Wife IV (Capt. Buck Wilde) and *Sea Wife III* (Capt. Hugh L. Wilde), Rt. 2, Box 614 28516 (919/728-5670).
Benson: Vicky Joe Fishing Team, Box 248 27504 (919/278-6393).
Calabash: Captain Jim's, P.O. Box 4300 28459 (919/579-3660). Capt. Sam's *Mary B. III,* Rt. 7, Box 248 28459 (919/577-3141).
Carolina Beach: Town Marina: *Fired-Up* (919/458-5712). *Fish Witch* (Capt. Carl S. Snow Jr.), P.O. Box 1700 28428 (919/458-5855). *Flapjack* (Capt. Chuck Harrill), P.O. Box 2120 28428 (919/458-4362). *Lady Frances* (Capt. Don Donaldson) (919/458-5228). Capt. Rick (919/458-4458). *Flo-Jo* (Capt. Ray Rothrock) (919/458-5454); *Winner Queen* (919/458-5356); *Cruise Queen* (919/458-5356). Pirate Fishing and Cruise Boats, P.O. Box 1207 28428 (919/458-5626 or 800/234-7322).
Duck: Bob's Bait & Tackle, Duck Rd., Duck 27949 (919/261-8589).
Durham: Tom N Jerry (Capt. Tom Talton), P.O. Box 749 27702 (919/489-9688).
Harkers Island: Sensation (Capt. Randy Ramsey or Capt. Jim Luxton), P.O. Box 376 28531 (919/728-6571). *Ashley Renaie* (Capt. Tommy Fletcher), Calico Jacks Marina 28531 (919/728-3676).
Hatteras: Albatross Fleet, P.O. Box 85 27943 (919/986-2515). Hatteras Connection Inc., P.O. Box 469 27943 (919/966-2163).
Holden Beach: Swag Charters (Capt. Ron Arvidson) P.O. Box 1615, Shallotte 28459 (919/842-4930).
Long Beach: Drifter, 306 45th St. NE 28465 (919/278-6257). *The Fugitive,* 138 NW 17th St. 28465 (919/276-3796). *Hot Pursuit* (Capt. Jeff Burns), 106 W. Island Dr. 28465 (919/278-7272). *Predator,* 205 NE 61st St. 28465 (919/278-4754).
Manteo: Dreamkeeper, Dough Creek Marina 27954 (919/473-3515).

Miss Oregon Inlet, Oregon Inlet Fishing Center, P.O. Box 533 27954 (919/441-6301). *Crystal Dawn, Country Girl,* Pirate's Cove Yacht Club, 4600 Roanoke Way, Nags Head 27959 (919/473-5577). *Island Lady,* P.O. Box 2119 27954 (919/473-6242).

Marshallberg: Offshore III (Capt. Buddy Harris), P.O. Box 34 28553 (919/729-2431).

Morehead City: Captain Stacy IV, P.O. Box 1283 28557 (919/726-4675). *Carolina Princess,* P.O. Box 1663 28557 (919/726-5499). *Triple Header* (Capt. Ken Wagner), P.O. Box 1495 28557 (919/726-3844). *C-Oats* (Capt. Don Coats), P.O. Box 451 28557 (919/726-3565). *Sea Mistress* (Capt. Walt Johnson), 1304 Wicklow Drive, Cary 27511 (919/726-3032). *Wave Runner,* 2798 Evans Street 28557 (919/726-7641). *Southwind* (Capt. Ken Kramer), P.O. Box 264 28557 (919/726-2476).

Nags Head: Crystal Dawn Fishing Parties, P.O. Box 879, 27959 (919/473-5577). Outer Banks Fishing Unlimited, Nags Head Causeway at Little Bridge 27959 (919/441-5028).

Newport: Kathi "T" (Capt. Ron Tong), P.O. Box 391 28570 (919/223-5238).

Ocean Isle Beach: Adam's Apple, Ocean Isle Beach 28459 (919/579-3599 or 919/579-5515).

Snead's Ferry: Swan Point, P.O. Box 10 28460 (919/327-1081).

Southport: Trophy Hunter (Capt. "Ski" Sherfinski), Rt. 1, Box 215 28461 (919/457-5392). *Watts,* 318 W. Brunswick St. 28461 (919/457-5441).

Topsail Beach: King Fisher Charters, P.O. Box 3298 28445 (919/328-2659).

Wrightsville Beach: Hanover Fishing Center, *Sea Lady* (Capt. Lloyd Eastback), Airlie Road 28480 (919/452-9955). Sport Fishing Center, *Top Gun, Happy Day* (Capt. Jim Mixon) (919/799-2766), *Richochet, Hattarest* (919/256-9610).

Golf

ASSOCIATIONS

Crystal Coast Golf & Recreation Assn., 152 Oakleaf Dr., Pine Knoll Shores 28557 (919/729-1661).

COURSES

Cape Carteret: Star Hill, Highway 25 (919/393-8111).

Cape Fear Coast: Beau Rivage (919/392-9022). Duck Haven (919/791-7983). Wilmington (919/791-0558).

Outer Banks: Nags Head, 5616 South Seachase Dr., Nags Head 27959 (919/441-8074). Ocean Edge, Frisco 27936 (919/995-4100). Sea Scape, Kitty Hawk 27949 (919/261-2158).

Hertford: Sound Golf Links at Albemarle Plantation, P.O. Box 49 27944 (919/426-5555 or 800/535-0704).
Snead's Ferry: North Shore Country Club, Highway 210 28460 (919/327-2410).
South Brunswick: Brick Landing Plantation, Rt. 2, Box 210, Ocean Isle Beach 28459 (919/754-5545). Brierwood, P.O. Box 100, Shallotte 28459 (919/754-4660). Carolina Shores, 99 Carolina Shores Drive, Calabash 28459 (919/579-2181). Lockwood, 100 Club House Dr., Holden Beach 28462 (919/842-5666). Marsh Harbour, 10155 Beach Rd., Calabash 28459 (919/579-3161). Ocean Harbour, 10301 Somersett Dr., Calabash 28459 (919/579-3588). Pearl, Rt. 8, Sunset Lakes Blvd., Calabash 28459 (919/579-8132). Sandpiper, 6660 Sandpiper Bay Dr., Calabash 28459 (919/579-9021). Sea Trail, P.O. Box 102, Sunset Beach 28459 (919/579-4350).

History
North Carolina Division of Archives and History
109 E. Jones St., Raleigh 27611 (919/733-2290).

HISTORICAL ORGANIZATIONS
Chicamacomico Historical Association, Yucca Perch Way, Waves, NC 27982 (919/978-2203).
Fort Branch Battlefield Commission, P.O. Box 355, Hamilton 27840.
Historic Hamilton Commission Inc., P.O. Box 504, Hamilton 27840.
Historic Wilmington Foundation, 209 Dock St., Wilmington 24801 (919/762-2511).
Lower Cape Fear Historical Society, 126 South 3rd St., Wilmington 28401 (919/762-0492).
Outer Banks History Center, P.O. Box 250, Manteo 27954 (919/473-2655).
Roanoke Island Historical Assn., P.O. Drawer 40, Manteo 27954 (919/473-2127).

HISTORIC SITES
Brunswick Town State Historic Site, Rt. 1, Box 55, Winnabow 28479 (919/371-6613).
Charles B. Aycock Birthplace, P.O. Box 207, Fremont 27830 (919/242-5581).
Elizabeth II State Historic Site, P.O. Box 155, Manteo 27954 (919/473-1144).
Fort Branch Battlefield, Box 220, Jamesville 27846 (919/792-3001).
Fort Fisher State Historic Site, P.O. Box 68, Kure Beach 28449 (919/458-5538).

Fort Macon State Park, Highway 58 (Fort Macon Rd.), Atlantic Beach 28512 (919/726-3775).

Historic Bath, P.O. Box 148, Bath 27808 (919/923-3971).

Historic Edenton, P.O. Box 474, Edenton 27932 (919/482-3663).

Historic Halifax State Historic Site, P.O. Box 406, Halifax 27839 (919/583-7191).

Historic Hamilton, Box 218, Hamilton 27840 (919/798-7461).

Historic Murfreesboro, P.O. Box 3, Murfreesboro 27855 (919/398-5922).

Historic Tarboro, 130 Bridgers St., Tarboro 27886 (919/823-4159).

Historic Washington, P.O. Box 1968, Washington 27889 (919/946-1033).

Hope Plantation Inc., P.O. Box 601, Windsor 27983 (919/794-3140).

Moore's Creek National Battlefield, P.O. Box 69, Currie 28435 (919/283-5591).

Newbold-White State Historic Site, P.O. Box 103, Hertford 27944 (919/426-7867).

Poplar Grove Historic Plantation, Rt. 1, Box 496-A, Wilmington 28405 (919/686-9518).

Somerset Place, P.O. Box 215, Creswell 27928 (919/797-4560).

Tryon Palace, 610 Pollock St., New Bern 28563 (919/638-1560).

Hunting

REGULATIONS

North Carolina Wildlife Resource Commission, 512 Salisbury St., Raleigh 27604 (919/733-3391); to report wildlife violations: 800/662-7137.

GAME LANDS

Bachelor Bay, Bertie and Washington counties. Bertie, Bertie County. Chowan, Chowan County. Bull Rock, Hyde County. Croatan, Carteret, Craven, and Jones counties. Dare, Dare County. Goose Creek, Beaufort and Pamlico counties. Holly Shelter, Pender County. Hoffman Forest, Jones and Onslow counties. Neuse River, Craven County. New Lake, Hyde and Tyrell counties. Pungo River, Hyde County. North River, Currituck County. Northwest River, Currituck County. Roanoke River, Bertie, Halifax, and Martin counties. Sutton Lake, New Hanover County. Tuscarora, Craven County. White Oak River, Onslow County.

Information Sources

North Carolina Travel & Tourism Division,
410 N. Salisbury St., Raleigh 27603 (919/733-4171).

CHAMBERS OF COMMERCE

Carteret County, P.O. Box 1198, Morehead City 28557 (919/726-6350).

Edenton-Chowan, Drawer F, Edenton 27932 (919/482-3400).

Greater Washington, P.O. Box 665, Washington 27889 (919/946-9168).

Greater Jacksonville/Onslow County, P.O. Box 765, Jacksonville 28541 (919/347-3141).

Greater Wilmington, 514 Market St., Wilmington 28401 (919/762-2611).

Lenoir County, P.O. Box 157, Kinston 28502 (919/527-1131).

The Outer Banks, P.O. Box 1757, Kill Devil Hills 27948 (919/995-4213 Hatteras Island, 919/441-8144 north beaches).

Pamlico County, P.O. Box 23, Bayboro 28515 (919/249-1851).

Southport-Oak Island, Rt. 5, Box 52, Southport 28461 (919/457-6964).

Tarboro Area, 112 West Church St., Tarboro 27886 (919/823-7241).

Wayne County, 308 N. William St., Goldsboro 27533 (919/734-2241).

Wrightsville Beach, P.O. Box 366, 28480 (800/232-467 or 919/395-2965).

TOURISM ORGANIZATIONS

Cape Fear Coast Convention & Visitors Bureau, 24 North Third St., Wilmington 28401 (919/341-4030; 800/222-4757 Eastern U.S.; 800/922-7171 in NC).

Cartaret County Tourist Development Bureau, P.O. Box 1406, Morehead City 28557 (800/786-6962).

Craven County Convention & Visitors Bureau, P.O. Box 1413, New Bern 28563 (919/637-9400).

Dare County Tourist Bureau, P.O. Box 399, Manteo 27954 (919/473-2138).

Fayetteville Area Convention & Visitors Bureau, 515 Ramsey St., Fayetteville 28301 (919/483-5311 or 800/446-8604).

Gates County Industrial Development Commission, P.O. Box 141, Gatesville 27938 (919/357-1240).

Greenville-Pitt County Convention & Visitors Bureau, P.O. Box 8027, Greenville 27835 (919/752-8044 or 800/537-5564).

Historic Albemarle Tour Inc., P.O. Box 759, Edenton 27932 (919/482-7325).

North Carolina Travel & Tourism Division, 430 N. Salisbury St., Raleigh 27603 (919/733-4171).

Johnson County Convention & Visitors Bureau, P.O. Box 1990, Smithfield 27577 (919/989-8687 or 800/441-7829).

Onslow County Tourism Committee, P.O. Box 1226, Jacksonville 28541 (919/455-1113).

OTHER GOVERNMENTAL AGENCIES
Brunswick County Parks and Recreation, P.O. Box 249, Bolivia 28422 (919/253-4357).
County of Hyde, Courthouse Square, Swan Quarter 27885 (919/926-5711).
North Carolina Department of Cultural Resources, 109 East Jones St., Raleigh 27601 (919/733-5723).
North Carolina Department of Transportation, P.O. Box 25201, Raleigh 27611 (919/733-2804).

Miscellaneous

HANG GLIDING/PARAGLIDING
Corolla Flight, P.O. Box 1021, Kitty Hawk 27949 (919/261-6166).
Kitty Hawk Flight, P.O. Box 340, Nags Head 27959 (919/441-4124).
Kitty Hawk Kites, P.O. Box 1839, Nags Head 27959 (919/441-4124).
Ocean Winds Parasail, MP 13, Nags Head 27959 (919/441-6800).

KITES
Kite Kingdom, Sea Holly Square, Beach Rd., Kill Devil Hills 27949 (919/441-7709).
Outer Banks Stunt Kite Competition, P.O. Box 1839, Nags Head 27939 (919/441-4124).

HORSEBACK RIDING
Buxton Stables, Buxton, Hatteras Island 27943 (919/995-4656).
Whitesand Trail Rides, P.O. Box 1040, Atlantic Beach 28512 (919/729-0911).

Nature Sites

NATIONAL PARKS, REFUGES, AND FORESTS
Cape Hatteras National Seashore, U.S. National Park Service, Manteo 27954 (919/473-2111).
Cape Lookout National Seashore, P.O. Box 690, Beaufort 28516 (919/728-2250).
Cedar Island National Wildlife Refuge, Cedar Island 28520 (919/225-2511).
Croatan National Forest, 141 E. Fisher Ave., New Bern 28560 (919/638-5628).
Matamuskeet National Wildlife Refuge (also headquarters for Swan-

quarter and Cedar Island NWR), Rt. 1, Box N-2, Swanquarter 27885 (919/926-4021).

Pocosin Lakes National Wildlife Refuge, Rt. 1, Box 195-B, Creswell 27928 (919/797-4431).

STATE AND LOCAL PARKS

North Carolina Division of Parks and Recreation
P.O. Box 27687, Raleigh 27611 (919/733-7275).

Carolina Beach State Park, P.O. Box 475, Carolina Beach 28428 (919/458-8206).

Cliffs of Neuse State Park, Route 2, Box 50, Seven Springs 28575 (919/778-6234).

Fort Fisher State Recreation Area, P.O. Box 475, Carolina Beach 28428 (919/458-8206).

Fort Macon State Park, P.O. Box 127, Atlantic Beach 28512 (919/726-3775).

Goose Creek State Park, Rt. 2, Box 372, Washington 27889 (919/923-2191).

Hammocks Beach State Park, Route 3, Box 295, Swansboro 28584 (919/326-4881).

Jockey's Ridge State Park, P.O. Box 592, Nags Head 27959 (919/441-7132).

Jones Lake State Park, Rt. 2, Box 945, Elizabethtown 28337 (919/588-4550).

Lake Waccamaw State Park, Rt. 1, Box 63, Kelly 28448 (919/669-2928).

Merchants Millpond State Park, Rt. 1, Box 141A, Gatesville 27938 (919/357-1191).

Pettigrew State Park, Rt. 1, Box 336, Creswell 27928 (919/797-4475).

Singletary Lake State Park, Rt. 1, Box 63, Kelly 28448 (919/669-2928).

Waynesborough State Park, Rt. 2, Box 50, Seven Springs 28578 (919/776-6234).

GARDENS

Airlie Gardens (Airlie Rd. off Rt. 72-74), 1200 Castle Hayne Road, Wilmington 28405 (919/763-9991).

Elizabethan Gardens of the Garden Club of North Carolina Inc., P.O. Box 1150, Manteo 27954 (919/473-3234).

New Hanover County Arboretum, 6206 Oleander Dr., Wilmington 28403 (919/350-0010).

Orton Plantation Gardens, Rt. 1, Box 57, Winnabow 28479 (919/371-6851).

Tours

AERIAL

Aerotours, Kitty Hawk 27948 (919/441-4460).

Outer Banks Airways, P.O. Box 1976, Manteo 27954 (919/441-7677).

Wright Brothers Tours, P.O. Box 1036, Kill Devil Hills 27948 (919/441-5909).

SIGHTSEEING

Beaufort: Beaufort Tours Inc., Front St., 28516 (919/728-7827 or 919/223-4551).

Outer Banks: Outer Banks Cruising, NC Route 12, Duck 27949 (919/261-8620).

Wilmington: Cape Fear Riverboats Inc., P.O. Box 1881, 28402 (919/343-1611). Maffitt Cruises, 2 Ann St., 28401 (919/343-1776). North Carolina Azalea Festival (Wilmington Area), 28402 (919/763-0905). Port Facilities, P.O. Box 9002, 28401 (919/763-1621).

South Carolina

Accommodations

HISTORIC HOTELS, B&BS, AND INNS

Beaufort: Bay Street Inn, 601 Bay St. 29902 (803/524-7720). Old Point Inn, 212 New St. 29902 (803/524-3177). Rhett House Inn, 1009 Craven St. 29902 (803/524-9030).

Bluffton: Fripp House Inn, P.O. Box 857, 29910 (803/757-2139).

Charleston: The Anchorage Inn, 26 Vendue Range 29401 (803/723-8300 or 800/421-2952). Ansonborough Inn, 21 Hasell St. 29401 (800/522-2073 outside SC, 800/723-1655 in state). Church Street Inn, 177 Church St. 29401 (803/722-3420 or 800/552-3777). Maison Du Pre, 317 East Bay St. 29401 (800/533-4667). Indigo Inn, 1 Maiden Lane 29401 (800/845-7639 outside SC, 800/922-1340 in state). The Jasmine House, 64 Hassell St. 29401 (800/845-7639 outside SC, 800/922-1340 in state). John Rutledge House Inn, 116 Broad St. 29401 (803/723-7999 or 800/476-9741). Kings Courtyard Inn, 198 King St. 29401 (803/723-7000 or 800/845-6119). The Lodge Alley Inn, 195 East Bay St. 29401 (800/845-1004 outside SC, 800/821-2791 in state). Meeting Street Inn, 173 Meeting St. 29401 (803/723-1882 or 800/842-8022). Mills House, P.O. Box 1013 29402 (803/577-2400 or 800/874-9600). Planters Inn, 122 N. Market St. 29401 (803/722-2345 or 800/845-7082).

Edisto Island: Cassina Point Plantation, P.O. Box 535 29438 (803/ 869-2535).
Georgetown: Five Thirty, 530 Prince St. 29440 (803/527-1114). 1790 House, 630 Highmarket St. 29440 (803/546-4821).
Mt. Pleasant: Guild's Inn, 101 Pitt St. 29464 (803/881-0510).
Sullivan's Island: The Palmettoes, P.O. Box 706 29482 (803/883-3389).
Summerville: Bed and Breakfast of Summerville, 304 South Hampton St. 29483 (803/871-5275). Gadsden Motor Inn, 329 Postern Rd. 29484 (803/873-2333).

RESORTS
Edisto Island: Fairfield Ocean Ridge Resort 29438 (803/869-2561 or 800/922-3330).
Fripp Island: Fripp Island Resort, 1 Tarpon Rd. 29920 (803/838-3535 or 800/845-4100).
Garden City: Dunes Golf Villas and Village, Atlantic Avenue 29576 (803/651-2116 or 800/845-8191).
Hilton Head Island: Palmetto Dunes, P.O. Box 5606 29938 (803/785-1161 or 800/845-6130). Port Royal Plantation 29925 (803/686-9099 or 800/428-2228). Sea Pines 29928 (803/785-3333 or 800/845-6131). Shipyard Plantation 29925 (803/785-3333 or 800/845-6135).
Kiawah Island: Kiawah Island Resort, P.O. Box 12910, Charleston 29412 (803/768-2121).
Litchfield Beach: Litchfield Inn 29585 (803/237-4211).
Myrtle Beach: Bluewater, P.O. Box 3000 29578 (803/626-8345 or 800/845-6994). Caravelle, 6900 N. Ocean Blvd. 29572 (803/449-2331). Carolina Winds, P.O. Drawer 7518 29578 (803/449-2477 or 800/523-4027). Driftwood, P.O. Box 275-AG 29578 (803/448-1544 or 800/942-3456). Myrtle Beach Martinique, P.O. Box 331 29578 (803/449-4441 or 800/542-0048). Sheraton Atlantic Shores, 2701 S. Ocean Blvd. 29577 (803/448-2518 or 800/992-1055). The Reef, 201 S. Ocean Blvd. 29577 (803/448-1765 or 800/845-1212).
Seabrook Island: Seabrook Island, P.O. Box 32099, Charleston 29417 (803/845-5531).

CAMPGROUNDS
Bluffton: Stoney Crest 29910 (803/757-3249).
Charleston Area: Comfort Inn and RV Park, St. George 29477 (803/563-4180); James Island County Park, Charleston 29412 (803/795-7275); KOA, 9494 Highway 78, Ladson 29456 (803/797-1045). Oak Plantation, 3540 Savannah Highway, Johns Island 29455 (803/449-3714). Waterloo Plantation, Maybank Highway, Johns Island 29455 (803/559-5934).

Edisto Beach: Edisto Beach State Park 29438 (803/869-2156).
Eutawville: Rocks Pond, Rt. 1, Box 432 29048 (803/492-7711).
Florence: KOA, Rt. 6, Box 125 29506 (803/665-7007). Swamp Fox, Rt. 5, Box 76 29501 (803/665-9430).
Folly Beach: Pelican Cove RV Resort, Box 299 29439 (803/588-2072).
Grand Strand: Apache, 9700 Kings Rd., Myrtle Beach 29877 (803/449-7323). Barefoot RV Resort, P.O. Box 2116, North Myrtle Beach 29598 (803/272-1790 or 800/272-1790). Briarcliff, 10495 Kings Highway, Myrtle Beach 29577 (803/272-4332). KOA North Sherwood, U.S. Route 17 North, North Myrtle Beach 29598 (803/272-6420). Lakewood, 5901 Business Highway 17 South 29577 (803/238-5181). Myrtle Beach KOA, 5th St. South, Myrtle Beach 29577 (803/448-3421). Myrtle Beach RV Resort, 5400 Little River Neck Rd., North Myrtle Beach 29582 (800/356-6278 or 803/249-1484). Myrtle Beach Travel Park, 9916 Kings Rd., North Myrtle Beach 29572 (803/449-3714). Myrtle Beach State Park 29577 (803/238-5325). Ocean Lakes, 6001 South Kings Highway, Myrtle Beach 29575 (803/722-1451 or 800/722-1451). Pebble Beach, 3000 South Ocean Blvd., Myrtle Beach 29577 (803/238-2830). Pirateland, 5401 South Kings Highway 29575 (803/238-5155 or 800/443-2267). Springmaid Beach, 3201 South Ocean Blvd., Myrtle Beach 28577 (803/238-5264).
Hilton Head: Outdoor Resorts (Motorcoach), 19 Arrow Rd. 29925. Outdoor Resorts (RV and Yacht Club), P.O. Box 21585 29925 (803/681-3256 or 800/845-9560).
Murrells Inlet: Huntington Beach State Park 29576 (803/237-4440).
Ridgeville: Givhans Ferry State Park 29472 (803/873-0692).
St. Helena Island: Hunting Island State Park 29920 (803/838-2011).
Summerton: Santee Lakes, Rt. 2, Box 542 29148 (803/478-2262).

Biking

Clubs
Carolina Cyclers, P.O. Box 1163, Columbia 29211. Coastal Cyclist, P.O. Box 32095, Charleston 29417. Beaufort Bicycle Club, P.O. Box 2081, Beaufort 29901.

Maps
South Carolina Department of Highways and Public Transportation Map Sales, P.O. Box 191, Columbia 29202 (803/737-1501).

Trails
Coastal (about 227 mi.): from North Carolina border on Routes 179 and 17 to Little River; 26/50, 26/111, 90, 26/31, 905 to Conway; 701, 261, 513, and 41 to Francis Marion National Forest; 51, 8/48,

8/125, 8/376, 8/171, 402, 17A, 0810, 8/791, 8/357, 8/413, 8/467, 176, 8/32, 18/182, 173, 27, 18/233, 18/19, and 18/30 to Givhans Ferry State Park; 18/30, 61, 16/21, 17A, 63/17A, 63, 25/50, 25, 168, 25/93, and 33 to Furman; 25/852, 27/50, 321, and 119 to Georgia border.

Savannah River (segment, about 41 mi.): from I-95 near Yemassee on Routes 68, 25/1, 7/3, 7/21, 21, and 7/348 to Hunting Island State Park.

Walter Ezell (segment, about 86 mi.): from I-95 at Santee on Routes 6 and 45 to McClellanville.

Boating

REGULATIONS

South Carolina Wildlife and Marine Resources Department, P.O. Box 167, Columbia 29202.

MARINAS

Beaufort: Dataw Island, P.O. Box 819 29901. Downtown, 1010 Bay St. 29902 (803/524-4422). Marsh Harbor 29902 (803/524-4797). Port Royal Landing, P.O. Drawer 1257 29901 (803/525-6664). Sea Island, 1105 Rogers St. 29902.

Bucksport: Bucksport Plantation, Rt. 1, Box 38 29527 (803/397-5566).

Charleston: Ashley, 33 Lockwood Drive 29401 (803/722-1996). Municipal, 17 Lockwood Blvd. 29401 (803/577-6970). Patriot's Point, P.O. Box 1426 29403 (803/881-3770).

Conway: Municipal Marina 29526 (803/248-4033).

Daufuskie Island: Freeport Marina, Daufuskie Island 29915 (803/785-8242). Cooper River Landing, P.O. Box 30 29915.

Edisto Beach: Edisto, P.O. Box 8 29438 (803/869-3503). Salty Mike's, 3702 Dock Site Rd. 29438 (803/869-3504).

Fripp Island: Fripp Island, 875 Bonita 29920 (803/838-2832).

Folly Beach: Folly, 46 West 9th St. Extension 29439 (803/588-6663). Mariner's Cay, 3-A Mariners Cay 29439 (803/588-2091).

Georgetown: Belle Island, P.O. Box 796 29440 (803/546-8491). Exxon, 18 St. James 29440 (803/546-4415). Georgetown Landing, P.O. Box 1704 29440 (803/546-1776). Gulf, 525 Front St. 29442 (803/546-4250). Hazard's 29440 (803/546-6604).

Hilton Head: Broad Creek Marina, P.O. Box 5184 29925 (803/681-7335). Harbour Town Yacht Basin, Sea Pines Plantation 29928 (803/671-2794 or 803/671-4334). Outdoor Resorts 29928 (803/681-2350). Palmetto Bay Marina, 164 Palmetto Bay 29928 (803/785-3910). Schilling Boathouse, 145 Squire Pope Rd. 29928 (803/681-2628). Shelter Cove Harbour, Shelter Cove Harbour,

P.O. Box 5628 29928 (803/842-7001). Skull Creek Marina, P.O. Box 2047 29925 (803/681-4234). South Beach Marina, 232 Sea Pines Dr. 29928 (803/671-6640). Windmill Harbour, 161 Harbour Passage 29928 (803/681-9235).
Isle of Palms: Cast-A-Way, 101 Palm Blvd. 29451 (803/886-4396). Isle of Palms, 101 Palm Boulevard 29451 (803/886-8003). Wild Dunes, P.O. Box 527 29451 (803/886-5100).
John's Island: Bohicket, 1860 Andell Bluff Blvd. 29455 (803/768-1280). Buzzard's Roost, 2408 Maybank Highway 29455 (803/559-5516). Stono, 2409 Maybank Highway 29455 (803/559-2307).
Little River: Little River, P.O. Box 365 29566 (803/249-5294).
McClellanville: Leland, P.O. Box 357 29458 (803/887-3641).
Mount Pleasant: Atlantis, 526 Mill St. 29464 (803/884-3211). Shem Creek, 526 Mill St. 29464 (803/884-3211). Toler's, 1610 Ben Sawyer Blvd. 29464 (803/881-0325).
Murrells Inlet: Capt. Dick's, P.O. Box 306 29576 (803/651-3676). Marlin Quay, P.O. Box 549 29576 (803/651-9938). Wacca Wachee, P.O. Box 570 29576 (803/651-7171).
Myrtle Beach: Briarcliff, 10495 Kings Highway 29577 (803/272-4332). Hague, P.O. Box 835 29577 (803/293-2141).
North Charleston: Dolphin Cove, 2079 Austin Ave. 29402 (803/744-2562). Duncan's, 1997 Bridge View Drive 29402 (803/744-2628).
North Myrtle Beach: Coquino Harbor, P.O. Box 4068 29597 (803/249-9333). Harbor Gate, P.O. Box 3197 29582 (803/249-8888). North Myrtle Beach, Rt. 1, Box 484 29582 (803/249-1222). Palmetto Shores, P.O. Box 3063 29582 (803/249-4131). Vereen's, Highway 17 North and 11th Ave. North 29582 (803/249-4333).

RAMPS

Beaufort Area: Broad River Boat Landing. Battery Creek Boat Landing, Shell Point. Combahee Boat Landing, Combahee River. Edgar C. Glen Boat Landing, Chechesee River. Factory Creek Boat Landing, Broad River. Fripp Island Marina. Grays Hill Boat Landing, Whale Branch. Henry C. Chambers Waterfront Park, Beaufort. Hunting Island State Park. Paige Point Boat Landing, Whale Branch. Sea Island Marine, Beaufort. Victoria Bluff Boat Landing, Colleton River. Wimbee Boat Landing, Wimbee Creek.
Charleston Area: Battery Island Boat Landing, Stono River. Charleston City Marina. Cherry Point Boat Landing, Bohicket Creek. County Farm Boat Landing, Ashley River. Dawhoo Boat Landing, Intracoastal Waterway, Edisto Island. Detco Boat Landing, Wando River. Filbin Creek Boat Landing, Cooper River. Folly Island Boat Landing, Folly River. Isle of Palms, 42nd St. Limehouse Boat

Landing, Stono River. Naval Station Marina. Northbridge Marina, Ashley River. Paradise Island Boat Landing, Wando River. Pier Point Boat Landing, Ashket River. Remley's Point Boat Landing, Cooper River. Shem Creek Boat Landing, Mount Pleasant. Steamboat Boat Landing, Edisto Island. Toogoodoo Boat Landing, Toogoodoo Creek. Wando Woods Boat Landing. Wappoo Cut Boat Landing, James Island. Wild Dunes Yacht Harbor, Isle of Palms. Willtown Bluff Boat Landing, Edisto River.

Edisto Island Area: Brickyard Ferry Landing, Ashpoo River. Edisto Beach State Park. Edisto Marina. West Bank, Edisto River. Live Oak Boat Landing, Big Bay Creek.

Georgetown Area: Belle Isle Marina. Buck Hall Landing, Francis Marion Forest, Cedar Hill Boat Landing. Georgetown County Parks. Gulf Auto Marina. Murrells Inlet. Georgetown Recreation Department, Morgan Park. Pawley's Island (North, Center, and South). Moore's Landing, McClellanville. Poleyard Boat Landing. South Island Ferry. Wacca Wache Marina.

Grand Strand Area: AIWW, Little River. North Myrtle Beach, Second Avenue, South Myrtle Beach, beach access points. Palmetto Shores, Little River. Municipal, Surfside Beach.

Hilton Head: All Joy Boat Landing, May River. Old House Creek Marina. Outdoor Resorts RV Resort & Yacht Club. South Beach Marina. Waterfront Park Marina. Windmill Harbour Marina.

ROWING
Palmetto Rowing Club, 101 Marshland Rd., Hilton Head 29925 (803/681-4207).

SCUBA DIVING & SNORKELING
Charleston Scuba & Trident Charters, 35 Lockwood Dr., Charleston 29401 (803/722-1120).

Conservation Organizations

Center for Forested Wetlands, 2730 Savannah Highway, Charleston 29414 (803/556-4860).
The Nature Conservancy Field Office, P.O. Box 5476, Columbia 29250 (803/254-9049).

Cultural Attractions

AQUARIUMS
South Carolina Aquarium/Marine Science Museum, 116 Meeting St., Charleston 29401 (803/724-3784).

ART MUSEUMS
Gibbes Art Gallery, 135 Meeting St., Charleston 29401 (803/722-2706).

EVENTS

Beaufort: The Gullah Festival of South Carolina (September), 803 Green St. 29902 (803/525-0628).

Charleston: Festival of Houses (March–April), 51 Meeting St. 29401 (803/723-1623). Lowcountry Oyster Festival (February), P.O. Box 975 29402 (803/577-2510). Plantation Days (November), Middleton Place, Ashley River Rd. 29414 (803/556-6020). Scottish Games and Highland Gathering (September), P.O. Box 21109 29413. Southeastern Wildlife Exposition (February), 701 E. Bay St., Control Data Bldg., 4th floor 29403 (803/723-1748). Spoleto Festival, USA (May–June), P.O. Box 794 29402 (803/722-2764).

Georgetown: Annual Plantation Tours (April), Prince George Winyah Parish, P.O. Box 674 29442 (803/546-5438).

Little River: Blue Crab Festival (May), P.O. Box 836 29566 (803/249-6604).

MUSEUMS

Beaufort: Beaufort Museum, 713 Craven St. 29902 (803/525-7471).

Charleston: American Military Museum, 115 Church St. 29401 (803/723-9620). Charleston Museum, 360 Meeting St. 29401 (803/722-2996). Confederate Museum, 188 Meeting St. 29401 (803/723-1541). Memorial Archives and Museum, The Citadel 29409 (803/792-6846).

Conway: Horry County Museum, 438 Main St. 29526 (803/248-6489).

Darlington: Darlington County Historical Museum of Ethnic Culture, P.O. Box 243 29532 (803/393-7052).

Florence: Florence Air & Missile Museum, P.O. Box 1326 29503 (803/665-5118). Florence Museum of Arts & Sciences, 558 Spruce St. 29501 (803/662-3351).

Georgetown: The Rice Museum, P.O. Box 902 29442-0902 (803/546-7423).

Hilton Head: Museum of Hilton Head Island, P.O. Box 5836 29938 (803/842-9197).

Moncks Corner: Berkeley County Historical Society Museum, 950 Stony Landing Rd. 29461 (803/899-5101).

Mt. Pleasant: Patriots Point Naval and Maritime Museum, 40 Patriots Point Rd. 29464 (803/884-2727).

Myrtle Beach: South Carolina Hall of Fame, P.O. Box 1828 29577 (803/448-4021).

Parris Island: Marine Corps Museum, Marine Corps Recruit Depot 29905 (803/525-2951).

THEATER

Young Charleston Theatre Company, 133 Church St., Charleston 29401 (803/577-5967).

Fishing

REGULATIONS

South Carolina Department of Wildlife & Marine Resources, P.O. Box 167, Columbia 29202 (803/734-3888).

GUIDES

Beaufort: Seawolf IV (Capt. Wally Phinney, Jr.), 5003 Luella St. 29902 (803/525-1174). *Charleston: Silver Dolphin* (Capt. Bill Grooms), 1311 Gilmore Rd., 29407 (803/556-3526). *Folly Beach:* Capt. Ivan's Island Charters, P.O. Box 1470 29439 (803/588-6060). *Georgetown:* Georgetown Landing, Marina Drive 29440 (803/546-1776). *Little River: Captain Juel II,* P.O. Box 541 29566 (803/249-7775). *Pride of the Carolinas,* P.O. Box 365 29566 (803/249-1100). *Swiftship I* (Captains Frank Juel and Robert Snall), P.O. Box 295, 29566 (803/249-1222). *Mullins: Chico* (Captain Mac Lewis), 606 Avon Circle 29574 (803/464-7786). *Murrells Inlet: Voyager's View,* Highway 17 (Business) 29576 (803/651-7033). *Myrtle Beach:* Hague, off Highway 17 at Intracoastal Waterway 29577 (803/293-2141). *North Myrtle Beach:* Hurricane, Highway 17 North and 11th Ave. North 29597 (803/249-3571).

PIERS

Beaufort Area: Wimbee Boat Landing, Wimbee Creek. Battery Creek Boat Landing. Hunting Island State Park. Windmill Harbour Marina, Mackeys Creek. *Charleston Area:* Bohicket Marina, 1860 Andell Bluff Boulevard 29455 (803/768-0880 or 800/845-2233). Charleston Waterfront Park. Dawhoo River Boat Landing. Detco Boat Landing, Wahoo River Bridge. Old Pitt Street Bridge, Mount Pleasant. North Bridge Marina, Ashley River. Pier Point Boat Landing, Ashley River near Drayton Hall. Pelican Cove RV Resort, Box 299 29439 (803/588-2072). John R. Limehouse Boat Landing, Stone River. *Edisto Beach Area:* Brickyard Ferry Boat Landing, Ashpoo River. *Grand Strand:* Cherry Grove, P.O. Box 3084, North Myrtle Beach 29597 (803/249-1625). Holiday Inn, 28th Ave. South, North Myrtle Beach 29597 (803/272-6632). Kingfisher Pier, Route 1, Garden City 29576 (803/651-9700). State Park, Highway 17 South, Myrtle Beach 29577 (803/626-35341). Surfside Pier Inc.,

11 South Ocean Blvd., Surfside Beach 29575 (803/238-0121). *Georgetown Area:* Santee Coastal Reserve. Moore's Landing, Cape Romain National Wildlife Refuge. *Hilton Head:* Outdoor Resorts RV Resort & Yacht Club. Shelter Cove Marina.

Golf

COURSES

Beaufort: Cat Island (803/542-0300).
Charleston Area: Charleston Municipal (803/795-6517). Charleston National (803/884-7799). Edisto (803/869-2361). Hope Plantation (803/768-7431). Kiawah Island courses (803/768-2121 or 800/654-2924). Links at Stono Ferry (803/763-1817). Patriot's Point (803/881-0042); Seabrook Island courses (803/768-1000). Shadowmoss Plantation (803/556-8251). Waterloo Plantation (803/559-5934). Wild Dunes (803/886-2164).
Conway: Conway (803/365-3621).
Dillon: Twin Lakes (803/774-3740).
Florence: Country Club of South Carolina (803/669-0920). Oakdale (803/662-0268). The Traces (803/662-7775).
Georgetown: Mount Hope (803/546-5582). Wedgefield Plantation (803/448-2124).
Hilton Head: National (803/842-5900). Hilton Head Plantation (803/681-4653). Palmetto Dunes (803/785-1138 or 800/827-3006). Port Royal Plantation (803/681-3671). Rose Hill courses (803/757-2160). Sea Pines (803/671-2446 or 803/671-2436). Shipyard Plantation (803/686-8802).
Little River: Marsh Harbour (803/249-3449). River Hills (803/249-8833).
Moncks Corner: Berkeley (803/899-9312).
Myrtle Beach Area: Bay Tree (803/249-1487). Burning Ridge (803/448-3141). Deeptrack (803/650-2146). Eagle's Nest (803/249-1449). Heather Glen (803/249-9000). Myrtlewood (803/449-5134). Myrtle Beach National (803/448-2308). River Oaks (803/236-2222). Waterway Hills (803/449-6488).
North Myrtle Beach: Azalea Sands (803/272-6191). Beachwood (803/272-6168). Buck Creek (803/249-5996). Eagle Nest (803/249-1449).
Pawleys Island: Heritage Club (803/626-3887). Litchfield (803/237-3411 or 800/922-6348). River Club (803/237-8755). Sea Gull (803/448-5931 or 800/833-0337).
Summerville: Kings Grant (803/873-7110). Miler (803/873-2210). Pine Forest (803/821-1582).
Surfside Beach: Deer Track (803/650-2146).

History
South Carolina Department of Archives & History,
1430 Senate St., Columbia 29211 (803/734-8591).

HISTORIC SITES
Beaufort: Elliott House and John Mark Verdier House, Historic Beaufort Foundation, Box 11 22902 (803/524-6334).
Charleston: Aiken-Rhett Mansion, 360 Meeting St. 29403 (803/722-2996). Boone Hall Plantation, Box 254, Mount Pleasant 29465 (803/884-4371). Calhoun Mansion, 16 Meeting St. 29401 (803/722-8205). Charles Towne Landing, 1500 Old Town Rd. 29407 (803/556-4450). Drayton Hall, 3380 Ashley River Rd. 29414 (803/766-0188). Edmonston-Alston House, 21 East Battery St. 29401 (803/722-7171). Heyward-Washington House, 87 Church St. 29403 (803/722-2996). Magnolia Plantation and Gardens, Ashley Cooper Road (Highway 61) 29414 (803/571-1266). Joseph Manigault House, 350 Meeting St. 29403 (803/722-2996). Middleton Place, Ashley River Road 29414 (803/556-6020). Nathaniel Russell House, 51 Meeting St. 29401 (803/723-1623). Old Exchange Building and Provost Dungeon, 122 East Bay St. 29401 (803/792-5020). Powder Magazine, 79 Cumberland St. 29402 (803/722-3767). Thomas Elfe Workshop, 54 Queen St. 29401 (803/722-2130).
Georgetown: Hampton Plantation State Park, 1950 Rutledge Rd., McClellanville 29458 (803/546-9361). Hopsewee Plantation National Historic Landmark, Rt. 2, Box 205 29440 (803/546-7891). Harold Kaminski House, 1003 Front St. 29440 (803/546-7706). Man-Doyle House, 528 Front St. 29440 (803/546-4612).
Hartsville: Jacob Kelly House, Highway S-16-12, Kelleytown Community 29550.

Hunting

REGULATIONS
South Carolina Department of Wildlife & Marine Resources, P.O. Box 167, Columbia 29202 (803/734-3888).

WILDLIFE MANAGEMENT AREAS
Bear Island, Colleton County. Cypress Creek, Hampton County. Ellerbee Bay, Ervin Dargan, and Horace Tilghman, Marion County. Lewis Ocean Bay, Horry County. Pee Dee, Florence County. Sandy Beach, Berkeley County. Samworth, Georgetown County. Santee Coastal Reserve, Charleston and Georgetown counties. Santee Coastal, Georgetown County. Tillman Sand

Ridge, Jasper County. Turtle Island, Jasper County. Victoria Bluff, Beaufort County. Webb, Hampton County.

Information Sources
South Carolina Department of Parks, Recreation & Tourism
1205 Pendleton St., Columbia 29201 (803/734-0127).

CHAMBERS OF COMMERCE
Conway Area, 203 S. Main St. 29526 (803/248-2273).
Dillon County, 202 West Harrison St. 29536 (803/774-8551).
Edisto, P.O.Box 206, Edisto Beach 29438 (803/869-3867).
Georgetown County, P.O. Box 1776 29442 (803/546-8436 or 800/777-7705).
Greater Beaufort, P.O. Box 90, Beaufort 29901 (803/524-3163).
Greater Summerville, P.O. Box 670, Summerville 29484 (803/873-2931).
Hardeeville, P.O. Box 307 29927 (803/784-3606).
Jasper County, P.O. Box 1267, Ridgeland 29936 (803/726-8126).
Little River, P.O. Box 400 29566 (803/249-6604).
Myrtle Beach Area, P.O. Box 2115, Myrtle Beach 29578-2115 (803/626-7444).
North Myrtle Beach, P.O. Box 754 29597 (803/249-3519).
Pawley's Island, P.O. Box 569 29585 (803/237-1921).
South Strand, P.O. Box 650, Murrells Inlet 29576 (803/651-1010).
Summerville, 106 E. Doty Ave. (Box 670), Summerville 29483 (803/873-2931).
Walterboro-Colleton, 218 Jefferies Blvd., Walterboro 29488 (803/549-9595).

CONVENTION & VISITORS BUREAUS
South Carolina Division of Tourism, P.O. Box 71, Columbia 29602 (803/734-0235).
Charleston Trident Convention & Visitors Bureau, P.O. Box 975, 81 Mary St., Charleston 29402 (803/577-2510 or 800/868-8118).
Dorchester County Information Office, 520 Main St., Summerville 29483 (803/871-4636).
Hilton Head Island Convention & Visitors Bureau, P.O. Drawer 5647, Hilton Head Island 29938 (803/785-3673).
Lowcountry and Resort Island Tourism Commission, P.O. Box 366, Hampton 29924 (803/943-9180).
Myrtle Beach Area Convention Bureau, 710 N. 21st Ave., North Suite 1, Myrtle Beach 29577 (803/448-1629).
Pee Dee Tourism Commission, P.O. Box 3093, Florence 29502 (803/669-0950).

Santee-Cooper Counties Promotion Commission, P.O. Drawer 40, Santee 29142 (803/854-2131).
Summerton Area Promotion Committee, P.O. Box 1031, Summerton 29148 (803/485-2525).

OTHER GOVERNMENT OFFICES
South Carolina Department of Parks, Recreation and Tourism, 1205 Pendleton St., Columbia 29201 (803/734-3950).
South Carolina Marine Resources Center, Recreational Fisheries, P.O. Box 12559, Charleston 29412 (803/795-6350).
Waddell Mariculture Center, P.O. Box 809, Bluffton 29910 (803/837-3795 or 803/837-7174).

Miscellaneous

HORSEBACK RIDING
Georgetown: Equestrian Center, Rt. 4, Box 531 29440 (803/546-3685).
Rebel Ranch, P.O. Box 2137 29442 (803/546-2516).

Nature Sites

NATIONAL PARKS, REFUGES, AND FORESTS
Cape Romain National Wildlife Refuge, 390 Bulls Island Rd., Awendaw 29429 (803/928-3368).
Fort Moultrie, 1214 Middle St., Sullivans Island 29482 (803/883-3123).
Fort Sumter National Monument, Drawer R, Sullivans Island 29482 (803/883-3123).
Francis Marion National Forest: Wambaw District, P.O. Box 788, S. Pinckney St., McClellanville 29458 (803/887-3257); Witherbee District, HC 69 Box 1532, Highway 125, Moncks Corner 29461 (803/336-3248).
Santee National Wildlife Refuge, Rt. 2, Box 66, Summerton 29148 (803/478-2217).

STATE PARKS & REFUGES
Colleton, Canadys 29433 (803/538-8206).
Edisto Beach, 8377 State Cabin Rd., Edisto Island 29438 (803/869-2156).
Givhans Ferry, Rt. 3, Box 327, Ridgeville 29472 (803/873-0692).
Hampton Plantation State Park, 1950 Rutledge Rd., McClellanville 29458 (803/546-9361).
Hunting Island, 1775 Sea Island Parkway, St. Helena Island 29920 (803/838-2011).

Huntington Beach, Murrell's Inlet 29576 (803/237-4440).
Little Pee Dee, Rt. 2, Box 250, Dillon 29536 (803/774-8872).
Myrtle Beach, U.S. Highway 17 South 29577 (803/238-5325).
Old Dorchester, 300 State Park Rd., Summerville 29485 (803/873-1740).
Old Santee Canal State Park, 900 Story Landing Rd., Moncks Corner 29461 (803/899-5200).
Santee Coastal Reserve, 270 Santee Gun Club Rd., McClellanville 29458 (803/546-5990).

CITY/COUNTY PARKS
Beachwalker Park, Kiawah Island (803/722-1681). City of Charleston (803/724-7327). Charleston County (803/762-2172). Folly Beach (803/722-1681).

OTHER NATURE AREAS
Audubon Swamp Garden, Rt. 4, Highway 61, Charleston 28414 (803/571-1266).
Bellefield Nature Center (Hobcaw Barony), Rt. 5, Box 1003, Georgetown 29440 (803/546-4623).
Edisto Nature Trail, Westvaco Timberlands Division, Southern Woodlands, P.O. Box 1950, Summerville 29484.
Francis Beidler Forest, Rt. 1, Box 600, Harleyville 29448 (803/462-2150).
Tom Yawkey Wildlife Center, Rt. 2, Box 181, Georgetown 29440 (912/546-6814).
Waccamaw River Tract, The Nature Conservancy, P.O. Box 5475, Columbia 29250 (803/254-9049).

GARDENS
Brookgreen Gardens, Murrells Inlet 29576 (803/237-4218).
Cypress Gardens, 3030 Cypress Gardens Rd., Moncks Corner 29461 (803/553-0515).
Magnolia, Ashley Cooper Rd. (Highway 61), Charleston 29414 (803/571-1266).
Middleton, Ashley River Rd., Charleston 29414 (803/556-6020).

Tours

AERIAL
Carolina Sailplanes Inc., Highway 17, Little River 29566 (803/249-4523).
Eagle Balloons, P.O. Box 60744, Charleston 29419 (803/552-3782).

Rainbow Helicopter Tours, 27th Ave. S., North Myrtle Beach 29597 (803/626-6918).

SIGHTSEEING
Beaufort: Carriage Tours, 1006 Bay St. 29902 (803/524-3163).
Cape Romain National Wildlife Refuge: Capt. John Pryor, 1222 Calais Dr., Mt. Pleasant 29464 (803/884-0448).
Charleston: American Sightseeing International, P.O. Box 31485 29417 (803/767-7115). Annual Fall House and Garden Candlelight Tours, The Preservation Society, P.O. Box 521 HV 29402 (803/722-4630). Architectural Walking Tour, Rt. 1, Box 1228, Roundo 29474 (803/893-2327). Carolina Lowcountry Tours, Inc., Charleston KOA, Ladson 29456 (803/797-1045). Charleston Carriage Co., 96 North Market St. 29401 (803/577-0042). Civil War Walking Tour, 17 Archdale St. 29401 (803/722-7033). Colonial City Tours Inc., P.O. Box 20996 29413 (803/871-2828 or 800/272-8422). Doin' the Charleston, P.O. Box 31338 29417 (803/763-1233). Fort Sumter Tours Inc., 205 King St., Suite 204 29401 (803/722-1691). Gray Line Water Tours, P.O. Box 861 29402 (803/722-1112 or 800/344-4483). Kiawah Island Tours, P.O. Box 31485 29417 (803/768-1111). Old South Carriage Co., 14 Anson St. 29401 (803/723-9712). Palmetto Carriage, 40 N. Market St. 29401 (803/723-8145). Southern Windjammer (Capt. Bob Marthai), 2044 Wappoo Hall Rd. 29412 (803/895-1180).
Georgetown: Captain Sandy's, 600 Front St. 29442 (803/527-4106). Hobcaw Barony Tours, Bellefield Nature Center, Rt. 5, Box 1003 29440 (803/546-4623). *Island Queen,* P.O. Box 1775 29585 (803/527-3160). Swamp Fox Tram, 709 Front St. 29442 (803/527-4106).
Hilton Head: Adventure Cruises, Shelter Cove Harbour, 29928 (803/785-4558). Vagabond Sightseeing Cruises, Harbour Town Marina, 29928 (803/842-7581).
Murrells Inlet: Captain Dick's, P.O. Box 306 29576 (803/651-3676).
Myrtle Beach: Gray Line, 708 Main St. 29577 (803/448-9483). *Southern Star* (803/650-6600).
North Myrtle Beach: Hurricane Fleet, Highway 17 North and 11th Ave. North 29597 (803/249-3571).

Georgia

Accommodations

HISTORIC HOTELS, B&BS, AND INNS
Brunswick: Brunswick Manor, 825 Egmont St. 31520 (912/265-6889).

APPENDICES

Darien: Open Gates: Vernon Square 31305 (912/437-6985).
Savannah: R.S.V.P. Savannah Historic Inns and Guest Houses, 147
Bull St. 31401 (912/233-7666 or 800/262-4667). Ballastone Inn,
14 E. Oglethorpe 31401 (912/238-1225 or 800/822-4553). East
Bay Inn, 225 East Bay St. 31401 (912/238-1225 or 800/634-5488).
Eliza Thompson House, 5 W. Jones St. 31401 (912/236-3620 or
800/845-7638). Foley House, 14 West Hull St. 31401 (912/232-
6622, or 800/647-3708 outside of Georgia). The Gastonian, 220
E. Gaston St. 31401 (912/232-2869). Haslam-Fort House, 417
E. Charlton St. 31401 (912/233-6380). Liberty Inn-1834, 128 W.
Liberty St. 31401 (912/233-1007 or 800/637-1007). The Mulberry, 801 East Bay St. 31401 (912/238-1200, 800/554-5544, and
in Georgia 800/282-9198). Olde Harbour Inn, 508 East Bay St.
31401 (912/234-4100). Planters Inn, 29 Abercorn St. 31401
(800/554-1187 outside Georgia, 800/554-1188 in state). Rems-
hart-Brooks House, 106 W. Jones St. 31401 (912/234-6928). River
Street Inn, 115 East River St. 31401 (912/234-6400 or 800/533-
4667).
St. Marys: The Goodbread House, 209 Osborne St. 31558 (912/882-
7490). Riverview Hotel, 105 Osborne St. 31558 (912/882-3242).
St. Simons Island: Gaubert, 521 Oglethorpe 31522 (912/638-9424).

RESORTS
Beach Club, 1440 Ocean Blvd., St. Simons Island 31522 (912/638-
5450 or 800/627-6850).
The Cloister, Sea Island 31561 (912/638-3611 or 800/732-4752).
Jekyll Island Club Hotel, 371 Riverview Dr., Jekyll Island, 31520
(912/635-2600 or 800/333-3333).
Jekyll Island Inn, 975 N. Beachview Dr., Jekyll Island 31520 (912/
635-2531 or 800/342-1046).
King & Prince, 311 Arnold Rd., St. Simons Island 31522 (912/638-
3631 or 800/342-0212).
Little St. Simons Island, P.O. Box 1018, St. Simons Island 31522
(912/638-7472).
Savannah Beach, P.O. Box 938, Tybee Island 31328 (912/786-4699).
Sea Island, Sea Island Company, Sea Island, 31361 (912/638-3611).
Sea Palms Golf & Tennis Resort, 5445 Frederica Rd., St. Simons Island 31522 (912/638-3351 or 800/841-6266, in Georgia 800/282-
1226, in Canada 800/344-1123).
Sheraton Savannah Resort and Country Club, 612 Wilmington Island Rd., Savannah 31410 (912/897-1612).

COTTAGE RENTALS
Jekyll Island: Vacation Cottages, 22 Beachview Dr. 31520 (912/635-
2512).

Camping

Brunswick: Altamaha Park, Rt. 3, Box 161 31520 (912/264-2342). Blythe Island Regional Park, Rt. 6, Box 224 31520 (912/267-9200). Golden Isles, Rt. 6, Box 153 31520 (912/265-5429).

Georgia State Parks: Georgia Department of Natural Resources, 205 Butler St. SE, Atlanta 30334 (404/656-3520).

Jekyll Island: Jekyll Island, North Beachview Dr. 31520 (912/635-3021 or 800/841-6586).

Riceboro: Pinewood Lake, Rt. 2 31323 (912/832-5407).

Savannah: Bellaire Woods, 805 Fort Argyle Rd. 31419 (912/748-4000).

Skidaway State Park: Savannah 31406 (912/356-2523).

Townsend: Belle Bluff, Rt. 2 31331 (912/832-5323).

Tybee Island: River's End, 915 Polk 31328 (912/786-5518).

Biking

Organizations
Coastal Bicycle Touring Club, 1326 Grace Dr., Savannah 31406.

Dedicated Trails
Coastal Route: from Clyo on state Route 119 near the South Carolina border, along state Route 21 to Garden City, then U.S. 17 Alternate to Savannah's historic district (to bypass Savannah take state Route 80 to Chatham Parkway to Route 17), then follow Route 17, with diversions as desired to places such as Skidaway Island, Sunbury Historic Site, Darien and Fort King George, Brunswick and St. Simons Island, Jekyll Island, Crooked River State Park, St. Marys, and Cumberland Island.

Savannah River Run (coastal segment): from Sylvania parallel the railroad tracks and the Savannah River along state Route 21 to U.S. 17 Alternate to Savannah's riverfront and historic district.

Boating

Canoeing
Altamaha River Excursion, Ft. King George Historic Site, P.O. Box 711, Darien 31305 (912/437-4770).

John L. Frank, Barrier Island Enterprises, P.O. Box 1467, Darien 31305 (912/832-4730).

Diving
Judy's Island Dive Center, 1610½ Frederica Rd., St. Simons Island 31522 (912/638-6590).

SAILING INSTRUCTION
Sail Harbor Academy, 618 Wilmington Island Rd., Savannah 31410 (912/897-2135).
Sailing School Blackbeard, 6000 Peachtree Rd. NE, Atlanta 30319 (404/233-9463).

MARINAS
Brunswick: Brunswick, P.O. Box 802 31523 (912/265-2290). Harry Jones, Georgia Route 3093 31520 (912/264-1757). Joiner Creek, Route 1, Box 1 31520 (912/265-7611). Troupe Creek, Route 2, Box 3 31520 (912/264-3862). Two-Way, Route 2, Box 84 31520 (912/265-0410).
Darien: Mcintosh County Rod & Gun Club, P.O. Box 602 31305 (912/437-4677).
Jekyll Island: Jekyll Island, 1 Pier Rd. 31520 (912/635-2891).
Midway: Jordan's Half Moon, Route 1, Box 207-H 31320 (912/884-6819). Yellow Bluff, Route 1, Box 215 31320 (912/884-5448).
Richmond Hill: Fort McAllister Historic Park, Rt. 2, Box 394-A 31324 (912/727-2339). Kilkenny, Route 2, Box 216 31324 (912/727-2215).
Savannah: Bona Bella, 2740 Livington Avenue 31406 (912/355-9601). Coffee Bluff, 14915 White Bluff Rd. 31419 (912/925-9030). Delegal Creek, P.O. Box 14606 31416 (912/598-0023). Harrison's, Route 3, Box 258-B 31406 (912/355-0232). Isle of Hope, 50 Bluff Dr. 31406 (912/355-2310). Landings Harbor, P.O. Box 14606 31416 (912/598-1901). Turner's Creek, 34 Wilmington Island Rd. 31410 (912/897-5495). Tuten's, 7460 LaRoche Avenue 31406 (912/355-8747).
Skidaway Island: The Landings 31406 (912/938-1902).
St. Marys: Crooked River State Park, 3092 Spur 40 31558 (912/882-5256). Lang's, 307 West Marys St. 31558 (912/882-4452 or 912/882-4901).
St. Simons Island: Golden Isles, P.O. Box 1715 31522 (912/638-7717). Hampton River Club Marina, 1000 Hampton River Club Dr. 31522 (912/638-1210). St. Simons, 1000 Arthur Moore Dr. 31522 (912/638-9146). Taylor's, Lawrence Rd. 31522 (912/638-8201).
Thunderbolt: Fountain, 2812 River Dr. 31404 (912/354-2283). Tidewater, Old Tybee Rd. 31404 (912/352-1335).
Townsend: Belle Bluff Island, Route 2, Box 204-B 31331 (912/832-5323). Dallas Bluff, Route 2, Box 180 31331 (912/832-5116). Fisherman's Lodge, Route 2 31331 (912/832-4671). Pine Harbor, Route 2, Box 34-C 31331 (912/832-5999).
Tybee Island: Chimney Creek Fishing Camp, 40A Estill Hammock Rd. 31328 (912/786-9857). Lazaretto Creek Boat Club, 6 Schwartz

Pl., Savannah 31414 (912/879-9974). Tybee Island, 1315 Venetian Dr. 31328 (912/780-7508). *Wilmington Island:* Wassaw Water Taxi, 112 Palmetto Dr. 31410 (912/897-2277).

RAMPS

Brunswick: Altamaha Fish Camp, Everett off U.S. Route 341. Blythe Island, Blythe Island Drive off state Route 303. South Brunswick River, off Route 303. Turtle River, off Route 303.
Darien Area: Harris Neck Creek.
Savannah Area: Bell's Landing, Apache Road off Abercorn on Forest River. Islands Expressway, Frank W. Spencer Park on Wilmington River. Kings Ferry, Highway 17 on Ogeechee River. Lazaretto Creek, Tybee Island Causeway (Route 80E). Montomery, end of Whitfield Avenue on Vernon River. Port Wentworth, Route 17 on Savannah River. Salt Creek, Route 17 at Silk Hope. Skidaway Narrows, Diamond Causeway to Skidaway Island. Thunderbolt, Wilmington River. Tybee, Back River and 16th St.
St. Marys: St. Marys River (U.S. Route 17), Satilla River, White Oak Creek.
St. Simons Island: Harrington, at Village Creek off Frederica Road. MacKay River, St. Simons Causeway. South Riverview Drive.

Conservation Organizations

Bartram Trail Conference, c/o Elliott O. Edwards, Jr., 431 E. 53rd St., Savannah 31405 (912/354-5014).
Coastal Heritage Society, Old Fort Jackson, 1 Ft. Jackson Rd., Savannah 31404 (912/232-2945).
Historic Savannah Foundation, P.O. Box 1733, Savannah 31402 (912/233-7787).
The Nature Conservancy Field Office, 1401 Peachtree St. NE, Atlanta 30309 (404/873-6946).
Oatland Island Education Center, Savannah-Chatham Board of Education, 711 Sandtown Rd., Savannah 31410 (912/897-3773).
Okefenokee Wildlife League Inc., Rt. 2, Box 338, Folkston 31537.
University of Georgia Marine Extension Service, P.O. Box 13687, Savannah 31416 (912/356-2496).

Cultural Attractions

ORGANIZATIONS
Office of Cultural Affairs, City of Savannah, P.O. Box 1027, Savannah 31402 (912/651-6417).

Savannah Scottish Games and Highland Gathering, P.O. Box 13435, Savannah 31416 (912/964-4951).

Savannah Symphony Orchestra, P.O. Box 9505, Savannah 31412 (912/236-9536).

ART MUSEUMS

City Market Art Center, Jefferson at W. Julian St., Savannah 31401 (912/234-2327).

Coastal Center for the Arts, 2012 Demere Rd., St. Simons Island 31522 (912/638-8770).

Jekyll Island Arts Assn., Riverview Dr., Jekyll Island 31520 (912/635-3920).

Telfair Academy of Arts & Sciences, 121 Barnard St., Savannah 31401 (912/232-1177).

EVENTS

Brunswick: Blessing of Shrimp Fleet (April), 4 Glynn Ave. 31520 (912/265-0620).

Jekyll Island: Beach Music Festival (August), 5K and 10K Runs (February), Spring Arts Festival (March), P.O. Box 3186, Jekyll Island 31520 (912/635-3636).

Savannah: St. Patrick's Day (March), 222 W. Oglethorpe Ave. 31499 (912/944-0456 or 800/444-2427). A Night in Old Savannah (April), Alee Shrine Temple, P.O. Box 14147 31416 (912/355-2422). Scottish Games (May), P.O. Box 13433 31416 (912/352-9959). Fireworks at Tybee Island (July 4), Tybee City Hall 31328 (912/786-5444). Fourth of July, Old Fort Jackson, 1 Fort Jackson Rd. 31404 (912/232-3945). Savannah Jazz Festival (September) (912/944-0456). Georgia Heritage Celebration (February), P.O. Box 1733 31402 (912/233-7787).

Sea Island: Weekend for Wildlife (February), Dept. of Natural Resources, 209 Butler St. SE, Suite 1258, Atlanta 30334 (404/656-0772).

St. Marys: Rock Shrimp Festival (October), P.O. Box 1291 31558 (912/882-6200).

St. Simons: Jazz-in-the-Park (September), Christmas Tour of Homes, 4 Glynn Ave. 31520 (912/265-0620).

Woodbine: Annual Crayfish Festival (April), P.O. Box 26, 31569 (912/576-3211).

HISTORIC MUSEUMS

Augusta: Augusta-Richmond County Museum, 540 Telfair St. 30901 (404/722-8454).

Brunswick: Mary Miller Doll Museum, 1523 Glynn Ave. 31520 (912/267-7569).

Fort Stewart: 24th Infantry Division (Mechanized) and Fort Stewart Museum 31314 (912/767-4891).
Jekyll Island: Jekyll Island Museum, 375 Riverside Dr., Jekyll Island 31520 (912/635-2762).
Midway: Midway Museum, P.O. Box 195, 31320 (912/884-5837).
Savannah and Vicinity: Beach Institute/African-American Cultural Center, 502 E. Harris St., Savannah 31401 (912/234-8000). Central of Georgia Roundhouse Complex, 601 West Harris St., Savannah 31401 (912/238-1779). Georgia Salzberger Society Museum, 9175 Whitfield Ave., Savannah 31406 (912/754-6333). Massie Heritage Interpretation Center, 207 E. Gordon St., Savannah 31401 (912/651-7380). Savannah History Museum, 303 Martin Luther King Blvd., Savannah 31499 (912/238-1779). Ships of the Sea Museum, 503 E. River St., Savannah 31401 (912/232-1511).
St. Simons Island: Museum of Coastal History, P.O. Box 1136 31522 (912/638-4666). Arthur J. Moore Methodist Museum, 99 Arthur J. Moore Dr., Epworth-by-the-Sea 31522 (912/638-4050).
Tybee Island: Lighthouse, P.O. Box 366, Tybee Island 31328 (912/786-5801). Tybee Island Museum (Fort Screven), Tybee Island 31328 (912/786-4077).

SCIENCE MUSEUMS
Savannah Science Museum, 4405 Paulsen St., Savannah 31405 (912/355-6705).
Skidaway Marine Science Complex, Skidaway Island 31411 (912/356-2496).

Fishing

GUIDES
Brunswick Area: Capt. Rick Causey (912/265-0275). Capt. Ken Doss (912/994-4264). Capt. David Blackshear (912/638-2513 or 912/638-8132). Capt. Jim Geeslin (912/638-2900). Capt. Charlie Griffis (912/638-7460). Capt. Frank Mead (912/638-4261). Capt. Jeanne Pleasants (912/638-9354). Capt. Vernon Reynolds (912/265-0392). Capt. Tracey Youmans (912/638-2308). Capt. Bob Torras (912/638-8799). Capt. Larry Kennedy (912/638-3214). Capt. Dan Simpson (912/635-2821). Capts. George Counts and Jeff Counts (912/264-5813). Capts. Harry Butts, Cap Fendig, Richard Malone (912/635-2891). Capt. Frankie Denmark (912/264-0410). Capt. Dan Drummond (912/264-1733). Capt. Jimmy Durrance (912/437-2012). Capt. Mike Evans (912/264-3807). Capt. Adam Johnson (912/638-6352). Capt. James McVeigh (912/265-1485). Capt. Terry Mathis (912/265-4382). Capt. Donnie

Sikes (912/832-5737). Capt. Rick Smith (912/264-9561). Dunbar Charters (912/638-8573).

Darien Area: Capt. Ken Ammerman (912/832-6122). Capt. Robert Crowell (912/437-4339). Capt. Suzanne Forsythe (912/632-4748). Capt. Jimmy Hyers (912/832-4671). Capt. Tim Taver (912/654-4073). Capt. David Wallace (912/986-6162).

Savannah Area: Capt. Mark Covington (912/354-9651). Capt. Jeff Glenn (912/354-6528). Capt. Paul Glenn (912/352-8454). Capt. Brian Roux (912/355-9525). Capt. Judy Helmey (912/897-4921). Capt. Bob Morrissey (912/598-1814).

Sea Island: Inland Charter Boat Service, North First St. 31561 (912/638-3611).

St. Marys: Capt. Calvin Lang (912/882-4901).

St. Simons: B&D Marina, 209 Marina Dr. 31522 (912/638-7981). Golden Isles Charter, 205 Marina Dr. 31522 (912/638-7717).

Tybee Island: Capt. Cecil Johnson (912/786-4801). Capt. Jack Flanagan (912/786-9857).

PIERS/DOCKS/BEACHES

Brunswick Area: Back River Pier. Blythe Island Regional Park, Blythe Island. Little River Catwalk. MacKay River Pier. Gould's Inlet at East Beach. Back River, Torras Causeway to St. Simons Island. Satilla River Waterfront Park, off U.S. 17.

Darien Area: Blue-N-Hall Public Dock, Champney River Park, Harris Neck.

Jekyll Island: Clam Creek Rd., St. Andrews picnic area. Jekyll Island Pier. Jekyll Island Beach.

Midway/Richmond Hill Area: Liberty County Park, Riceboro River Dock. Tivoli River Park.

Savannah Area: Frank W. Spencer Park on Islands Expressway. Port Wentworth on Route 17, Salt Creek Park on Route 17 at Silk Hope. Bull River (Route 80). Diamond Causeway. Morgan Bridge on Old Route 204 at Ogeechee River.

Skidaway Island: Moon River.

St. Marys: Crooked River State Park. Harriett's Bluff. Woodbine Park. Waterfront Pavilion.

St. Simons Island: East Beach. Mallory St. St. Simons Island Beach.

Tybee Island: Lazaretto Creek, Tybee Island Causeway. Chatham Avenue. North End Beach. South End Beach. Chimney Creek Marina.

Golf

PUBLIC COURSES

Folkston: Folkston Golf Club (912/496-7155).

Jekyll Island: Pine Lakes, Indian Mounds, Oleander (912/635-3464).
Savannah Area: Bacon Park (912/354-2625). Meadow Lakes (912/839-3191). Sheraton Savannah (912/897-1612). Willowpeg (912/236-5884). See also Beaufort, Bluffton, and Hardeeville, SC.
Sea Island: Sea Island Golf Club (912/638-5118).
St. Marys Area: Deerfield Lakes (Callahan, FL) (904/359-0404). Osprey Cove (912/882-5575). Pine Lakes (Jacksonville, FL) (904/757-0318).
St. Simons Island: St. Simons Island Club (912/638-5130). Sea Palms Golf & Tennis Resort (912/638-3351). The Hampton Club (912/634-0255).

History

ORGANIZATIONS
Coastal Georgia Historical Society, 610 Beachview Dr., St. Simons Island 31522 (912/638-4666).
Georgia Historical Society, 501 Whittaker St., Savannah 31401 (912/651-2128).

HISTORIC SITES
Toll-free number for Georgia Parks: 800/542-7275 outside Georgia; 800/342-7275 inside the state.
Andrew Low House, 329 Abercorn St., Savannah 31401 (912/233-6854).
Flannery O'Connor House, 207 E. Charlton, Savannah 31401 (912/927-5289).
Fort Frederica National Monument, Route 9, Box 2876-C, St. Simons Island 31522 (912/638-3639).
Fort King George, P.O. Box 711, Darien 31305 (912/437-4770).
Fort McAllister Historic Park, Rt. 2, Box 349A, Richmond Hill 31324 (912/727-2339).
Fort Pulaski National Monument, P.O. Box 98, Tybee Island 31328 (912/786-5787).
Historic Augusta Inc., P.O. Box 37 30903 (404/724-0436).
Hofwyl-Broadfield Plantation State Historic Site, Rt. 10, Box 83, Brunswick 31520 (912/264-9263).
Isaiah Davenport House, 324 E. State St., Savannah 31401 (912/236-8097).
Juliette Gordon Low House, 142 E. Bull St., Savannah 31401 (912/233-4501).
King-Tisdell Cottage, 514 E. Huntingdon St., Savannah 31401 (912/234-8000).
LeConte-Woodmanston Plantation, P.O. Box 356, Minesville 31313 (912/884-5837).

Old Fort Jackson, 1 Fort Jackson Rd., Savannah 31404 (912/232-3945).

Owens-Thomas House, 124 Abercorn St., Savannah 31401 (912/233-9743).

Savannah History Museum, Visitors Center, 303 Martin Luther King Jr. Blvd., Savannah 31401 (912/238-1779).

Sunbury Historic Site, Rt. 1, Box 236, Midway 31320 (912/884-5999).

Wormsloe Historic Site, 7601 Skidaway Rd., Savannah 31406 (912/352-2548).

Information Sources

Tourism Division
Georgia Department of Industry, Trade & Tourism
285 Peachtree Center Ave., Atlanta 30301-1776 (404/656-3590).

CHAMBERS OF COMMERCE

Camden/Kings Bay Area Chamber of Commerce, P.O. Box 130, Kingsland 31548 (912/729-5999).

Folkston-Charlston County Chamber of Commerce, 202 West Main St., Folkston 31537 (912/496-2536).

McIntosh County Chamber of Commerce, P.O. Box 1497, Darien 31305 (912/437-4192 or 912/437-6684).

Pooler Area Chamber of Commerce, P.O. Box 647, Pooler 31322 (912/748-5204).

Savannah Area Chamber of Commerce, 222 West Oglethorpe Avenue, Savannah 31499 (912/944-0444).

St. Simons Island Chamber of Commerce, Neptune Park, St. Simons Island 31522 (912/638-9014).

Tybee Island Chamber of Commerce, 209 Butler Ave., Tybee Island 31328 (912/786-5444).

Waycross Chamber of Commerce, P.O. Box 137 31592 (912/283-3742).

TOURIST ORGANIZATIONS

Brunswick-Golden Isles Convention & Visitors Bureau, 4 Glynn Ave., Brunswick 31520 (912/265-0620).

Coastal Georgia Regional Development Center, P.O. Box 1917, Brunswick 31520 (912/264-7363).

Jekyll Island Convention & Visitors Bureau, P.O. Box 3186, Jekyll Island 31520 (912/635-3636).

Kingsland Tourist & Convention Bureau, P.O. Box 1928, Kingsland 31548 (912/729-5999).

Savannah Area Convention & Visitors Bureau, 222 W. Oglethorpe Ave., Savannah 31499 (912/944-0456 or 800/444-2427). (Mail address: P.O. Box 1628, Savannah 31402-1628.)

St. Marys Tourism Council, P.O. Box 1291, St. Marys 31558 (912/ 882-6200 or 912/882-4000).
Tybee Island Visitors Center, P.O. Box 491, Tybee Island 31328 (912/944-0456 or 800/868-2322).

Miscellaneous

Horseback Riding: Sea Island Stables, 3001 Frederica Rd., St. Simons Island 31522 (912/638-5170).

Nature Areas

NATIONAL

Blackbeard Island National Wildlife Refuge, U.S. Fish & Wildlife Service, Georgia Coastal Refuge Complex, P.O. Box 8487, Savannah 31412 (912/944-4415).
Cumberland Island National Seashore, P.O. Box 806, St. Marys 31558 (912/882-4335).
Grey's Reef National Marine Sanctuary (Sapelo Live Bottom), Coastal Resources Division, Georgia Department of Natural Resources, 1200 Glynn Ave., Brunswick 31522 (912/264-7218).
Harris Neck National Wildlife Refuge (same as Blackbeard Island above).
Okefenokee National Wildlife Refuge and Suwanee Canal Recreation Area, U.S. Fish & Wildlife Service, Rt. 2, Box 337, Folkston 31537 (912/496-7836).
Sapelo Island National Estuarine Sanctuary and R. J. Reynolds Wildlife Refuge, Darien Welcome Center, P.O. Box 1497, Darien 31305 (912/437-6684).
Savannah Natural Wildlife Refuge (same as Blackbeard Island above).
Tybee Island National Wildlife Refuge (same as Blackbeard Island above).
Wassaw Island National Wildlife Refuge (same as Blackbeard Island above).
Wolf Island National Wildlife Refuge (same as Blackbeard Island above).

STATE

Toll-free number for Georgia Parks: 800/542-7275 outside Georgia; 800/342-7275 inside the state.
Altamaha River Waterfowl Area, Georgia Department of Natural Resources, P.O. Box 19, Sapelo Island 31327 (912/485-2251).
Crooked River State Park, Georgia Department of Natural Resources, 3092 Spur 40, St. Marys 31558 (912/882-5256).

APPENDICES

Jekyll Island State Park, Jekyll Island Authority Convention & Visitors Bureau, One Beachview Dr., Jekyll Island 31520 (800/841-6586 outside Georgia, 800/342-1042 or 912/635-3400 inside Georgia).

Laura S. Walker State Park, Georgia Department of Natural Resources, Rt. 6, Box 205, Waycross 31501 (912/283-4424).

Ossabaw Island, Georgia Department of Natural Resources, P.O. Box 14565, Savannah, 31416 (912/232-0394).

Skidaway Island State Park, Diamond Causeway, Savannah 31411 (912/356-2523).

Stephen C. Foster State Park, Georgia Department of Natural Resources, Rt. 1, Fargo 31631 (800/542-7275 outside Georgia, 800/342-7275 or 912/637-5274 inside Georgia).

Suwannee Canal Recreation Area, Okefenokee National Wildlife Refuge, Rt. 2, Box 338, Folkston 31537 (912/496-3331).

Williamson Island, Georgia Department of Natural Resources, 270 Washington St. SW, Atlanta 30334 (912/267-7330).

OTHER

Little St. Simons Island, P.O. Box 1078, St. Simons Island 31522 (912/838-7472).

Okefenokee Swamp Park, Waycross 31501 (912/283-0583).

St. Catherines Island, St. Catherines Island Foundation, Route 1, Box 207-Z, Midway 31320 (912/884-5002).

St. Simons Island, St. Simons Island Chamber of Commerce, Neptune Park, St. Simons Island 31522 (912/638-9014).

TOURS

Blackbeard Island: Forsyth Charter Service, Cedar Spring, Valona 31332 (912/832-4748).

Jekyll Island: Jekyll Island Marina (sunset cruises and dolphin watch), 1 Pier Road 31520 (912/635-2891).

Sapelo Island: Darien Welcome Center, P.O. Box 1497 31305 (912/437-6684).

Savannah: Adventure Savannah Tours Inc., P.O. Box 9973 31412 (912/656-2000). Associated Guides of the Low Country (912/234-4088). Black Heritage Tour (912/234-8000). Cap'n Sam's Riverboat Cruises, P.O. Box 1131, 31402-1131 (912/234-7248). Carriage Tours of Savannah, 10 Warner St. 31401 (912/236-6756). Coastal Cruise Line, 314 East River St. 31401 (912/232-3382). Coastal Excursions, 54 Jackson Blvd. 31405 (912/355-5282). Colonial Historic Tours Inc., P.O. Box 9704 31401 (912/233-0083). Cycle Carriage Company, City Market, Jefferson & Congress 31401 (912/234-8277). Daufuskie Island Escape (800/389-7687).

Gray Line Savannah/Landmark Tours, Inc., 215 W. Boundary St. 31401-2207 (912/236-9604). NOGS Garden Tours (mid-April), Garden Club of Savannah, 425 East 56th St. 31405 (912/238-0248). Oglethorpe Tours, P.O. Box 13008 31416 (912/352-0710). Helen Salter's Tours, 1113 Winston Ave. 31404 (912/355-4296). Historic Savannah Foundation Tours, P.O. Box 1733 31402 (912/233-7703). Helen Bryant's Shoppers Walk (912/355-7731). Historic Horse Tours, 2805 Bull St. 31405 (912/927-2050). Old Savannah Tours, 516 Lee Blvd. 31406 (912/354-7913). Savannah Walking Tours, 6 Illinois Ave. 31404 (912/232-3905). Savannah River Cruise Lines, P.O. Box 2062 31402 (912/234-4011). *Spirit of Savannah* Paddleboat, Hyatt Regency, River St. 31401 (912/238-1234). Square Routes, P.O. Box 10371 31412 (912/232-3905 or 800/627-4080). Tours by BJ, P.O. Box 3834 31404 (912/233-2335). Tours on Tape, 313 Abercorn St. 31401 (912/232-0582).

St. Marys: Guale Tours, P.O. Box 1091 31558 (912/673-6110).

St. Simons Island: Goldline Cruises, 208 Marina Dr. 31522 (912/638-8537).

Sea Island: Island Charter Marsh Boat Ride, North First St. 31561 (912/638-3611).

Wassaw Island: Helmey Charters, 124 Palmetto Dr., Wilmington Island 31410 (912/897-4921). Salt Water Charter, 1111 Wickersham Dr., Skidaway Island 31411 (912/598-1814).

Index

ACE Basin Plan, 205-206
Adventure, 196
Airlie Garden, 107
Alamance, Battle of, 79
Albemarle Region, 24, 47-74
Albemarle Sound, 4, 17, 18, 46, 48, 53, 58
Alexander, Charles A., 292
Algonkian Indians, 52, 57
Alligator River, 62, 63, 69
Alligator River Wildlife Refuge, 46, 48, 64-65
Allston, Washington, 153
Alston, Charles, 187
Altamaha River, 4, 230, 231, 271, 276-277, 281, 283, 284, 287
American Forestry Association, 62
Anderson, Maj. Robert, 179, 194
Anderson, William P., 294
Armstrong, Maitland and Helen, 295
Ashley River, 4, 174, 195, 198
Ashpoo River, 141, 205
Atlantic Beach, NC, 92, 95, 150
Audubon, James J., 199; and Audubon Swamp Garden, 199
Aurora, NC, 74, 75
Avon, NC, 37
Awendaw Creek, 166
Awendaw, SC, 139

Baker, Frederick, 295
Bald Head Creek, 112
Bald Head Lighthouse, 112, 113
Barker, Thomas, 56
Barlowe, Capt. Arthur, 3

Barnwell, John, 215
Bartram, William, 140, 309
Bartram Trail, 240
Baruch, Bernard and Belle, 157
Bateman, Hester, 187
Bath Creek, 71
Bath, NC, 48, 61, 70-71, 75
Battery Island, 112
Battle, Elisha, 127
Batts, Nathaniel, 18
Baum, Carolista, 32
Bayley, John, 215
Bear Island, 9
Beaufort, NC, 12, 85, 87-89, 92, 95
Beaufort, SC, 206-208, 209
Beauregard, Gen. P.G.T., 183, 186
Bee Tree Canal, 62
Beidler, Francis, 203
Belhaven, NC, 70
Belle Isle Garden, 160-161
Bentonville Battlefield, 129, 130
Berkeley, Sir William, 18
Berolzheimer, Philip, 291
Big Bay Creek, 204
Big Davis Canal, 118
Biggin Creek, 173, 174
Big Kill Devil Hill, NC, 30, 31
Billy's Island, 309
Bird Island, 120
Bischoff, William, 244
Black Banks River, 291
Blackbeard (Edward Teach), 8, 14, 19, 20, 40, 71, 75
Blackbeard Creek, 281

Blackbeard Island, 234, 236, 237, 280–281
Black River, 141, 158
Bladen Lakes State Forest, 133–134
Bliss, Cornelius, 295
Bloody Marsh, Battle of, 229, 282, 287, 288, 295
Blount, Thomas, 128
Blue Ridge Mountains, 125
Bluffton, SC, 211
Bogue Banks, 95–96, 107
Bogue Sound, 87, 97
Bodie Island, 34–36
Bodie Island Lighthouse, 36
Boiling Springs Lake, 113
Bonaventure Plantation, 255
Bonneau, SC, 168
Bonner, James, 72
Bonnet's Creek, 113
Bonnet, Stede, 8, 19, 20, 113
Boone Hall Creek, 171
Boone Hall Plantation, 174, 176–177
Boone, John, 176, 177
Bradham, Caleb D., 81
Bradley Creek, 107
Briar Creek, 232, 270
Brice Creek, 83
Bridgers, Capt. John, 128
Brookgreen Garden, 151–153; Plantation, 152
Brunswick, GA, 12, 240, 272, 285–287, 289
Brunswick, NC, 99, 115
Brunswick State Historic Site, 115–116
Buckner, Ken, 121
Bulls Island, 141, 170
Burnside, Gen. Ambrose, 79, 80
Burr, Theodosia, 159
Burton, SC, 139
Butler Island, 277, 284

Calabash, NC, 117, 123
Calabash River, 123
Calhoun, John C., 189
Calibogue Sound, 220
Camp Le Jeune, 97

Cape Carteret, NC, 96
Cape Fear, 5, 6, 7, 17, 18
Cape Fear Area, 99–116
Cape Fear River, 8, 20, 100, 105, 106, 107, 108, 112, 116, 135
Cape Fear River Valley, 18
Cape Hatteras, 5, 20, 21, 38, 232
Cape Hatteras Lighthouse, 38–40
Cape Hatteras National Seashore, 23, 34–42
Cape Hatteras Point, 34
Cape Island, 170
Cape Lookout, 5
Cape Lookout Lighthouse, 92, 93, 95
Cape Lookout National Seashore, 12, 42, 90, 91–95
Cape Romain, 4, 171
Cape Romain National Wildlife Refuge, 166, 169, 170
Capers Island, 170–171
Carnegie, Andrew, George Lauder, and Lucy 302; Thomas 302, 304
"Carolina Bays," 132–135, 166
Carolina Beach, NC, 106, 107
Carolina Beach State Park, 109–110
Carson, Rachel, 230
Cashie River, 58, 60
Caswell, Gov. Richard, 132
Cat Island, 162, 163
Causey, W. Jackson, 207
Cedar Island, 27, 42, 163
Cedar Island National Wildlife Refuge, 90
Central of Georgia Railroad, 242, 245
Charles B. Aycock Birthplace, 130
Charleston Naval Base, 195
Charleston, SC, 6, 7, 8, 9, 10, 11, 12, 20, 72, 139, 141, 142, 143, 159, 161, 166, 173, 176, 177, 178, 179, 180–196, 229, 240, 266
Charles Towne 18, 182; Landing, 195–196
Chatham Artillery, 247

Chechesse River, 212
Cherry Point Marine Air Station, 85
Chesapeake Bay, 42, 43
Chesser Island, 308, 310
Chicamacomico Lifesaving Station, 38
Chicora, 147
Chicken Creek, 166
Chief Manteo, 17
Chimney Creek, 262
Chowan College, 126
Chowan River, 4, 48
Chocoyotte Creek, 125
Churchill, Winston, 157
Citadel, The, 191
Civil War, 39, 40, 42, 46, 51, 59, 61, 72, 73, 78, 80, 82, 92, 95, 102, 103, 109, 112, 113, 115, 118, 124, 127, 128, 130, 143, 146, 147, 154, 157, 160, 161, 163, 167, 173, 179, 180, 183, 184, 186, 187, 191, 194, 199, 206, 207, 208, 210, 211, 215, 216, 219, 229, 230, 231, 242, 244, 247, 251, 254, 255, 257, 258, 261, 263, 266, 268, 279, 282, 285, 286, 288, 289, 291, 305
Civilian Conservation Corps (CCC), 37, 67, 150, 168
Clamagore (ship), 178
Clam Creek, 296
Clemson University, 156
Cleveland, Pres. Grover, 163
Cliffs of Neuse State Park, 130–132
Clyo, GA, 240
Cochran, James, 144
Cockspur Island, 259
Coffin, Howard Earle, 291, 292
Colington Bay, 27
Colington Island, 30, 32
College of Charleston, 203
Colleton River, 211
Colleton State Park, 201
Collins, Josiah, 63
Congaree River, 4
Conservation Fund, 69

Continental Congress, 124, 200, 212, 275
Continental Shelf, 235
Conway, Gen. Robert, 146
Conway, SC, 146–147
Cooper River, 4, 141, 162, 168, 169, 173, 174, 178
Coosawatchie River, 4
Coquina Beach, NC, 36
Core Banks, 91, 92, 93
Coree Indians, 94
Cornwallis, Lord, 102, 104, 124, 183
Corolla, NC, 27, 28, 29
Cotton, Joseph, 113
Couper, James Hamilton, 287
Cowhouse Island, 308
Crane, Richard T., Jr., 295
Crane, Roy, 301
Croatan National Forest, 77, 83–84
Croatan Sound, 46, 64
Crooked River, 231
Crooked River State Park, 298
Crusoe, NC, 121
C.S.S. Albemarle, 161
C.S.S. Florida, 105
C.S.S. Nashville, 267
C.S.S. Neuse, 131
Cumbahee River, 205
Cumberland Island, 11, 228, 234, 235, 236, 239, 271, 299, 302–305, 311
Cumberland Island National Seashore, 12, 235
Cumberland Sound, 236
Cunningham, Maj. Alfred A., 85
Currituck Beach Lighthouse, 29
Currituck National Wildlife Refuge, 28
Currituck Sound, 27, 39, 46, 88
Curtis, David, 73
Cypress Garden, 172–173

Dare, Virginia, 17
Darien, GA, 7, 239, 281–284, 287; River, 282
Daufuskie Island, 220–221
Davis, James, 77

Dean Hall Plantation, 172
de Aviles, Pedro Menendez, 209
d'Estaing, Comte, 252
deGraffenreid, Baron Christopher, 78
Del Mar Beach, NC, 98
De Soto, Hernando, 6, 228, 256
De Weldon, Felix, 248
Diamond City, NC, 94, 95
Diamond Shoals, 5, 20, 39
Dillard, GA, 239
Dillon, James W., 144
Dillon, SC, 143, 144
Dingle, Edward Von Seibold, 199
Dixon, George, W., 78, 94
Dixon Memorial State Forest, 310
Doboy Sound, 278
Doctor's Creek, 94
Dodge, Anson Green Phelps, Jr., 288–289; Rev. Anson Phelps, 301
Drayton Hall Plantation, 196–198
Drayton, John, 196, 198, 199–200; Thomas, Jr., 199
Drummond Lake, 49
Drunken Island, 154
Drysdale, Isabelle, 299
du Bignon, Christophe Poulain, 293
Duck, NC, 28, 29
Ducks Unlimited, 206
Duke University Marine Laboratory, 89
Duplin River, 278

Eagle Pencil Company, 290
East Carolina University, 74
East Lake, 65
Ebenezer Creek, 232
Echaw Creek, 166
Eddy, Mary Baker, 103
Eden, Gov. Charles, 19, 57, 71
Edenton, NC, 19, 22, 23, 48, 55–57, 63; Edenton Bay, 55
Edisto Beach, SC, 139
Edisto Beach State Park, 204
Edisto Island, 180, 203, 204
Edisto River, 4, 140, 141, 201, 202, 205

Edmonston, Charles, 186
Edwards, Elliott O., Jr., 240
Egg Island, 284
Elfe, Thomas, 186
Elizabeth II (sailing ship), 44–46
Elizabeth II State Historic Site, 49
Elizabethan Garden, 44
Elizabeth City, NC, 50–53
Elizabeth River, 47
Elizabethtown, NC, 133
Elizafield Plantation, 287
Elliott, William, 215
Emerald Isle, NC, 95
Englehard, NC, 12, 66
Exum, NC, 121

Fayetteville, NC, 99
Fearing, Fred, 52
Fernandina Beach, FL, 310
Field, Marshall, 293
Fisher, James Robinson, 66
Fishermans Island National Wildlife Refuge, 46
Florence, SC, 12
Florida Central and Peninsula Railroad, 297
Folkston, GA, 306, 308
Folkstone, NC, 98
Forsyth, John, 244; Capt. Suzanne, 281
Fort Anderson, 115, 116
Fort Argyle, 236
Fort Beauregard, 211
Fort Caswell, 118
Fort Defiance, 268
Fort Fisher, 102
Fort Fisher State Historic Site, 109
Fort Frederica National Monument, 288, 289
Fort Holmes, 112
Fort Johnson, 113
Fort King George, 283–284
Fort Macon, 95, 129
Fort McAllister, 266–267
Fort Mitchell, 316
Fort Morris, 268
Fort Moultrie, 143, 179–180
Fort Pulaski, 229, 242, 258–259

Fort Raleigh National Historic Site, 43
Fort Screven, 261
Fort Sherman, 216
Fort Stewart, 231, 267
Fort Sumter, 143, 179; National Monument, 194–195
Fort Walker, 216
Fort Watson, 172
Four Hole Swamp, 203, 210
Fox, George, 55; Stephen, 199
Francis Beidler Forest, 201–203
Francis Marion National Forest, 12, 141, 142, 164, 166–169
Franklin, Benjamin, 240
French and Indian War, 229
French, Daniel Chester, 244
Fripp Island, 140, 210
Frisco, NC, 12, 38
Frogmore, SC, 139
Front River, 221, 222
Frying Pan Lake, 69

Garden City, SC, 3, 148, 150
Garden Club of North Carolina, 44
Gatesville, NC, 126
General Sherman (ship), 140
Georgia Bight, 3
Georgia Department of Natural Resources, 239, 272, 275, 277, 283, 287, 296
Georgia Historical Society, 243
Georgia Salzberger Society, 269
Georgia Southern University, 275
Georgetown, SC, 147, 156, 158–160, 161, 187
German Heritage Society, 245
Gershwin, George, 189
Gibbs, Henry W., 66
Gilman Paper Company, 299
Givhans Ferry State Park, 201
Goldsboro, NC, 129–130
Goldsborough, Maj. Matthew T., 129
Goose Creek, 73
Goose Creek Island, 75, 76
Goose Creek State Park, 73–74
Gorges, Will, 81

Gould, Edwin, 294
Grady, Henry W., 230; Pvt. John, 99
Grahamsville, SC, 211
Grand Strand, 4, 123, 139, 143–161
Grantsboro, NC, 76
Gray, Dr. Milton B., 238
Gray's Reef (Sapelo Live Bottom), 13, 238, 260, 261, 263
Great Dismal Swamp, 14, 47, 49; Canal, 47, 48, 49, 50
Great Dismal Swamp National Wildlife Refuge, 49
Great Pee Dee River, 4, 140, 157
Green Swamp, 120–121
Greene, Gen. Nathaniel, 304
Greenville, NC, 74
Grenville, Sir Richard, 40
Guale Indians, 284, 290, 293
Gulf Stream, 5, 9, 13, 144, 151, 238, 262
Guillard Lake, 166
Gullah Festival, 208; dialect, 220
Guthrie, Julian, 90
Gwinnett, Button, 250, 275

Hagley Plantation, 160
Halifax, NC, 22, 48, 124; Historic Halifax, 22, 48, 124–25
Hall, Dr. Lyman, 268
Hamilton, NC, 59–60
Hammocks Island State Park, 97–98
Hampstead, NC, 98
Hampton, Gen. Wade, 147
Hampton Plantation, 290
Hampton Plantation State Park, 164, 165
Hampton Roads, VA, 10, 26
Harding, Thomas, 71
Harker's Island, 89, 92, 95
Harris Neck Creek, 275
Harris Neck National Wildlife Refuge, 274–275
Harleyville, SC, 201
Harvest Moon, 161
Hatteras Island, 27, 28, 34, 36–40

Hatteras Village, NC, 12, 27, 28, 40
Havelock, NC, 77, 85
Haws Run, NC, 97
Heath, Sir Robert, 17
Hertford, NC, 12, 53–54
Heyward, Daniel, 186; Thomas, 186; DuBose, 189
Hilton, Capt. William, 215
Hilton Head, SC, 11, 139, 140, 141, 211, 212–220, 258
Hilton Head Plantation, 217
HMS Bedfordshire, 49
Hobcaw Barony, 155–156
Hobucken, NC, 74, 75, 76
Hoffman State Forest, 84
Hofwyl-Broadfield Plantation, 285
Holden Beach, NC, 118
Holden Island, 116, 119
Holly Ridge, NC, 98
Honey Hill, Battle of, 211
Hope Island, 256–257
Hope Plantation, 58–59
Hopeton Plantation, 287
Hopsewee Plantation, 164–165
Horry, Gen. Peter, 146
Horton, William, 295
Hudson Creek, 278
Huger Creek, 166
Hunting Island, 140, 141, 209–210
Hunting Island Lighthouse, 210
Hunting Island State Park, 12, 209–210
Huntington, Archer M. and Anna Hyatt, 151, 152, 154
Huntington Beach State Park, 153–154
Hurricane Hugo, 6, 116, 162, 168, 173, 174, 185, 202
Hyde, Henry B., 294

Indian Beach, NC, 95
Intracoastal Waterway, 12, 52, 60, 65, 70, 74, 76, 82, 109, 113, 117, 118, 140, 162, 164, 166, 176, 255, 260, 262
Iredell, James, 56; James Jr., 56

Isle of Palms, 174, 180

Jack Creek, 170
Jackson, Charles, 299; Cynthia, 133
Jacksonboro, SC, 205
Jacksonville, FL, 12, 310–311
Jacksonville, NC, 12, 97
James, Dr. Walter B., 295
James Island, 193, 203
Jamestown, SC, 168
Jamestown, VA, 17, 47, 227
Jay, William, 248, 249
Jekyll Creek, 294
Jekyll Island, 8, 9, 235, 239, 292–296
Jekyll Island Club, 292, 293, 295
Jekyll River, 296
Jerico River, 231
Jesup, GA, 259
Jockey's Ridge State Park, 32–33
Johnson's Creek, 207
Johnston, Gen. Joseph E., 130
Jones, Alfred, 292; Hugh, 66; Noble, 256, 257
Jones Creek, 163
Jones Island, 308
Jones Lake, 134, 135
Jones Lake State Park, 134
Joyner's Bank, 220

Kemble, Fanny, 229, 290
Kenansville, NC, 12
Kiawah Island, 180, 203
Kill Devil Hills, NC, 27, 30
King Charles I, 17; Charles II, 17, 142
King George II, 81
King, John, 297; William Henry, 297
King's Highway, 12, 78, 169, 205
Kingsland, GA, 240, 297–298
Kingstree, SC, 158
Kinston, NC, 132
Kittredge, Benjamin R., 173
Kitty Hawk Bay, 27
Kitty Hawk, NC, 12, 26, 28, 30, 31
Knotts Island, 24, 25

Kramer, Joe, 52
Kure Beach, NC, 106, 107

Lafayette, Marquis de, 125, 163, 206, 248
Lake Landing, NC, 66–67
Lake Waccamaw State Park, 134
Lane, Gov. Ralph, 44
Lanier, Sidney, 229, 241, 254, 286
Lavra A. Barnes (sailing ship), 36
Laura S. Walker State Park, 310
Lawson, John, 71
Lazaretto Creek, 260, 265
LeConte, John Eatton, 268; Joseph, 268; Louis, 268
LeConte-Woodmanston Plantation, 240, 268
Lee, Henry "Light-horse Harry," 305; Gen. Robert E., 60, 95, 194, 258
Lewis Island, 232, 276
Lighthouse Island, 170
Lincoln, Pres. Abraham, 194, 230, 242
Lindbergh, Charles A., 279
Litchfield Beach, SC, 148, 151
Little Cumberland Island, 305
Little Egg Island, 284
Little David, 173
Little Pee Dee River, 141
Little River, SC, 123, 140, 144
Little St. Simons Island, 234, 290–291
Locke, John, 18
Lockwood Folly, 121, 122
Long Island, NY, 72
Longwood, The, 297
Lorillard, Pierre, 274, 293
Lost Colony, 17, 40, 43
Low, Andrew, 249; Juliette Gordon, 249
Lowland, NC, 75
Lynch, Thomas, Jr., 164

Mackay Creek, 212
Mackay Island, 24
Mackay Island National Wildlife Refuge, 24–25, 28
Macon, GA, 245

Maddocks, Sean, 193
Magnolia Plantation, 186, 198–199
Mallard Creek, 73
Manning, Gen. Thomas Courtland, 57
Manns Harbor, NC, 61
Mansfield Plantation, 159
Manteo, 27, 44
Marion, Gen. Francis, 143, 160
Marion Lake, 164, 171–172, 173
Marshes of Glynn, 233, 286, 294
Martin, Howard H., 230; Gov. Josiah, 78, 99
Martus, Florence, 248
Masonboro Island, 108–109
Mattamuskeet Lake, 66, 67, 68, 69, 70
Mattamuskeet National Wildlife Refuge, 12, 67–68
Maurice, Charles Stewart, 294
Maynard, Lt. Robert, 19, 40
McAllister/Richmond Hill State Park, 266–267
McCartan, Edward, 152
McClellanville, SC, 139, 166, 167, 168, 169
McCrady, Capt. John, 266
McKay, Gordon, 293, 294
McKinley, Pres. William, 295
Medway River, 231
Mercer, Johnny, 250
Merchants Millpond State Park, 49–50
Meridian, GA, 278
Methodist Church, 41, 42, 259, 288
Middleburg Plantation, 169
Middleton, Henry, 200
Middleton Place, 196, 200–201
Middletown, NC, 66
Midway, GA, 240, 267
Midyette, Louis B. and Robert P., 77
Mill Creek, 131
Milledge, John, 264; John Jr., 264
Milles, Carl, 152
Millionaire's Village Historic District, 294

Mills, Robert, 146, 160
Milltrail Creek, 65
Minnesott Shores, NC, 77
Mitchell, Gen. Billy, 26;
  Margaret, 187
Moccasin Canal Overlook, 62
Moncks Corner, SC, 166, 171,
  173, 174
Monroe, Pres. James, 250
Moore, Roger, 115; Maurice, 115
Moore's Creek National Battle-
  field, 99–100
Morehead City, NC, 77, 86–87, 95
Morehead, Gov. John Motley, 86
Morgan, J. P., 293, 294
Morris Island, 194
Mosquito Creek, 290
Moultrie Lake, 171, 173
Mount Airy, NC, 31
Mount Olive, NC, 12
Mount Pleasant, SC, 174, 176
Muir, John, 254
Mulryne, Colonel, 255; Mary,
  255
Murfree, William, 126
Murfreesboro, NC, 22, 126
Murphy Island, 163
Murrells Inlet, SC, 148, 151
Musgrove, Mary, 279
Myrtle Beach, SC, 9, 12, 140,
  143, 148–150
Myrtle Beach State Park, 150

Nags Head, NC, 26, 28, 33–34,
  46
Nags Head Woods Ecological
  Reserve, 33
National Audubon Society, 29,
  201, 217
National Oceanic and At-
  mospheric Administration, 261
National Park Service, 39, 94,
  258, 302
National Trust for Historic
  Preservation, 198
National Wilderness Preservation
  System, 69
Native American Museum and
  Natural History Center, 38

Nature Conservancy, 28, 35, 121,
  164, 201, 206, 275
Nebraska, NC, 66
Neuse River, 4, 47, 74, 76, 81,
  82, 83, 84, 130
New Bern, NC, 22, 23, 77–83,
  84; Academy, 79; Historical
  Commission, 80
Newport, NC, 85
Newport River, 87
Newton Grove, NC, 130
New York Zoological Society,
  275
Nicholson Creek, 166
Norfolk, VA, 30
North Carolina Aquarium, 46, 96,
  110–111
North Carolina Baptist Assem-
  blies, 118
North Carolina Beach Buggy As-
  sociation, 34
North Carolina Gazette, 77
North Carolina Maritime
  Museum, 88–89
North Carolina National Estuarine
  Research Reserve, 108
North Carolina Wildlife Commis-
  sion, 76
North Charleston, SC, 174
North Island, 162, 163
North Island Lighthouse, 163
North Landing River, 25
North Myrtle Beach, SC, 148, 149
North River, 89, 299
N.S. Savannah, 178
Nunis, Dr. Samuel, 228

Oak Creek, 153
Oak (Long) Island, 112, 116,
  118–119
Oak Island, Lighthouse, 112, 118
Ocean Island, 116
Ocean Island Beach, 117,
  119–120
Ocean View Railroad, 107
Ocmulgee River, 230
Oconee River, 230, 232
Ocracoke Island, 19, 26, 27, 28,
  34, 40–47, 90, 92

Ocracoke Lighthouse, 41
Ogeechee River, 4, 231, 267, 270
Oglethorpe, Gen. James, 228, 229, 230, 231, 241–242, 243, 244, 282, 287, 288
Okefenokee Swamp, 11, 233, 240, 298, 305–310
Okefenokee Swamp National Wildlife Refuge, 308
Old Dorchester State Park, 201
Old Fort Jackson, 257
Old Ironsides, 287
Old Santee Canal State Park, 173–174
Old Town Brunswick Preservation Association, 286
Olympic Games, 254
Onslow Bay, 92
Oriental, NC, 74, 76–77
Orton Garden, 114, 115
Osceola, Chief, 180
Ossabaw Island, 272–274
Ossabaw Sound, 272
Outer Banks, 5, 10, 11, 20, 23, 24, 25–42, 48, 49, 61, 93, 107
Outer Banks History Center, 45

Palmer, Col. Robert, 71
Pamlico River, 74, 75
Pamlico Sound, 4, 18, 23, 34, 37, 40, 66, 69
Parris, Alexander, 208
Parris Island, 7, 142, 208–209
Parris Island Marine Depot, 208–209
Pasquotank River, 47, 50
Patriot's Point, SC, 174, 176, 177–178, 195
Pawley's Island, NC, 148, 154–156
Pea Island, 34
Pea Island National Wildlife Refuge, 37, 46
Perquimans County Restoration Association, 55
Perquimans River, 53, 55
Pettigrew, Gen. James J., 62
Pettigrew State Park, 61–64
Phelps Lake, 61, 63, 135

Phillips Island, 89
Pigott, Emaline, 80
Pinckney, Charles Cotesworth, 212
Pinckney Island, 212
Pinckney Island National Wildlife Refuge, 211, 212
Pine Island Sanctuary, 29
Pine Knoll Shores, NC, 95, 96
Pinopolis, SC, 171
Plymouth, NC, 60, 61
Pocosin Lakes (Pungo) National Wildlife Refuge, 69
Poinsett, Elijah, 191
Pope, Miller, 117
Poplar Grove, 100, 106
Porter, Noah, 41; Henry Kirke, 295
Port Royal Bay, 208
Port Royal Plantation, 214, 216
Port Royal, SC, 283
Port Royal Sound, 140, 209
Portsmouth Island, 42
Portsmouth Village, NC, 26, 92, 93–94
Potter, T. T., 84
Powers, Hiram, 152
Pratt, Rev. Horace, 299
Preservation 2000, 237
Price, Eugenia, 301
Pritchard's Island, 210–211
Pulaski, Gen. Casimir, 250, 252
Pulitzer, Joseph, 293
Pungo Lake, 69
Purcell, Rev. Henry, 215

Queen Anne's Revenge (sailing ship), 281

Rabb, Jesse, 94
Raccoon Key, 170
Rachel Carson Estuarine Sanctuary, 89
Raleigh/Durham, NC, 12
Raleigh, Sir Walter, 17, 40, 42, 72
Recess Island, 222
Reed, Dr. Walter, 126
Retreat Plantation, 289, 291, 292

Revolutionary War, 56, 72, 78, 81, 82, 89, 99, 100, 112, 115, 124, 132, 143, 159, 160, 161, 166, 179, 180, 182–183, 184, 201, 204, 208, 229, 242, 245, 250, 252, 255, 268, 269, 286, 301
Reynolds, Gov. John, 229; Richard J., Jr., 279
Rhett, Col. William, 19, 20
Ribault, Jean, 228
Richardson Creek, 259
Richardson, Richard, 248
Ridgeville, GA, 284
Rincon, GA, 240
Roanoke Canal Trail, 125–126
Roanoke Island, 17, 25–26, 27, 34, 40, 42–46, 61, 65
Roanoke Rapids, NC, 124
Roanoke River, 4, 48, 60, 61
Roanoke River Valley, 124
Roanoke Sound, 32, 43
Robert E. Lee (ship), 110
Rockefeller, William, 294
Rockville, SC, 139
Rocky Mount, NC, 127
Rodanthe, NC, 37
Roosevelt, Pres. Franklin D., 157, 310
Rose Bay Canal, 68
Rutledge, Dr. Archibald, 165

St. Augustine, FL, 7, 215
St. Catherines Island, 7, 8, 12, 228, 229, 268, 275
St. Catherines Sound, 269
St. Helena Island, 209
St. John's River, 8, 229, 310
St. Mary's, GA, 297, 298–301, 311
St. Marys Railroad, 299
St. Marys River, 4, 231, 232, 297, 298, 306
St. Simons Island, 229, 234, 242, 282, 286, 290, 291, 295
St. Simons Sound, 296
Salkahatchie River, 4
Salter Path, NC, 95
Salvo, NC, 37

Sampit River, 159
San Diego de Ocone, 293
Santa Cataline de Guale, 7, 228, 275
Santa Elena, 7, 208, 209
Santee National Wildlife Area, 172
Santee River, 4, 141, 161, 162, 164, 165, 166, 167, 168
Santee State Park, 171–172
Sapelo Island, 234, 235, 236, 238, 277–280; National Estuarine Research Reserve, 278
Saponi Indians, 131
Savannah, GA, 7, 9, 11, 12, 72, 229, 240, 241–254, 255, 257, 258, 260, 261, 264, 271, 311
Savannah National Wildlife Area, 221–223
Savannah River, 4, 220, 221, 222, 223, 227, 230, 231, 232, 237, 270, 271
Savannah State University, 255
Scott, Joseph, 55
Screven, Rev. Elisha, 158
Scrymser, James A., 294
Scuppernong River, 63, 69
Sea Island, 11, 234, 292–296, 311
Sea Pines Plantation, 214, 217
Seven Springs, NC, 131
Seymour Johnson Air Force Base, 129
Shackleford Banks, 89, 91, 94
Shackleford, John, 94
Shallotte, NC, 117, 122–123
Shallotte River, 122
Shell Castle Island, 41
Sherman, Gen. Thomas W., 217
Sherman, Gen. William Tecumseh, 8, 129, 184, 194, 242, 250, 266
Shrady, George F., 295
Sierra Club, 254, 268
Singletary Lake, 135
Singletary Lake State Park, 134
Singletary, Richard, 134
Skidaway Island, 254, 262–264, 265
Skidaway Island State Park, 262, 263

Skull Creek, 212
Slocum, Molly, 99
Smith/Bald Head Island, 111–112
Smithsonian Institution, 31
Snapper Banks, 13
Snead's Ferry, NC, 98
Somerset Place, 63–64
South Brunswick, NC, 11, 12, 116–123, 147
South Carolina Hall of Fame, 149–150
South Carolina Institute of Archaeology and Anthropology, 209
South Carolina Wildlife and Marine Resources Department, 163, 219
South Island, 162, 163
South Newport River, 274
Southport, NC, 23, 112–114, 115, 118
Spanish-American War, 95, 118, 194, 244, 264
Sparrow, Dr. William T., 66
Spotswood, Gov. Alexander, 19
Sprunt, Alexander, 102; James and Luola, 115
Stanly, John Wright, 81
Stephen C. Foster State Park, 308, 309
Stickney, Joseph, 294
Stone, Gov. David, 58, 59; Jedekiah, 58
Stoney-Baynard Plantation, 216
Stono River, 203
Stuart Creek, 168
Styron, Ed, 94
Sullivans Island, 174, 176, 180
Summerhouse Creek, 170
Summerville, SC, 199, 201
Sunbury, GA, 240, 268–269
Sunset Island, 116
Surf City, NC, 98
Surfside Beach, SC, 148, 150
Suwanee River, 233, 306
Swanquarter National Wildlife Refuge, 69
Swan Quarter, NC, 27, 42, 67

Swansboro, NC, 97, 133
Sweat, J. L., 310

Talahi Island, 260
Tarboro, NC, 22, 127–128
Tar River, 4, 72
Tattnall, Josiah, 255
Telfair, Mary, 243
Thackery, William Makepeace, 249
Thunderbolt, GA, 255–256
Tiffany, Louis Comfort, 295
Timucuan Indians, 305
Toccoa Falls, GA, 237
Tompkins, John F., 71
Tom Yawkey Wildlife Center, 162–163
"Toonerville Trolley," 301
Topping, Solomon J., 70
Topsail Beach, NC, 98
Torrey, Dr. H. N., 274
Totten, Joseph C., 258
Town Creek, 116
Turtle Island, 221
Trent River, 81, 82, 83
Tryon, Gov. William, 71, 78, 79, 115
Tryon Palace, 78–80
Turkey Creek, 166
Turnbull Creek, 133
Turner, David H., 152
Tuscarora Indians, 131; War, 47
Tybee Island, 233, 234, 258, 260–262, 269
Tybee Island National Wildlife Refuge, 223
Tybee Lighthouse, 261
Tyler, John, 58

Union Camp Corporation, 221
University of Georgia, 14, 264, 278, 279
University of South Carolina, 156
U.S. Army Corps of Engineers, 222, 223, 239, 262
U.S. Coast Guard, 23, 38, 39, 53
U.S. Fish and Wildlife Service, 206, 261, 264, 281
U.S.S. Constitution, 218

U.S.S. North Carolina, 105, 106
U.S.S. Yorktown, 177–178

Vail, Theodore N., 293
Vera Cruz II (ship), 94
Vereen Memorial Garden, 122
Van Sant, Jack, 52
Vernezobre Creek, 222
Verrazano, Giovanni da, 6
Virginia Beach, 24
Virginia Coastal Drift, 5, 20
von Reck, Philip Georg Frederick, 256

Waccamaw Indians, 147
Waccamaw Lake, 135
Waccamaw Neck, 151–158
Waccamaw River, 4, 121, 122, 135, 146, 157
Waddell Mariculture Center, 211
Wallace, John, 94
Wambaw Creek, 141, 164, 166, 167
Wampacheone Creek, 177
Wanchese, NC, 46
War of 1812, 50, 184, 194, 267, 268, 269
Washington, DC, 31, 258
Washington Monument, 146
Washington, Pres. George, 49, 56, 72, 78, 82, 144, 150, 153, 154, 164, 165, 186, 187, 247
Washington, NC, 12, 60, 61, 70, 72–73, 75
Wassaw Creek, 264, 265
Wassaw Island, 234, 262, 263, 264–265
Wassaw Island National Wildlife Refuge, 235
Watermelon Creek, 277
Waves, NC, 37
Waycross, GA, 308, 310
Weed, Jacob, 299
Weil, Lionel, 131
Weldon, NC, 124
Wesley, John, 249, 259, 264, 288, 289; Charles, 288, 289
West, Mrs. Eleanor Torrey, 274
Weston, Plowden C. J., 147

West Onslow Beach, NC, 98
Whaleboat Junction, NC, 34
White, John, 41, 44, 66
White Lake, 134
White Marsh Island, 260
White Oak Creek, 296
White Oak River, 84, 89, 97
Wilde, Oscar, 184
Wilkinson, John A., 70
Williams, George, Jr., 187
Williamson Island, 234, 260, 265–266
Williamson, Odell, 119; Jimmy 266
Williamston, NC, 60
Wilmington Island, 265
Wilmington, NC, 9, 21, 23, 100–107, 112, 115, 123
Wilmington Railroad Museum, 105
Wilmington River, 231, 255
Wilmington to Weldon Railroad, 105, 129
Wilson, NC, 128
Wilson, Pres. Woodrow, 103
Windsor, NC, 57–59
Winyah Bay, 14, 140, 142, 151, 157, 161
Winyah Indians, 147
Wolf Island, 271, 284
Wolf Island National Wildlife Refuge, 284–285
Wood, John, 299; Jane, 299
Woodbine, GA, 297
Woodbine Plantation, 297
World War I, 118, 179, 253, 261; World War II, 41, 92, 118, 127, 129, 130, 154, 178, 179, 180, 192, 230, 255, 258, 261, 274, 279, 290, 293
Wormsloe National Wildlife Refuge, 245
Wormsloe Plantation, 255
Wormsloe State Park, 256
Wright Brothers National Memorial, 30
Wright, Frank Lloyd, 193
Wright, Wilbur and Orville, 26, 30, 31

Wrightsville Beach, NC, 10, 107, 108

Yawkey, Tom, 163
Yemassee Indians, 202, 209

Yemassee, SC, 139
Yeopim Indians, 53
Yorktown, VA, 183, 247

Zeke's Island, 111